WHAT IF JESUS CARRIED A BRIEFCASE?

Wise leaders spend time each day in quiet reflection. If they only keep their eyes focused on the problems of the day, and never look at deeper things, they will never be great leaders. *What if Jesus Carried a Briefcase* is an excellent guide to prepare leaders to become more effective in the workplace.

—Roger Hall, Ph.D.
Compass Consultation Ltd.

God speaks to us in many ways and when we listen to His voice we receive blessings. The messages of hope and encouragement in *What if Jesus Carried a Briefcase* will inspire leaders to actively listen for God's voice as they make decisions and lead their organizations.

—Dr. Tom Hill
Author, Speaker, Businessman, and Co-Founder
of the Tom Hill Institute

What if Jesus Carried a Briefcase provides God-centered practical advice for Christian business leaders seeking to harmonize their principles of faith with their leadership roles at work. Relevant and timely, it is both thought-provoking and uplifting to read.

—Mark Whitacre, PhD
Author and Speaker

A CHRISTIAN DEVOTIONAL FOR BUSINESS LEADERS

WHAT IF JESUS CARRIED A BRIEFCASE?

DONALD C. MOORE

Ambassador International
Greenville, South Carolina & Belfast, Northern Ireland
www.ambassador-international.com

What if Jesus Carried a Briefcase?
A Christian Devotional for Business Leaders
© 2015 by Donald C. Moore
All rights reserved

ISBN: 978-1-62020-518-1
eISBN: 978-1-62020-425-2

Scripture marked NKJV taken from the New King James Version®. Copyright © 1982 by Thomas Nelson, Inc. Used by permission. All rights reserved.

Scripture marked NIV taken from The Holy Bible, New International Version®, NIV® Copyright © 1973, 1978, 1984, 2011 by Biblica, Inc.® Used by permission. All rights reserved worldwide.

Scripture marked NRSV taken from the New Revised Standard Version of the Bible, copyright 1952 [2nd edition, 1971] by the Division of Christian Education of the National Council of the Churches of Christ in the United States of America. Used by permission. All rights reserved.

Scripture marked ESV taken from The ESV® Bible (The Holy Bible, English Standard Version®) copyright © 2001 by Crossway, a publishing ministry of Good News Publishers. ESV® Text Edition: 2011. The ESV® text has been reproduced in cooperation with and by permission of Good News Publishers. Unauthorized reproduction of this publication is prohibited. All rights reserved.

Scripture marked NASB taken from the New American Standard Bible®, Copyright © 1960, 1962, 1963, 1968, 1971, 1972, 1973, 1975, 1977, 1995 by The Lockman Foundation Used by permission.

Scripture quotations marked NLT are taken from the Holy Bible, New Living Translation, copyright © 1996, 2004, 2007 by Tyndale House Foundation. Used by permission of Tyndale House Publishers, Inc., Carol Stream, Illinois 60188. All rights reserved.

Cover Design & Typesetting by Hannah Nichols
Ebook Conversion by Anna Riebe Riebe Raats

AMBASSADOR INTERNATIONAL
Emerald House
427 Wade Hampton Blvd.
Greenville, SC 29609, USA
www.ambassador-international.com

AMBASSADOR BOOKS
The Mount
2 Woodstock Link
Belfast, BT6 8DD, Northern Ireland, UK
www.ambassadormedia.co.uk

The colophon is a trademark of Ambassador

This book would not have been completed without the uplifting encouragement and support of my wife, Elizabeth. Her insights added clarity, her pursuit of godly wisdom added depth, and her perseverance in all things spurred me on to completion. I have been richly blessed.

CONTENTS

FOREWORD	10
JANUARY	18
FEBRUARY	40
MARCH	62
APRIL	96
MAY	130
JUNE	160
JULY	202
AUGUST	252
SEPTEMBER	300
OCTOBER	354
NOVEMBER	398
DECEMBER	444
NOTES	482
INDEX	490

FOREWORD

Before I first began a serious study of the Bible, but after I had accepted Jesus as my Savior, certain passages of Scripture had a tendency to trouble me whenever I heard them preached or came across them in the Bible. A number of them appeared in the Sermon on the Mount (Matthew 5:1–7:27), such as the admonition to store up treasures in heaven, the inescapable reality that you cannot serve both God and money (Matthew 6:19–24), and the wise and foolish builders (Matthew 7:24–27). These passages caused me to question the depth of my faith, particularly with respect to my career and my self-guided career choices. But there were others—the parable of the workers in the vineyard (Matthew 20:1–16), the reluctance of the rich young man (Mark 10:17–25), and the parable of the rich fool (Luke 12:14–21)—that also led me inexorably to conclude that I was caught up in the things of the world and not God.

I saw myself in those verses, and the image was troubling.

Professionally, my career had moved progressively upward. I had not broken any laws, I had not violated any "public trust," and I did not think of myself as driven to succeed at any cost, but there was a tension in my life. There was something going on in the quiet of my soul that said I was pursuing goals that really didn't matter in the big scheme of things. I wanted to know with certainty that my life mattered, but the world's response was unhelpful.

So, heeding the quiet voice within my heart, I embarked upon a diligent study of the Bible, reading it cover to cover and then reading it again. With each day's efforts I found encouragement, and reading the Bible became a habit I have maintained ever since. As I read the Bible, I prayed about the tension in my heart and my sincere desire to know Jesus better than I knew Him then. Where once the Sermon on the Mount caused me to feel incomplete, now the promise of Matthew 7:7–12 beckoned me to "seek, ask, and knock."

I participated in five different long-term Bible studies and eagerly listened to television and radio pastors, such that some weeks it was as if I had attended church every single day. I also sought out other believers and became active in my church, and I began to keep a journal record of my prayers, my questions, my concerns, my fears, and my faith.

The more time I invested in the Scriptures, the more I learned. And the more I learned, the stronger the impressions on my heart that my work and my career remained part of the problem, such that I daydreamed about leaving my business and my career and enrolling in a seminary. But the call to be a full-time pastor in pastoral care did not seem to be what I was missing. Frankly, I was adept at business, and I enjoyed so many aspects of business that the prospect of giving it up was difficult to comprehend as being the right choice for me.

My work requires that I travel. That has been a blessing because I have long stretches of uninterrupted time perfectly suited to reading and meditating on the Bible. One day, in 2003 or 2004, on a trip to Colorado, I had my Bible in hand when a passenger sat down beside me and remarked, "Oh, you have a Bible just like mine." And he produced a slim travel Bible like mine from his carry-on bag. It turned out he was an Air Force chaplain on his way out to California for a new assignment. I do not remember much about what we discussed other than I asked him questions about theological matters that were on my mind. After all, I had a captive pastor sitting next to me for a three-hour ride. But somewhere in the air, my heart urged me to ask him about being of use to God, and I asked him, "What about someone like me? How can God use someone like me?"

I remember he looked at me in surprise, but without hesitation he answered my question. He said, "God can use businessmen too." His answer was so unexpected and such a relief that I had to look away as tears welled up in my eyes. I had come to believe that God gifts each person in certain ways, but I was struggling to feel comfortable as a Christian inside my business talents. Now, to discover I could use my calling as a businessman in God's service made my joy so overwhelming that I think I could have flown the rest of the way to Denver without the airplane!

From that moment on, I began to concentrate my meditations and study of the Bible to discover how I could involve God in my business career. The results have been miraculous for me. I am no longer troubled by questions of self-worth and purpose because I know I am using the talents God gave me to do His will and to grow more and more into the likeness of Christ. I can say with the psalmist, "God is (my) refuge and strength, an ever-present help in trouble" (Psalm 46:1 NIV).

Perhaps you find yourself where I was before. Perhaps the siren call of the secular world's definition of morality and success no longer appeals to you—you hear it as the lie it is. Perhaps God, in the stillness of the night, is whispering in your inner consciousness that something is just not right.

It is interesting to note that the word integrity is listed as the ninth most frequently searched word on the Merriam-Webster online dictionary. That disquieting statistic and the popularity of Rick Warren's *The Purpose Driven Life: What on Earth Am I Here For?* and movies like *Courageous* lead me to conclude many Christians feel a similar longing in their hearts. And I think I know why.

Christian business leaders often struggle with living professional careers that are in harmony with their principles of faith. The messages of peace, joy, self-sacrifice, and hope we hear preached on Sunday are soon forgotten on Monday amid an environment of constant change, anxiety, self-interest, and uncertainty that any business operates within. Rather than being one among many like-minded individuals, we must lead people of different faiths, or no faith at all, in an increasingly secular world where we are pressured to balance who we are (Christians) and what we believe in (the Bible) with practicalities, compromises, and a moral relativism that believes nothing is ever truly right and very seldom is anything truly wrong.

Nonetheless, Christians are called to follow the teachings of Jesus 24/7/365—at work, at home, and anywhere else. And Christian business leaders, in spite of a worldview that speaks otherwise, know that business decisions and actions always include making choices of behavior that include the elements of being right or wrong, good or evil, and fair or unfair. The result: we can experience tension, stress, doubt, and loneliness at work. And, we can make bad decisions.

But God does not want it to be that way! God is in the business of guiding, training, uplifting, blessing, and transforming His people so that they more and more grow into the likeness of Jesus and fully realize their life's purpose. Our responsibility is to allow Him the opportunity to complete us by investing the time and passion to grow in our relationship with Him. God is not apart from our work. The messages in this devotional are specifically designed to reveal God's hand in the part of your life where you feel the most pressure to exclude Him—your career.

This devotional is, in part, my personal reflections on the essential activities of business leaders and what guidance can be found in Scripture for those activities. It is also, in part, my response to Paul's advice when he said, "Blessed be the God and Father of our Lord Jesus Christ, the Father of mercies and God of all comfort, who comforts us in all our tribulation, that we may be able to comfort those who are in any trouble, with the comfort with which we ourselves are comforted by God" (2 Corinthians 1:3-4 NKJV).

The devotionals in this book are designed to be read on a weekly basis, usually only one message each week, and have been organized around activities that I believe are essential for a leader in a business setting. There may be other activities you consider to be important that I have omitted, but this is a journey for the heart more than a "how to run a company" book. If there are other activities you believe are relevant, I trust you will be encouraged to search the Scriptures to guide your diligent pursuit of them.

The activities I have chosen are:

- Defining the mission of the organization—its reason for being in existence;

- Establishing the values and the culture of the organization—the way in which it will achieve its mission;
- Determining priorities, setting goals, and communicating them to others;
- Holding yourself and others accountable to keep promises and commitments;
- Accumulating sufficient resources to achieve the goals and objectives of the organization;
- Practicing good stewardship through the diligent management and allocation of resources;
- Retaining and recruiting talented employees;
- Increasing sales and revenues;
- Managing the balance sheet and anticipating trouble;
- Protecting the reputation of the organization;
- Recognizing when change is necessary; and
- Harvesting and pruning the organization.

Due to the dynamic changes in situations all businesses experience, these twelve activities seldom occur in a linear fashion. Perhaps the first activity, defining the mission of the enterprise, is a natural "first" on the list, but I believe even this activity requires continuous evaluation and justification. My experience is that these twelve activities have a way of cropping up at various times throughout the year. As a result, the devotionals and Scripture references have not been collected and presented sequentially by topic, but have been broken up so they appear at different times during the 52 weeks of the book.

Each devotional message begins with a longer passage of Scripture than is typically found in devotionals, and this is by design. Paul, in writing to Timothy, notes: "All Scripture is given by inspiration of God, and is profitable for doctrine, for reproof, for correction, for instruction in righteousness, that the man of God may be complete, thoroughly equipped for every good work" (2 Timothy 3:16–17, NKJV). My belief is that you, by virtue of your role as a leader of others, are a person who examines things carefully with respect to both your business and your life. It was to honor that characteristic in you that enough material has been provided to allow you to gain personal insight into the context in which the Scripture is found. Additionally, Scripture sings in God's own voice the truth that He loves you, has a plan for you, and is keenly interested in your life and your career.

The devotionals are grouped following a retail business calendar of thirteen-week quarters, with the three months of each quarter consisting of four weeks, four weeks, and five weeks. In addition, there are twelve calendar-month introductory devotionals to center the business messages that follow within the seasons of the year. Thus, the first week of each new month entails two messages; thereafter, one message is to be read each week.

Finally, the questions at the end of each weekly message will ask you to deeply reflect on the message, the Scripture, the application of the message to your life, and to explore new insights into God and His desire to reveal His blessings in your life through relationship, trust, and faith.

I can testify that if you devote yourself to a diligent pursuit of God, you will find Him. The messages in this book will teach you how to apply godly principles and spiritual discernment in reaching business decisions and choosing among alternative courses of action. You will become a better leader because you will make better decisions. God will not disappoint you, and He will not bring you any shame.

My prayer for you is that God will richly bless your study and the questions of your heart so that you may know Him more fully and that you may become more and more grounded in a deep and personal relationship with Him. I am confident He will do this and more for you.

Don Moore

December 2014

JANUARY

Blessed is the one
who does not walk in step with the wicked
or stand in the way that sinners take
or sit in the company of mockers,
but whose delight is in the law of the Lord,
and who meditates on his law day and night.
That person is like a tree planted by streams of water,
which yields its fruit in season
and whose leaf does not wither—
whatever they do prospers.
Not so the wicked!
They are like chaff
that the wind blows away.
Therefore the wicked will not stand in the judgment,
nor sinners in the assembly of the righteous.
For the Lord watches over the way of the righteous,
but the way of the wicked leads to destruction.
~ Psalm 1:1–6 NIV

Where I live, January is an impostor. The dark and dreariness of winter with its bone-chilling frigid mornings and icy blasts of raw cutting air hardly ever bother us here in New Orleans, where the probability of sunshine stands at 46 percent and the average temperature is 53 degrees Fahrenheit.

Houses here have fireplaces (I have one), but they are as absurd as a racing stripe on a 1976 Chevy Vega (I had one). Yes, January in New Orleans is an impostor, and that is a shame.

There is something good for our human souls to see the physical world overcome with dreariness, darkness, stillness, and death. We need to be reminded that winter will come to us someday, and it will come on its own terms. We cannot control the seasons of our life any more than we can control the natural weather.

Our business careers can stand as impostors, too. Our rank, our status, our responsibility, our ambitions, our competitiveness, our fortune, and even our folly can enchant us to believe *we* are to be found, known, and considered worthy of love, or respect, or admiration, or honor in what we do rather than in what we believe or, to be more precise, in whom we believe. After all, most of our waking hours are spent working and associating with others similarly working. Work is what keeps our families fed, clothed, educated, and otherwise provisioned. If we work hard enough, smart enough, and long enough, and if we are careful about our lifestyles and spending habits, work will propel us into our golden years of retirement.

It is very easy to become self-absorbed and self-identified in our work.

We are called to work by God (Genesis 2:15). Since work is from God, it is reasonable to expect work can help each of us fulfill our purpose in life. But just because work is from God does not mean we will use work as God intended—we can abuse work just as we can abuse any gift of God.

It is possible that our work, standing as an impostor, can hinder us in finding our purpose in life. We know this to be true because we can see how work is exhilarating and uplifting to some, and debilitating and fatiguing to others. Charles Dickens' Ebenezer Scrooge is hateful to us, but he is not so much a caricature as to be unrecognizable. The ghost of Christmas Future reminds us that the trappings of this life are fleeting. Intellectually, we may know that work, albeit important, is not the whole of our being; nonetheless, we remain susceptible to succumbing to the siren call of success.

One of my favorite poems is Robert Frost's "The Road Not Taken". Frost, like the psalmist, speaks with certainty that our choices matter. Frost instructs that one step can inexorably lead on to other steps such that direction becomes difficult or impossible to change. His poem draws us into self-reflection about our own roads taken or not taken: did we choose wisely? Will we find ourselves, somewhere ages and ages hence, sighing because of the road not taken? Perhaps that question is what prompted you to open this book; you want to know that what you do and who you are matters in the big scheme of things. You want to discover how to live a professional life filled with meaning and purpose, because sometimes work seems out of touch with God.

Those questions and concerns are what prompted me to write this book, and in the weeks ahead you will discover God is keenly interested in what you do at work and in your role as a leader.

The psalmist speaks to us in the dead of winter about two types of men. One of them lives and is destined to live in winter, and the other lives and is destined to live in spring where his "leaf does not wither." What separates these men from each other; what dictates their respective fates? One of them knows God, and the other knows Him not. One longs to spend time with God, and the other mocks Him. One stands under God's blessings; one stands under judgment.

The psalmist does not acknowledge what Christians know: that once, each one of us sat in the seats of mockers and was under judgment. Neither does he inform us what Christians know: that hope exists, even for the sinner. But he does inform us of a spiritual truth that Jesus spoke to His disciples when He said, "apart from me you can do nothing" (John 15:5b NIV).

God gave us work, and He wants to bless the work of our hands. God gave us the desires of our hearts, and He wants to fulfill them for us. God gave us Jesus, and for us, the blessed New Thought for a Christian New Year is we can choose wisely; we can find a new path; we can come home and can stand under God's blessings. Jesus Christ made that possible.

As you begin this study, I pray that God will use it to draw you into a deeper and more personal relationship with Him, because our purpose in life is known only in the context of our relationship with God. God sees you at work just as He sees you on Sunday at church. God has a purpose and a plan for your life, and He does not want it to remain a secret from you. The psalmist reminds us that "the Lord knows the way of the righteous" (Psalm 1:6a NKJV). Jesus said, "He who abides in Me, and I in him, bears much fruit; for without Me you can do nothing" (John 15:5b NKJV).

In January, when winter still holds fast to the world, the psalmist sings of spring, of bearing fruit in season, and leaves that do not wither. Such is the life-giving, breathtaking, awesome wonder of the God who is Creator and who is still creating newness of life in those He loves. As you contemplate your godly role of leadership in your company and in your family, delight yourself in God's love and meditate on His promises so that all who come in contact with you get the sense of spring.

REFLECTIONS FOR JANUARY

1. As you reflect on the year just past and the hope for the year to come, consider how you feel about your relationship to God.

2. Thinking only about yesterday, write down the primary activities and work-related activities that you can recall. Now write down beside each one how you included God in that activity, how you asked Him to provide you with wisdom and insight, and how you thanked Him for the blessings He provided.

3. Now, think about those things that will face you today. How will you include God in your plans and decisions today?

4. Do you include God in every aspect of your life, or do you exclude Him from some aspects of your life?

5. If you were asked to give an account of your relationship with God, how would you describe it? Is it warm and cordial, trusting and full of hope, or is it something else? Would you care to change the relationship if you could?

6. Finally, ask yourself how others who know you would respond to the question, "I know that (insert your name) is a Christian because_____."

PRAYER

Father God, Creator of all things, here at the start of a New Year, let me rejoice that You have made me in Your own image—You have given me intelligence, desires, drive, ambition, compassion, and work. You have also given me a mind and a conscience so that I can hear and respond to Your call in my life to build a life that is pleasing to You. You will fully equip me to accomplish all that is set before me. You desire obedience; Lord, grant me a willing spirit to hear and obey. You desire relationship; Lord, grant me a deep desire and the courage to include You in all aspects of my life. If You do not reveal Yourself to me, I shall not find You; Lord, be near to me, and in Your love and mercy, teach me Your ways. I pray all of this in the name of Your Son, Jesus.

Amen

JANUARY—WEEK ONE

PRACTICING GOOD STEWARDSHIP THROUGH THE DILIGENT MANAGEMENT AND ALLOCATION OF RESOURCES

> Then God said, "Let there be lights in the firmament of the heavens to divide the day from the night; and let them be for signs and seasons, and for days and years; and let them be for lights in the firmament of the heavens to give light on the earth"; and it was so. Then God made two great lights: the greater light to rule the day, and the lesser light to rule the night. He made the stars also. God set them in the firmament of the heavens to give light on the earth, and to rule over the day and over the night, and to divide the light from the darkness. And God saw that it was good. So the evening and the morning were the fourth day.
>
> ~ Genesis 1:14–19 NKJV

Has it been a while since you read the account of creation as set forth in Genesis? If so, I urge you to reacquaint yourself with the story because it sheds great light on who we are and who God is, how we are to relate to Him and understand Him, and His desire for our good. What strikes me as I read the story is just how firm God's plans were from the outset.

The chronology of each of the days of creation in sequence is fascinating. God observed the formless emptiness of the earth and set in motion an order to our world and the universe, an order full of promise and goodness. On the first day, God created light, and light forevermore separated the darkness. The source of the light was God Himself, since the stars and the sun and the moon had not yet been created. Hold onto that thought as we move through days two and three.

On the second day, God created the sky, separating it from the primordial waters. On the third day, God gathered the water under the sky into one place so that dry ground might appear. From the ground God then created all vegetation, each according to their various kinds and each with the ability to reproduce. By the end of the third day, the earth was alive with plants, thriving and growing, covering the land.

Consider carefully this chronology of the order of creation. God had not yet created the sun. Plants need light to live. On the earth without the sun hanging in the heavens we see God has created the earth and filled it with vegetation. God was the light for the plants. There were no seasons and no end of the growing season while God provided the light. On the fourth day, God created the sun, the moon, and the stars. After the creation events of the fourth day, the earth was prepared for seasons and for marking the passage of time, before there was any need for such things. Why?

On the sixth day, God capped off His mighty works of creation by making man in His own image—an image that included free will. The use of that free will soon resulted in a breach of the harmony of creation with its Creator, and man forevermore needed the seasons, the marking of time, and the pull of the tide and the delicate balance of gravitation to sustain life.

God knew what we are made of and how we would behave with our gift of free will. And He made sure, before it happened, that we would have what we needed to live when we separated from the one true light.

We see in Genesis 1:26–31, and also in Genesis 2:15–23, that God set clear goals and communicated them to the man and woman. Tragically, in Genesis 3 we read about man's disobedience and expulsion from the Garden of Eden. Thankfully, God provided the sun and the moon and the stars on the *fourth* day in anticipation of the time when Adam and Eve would fall away from the one true light and would need the seasons and the passage of time to live in the world outside the Garden.

Leaders are often faced with decisions to allocate the resources of their business, and those resources are invariably scarcer than one would like. A key aspect of successful leadership (and a godly characteristic as well) is to demonstrate an ability to be a good **steward** of the business's available resources. Making judicious choices in the allocation of resources among mutually exclusive opportunities often leads to success.

Also associated with good stewardship is a recognition that events do not always turn out as we had hoped or anticipated. Because of inherent uncertainty in the outcomes of our stated objectives, good stewards will consider and develop contingency plans in the event that actual results differ significantly with planned results.

Our human inability to anticipate the future needs of the enterprise in times of change and uncertainty can create tension in our businesses and in our lives. As we see in the account of Genesis, God is never confused or in doubt about the future. On the contrary, God has seen everything that will happen and is working His purposes in the lives of all of His creation. As you approach the decisions of being a good steward and managing the resources under your control, avail yourself of the willingness of God to guide your decisions and to bless them.

REFLECTIONS FOR THE WEEK

1. How have you solicited, through prayer, God's wisdom and blessings on your decisions to allocate resources to various goals and objectives of your business?

2. What would you say to someone if asked to explain how God is involved in the day-to-day activities of your business?

3. What might be the outcome if you included in your prayer life a daily discussion with God of your plans and objectives, both for business and personally?

PRAYER

Lord, help me never cease to be amazed and in awe that the Creator of the universe actually cares about the wants and the needs of humans. You are never confused. You are never in doubt. You know the choices that are before me each day, and You know the ones that will bring me closer to You. I pray that You will illuminate my mind to Your desires and guide my thoughts to reach right decisions in harmony with Your will. As I struggle with daily choices, forgive my errors and judge my heart, for my heart desires to please You.

Amen

JANUARY—WEEK TWO

HOLDING YOURSELF AND OTHERS ACCOUNTABLE TO KEEP PROMISES AND COMMITMENTS

> The Pharisees and Sadducees came to Jesus and tested him by asking him to show them a sign from heaven.
>
> He replied, "When evening comes, you say, 'It will be fair weather, for the sky is red,' and in the morning, 'Today it will be stormy, for the sky is red and overcast.' You know how to interpret the appearance of the sky, but you cannot interpret the signs of the times. A wicked and adulterous generation looks for a sign, but none will be given it except the sign of Jonah." Jesus then left them and went away.
>
> ~ Matthew 16:1–4 NIV

When was the last time you were tested in your faith—a time when problems seemed overwhelming or life particularly harsh and unfair? Recall those circumstances and your response to the time of testing. Did you wonder if God cared? Did you wonder where God was in the midst of your time of testing?

Such questions are important to ask because they are honest and real. If God truly wants for us to have fellowship with Him, such questions must be asked.

A truth of Scripture is that God uses tests to teach, encourage, admonish, and strengthen His people. A time of testing—in fact, many times of testing, will face all of us. Some of those tests will affect our personal lives, but others will affect our businesses and careers.

It is wishful thinking to hope that all tests reveal themselves and call out when they approach us, but that is not always the case. Leaders are wise who stay alert to the times of testing, praying to have them quickly pass and for their responses to remain true to the Lord and His call. Consider Jesus in the garden when He admonished His disciples,

"Couldn't you men keep watch with me for one hour?" He asked Peter. "Watch and pray so that you will not fall into temptation. The spirit is willing, but the flesh is weak" (Matthew 26:40b-41 NIV).

Sadly, the disciples did not follow Jesus' advice but returned again to sleep. It is speculation to wonder how the events of the next few hours might have turned out for them had they heeded His advice. But recall also that Peter, years later, could say with certainty to others, "Be of sober spirit, be on the alert. Your adversary, the devil, prowls around like a roaring lion, seeking someone to devour. But resist him, firm in your faith, knowing that the same experiences of suffering are being accomplished by your brethren who are in the world. After you have suffered for a little while, the God of all grace, who called you to His eternal glory in Christ, will Himself perfect, confirm, strengthen and establish you" (1 Peter 5:8-10 NASB).

In looking at the passage from Matthew 16 above, we see one of the tests Jesus faced in His earthly ministry. It was very real and not unlike tests all people face. Just as Satan had tested Jesus in the wilderness with promises to shorten His path to victory by displays of His strength, now here come these successful and highly respected leaders of society asking Jesus to display signs to prove to them who He is. "Here," we can almost hear Satan say, "is the way to gain the influence and popularity you long for and could use in your work." It was not as if Jesus did not perform miracles and show signs of who He was. On the contrary, He displayed the power of God in His life to reveal the Father to the world.

But He would not display His power for crowd appeal and self-aggrandizement. Jesus knew the hearts of men, and these men would not see, nor would they believe. Jesus concluded being a part of the influential crowd was not important to His work, and displaying His power to this group of men would certainly not get Him closer to His goals.

Jesus faced a true test of His obedience and courage. This particular situation presented the opportunity for Jesus to choose to act in a way contrary to God's will, in essence to break His promise to obey God completely. However, Jesus held firm to the vision he had from God that the

JANUARY—WEEK TWO

cross was the way of His ministry. Later, He instructed His disciples to beware of the yeast of the Pharisees and Sadducees, although they were not able to follow His thinking without further explanation.

Jesus kept His promise to God to fulfill the mission set out for Him. Jesus was accountable for His actions and His choices. Through His response we see that what we say and do matters to our mission and to others.

You too, at some point, will be approached by society. You will see how society conducts business and be tempted to stray from the righteous thing to do. You will be tempted to break a promise. You will be tempted to avoid accountability. You will be tempted to compromise on your ethical position. The Christian band Casting Crowns recorded a song written by Mark Hall about the sly and pernicious way that compromise compromises a person—warning about the risks when one thing leads to another. As the song says, "a price will be paid when you give yourself away."[1]

Keeping promises and being accountable begins with you, as leader. Somewhere in the future, you will act or behave in a way that you wish you had not. Because you are a leader, your actual behavior or actions will be noticed by others. This is the way of the world—followers watch leaders. In the future, when you stumble, when you break a promise or commitment, you will run a great risk of putting others in harm's way by your actions.

But when you become aware of your failures, remember that Jesus loves you anyway. Let your prayer life include asking the Lord through the Spirit to illuminate your life as God sees it so that times of falling away will become the opportunity for great growth and change.

And as you recover from your error, prayerfully consider how to restore others through the wisdom you have gained by the time of testing. The book of Hebrews encourages leaders to take up the mantle of leadership again, to once again be an example of godly leadership, when it says, "Therefore, strengthen the hands that are weak and the knees that are feeble, and make

---

[1] Casting Crowns. *Slow Fade*. Producer: Mark A. Miller, 2007. CD.

straight paths for your feet, so that the limb which is lame may not be put out of joint, but rather be healed" (Hebrews 12:12–13 NASB).

REFLECTIONS FOR THE WEEK

1. Can you envision any reason or circumstance involving a broken promise or commitment that would not also be considered as a broken promise to God?

2. Reflect upon a recent circumstance where someone broke a promise to you. What was the outcome? How has the event changed your relationship?

PRAYER

Lord, You were tempted, but You overcame each temptation that came Your way. You said that the student is not above the Master, and that we can expect no better treatment in this world than You received. Help me to see the time of testing as a chance to grow and provide leadership to others. If I fall, help me quickly recover, admit my errors, and find forgiveness and newness of spirit through Jesus who stands as my Advocate before You. In His precious name I pray.

Amen

JANUARY—WEEK THREE

DETERMINING PRIORITIES, SETTING GOALS, AND COMMUNICATING THEM TO OTHERS

*Trust in the Lord with all your heart
And do not lean on your own understanding.
In all your ways acknowledge Him,
And He will make your paths straight.
Do not be wise in your own eyes;
Fear the Lord and turn away from evil.
It will be healing to your body
And refreshment to your bones.
Honor the Lord from your wealth
And from the first of all your produce;
So your barns will be filled with plenty
And your vats will overflow with new wine.
My son, do not reject the discipline of the Lord
Or loathe His reproof,
For whom the Lord loves He reproves,
Even as a father corrects the son in whom he delights.
How blessed is the man who finds wisdom
And the man who gains understanding.
For her profit is better than the profit of silver
And her gain better than fine gold.
She is more precious than jewels;
And nothing you desire compares with her.
Long life is in her right hand;
In her left hand are riches and honor.
Her ways are pleasant ways
And all her paths are peace.
She is a tree of life to those who take hold of her,
And happy are all who hold her fast.*

~ Proverbs 3:5–18 NASB

Have you ever been surprised by some passages of Scripture that seem paradoxical—that convey insights and instructions so unexpected as to appear upside down to traditional thinking? Of course, not all Scripture is that way; some seems very straight forward. But not infrequently, Scripture will instruct the reader to think or do something that is definitely not in accordance with human common sense. Consider, for example, the implications of the passages above against one of the highest and hardest aspects of being a leader—determining priorities, setting clear goals, and communicating them to your subordinates.

Leadership has consequences; leaders are accountable not only for their own actions and results, but also for the actions and the results of those they lead. One great task and responsibility for you is to set the goals and objectives for your company and the people you lead, and this role is filled with risks and rewards.

If you choose the wrong goals and objectives, your company will not be as successful as it might have been had you chosen other, more appropriate goals and objectives. And there is a ripple effect that flows from the choices you make: Your choice of goals and objectives will, in turn, lead to other choices by subordinates who are making their own goals to try and align with yours. As a result, the effect of choosing rightly will propel the enterprise toward achievement, and choosing wrongly will lead to difficulty.

How might you enhance your ability to choose rightly? The Bible says we are to ask God to reveal His will for us, and to then act as if we trust Him by obeying Him. In other words, a wise leader would begin by asking God for wisdom and then demonstrate trust and obedience by following the wisdom provided by God.

As a leader, it is difficult to lay the obvious purview of leadership at the door of someone else—even if that someone is God. Trusting God with the responsibility of providing wisdom in selecting goals and objectives is never easy, and there may be times of trial and error to experience.

I would urge you, however, to lay hold of the promises of God in the Proverbs passage set forth earlier, because the benefits of doing so are superb to consider. If you are open to consider the benefits of allowing God to guide your choices in setting goals and objectives, the passages at the beginning of this chapter provide a summary of how trust is developed and the benefits derived from trusting God.

As we consider Proverbs 3, right from the start, we are urged to trust in the Lord with all our heart and lean not on our own understanding. There is a promise that if we trust in the Lord, He will guide our paths—in fact, He will set them straight. But the promise is clearly conditional. **You must trust in the Lord to have Him set your paths straight.**

As you ponder that instruction and the resultant benefit against the backdrop of whatever business you are in with whatever constraints, hopes, issues, opportunities, and strengths and weaknesses your business possesses and faces, the next verse anticipates your surprise and concern: Don't be too smart or too full of yourself. Here again is instruction with a promise, for if you are not wise in your own eyes, if you fear the Lord and shun evil, this will bring health to your body and nourishment to your bones. I believe the evil referred to here is one of disbelief and failure to trust the Lord—to not trust the Lord is sinful. So, back to back, we hear that we are to trust God, and it will bring us benefits.

The next verses reflect a conscious act that will demonstrate a sense of trusting God. We are instructed to bring sacrifices to the Lord, and to attribute what we obtain materially in this world to the Lord. If we do our part, God promises He will bless our work.

We might be tempted to think this instruction is easier than the first ones—that giving gifts, or offerings, or charity, is natural and good, and we all should do that. But Cain found this hard to do (Genesis 4:2–5). So did the rich young ruler who inquired of Jesus what must he do to inherit eternal life (Matthew 19:16–22). As you set goals and objectives, prayerfully contemplate how you can be a faithful steward of God's blessings to you and to your business, returning a portion of its "first fruits" to the Lord.

The next passage offers some practical advice on what to do when the Lord treats us as His children and disciplines us from time to time. I believe this passage is placed here because the proverbs leading up to this section are difficult for us to accomplish. Since our God cares for us and desires a specific and wonderful future that He had in mind when He created us, He will take care to give us discipline when it is needed. A paradoxical effect of this is that the time of testing and discipline to come is really God's overarching love for you at work in your life. As such, it is wise and godly to approach all trials and discipline with thanksgiving instead of fear and despair.

The final passage in the Scripture selection from Proverbs is the culmination of the sequence of events, start to finish. Out of the pursuit of God in our daily lives and in our businesses—a diligent pursuit—a purposeful, thoughtful, loving, wondering, contemplative, honoring pursuit, we will gain wisdom. The benefits of wisdom are defined as better than anything the world might offer up in terms of wealth and value. And that completes the circle to the first passage, trust in the Lord and lean not on your understanding.

REFLECTIONS FOR THE WEEK

1. Reflect on an area in your life or your business where you are choosing to rely on your own insights and wisdom in making choices rather than asking God to participate in your decisions.

2. What might be the outcome if you believed that God had an opinion on such matters that He wished to share with you?

PRAYER

Almighty God, You will not accept a lesser role in any aspect of my life other than that of King and Savior. I acknowledge that though I lose sight from time to time, you are involved in all aspects of my life, and nothing escapes Your notice or Your love. Forgive my instances of trying to do anything without considering what You would have me do, and embolden me to trust You.

Amen

JANUARY—WEEK FOUR

DETERMINING PRIORITIES, SETTING GOALS, AND COMMUNICATING THEM TO OTHERS

> If any of you lacks wisdom, you should ask God, who gives generously to all without finding fault, and it will be given to you. But when you ask, you must believe and not doubt, because the one who doubts is like a wave of the sea, blown and tossed by the wind. That person should not expect to receive anything from the Lord. Such a person is double-minded and unstable in all they do.
>
> ~ James 1: 5–8 NIV

> Who is wise and understanding among you? Let them show it by their good life, by deeds done in the humility that comes from wisdom. But if you harbor bitter envy and selfish ambition in your hearts, do not boast about it or deny the truth. Such "wisdom" does not come down from heaven but is earthly, unspiritual, demonic. For where you have envy and selfish ambition, there you find disorder and every evil practice.
>
> But the wisdom that comes from heaven is first of all pure; then peace-loving, considerate, submissive, full of mercy and good fruit, impartial and sincere. Peacemakers who sow in peace reap a harvest of righteousness.
>
> ~ James 3:13–18 NIV

Last week we considered in Proverbs 3 that trusting God yields great benefits to us. The passage from James above reveals that we can also trust God to provide us with wisdom when we are choosing among alternative courses of action. The pre-requisite for obtaining godly wisdom is to ask God for it; the final step is to believe (trust) God to provide it.

You might be wondering how God feels about His children asking Him questions. Can we ask Him about everything, or should we only ask Him about the really important stuff?

That is not a trick question. When I was a young man, I held the opinion that God was too busy to be involved in my daily activities or my work. I cannot explain the reasons I felt that way at the time other than I was rationalizing my own rebellion against God. But I no longer believe God is uninvolved or uninterested in every aspect of our lives. The psalmist notes:

> *O Lord, You have searched me and known me.*
> *You know when I sit down and when I rise up;*
> *You understand my thought from afar.*
> *You scrutinize my path and my lying down,*
> *And are intimately acquainted with all my ways.*
> ~ Psalm 139:1–3 NASB

Here is another thought about choosing to withhold some question from God. You are finite and not omniscient. On the other hand, God is infinite and omniscient. Only God is in a position to know which of your questions are really important. Since you do not, ask them all.

Coming to grips with the idea that God is deeply interested in all that I do and that He desires a personal relationship with me has made a profound difference in my life and my outlook on life. My life is more peaceful now because I know that God cares about me and for me in ways that are, frankly, unimaginable to me.

In the passage from James above, we clearly see that God encourages us to seek His wisdom in our lives, and we can scarcely do that without asking Him for wisdom. But just as in last week, where God's promise in Proverbs 3 was conditional, the author of James points out that we need to believe that God will answer us, and we must be prepared for the answer that we get and to not doubt it; otherwise, we can expect to hear and receive nothing. This leads to a more difficult problem: how do we know what we hear is truly from God?

Often, after bringing concerns to the Lord and seeking His wisdom, I have felt uncertain that what my heart is hearing is not what God really wants me to do; it is just my "earthly" heart superimposing its thoughts on the quiet voice of God. Then I run smack into the admonition about being a doubter, an unstable man who should not expect anything from

God. The passages in Chapter 3 of James above have helped me to gain more confidence in listening to and interpreting the things my heart is telling me.

James tells us what godly wisdom looks like—and contrasts that with worldly wisdom. As you order and select priorities and set goals and objectives for yourself and others in your business, or as you contemplate what your heart is hearing about choosing among alternative courses of action, it will be helpful to screen them through the following list of godly attributes.

GODLY WISDOM IS:

PURE

> If you have a dictionary, look up the word *pure*. You will find the definition includes the concepts of being free from anything that adulterates, unmixed, simple, mere, utter, absolute, free from defects, and faultless. God's wisdom is pure—it is not conflicted. God's wisdom is complete unto itself and needs nothing else to make it complete.

PEACEABLE

> God's wisdom provides quiet assurance. It will seek the good of others. It will not be contentious. God's wisdom does not reflect any pride, but is humble in nature.

GENTLE

> God's wisdom should come to you without anger or rancor involved. God's wisdom will have no arrogance. Rather, it will be loving, kindly, and godly.

WILLING TO YIELD

> God's wisdom will not be directed toward a self-serving end, but will be considerate of the effects on others. Sometimes, God's wisdom will ask us to yield our objectives and goals. Such a conclusion will be difficult to accept and do.

FULL OF MERCY

> By being aware of the effects on others, God's wisdom will guide and direct toward mercy. God's wisdom will harbor no grudges, but will be full of forgiveness and reconciliation.

DEMONSTRATES GOOD FRUIT
> The book of Galatians describes the fruit of the Spirit as "love, joy, peace, patience, kindness, goodness, faithfulness, gentleness and self-control" (Galatians 5:22–23a NIV). Godly wisdom will be rich and filled with the outcomes of the fruit of the Spirit—for you, the decision maker, and for those affected by your decisions.

IMPARTIAL
> God's wisdom does not seek "favorites," placing one person above another. God's wisdom is imminently fair to all.

WITHOUT HYPOCRISY
> Jesus was relentless in calling out the hypocrisy of His generation. The Old Testament is also relentless in revealing the hypocrisy of human behavior toward God and toward each other. God's wisdom will not be hypocritical, but will stand fully in the light without cause for concern about motives or double-dealing.

As a leader, ask God to guide your choices. Then ask God, through the meditations of your heart, to prove the wisdom you hear is godly wisdom.

REFLECTIONS FOR THE WEEK

1. Choose a concern or opportunity that has recently appeared in your life or your business where your final decision is still uncertain. Present the issue to God in prayer and reflect upon the list of attributes that accompany godly wisdom as you reflect on your decision.

2. Record your thoughts and your decision in a journal so that with the passage of time you can reexamine the circumstances and see how God acted in your life in this moment of opportunity to rely on God's promises and your desire to hear His voice.

PRAYER

Lord, Your Word is full of life. I pray that each day Your Word takes deeper root in my heart, guiding and protecting me, and allowing me to make choices consistent with Your hopes and desires for me. Forgive me when I am deaf, and through Your Spirit, call the louder to bring me back to godly wisdom.

Amen

FEBRUARY

> Beloved, let us love one another, for love is from God; and everyone who loves is born of God and knows God. The one who does not love does not know God, for God is love. By this the love of God was manifested in us, that God has sent His only begotten Son into the world so that we might live through Him. In this is love, not that we loved God, but that He loved us and sent His Son to be the propitiation for our sins. Beloved, if God so loved us, we also ought to love one another.
>
> ~ 1 John 4:7–11 NASB

In America, this is the month of love and chocolates. For most of the country, February is cold and gray, snowy and without much of the promise of spring. The joy of the Christmas season is long past, and in February, winter is in full possession of the weather reports, the traffic reports, school closings reports, and our wardrobes. Valentine's Day provides celebration and relief to the fullness of winter. Valentine's Day reminds us that love can conquer even the effects of winter.

From God's perspective, a type of winter fell upon all of creation when Adam and Eve disobeyed. Sin supplanted paradise, replacing it with a form of perpetual winter. The promise and beauty that had once existed and had been proclaimed "good" was now trapped under the wintry shroud of death; man's disobedience, even though it was clothed in ignorance and initiated by the Serpent's deception, subjected the earth and all that was in it to the cold and death of winter.

But because God is love, He would not leave His creation to its self-selected fate. Rather than irrevocable abandonment from all that God intended or continual and forever judgment, God chose to continue to love us. And His all-surpassing love conquered the winter of our souls.

Consider what Paul says about God's love:

> For while we were still helpless, at the right time Christ died for the ungodly. For one will hardly die for a righteous man; though perhaps for the good man someone would dare even to die. But God demonstrates His own love toward us, in that while we were yet sinners, Christ died for us.
>
> ~ Romans 5:6–8 NASB

The extent of God's love and His unwillingness to abandon His creation was demonstrated in the atoning sacrifice of His perfect Son, Jesus. Through Jesus and His story of life, death, and resurrection from the dead, God revealed to the world the full expression of His love toward us, and the effects such love would bring to us and to our world.

As you prepare for the month of February, still gripped by winter but with the joy of love and chocolates embedded within the month, remember that God loves you every day and has perfect plans for you.

REFLECTIONS FOR FEBRUARY

1. The Bible says in Deuteronomy 6:5–7 (NASB), "You shall love the Lord your God with all your heart and with all your soul and with all your might. These words, which I am commanding you today, shall be on your heart. You shall teach them diligently to your sons and shall talk of them when you sit in your house and when you walk by the way and when you lie down and when you rise up." What might be the outcome if we were to take these words literally during the month of February?

2. Society today attempts to seek a "political correctness" in all areas where past societies were comfortable in reaching conclusions of right and wrong. In a work environment, the threat of litigation hangs heavy such that sincere and honest discussions of personal faith can be unwelcome. In spite of this, the knowledge of God is worth sharing because it is good news in a difficult world. How do

you feel about initiating or participating in a conversation about God with others? What are your greatest fears?

PRAYER

Almighty God, You are love—it is an essential characteristic of Your holy nature. When we love others, we participate in a supernatural way with the plan that You conceived at Creation. Make me glad to share Your love with others. Make me willing to open myself to the possibilities of loving my neighbors as myself.

Amen

FEBRUARY—WEEK ONE

INCREASING SALES AND REVENUES

> I am the true vine, and My Father is the vinedresser. Every branch in Me that does not bear fruit, He takes away; and every branch that bears fruit, He prunes it so that it may bear more fruit. You are already clean because of the word which I have spoken to you. Abide in Me, and I in you. As the branch cannot bear fruit of itself unless it abides in the vine, so neither can you unless you abide in Me. I am the vine, you are the branches; he who abides in Me and I in him, he bears much fruit, for apart from Me you can do nothing. If anyone does not abide in Me, he is thrown away as a branch and dries up; and they gather them, and cast them into the fire and they are burned.
>
> ~ John 15:1–6 NASB

For any organization, revenues are the fuel that powers the business. Businesses are expensive to develop and operate. Revenues must be sufficient to cover these costs, or the organization will fail. As a leader, one of your essential responsibilities is to make sure the organization has revenues sufficient for its purposes.

If this were simply a business book, a chapter on increasing revenues would spend a lot of time discussing such things as marketing and channels of distribution, pricing theory, the theory of constraints, motivation and bonus structures, share of market, share of voice, innovation and time to market, differentiation and segmentation—we'd have a lot to talk about with respect to increasing revenues and growing the business.

But this is not simply a business book. This book seeks to strengthen your soul, awakening in you a desire for God that will align your will with His not only away from work but also in your work life. What I want to do is increase your worth to God as a leader in whatever circumstances in which you find yourself. I want to increase your success, and by doing that to increase the success of others you lead or come in contact with.

FEBRUARY—WEEK ONE

Success, as defined by Merriam-Webster's online dictionary, is to achieve a favorable or desired outcome from an attempt. While that is a simple definition and one that I believe is fair from a godly perspective, success seems more difficult in practice or in conversation to define because what we each believe to be a "favorable outcome" can vary significantly from individual to individual.

Consider the following simple example. If you take a test and score 100 out of 100, is the outcome successful for you? Would your answer differ if the score you achieved was 99 out of 100? How about 95 out of 100? How about 90 out of 100? How about 85 out of 100? This simple example indicates that success is often solely in the eye of the beholder. At some point, we each will view success from a personal and relative perspective.

Defining success becomes more difficult when God's opinion is considered. How does God view success? In answering this question, let's consider the following ideas: (1) God intensely desires for us to become *fruitful* in our lives; (2) God's definition of success (i.e. *fruitful*) does not conform to the world's view of success; and (3) Scripture says that we will not be fruitful unless we *abide* in Jesus.

With respect to God's desire for us to become fruitful in our lives, consider the following Scriptures:

> The Lord was with Joseph so that he prospered.
> ~ Genesis 39:2a NIV

> "For I know the plans I have for you," declares the Lord, "plans to prosper you and not to harm you, plans to give you hope and a future."
> ~ Jeremiah 29:11 NIV

With respect to God's view of success versus a worldly view of success, consider the following passages of Scripture:

> Do not love the world or anything in the world. If anyone loves the world, love for the Father is not in them. For everything in the world—the lust of the flesh, the lust of the eyes, and the pride of life—comes not from the Father but from the world.
> ~ 1 John 2:15–16 NIV

> Do not store up for yourselves treasures on earth, where moths and vermin destroy, and where thieves break in and steal. But store up for yourselves treasures in heaven, where moths and vermin do not destroy, and where thieves do not break in and steal. For where your treasure is, there your heart will be also.
>
> ~ Matthew 6:19-21 NIV

> What good will it be for someone to gain the whole world, yet forfeit their soul? Or what can anyone give in exchange for their soul?
>
> ~ Matthew 16:26 NIV

> You know that the rulers of the Gentiles lord it over them, and their high officials exercise authority over them. Not so with you. Instead, whoever wants to become great among you must be your servant.
>
> ~ Matthew 20:25-26 NIV

These passages reflect some examples of worldly success, contrasted with God's perspective. For some, success means power and position when they compare themselves to others. For some, success can mean recognition, again in relation to how one compares to others. For others, success is measured in victory, again in relation to how one compares to others. Success can mean having enough money to purchase things that are desired or wanted, but usually success means having more than what is needed.

Worldly success is not always synonymous with greed. Success, in a worldly view, can also be interpreted more altruistically such that we want more in order to do more for others. Success can also be personal, as in seeking our personal best knowing (and often in spite of) the raw ingredients that we possess. Sometimes we gain tremendous wealth and no evil is attached to it—we simply do things in such a way that the result is our wealth grows.

Regardless how you define success or measure the degree of success attained from attempts made, has it occurred to you that only God can accomplish for you what you want for your company, your family, or yourself? Think of it this way: if God is sovereign over all things, if God is interested in all things, and if God has a plan for all things, then God is exercising His sovereign control over every act and thing that occurs in your life, my life, and every life.

And if God is sovereign, it does not matter whether the lives involved in His exercising divine sovereign control acknowledge Him or not.

Some people struggle with this idea for many reasons. For example, some people believe God is not a micro-manager of human affairs and really doesn't concern Himself in individual lives. Some people think that God just allows us to make our own choices (a true statement) and that as a result, **our** choices are responsible for **our** outcomes—ending in either success or failure as defined by the person involved (not necessarily true from a biblical point of view).

Other people struggle with this idea because it is discomforting to think that God will choose whom to bless with certain forms of "success" while withholding "success" from others. Any such questions are fruitful to explore, and I encourage you to consider how you feel about God's role in directing human affairs as a whole and **your** affairs in particular.

No matter the opinion you hold of how God is acting daily in the lives of all people, it is quite possible that "worldly success" will come to people from all backgrounds and beliefs, whether Christian, non-Christian, or even atheistic. In fact, winning worldly success is a strong possibility for you (or anyone) if that is what you are pursuing because the world loves to give good things to its own (cf. John 15:19).

But worldly success without a personal relationship with God can ring hollow to those who possess it. The teacher in Ecclesiastes describes his worldly knowledge and success as "vanity" and a "chasing after the wind" (cf. Ecclesiastes 1:2a, 12-18). The prophet Hosea notes that those who chase after the wind will "reap a whirlwind" (Hosea 8:7a). The rock singer and composer Don Henley wrote "Gimme What You Got," a song about greed that mentions our inability to take our belongings with us when we die. The things of this world do not last for you or anyone, because you don't last.

If *godly* success is or becomes a choice for you, how can you assure yourself of achieving it? The answer is found in John 15:5 (NRSV): "I am the vine, you are the branches. Those who abide in me and I in them bear much fruit, because apart from me you can do nothing." The Merriam-Webster's online dictionary defines the word *abide* as "to continue in place," "to bear patiently," and "to remain or continue." Those who pursue God diligently, who wait on the Lord to act, who place their trust in the Lord, bear much fruit. The reward comes at God's direction and does not result from any personal effort on your part other than diligent pursuit of a godly life in imitation of Jesus.

Rather than material wealth (which may or may not come in accordance with God's plan), Jesus promises that *you* will be made *fruitful* if you learn to abide in Him. The focus is on what you will become as opposed to what you will gain. Certainly, you might also come to possess material wealth, for there is no inherent evil in the things of the world. But all such things are temporary. However, bearing fruit and being fruitful where God is the object you desire with all your heart and all your mind and all your strength will lead to eternal blessings.

In Galatians, Paul says, "Do not be deceived, God is not mocked; for whatever a man sows, this he will also reap. For the one who sows to his own flesh will from the flesh reap corruption, but the one who sows to the Spirit will from the Spirit reap eternal life. Let us not lose heart in doing good, for in due time we will reap if we do not grow weary. So then, while we have opportunity, let us do good to all people, and especially to those who are of the household of the faith" (Galatians 6:7–10 NASB).

Psalm 127:1–2 (NIV) puts in perspective all the anxious moments that a leader in business will inevitably face at some point in the life of their business:

> *Unless the Lord builds the house,*
> *the builders labor in vain.*
> *Unless the Lord watches over the city,*
> *the guards stand watch in vain.*
> *In vain you rise early*
> *and stay up late,*
> *toiling for food to eat—*
> *for he grants sleep to those he loves.*

FEBRUARY—WEEK ONE

As a Christian leader, you will be blessed when you discover that striving (for absolutely anything) without abiding in Jesus is vanity, a "chasing after the wind." But the Father desires to make you fruitful beyond your wildest imaginations.

Abide in Jesus, and God will give you the desires of your heart. Trust in Jesus, and reap a harvest of spiritual fruit that will not fade away with the passing of time.

REFLECTIONS FOR THE WEEK

1. In Psalm 37:4, God promises that He will give you the "desires of your heart." Consider how you would define for yourself "the desires of your heart." Which ones are personal and which ones are focused on your career? In your journal, write down the ones that seem the most important to you.

2. What are you willing to spend (time, energy, money, resources, prayer) on in order to obtain the desires of your heart?

3. Imagine that you are a very old person approaching the end of your life. In looking back over your life, what areas of your life and your relationships can be considered "fruitful?" Why?

PRAYER

Father, as a Christian in a secular world, it is hard sometimes to remember that to you there is no separation of loyalty. Regardless of what the worldview is, you are always with us, and no aspect of our life is unimportant to you. Help me to remember to abide in Jesus and to be alert to your loving hand at work in my life to make me fruitful. Help me to carry over to my work the confidence that comes to those who trust you and seek to understand your purposes for their lives.

Amen

FEBRUARY—WEEK TWO

PROTECTING THE REPUTATION OF THE ORGANIZATION

You, O LORD, will not withhold Your compassion from me;
Your lovingkindness and Your truth will continually preserve me.
For evils beyond number have surrounded me;
My iniquities have overtaken me, so that I am not able to see;
They are more numerous than the hairs of my head,
And my heart has failed me.
Be pleased, O LORD, to deliver me;
Make haste, O LORD, to help me.
Let those be ashamed and humiliated together
Who seek my life to destroy it;
Let those be turned back and dishonored
Who delight in my hurt.
Let those be appalled because of their shame
Who say to me, "Aha, aha!"
Let all who seek You rejoice and be glad in You;
Let those who love Your salvation say continually,
"The LORD be magnified!"
Since I am afflicted and needy,
Let the Lord be mindful of me.
You are my help and my deliverer;
Do not delay, O my God.
~ Psalm 40:11–17 NASB

Have you ever thought that we all live constantly under a state of assault? Are there not times, and too many to count, where the day ends and you feel exhausted by the events of the day that seemed to assault your hopes, your dreams, your sense of justice, your friends, your family, your life? It is not about whether or not the glass is half empty or half full. It is not about your attitude, because attitude is different than circumstances. Our attitude helps shape our response to events, but does nothing to eradicate the circumstances of our lives.

In my opinion, the circumstances of our lives are more like an assault than a walk in the park. Consider the t-shirt saying, "Getting old ain't for sissies." If nothing else seems like an assault to you, then consider how age assaults us all. Eventually, we all face our own mortality.

Or consider any emotional attachment toward another person. No matter how sweet, how pure, how loving, or how faithful the relationship, that attachment will end when one person passes into eternity.

In a book by J. Ellsworth Kalas, *Easter from the Backside*, Kalas points out that once the serpent completed the assault on Eve, death entered the world, and the book of Genesis immediately records the march of death on the earth. First, the naked humans needed clothing for warmth, and God fashioned clothes for them from animal skins. Soon thereafter, Abel was reported to be making offerings of animals to God. And then Genesis records the first murder when Cain killed his brother Abel. Death assaults our world, and death assaults us all.

As Christian business people, we hopefully conduct a more godly assault on our competitors as we seek market share, better terms, better pricing, more customers, more repeat business, more innovation, more channels of distribution, better employees, better technology—just better stuff than the other guy or the other company has. We are competitive, and our businesses are competitive. As a result, we carry on our own assaults, and we are similarly assaulted.

As if what we do to each other isn't enough, Paul points out that we are also being assaulted by supernatural forces. In Ephesians, Paul writes by the Spirit, "For our struggle is not against flesh and blood, but against the rulers, against the authorities, against the powers of this dark world and against the spiritual forces of evil in the heavenly realms" (Ephesians 6:12 NIV).

We walk in a world that is fallen. Because of this, the world is corrupt (though we do not like to think so), we are susceptible to being corrupted (though we do not like to admit it), and we and the earth itself are melting away. That is our circumstance.

But, what should be our attitude? Joy, thanksgiving, praise, faith, endurance, perseverance, gentleness, love, abiding, patience, goodness, charity, humility, a spirit willing to yield to God, and a heart full of hope. Against the goodness of Jesus Christ, no assault can stand or prevail.

REFLECTIONS FOR THE WEEK

1. In his book *Make Today Count: The Secret of Your Success Is Determined by Your Daily Agenda,* John Maxwell says, "Your attitude is a choice. If you desire to make your day a masterpiece, then you need to have a great attitude. If it's not good now, you need to change it." Make it a point this week to record in your journal some disappointing events (assaults), and consider how those events affected your attitude. What was your response? Were you pleased with your response in retrospect?

2. What might you do when you become aware of someone who is experiencing a disappointment or a difficult situation that may bring them comfort or hope?

PRAYER

Jesus, You were assaulted by all the evil of this world, and You relied on the Father. You did not return the insults or seek the harm of others. Rather, You gave love to all You met, even Your enemies. And God, the Father, has placed You high above all others, in heaven and in earth, and we can claim You as our brother and our Savior. Praise to You, Almighty God, for defeating death and decay, and giving us salvation and hope. May You increase my strength in times of testing and hold fast to my hands so that I do not fall.

Amen

FEBRUARY—WEEK THREE

ACCUMULATING SUFFICIENT RESOURCES TO ACHIEVE THE GOALS AND OBJECTIVES OF THE ORGANIZATION

Do you not know? Have you not heard?
Has it not been declared to you from the beginning?
Have you not understood from the foundations of the earth?
It is He who sits above the circle of the earth,
And its inhabitants are like grasshoppers,
Who stretches out the heavens like a curtain
And spreads them out like a tent to dwell in.
He it is who reduces rulers to nothing,
Who makes the judges of the earth meaningless.
Scarcely have they been planted,
Scarcely have they been sown,
Scarcely has their stock taken root in the earth,
But He merely blows on them, and they wither,
And the storm carries them away like stubble.
"To whom then will you liken Me
That I would be his equal?" says the Holy One.
Lift up your eyes on high
And see who has created these stars,
The One who leads forth their host by number,
He calls them all by name;
Because of the greatness of His might and the strength of His power,
Not one of them is missing.
Why do you say, O Jacob, and assert, O Israel,
"My way is hidden from the LORD,
And the justice due me escapes the notice of my God"?
Do you not know? Have you not heard?
The Everlasting God, the LORD, the Creator of the ends of the earth
Does not become weary or tired.
His understanding is inscrutable.
He gives strength to the weary,
And to him who lacks might He increases power.

Though youths grow weary and tired,
And vigorous young men stumble badly,
Yet those who wait for the LORD
Will gain new strength;
They will mount up with wings like eagles,
They will run and not get tired,
They will walk and not become weary.
~ Isaiah 40:21–31 NASB

A vital responsibility of a leader is to accumulate sufficient resources to accomplish the organization's mission. The rub is that resources, particularly *valuable resources,* are scarce and hard to come by. Valuable resources can be both tangible (materials, people, money, land, etc.) and intangible (time, energy, insight, wisdom, innovation, creativity, opportunity, etc.).

A business requires some combination of both tangible and intangible resources, but the intangible ones (those dealing with people and their time, their willpower, their stamina, and their faith) often represent the most important scarce resource needed to achieve its goals. In an interesting irony, the very act of identifying and accumulating needed valuable resources for your business and its activities in turn consumes a portion of one of your most particular and valuable resources—your time.

If time were not limited, perhaps there would not be scarce resources at all; with enough time, the means or ways to obtain resources would eventually be solved. But time is finite, and there is never enough of it.

Most of the time, we act as if time were limitless. We plan our days as if they were never going to end. We pursue some dreams and abandon others. We postpone conversations. We end relationships abruptly. We simply move on. But, inevitably, we are jolted to the awareness that all things, time included, become exhausted, used up, and all the kings' horses and all the kings' men cannot put them back together again.

The psalmist notes, "If only we knew the power of your anger! Your wrath is as great as the fear that is your due. Teach us to number our days, that we may gain a heart of wisdom" (Psalm 90:11–12 NIV). The brevity of our lives is a great instructor of wisdom.

The context of Isaiah's words at the beginning of this chapter is set against the Jewish people's exile in Babylon. The history of the Jewish people, contained in nearly every book of the Old Testament, reveals they all, from kings to commoners, went through continuous cycles of time where they stopped following God and His commandments; they often forgot God and chased after the gods of the people and nations that surrounded them. Apart from God's blessings and protection, the people suffered hardship.

Eventually, the hardship that found them was the complete destruction of Jerusalem and the deportation of the Jewish survivors to Babylon. Years earlier, the Assyrians had destroyed the Northern Kingdom, Israel, because of a similar abandonment of God. Now, faced with the consequences of their own actions, the Jewish people wondered: would God even want to restore His people?

With God, there is always hope. Chapter 40 of Isaiah begins with the verse,

> *Comfort, comfort my people,*
> *says your God.*
> *Speak tenderly to Jerusalem,*
> *and proclaim to her*
> *that her hard service has been completed,*
> *that her sin has been paid for,*
> *that she has received from the Lord's hand*
> *double for all her sins.*
>
> ~ Isaiah 40:1–2 NIV

There is hope in God and in God alone, and the author of Isaiah spends many verses calling the people to return to God and to His strength.

Since your time and your resources are both limited, let the wisdom gained by the brevity of time guide you to pursue an inexhaustible resource. God has promised to be with you always. He has promised to provide you with strength if you will only have courage and faith. By all means, develop your important endeavors, seek to do well in your calling and work, but never lose sight of how close at hand are the inexhaustible resources of our infinite and loving God.

> May the favor of the Lord our God rest on us;
> establish the work of our hands for us—
> yes, establish the work of our hands.
>
> ~ Psalm 90:17 NIV

REFLECTIONS FOR THE WEEK

1. The psalmist says, "Teach us to number our days, that we may gain a heart of wisdom" (Psalm 90:12 NIV). Reflect upon what aspects of your life and relationships you might change if you knew with certainty when you would die.

2. Is there any unfinished emotional business between you and another that deserves your contemplation and wisdom from God? What would it take for you to begin a first step in restoring such a broken relationship?

PRAYER

Almighty God, Your promise is that those who wait on You will have their strength renewed at the crucial time. You are my Creator and You know just how weak and finite I am. In Your great love for me, guide and protect me when I do not know the way, and renew my strength so that I may finish the race set out for me. Let me enjoy each day as a gift, and in Your unfailing love toward me, help me to love others.

Amen

FEBRUARY—WEEK FOUR

RECOGNIZING WHEN CHANGE IS NECESSARY

Paul and his companions traveled throughout the region of Phrygia and Galatia, having been kept by the Holy Spirit from preaching the word in the province of Asia. When they came to the border of Mysia, they tried to enter Bithynia, but the Spirit of Jesus would not allow them to. So they passed by Mysia and went down to Troas. During the night Paul had a vision of a man of Macedonia standing and begging him, "Come over to Macedonia and help us." After Paul had seen the vision, we got ready at once to leave for Macedonia, concluding that God had called us to preach the gospel to them.

From Troas we put out to sea and sailed straight for Samothrace, and the next day we went on to Neapolis. From there we traveled to Philippi, a Roman colony and the leading city of that district of Macedonia. And we stayed there several days.

On the Sabbath we went outside the city gate to the river, where we expected to find a place of prayer. We sat down and began to speak to the women who had gathered there. One of those listening was a woman from the city of Thyatira named Lydia, a dealer in purple cloth. She was a worshiper of God. The Lord opened her heart to respond to Paul's message. When she and the members of her household were baptized, she invited us to her home. "If you consider me a believer in the Lord," she said, "come and stay at my house." And she persuaded us.

~ Acts 16:6–15 NIV

While the shortest distance between two points is a straight line, we very seldom can apply that law to our human circumstances and move in a straight line from point A (where we are now) to point B (where we want to be in the future). In the context of completing a mission or achieving a goal, we must anticipate that our path to success may have to change.

The art of managing change is important to develop in a leader. Stories of success inevitably include how obstacles were identified and how they were overcome. Successful leaders remain aware and adaptable to changing circumstances that require alternative methods when their first approach is thwarted.

The life and mission of Paul as recorded in the New Testament provides a comprehensive lesson on recognizing when change is necessary and then adapting to changing circumstances by modifying methods, all the while staying true to the primary goal. Not only was Paul often opposed in completing his mission by people who disagreed—often vehemently—with his purpose and message, but he was also subjected to the uncertainties of weather and geography, and the uncertainties of sufficient material resources in which to carry on. In chapter 16 of Acts alone, we see Paul recognizing that his plans to visit Asia and Bithynia to preach the gospel were not going to be allowed by the Holy Spirit, and then when he followed the leading of the Holy Spirit, he was beset upon by people and circumstances that threatened his life, abused his body, and had him incarcerated.

In 2 Corinthians 11:23–27 (NIV), Paul provides this account of the obstacles he faced in carrying out his mission:

> Are they servants of Christ? (I am out of my mind to talk like this.) I am more. I have worked much harder, been in prison more frequently, been flogged more severely, and been exposed to death again and again. Five times I received from the Jews the forty lashes minus one. Three times I was beaten with rods, once I was pelted with stones, three times I was shipwrecked, I spent a night and a day in the open sea, I have been constantly on the move. I have been in danger from rivers, in danger from bandits, in danger from my fellow Jews, in danger from Gentiles; in danger in the city, in danger in the country, in danger at sea; and in danger from false believers. I have labored and toiled and have often gone without sleep; I have known hunger and thirst and have often gone without food; I have been cold and naked.

It is inevitable that you will need to identify what new circumstances, either hindering or assisting you in achieving your goals and objectives, precipitate a need to adapt your methods and approach to reach your ultimate success. Part of our human condition is the reality that change is a real and certain part of life. But it is through changing circumstances that we see God's guiding hand. It is through changing circumstances that we test the veracity of our goals. It is through changing circumstances that we strengthen our lives and the ability to positively affect the lives of those who come in contact with us.

When circumstances change, these godly traits will serve you in overcoming obstacles and recognizing new opportunities, and help you to respond to change with a godly attitude:

FAITH

> Now **faith** is the assurance of things hoped for, the conviction of things not seen. For by it the men of old gained approval. By faith we understand that the worlds were prepared by the word of God, so that what is seen was not made out of things which are visible.
> ~ Hebrews 11:1–3 NASB

COURAGE

> Have I not commanded you? Be strong and **courageous**. Do not be afraid; do not be discouraged, for the Lord your God will be with you wherever you go.
> ~ Joshua 1:9 NIV

PERSEVERANCE

> Therefore, since we are surrounded by such a great cloud of witnesses, let us throw off everything that hinders and the sin that so easily entangles. And let us run with **perseverance** the race marked out for us, fixing our eyes on Jesus, the pioneer and perfecter of faith. For the joy set before him he endured the cross, scorning its shame, and sat down at the right hand of the throne of God.
> ~ Hebrews 12:1–2 NIV

ENDURANCE
> And not only that, but we also boast in our sufferings, knowing that suffering produces **endurance**, and endurance produces character, and character produces hope, and hope does not disappoint us, because God's love has been poured into our hearts through the Holy Spirit that has been given to us.
>
> ~ Romans 5:3–5 NRSV

PRAYER
> Do not be anxious about anything, but in every situation, by **prayer** and petition, with thanksgiving, present your requests to God. And the peace of God, which transcends all understanding, will guard your hearts and your minds in Christ Jesus.
>
> ~ Philippians 4:6–7 NIV

REFLECTIONS FOR THE WEEK

1. Consider an event in your past, at work or on a personal basis, that required a change in direction. Reflect upon the manner in which you responded to the event. Did your method of dealing with change include any of the attributes discussed above (faith, courage, perseverance, endurance, and prayer)?

2. What might have been different about the outcome, or about yourself, had you applied those godly attributes during the time of change?

PRAYER

Almighty God, who alone is unchanging, who alone is from everlasting to everlasting and in whom there is no shifting sand or shadow, encourage me with Your Spirit and Your wisdom as I encounter the changing circumstances of life. Guide me in making choices and enable me in Your strength to hold fast to godly objectives in the face of changing circumstances.

Amen

MARCH

"For it is just like a man about to go on a journey, who called his own slaves and entrusted his possessions to them. To one he gave five talents, to another, two, and to another, one, each according to his own ability; and he went on his journey. Immediately the one who had received the five talents went and traded with them, and gained five more talents. In the same manner the one who had received the two talents gained two more. But he who received the one talent went away, and dug a hole in the ground and hid his master's money.

"Now after a long time the master of those slaves came and settled accounts with them. The one who had received the five talents came up and brought five more talents, saying, 'Master, you entrusted five talents to me. See, I have gained five more talents.' His master said to him, 'Well done, good and faithful slave. You were faithful with a few things, I will put you in charge of many things; enter into the joy of your master.'

"Also the one who had received the two talents came up and said, 'Master, you entrusted two talents to me. See, I have gained two more talents.' His master said to him, 'Well done, good and faithful slave. You were faithful with a few things, I will put you in charge of many things; enter into the joy of your master.'

"And the one also who had received the one talent came up and said, 'Master, I knew you to be a hard man, reaping where you did not sow and gathering where you scattered no seed. And I was afraid, and went away and hid your talent in the ground. See, you have what is yours.'

"But his master answered and said to him, 'You wicked, lazy slave, you knew that I reap where I did not sow and gather where I scattered no seed. Then you ought to have put my money in the bank, and on my arrival I would have received my money back with interest. Therefore take away the talent from him, and give it to the one who has the ten talents.'

"For to everyone who has, more shall be given, and he will have an abundance; but from the one who does not have, even what he does have shall be taken away. Throw out the worthless slave into the outer darkness; in that place there will be weeping and gnashing of teeth.

~ Matthew 25:14–30 NASB

In business, the month of March comes with a lot of pressure. January and February have come and gone, the New Year is well underway, and March becomes the pivotal month in either achieving first quarter goals or falling short of them. Starting the year off with a good quarter sets the stage for a successful year, but a first quarter that fails to meet expectations means even more will have to be accomplished over the remaining months if the overall goals are to be achieved.

As a leader, you have watched the results of the business and paid close attention to the signs of progress or trouble. Depending on the size of your organization and your time management skills, you have spent time with various subordinates responsible for achieving results, inquiring as to obstacles, surprises, chance, and opportunity. You have also likely made inquiry and reviewed certain accounting records to evaluate the sources and uses of money, comparing the actual cash balances with the expected and hoped for cash balances.

In summary, you have been very busy, and your expectation is that everyone in your organization has also been busy.

Jesus taught the parable at the beginning of this chapter to his disciples when he was in Jerusalem in the week preceding the crucifixion as part of a discourse on signs of the end times. Chronologically, a number of events precede the story of the talents as presented in Matthew. First, Jesus confronts the teachers of the law and the Pharisees and pronounces seven "woes" on them (Matthew 23:1–36), calling these "leaders" to account for being in positions of knowledge and understanding and yet being false to the people of Israel, being full of hypocrisy and self-importance.

And as Jesus and the disciples were leaving the temple area, Jesus said, "Do you see all these things?" he asked. "Truly I tell you, not one stone here will be left on another; every one will be thrown down" (Matthew 24:2 NIV), a prophecy concerning the ultimate destruction of the temple by the Romans.

Later, when they were alone with Jesus on the Mount of Olives, the disciples ask Jesus for clarification and when Jesus' predictions would occur. In response, Jesus explains some signs of the end times and the coming of the Son of Man, and uses parables (including the selection used at the start of this chapter) to provide a description of what the world will be like at that time—some people will be ready, and some people will not be ready, including some who know better and should be ready.

The parable of the talents then, when read in context, is not about business, but rather depicts how people use their abilities. Some people are trustworthy and diligently pursue their responsibilities using their abilities in a right and godly manner. Others are not trustworthy and shirk, in one way or another, their responsibilities, failing to use their abilities in the process.

It is interesting to note that in the parable of the talents, each servant immediately set out to accomplish what they had purposed in their hearts. The diligent servants "went at once" and began to put the money to work. The lazy servant immediately went off and dug a hole in the ground and hid the money. The outcome was assured for the lazy servant. Risk awaited the diligent servants, but they were successful in their endeavors, and they were certainly pursuing the wishes of the Master.

The parable of the talents is also about how people behave when no one is looking. The Master was clearly gone, completely out of sight and removed from the area. In his absence, his servants acted in a manner consistent with their character because the parable says the Master gave to each "according to his ability." I'm not saying that people never change (praise God that I am living proof that people can change), but I am observing that the Master in this case had a clear understanding of the capabilities of his servants and trusted them with amounts consistent with that belief. What is important to me is that he allowed them to prove to themselves rather than to him what was their level of trust and accountability.

It's March, and it is natural to take time to reflect on how the year is progressing. As you push your team to achieve the goals set out for them, consider where they have invested the resources entrusted to them.

Be interested in their strengths and how they demonstrate using their abilities. Encourage those who are proving trustworthy, regardless of specific success or failure. Admonish and coach those who have decided to squander their talent.

REFLECTIONS FOR MARCH

1. When did you last meditate on the capabilities and performance of key members of your team at work? Have you identified both those who are achieving expected results and those who are missing their goals, and those who are working within the cultural framework of your organization and those who are not? Make it a point to include in your calendar specific one on one time with your key subordinates to evaluate their commitment and approach to their jobs.

2. Celebrate the activities of those who demonstrate the diligent pursuit of their jobs and responsibilities. Prayerfully consider how to respond as a Christian who is also a leader to those who appear to be failing.

PRAYER

Jesus, as the Son of God, You were able to discern the true motives and perspectives of everyone who appeared before You. Nothing was hidden from You. Yet, You loved everyone; even those who chose to betray, ignore, slander, and abuse You. You did not ignore wrong; rather, You chose to love even more. Help me with wisdom to be able to discern the abilities and motives of those I lead, to coach and counsel those in need of a deeper awareness of their own abilities and progress, and to celebrate with joy the works of those who are aligned with Your will.

Amen

MARCH—WEEK ONE

RECOGNIZING WHEN CHANGE IS NECESSARY

Now Ahab told Jezebel everything Elijah had done and how he had killed all the prophets with the sword. So Jezebel sent a messenger to Elijah to say, "May the gods deal with me, be it ever so severely, if by this time tomorrow I do not make your life like that of one of them."

Elijah was afraid and ran for his life. When he came to Beersheba in Judah, he left his servant there, while he himself went a day's journey into the wilderness. He came to a broom bush, sat down under it and prayed that he might die. "I have had enough, Lord," he said. "Take my life; I am no better than my ancestors." Then he lay down under the bush and fell asleep.

All at once an angel touched him and said, "Get up and eat." He looked around, and there by his head was some bread baked over hot coals, and a jar of water. He ate and drank and then lay down again.

The angel of the Lord came back a second time and touched him and said, "Get up and eat, for the journey is too much for you." So he got up and ate and drank. Strengthened by that food, he traveled forty days and forty nights until he reached Horeb, the mountain of God. There he went into a cave and spent the night.

And the word of the Lord came to him: "What are you doing here, Elijah?"

He replied, "I have been very zealous for the Lord God Almighty. The Israelites have rejected your covenant, torn down your altars, and put your prophets to death with the sword. I am the only one left, and now they are trying to kill me too."

The Lord said, "Go out and stand on the mountain in the presence of the Lord, for the Lord is about to pass by."

Then a great and powerful wind tore the mountains apart and shattered the rocks before the Lord, but the Lord was not in the wind. After the wind there was an earthquake, but the

> Lord was not in the earthquake. After the earthquake came a
> fire, but the Lord was not in the fire. And after the fire came a
> gentle whisper. When Elijah heard it, he pulled his cloak over
> his face and went out and stood at the mouth of the cave.
> Then a voice said to him, "What are you doing here, Elijah?"
> ~ 1 Kings 19:1–13 NIV

I find the story of Elijah in 1 Kings to be one of the most fascinating stories in the Bible. Out of obscurity, God called Elijah to denounce Ahab, king of Israel, for apostasy and for turning the hearts of the people to foreign gods.

Ahab was a very bad king, described by the author of 1 Kings in the following way: "Ahab son of Omri did more evil in the eyes of the Lord than any of those before him" (1 Kings 16:30 NIV). One of the evil things he did was to marry a very bad woman—Jezebel—and through that marriage the worship of Baal, the god of the Sidonians, came to Israel. In one story of the evils of Ahab and Jezebel, found in 1 Kings, chapter 21, Jezebel planned the murder of a man named Naboth in order to claim his vineyard for Ahab after Naboth had refused to sell it. The account reveals the depth of Jezebel's hatred and opposition to God.

The story of Elijah's courage in confronting the powerful in their evil ways offers great insight to God's concerns over how those in positions of power are expected to behave, and how God will use and equip those who hear His voice to deliver His message of warning and rebuke to those who abuse their power. However, I want to call your attention in this instance to how God calls us to a new direction when we are faced with uncertainty, and how patient He is with us when we doubt the call.

God called Elijah to be an agent of change in Israel. Under their corrupt king, the people had lost their love and fear of God and had adopted the practice of worshiping the false god Baal. God called Elijah to pronounce his anger over the actions of the people and to proclaim a drought on the land (1 Kings 17:1). Aware that the proclamation would inflame the king, God told Elijah to flee the kingdom. During the drought, God preserved Elijah's life in a number of miraculous ways, including providing him with food and water while he was in hiding, and then when the drought began to have full effect, by instructing him to go to Zarephath and seek food and water from a widow he would find there.

While living with the widow, God allowed Elijah to perform a great miracle by bringing back to life the widow's child who had died. After three years, God called Elijah to return to Israel to both end the drought and to confront the people with their unwillingness to serve God and God alone. In a great challenge to the people, Elijah said, "How long will you waver between two opinions? If the Lord is God, follow him; but if Baal is God, follow him" (1 Kings 18:21 NIV). Sadly, the people refused to respond. The verse ends with the phrase, "But the people said nothing."

Elijah, full of confidence and the power of God, challenged the priests of Baal to a "duel" between their gods and the God of Israel. God answered Elijah's prayer and displayed His power, sending fire from heaven to consume a water-soaked offering, proving to all of Israel that God alone was God over Israel. And God responded to Elijah's prayer to end the drought on the land, and it began to rain.

Brimming over with excitement, Elijah charged off to confront the king and Jezebel, but in this part of the story, things began to go poorly. Jezebel was not afraid of Elijah; in spite of the great miracles that had been performed, Jezebel threatened Elijah's life. And Elijah was stricken with fear—so fearful that he fled into the desert. Dejected, Elijah threw himself down and wished that he were dead. I imagine Elijah was very confused and wondered why God had allowed Jezebel to continue in power. Where was the happy ending? If ever there was a time for a change in direction, for Elijah, the time was now.

Perhaps you find Elijah's quick willingness to forget all he knew about God and to give up puzzling. I remember thinking these same thoughts many times in my reading the Bible about people and events in both the Old and the New Testaments. Why did the disciples so quickly desert Jesus? Why did David betray God with Bathsheba?

But then I get to me: How do I betray God when I choose to "forget" His claim on my life? The human condition is one of forgetfulness, pride, and self-confidence.

How did God respond to Elijah's pity party? He called Elijah back to mission, and He restored his confidence. He gave Elijah a helper, and He forgave Elijah for getting ahead of God's own plans (God had not asked Elijah to run to Jerusalem to confront the king and Jezebel).

During the period of Elijah's despair, Elijah was unaware of his own need to take a new direction. Elijah was unaware of his need to seek God's power and encouragement. Rather, he reacted with human hopelessness. Yet God continued to care for him and in a loving way revealed to Elijah that God does not always choose to move by visible strength. Importantly, God is found in a whisper.

Elijah responded to God and returned to his mission. As far as we know, Elijah was never shaken again.

As a leader, you need to be aware of changing circumstances and your response to them. In the process of choosing an appropriate direction, it is important to always consider the perspective you bring to the problem calling you to change. Is the perspective your own, or are the circumstances that confront you really an opportunity for God to change your perspective? Godly counselors, prayer, and the study of God's Word will increase your likelihood of correctly seeing the present circumstance and reacting to it in accordance with God's wishes.

As you approach a time of change, be encouraged that God is involved deeply in your life. "And we know that in all things God works for the good of those who love him, who have been called according to his purpose" (Romans 8:28 NIV).

REFLECTIONS FOR THE WEEK

1. God spoke to Elijah in an audible voice. How do you imagine that God speaks to us today? Can you remember a time when you were certain God was speaking to you?

2. Think of some situation, worry, problem, opportunity, or circumstance where God may be speaking to you now, if only you would listen.

3. Perhaps you struggle with accepting that God wants to speak to us, to guide us, and to allow us to see Him at work in our lives. If God wanted to speak to you, what would make you notice?

PRAYER

Lord, I confess that there can be so much noise in my mind, in my day, in my life, that I may miss Your whisper when you call. I may miss the person you place in my path to carry a message of hope. I may not read a particular situation correctly because my eyes are not focused on You. Forgive my arrogance. Allow me the discipline to rest and reflect on Your purposes for my life. Help me to hear. Give me eyes to see.

Amen

MARCH—WEEK TWO

ESTABLISHING THE VALUES AND THE CULTURE OF THE ORGANIZATION

Truly my soul finds rest in God;
  my salvation comes from him.
Truly he is my rock and my salvation;
  he is my fortress, I will never be shaken.
How long will you assault me?
  Would all of you throw me down—
  this leaning wall, this tottering fence?
Surely they intend to topple me
  from my lofty place;
  they take delight in lies.
With their mouths they bless,
  but in their hearts they curse.
Yes, my soul, find rest in God;
  my hope comes from him.
Truly he is my rock and my salvation;
  he is my fortress, I will not be shaken.
My salvation and my honor depend on God
  he is my mighty rock, my refuge.
Trust in him at all times, you people;
  pour out your hearts to him,
  for God is our refuge.
Surely the lowborn are but a breath,
  the highborn are but a lie.
If weighed on a balance, they are nothing;
  together they are only a breath.
Do not trust in extortion
  or put vain hope in stolen goods;
though your riches increase,
  do not set your heart on them.
One thing God has spoken,
  two things I have heard:

MARCH—WEEK TWO

> *"Power belongs to you, God,*
> *and with you, Lord, is unfailing love";*
> and, *"You reward everyone*
> *according to what they have done."*
>
> ~ Psalm 62 NIV

From a legal perspective, a business or enterprise is often considered to be and is treated like a person. Businesses can enter into contracts, hold property, and pay taxes. On a particular day they are born and come into existence; on another particular day they die and cease to exist. In many respects, businesses even have a personality. How a business exhibits its personality from a relational and moral point of view is determined by its values and culture. The values and culture of an enterprise, as embodied by its employees, form the underpinnings upon which all decisions that include an element of right or wrong, fairness or unfairness, and good or evil, are reached.

The values and culture of an enterprise provide the rules of engagement between coworkers and anyone else who has a relationship or dealing with the business. Even though a business personality is shaped by the collective "all" of its employees, its leaders hold significant power in establishing its rules of engagement.

Because I hold this opinion, it is impossible for me to separate how *my* business behaves toward its employees, customers, neighbors, competitors, lenders, suppliers, and anyone else who has any dealings with it, and how God has asked me to behave toward others. And God is very clear on the subject of how we are to behave toward each other.

> One of the teachers of the law came and heard them debating. Noticing that Jesus had given them a good answer, he asked him, "Of all the commandments, which is the most important?"
> "The most important one," answered Jesus, "is this: 'Hear, O Israel: The Lord our God, the Lord is one. Love the Lord your God with all your heart and with all your soul and with all your mind and with all your strength.' The second is this: 'Love your neighbor as yourself.' There is no commandment greater than these'"
>
> ~ Mark 12:28–31 NIV

> *He has shown you, O mortal, what is good.*
> *And what does the Lord require of you?*
> *To act justly and to love mercy*
> *and to walk humbly with your God.*
>
> ~ Micah 6:8 NIV

Love your neighbor as yourself? Act justly? Love mercy? Be humble?

I have not found these easy to do—in fact, I fail at doing these things more often than I care to admit. But my human failings do not obviate the need for me to persevere and try to live my life in a godly and righteous manner—both at home and at work. When Christ forgave my sins He did not consider that my work and my life away from work were somehow separate and distinct one from the other. And frankly, when that moment occurred, neither did I. My only thought that moment was how desperately I needed a Savior. I needed a Savior then 24/7/365—and I need Him now 24/7/365. So does everyone.

Psalm 62 (quoted at the start of this chapter) is powerful for pointing out God does not show favoritism. It also makes clear that God desires relationships with us. We cannot fellowship with God in the way He wants if we operate outside of His love. The Apostle John said: "We know that we have come to know him if we keep his commands. Whoever says, 'I know Him,' but does not do what He commands is a liar, and the truth is not in that person" (1 John 2:3-4 NIV). And Jesus said, "Anyone who loves me will obey my teaching. My Father will love them, and we will come to them and make our home with them. Anyone who does not love me will not obey my teaching. These words you hear are not my own; they belong to the Father who sent me" (John 14:23-24 NIV).

As a leader, you influence the values and the culture of all who work with you. If you are the chief executive, your influence is profound. But in any leadership capacity—chief executive to vice-president to department head to manager of employees—you can shape the godliness of your business. Allowing the instructions of God to shape both your work life and your personal life brings all of the comfort, the power, the confidence, and the protection that God has promised to His people to you. And often, those same attributes of comfort, power, confidence, and protection will overflow to others who come into contact with you.

REFLECTIONS FOR THE WEEK

1. Do the ideas that God is with you at work and cares about your business life bring you comfort or make you feel uncomfortable? Why?

2. In what types of situations at work would you find it easier to envision God being present, and in what types of situations at work would it seem more difficult to contemplate God's active involvement and concern?

3. Our God is a God of comfort and compassion who cares for us. Reflect upon those situations where you find it uncomfortable or struggle with the idea that God is involved. What could God's involvement accomplish that seems difficult or impossible to you?

PRAYER

Almighty God, in this moment, help me pause and reflect on Your sovereign nature and realize that You are present with me every moment of the day and through every hour of the night. When I read in the Bible accounts of Your interaction with Your people, so many of them occur in the "work" of the person rather than in their "home life." Help me to see You in all places, in all ways, and let me walk in comfort and strength of character as You have called me to do.

Amen

MARCH—WEEK THREE

ESTABLISHING THE VALUES AND THE CULTURE OF THE ORGANIZATION

Sacrifice thank offerings to God,
fulfill your vows to the Most High,
and call on me in the day of trouble;
I will deliver you, and you will honor me.
                              ~ Psalm 50:14–15 NIV

Those who sacrifice thank offerings honor me,
and to the blameless I will show my salvation.
                              ~ Psalm 50:23 NIV

Some people came and told Jehoshaphat, "A vast army is coming against you from Edom, from the other side of the Dead Sea. It is already in Hazezon Tamar" (that is, En Gedi). Alarmed, Jehoshaphat resolved to inquire of the Lord, and he proclaimed a fast for all Judah. The people of Judah came together to seek help from the Lord; indeed, they came from every town in Judah to seek him.

Then Jehoshaphat stood up in the assembly of Judah and Jerusalem at the temple of the Lord in the front of the new courtyard and said:

"Lord, the God of our ancestors, are you not the God who is in heaven? You rule over all the kingdoms of the nations. Power and might are in your hand, and no one can withstand you. Our God, did you not drive out the inhabitants of this land before your people Israel and give it forever to the descendants of Abraham your friend? They have lived in it and have built in it a sanctuary for your Name, saying, 'If calamity comes upon us, whether the sword of judgment, or plague or famine, we will stand in your presence before this temple that bears your Name and will cry out to you in our distress, and you will hear us and save us.'

"But now here are men from Ammon, Moab and Mount Seir, whose territory you would not allow Israel to invade when they came from Egypt; so they turned away from them and did not destroy them. See how they are repaying us by coming to drive us out of the possession you gave us as an inheritance. Our God, will you not judge them? For we have no power to face this vast army that is attacking us. We do not know what to do, but our eyes are on you."

~ 2 Chronicles 20:2–12 NIV

What "values" help describe the culture of your organization? Here are some samples from some well-known entities as published on their websites:

Ernst and Young, an international accounting firm, has as its values statement the following:

"People who demonstrate integrity, respect, and teaming.
People with energy, enthusiasm, and the courage to lead.
People who build relationships based on doing the right thing."

Brown Forman Corporation includes in its values statement the following:
"Over many years, Brown Forman has developed and nurtured a set of core values that have become deeply ingrained in our consciousness and our culture. These time honored values—integrity, respect, trust, teamwork and excellence—remain real and relevant today, guiding us in the conduct of our day-to-day business."

Berkshire Hathaway includes this quote from Warren Buffet in its Code of Business Ethics and Conduct:

"I want employees to ask themselves whether they are willing to have any contemplated act appear the next day on the front page of their local paper—to be read by their spouses, children and friends—with the reporting done by an informed and critical reporter."

Arby's, the roast beef fast food restaurant chain, has this as part of its values:
"Dream big, work hard, get it done, play fair, have fun, make a difference."

In today's society and business climate, the types of "values" a business professes and displays are relevant and significant. Some other words that convey a sense of ethical behavior that might be found in values statements are: fairness, responsibility, community-minded, ethical, trustworthy, high quality, open-minded, non-discriminatory, clear, transparent, honorable, socially conscious, above board, and faithful.

Values help define who we are as well as who is the collective organization for whom we work. Warren Buffet and Ernst and Young touch on this personal side of values and point out in their values statements that their organizations are defined by the actions of their employees. I believe it is also true that the actions of the corporations also define the employees through such means as establishing codes of conduct and rules for behavior between employees and with outsiders.

But if values are so important, and we can develop lists of words that describe values in a way that seems to homogenize them, do you think an employee at Ernst and Young would fit in at Arby's? How about at Berkshire Hathaway? Would a Brown Forman employee be able to transfer to a different organization with only his or her Brown Forman behaviors and values and fit seamlessly into the values culture of another corporation?

Perhaps, but the reality is culture in an organization is more about personal actions and beliefs than written statements. A friend of mine, Roger Hall, Ph.D., has noted, "Every time I walk into a room, I change the culture of the room. I bring my own culture with me wherever I go. What is the thing I always pick up and carry? The answer is me" (Roger Hall, Expedition. Arete Press, 2014, p. 126.) In my experience, while it is likely that "ethics," as conveyed to employees, are similar in many respects in all reputable businesses, differences will occur. Think Enron, Worldcom, and Bernie Madoff.

The history of Israel, as set forth in the Old Testament, provides compelling reading and frank assessment of some of the lapses in "values" displayed by the ancient Jewish people over hundreds of years. Time and time again, the Israelite people, often with the help of morally depraved leaders, would fall away from the Law of God. Only God would remain true, never changing His character or His righteousness. Whenever a drifting away occurred, a leader would become aware of the lapse in values and call the people to awareness and repentance (a change of direction).

Similarly, the history of Israel also provides many examples of how the people would respond to circumstances of adversity. Sometimes they would go their own way, and the consequences would not often work out for them. Sometimes they would turn to God with the help of a leader demonstrating values consistent with the Word of God, and when that occurred, the circumstances would often turn out much better for them.

In the longer passage from 2 Chronicles at the beginning of this chapter, Jehoshaphat, considered by the writer to be a good king who feared God and who led the people in righteousness, faced a significant threat from an opposing army. Here is an example where circumstances were not favorable for the people. By taking the problem to God, Jehoshaphat demonstrated to the people and to God that his **values** included relying on God to faithfully live up to the promises He had made over the centuries to Israel—His chosen people.

How profound for the people to witness their leader, in a situation of hopelessness from a human point of view, turning to God in humility and in eager anticipation of deliverance. As a leader, you will be called upon to demonstrate from time to time that the values of your organization mean something and are not just words on a page.

The shorter passages from Psalm 50 refer to "offering the sacrifice of thanks" to God. The concept of being "thankful" to God in all circumstances occurs often in the Bible—whether or not the circumstances are favorable or unfavorable. Linking the words "sacrifice" and "thanks" implies it is not always easy to be or remain thankful in all situations. However, a promise is contained in the Psalm for when a sense of thankfulness accompanies adverse circumstances. God says that He will hear and deliver us from adverse circumstances if we offer sacrifices of thanks and fulfill our vows to Him. God also says that we participate in the deliverance He provides when we offer sacrifices of thanks because He will prepare us for what lies ahead so that we will see the salvation of God.

Consider again Jehoshaphat's choices when confronted with a serious problem—an invading army. He first prepared himself and his people to approach God by ordering a fast. Then he demonstrated worship by recalling all that God had done and promised to do for His people. When the prayer was finished, God called upon a prophet to announce that the prayers had been heard and would be answered. All the king had to do was assemble the troops, go look for the enemy, and wait to see God act in a mighty way!

Right.

And all the Hebrews leaving Egypt had to do was march into the Red Sea.

All Abraham had to do was to get up early and take his son Isaac to the mountain and offer him as a sacrifice to God.

Sometimes, it is very difficult to listen and to obey, let alone to be able to say "thank you."

By going out early the next morning with hope and songs of thanksgiving, Jehoshaphat demonstrated his faith and his sacrifice of thanks. (I think leading a people toward a superior army with no prospect of defeating them by human needs qualifies as a tough situation in which to give thanks.) But in the act of going, singing as they went, God used Jehoshaphat's obedience and faith to "prepare the way" and show the world the salvation of God.

As a leader, you will be called upon to demonstrate godly integrity to your employees, and the clearest evidence of your true "values" will be during a time of uncertainty.

REFLECTIONS FOR THE WEEK

1. As you reflect on the values statements of your organization, how does your organization expect its employees to act in the face of adversity?

2. One thing is certain: adversity is going to come to your organization and to its employees. When adversity comes, what guidance can they expect to find for dealing with adversity in the workplace?

MARCH—WEEK THREE

PRAYER

Almighty God, thank You for the rich and unvarnished stories of the Bible that reveal troubles come to everyone in this world. Your Scriptures reveal truths about human reaction to times of trouble. Remind me that I should always bring my cares and concerns to You because You care for me and are aware of them even before I am aware of them. Help me also, as I read and study Scripture, to build a foundation now of values that are anchored in Your truth so that I can quickly overcome anxiety and doubt when trouble next comes my way. Give me the courage and wisdom to offer the sacrifice of thanks to You in difficult times so that Your power may be released into my life.

Amen

MARCH—WEEK FOUR

HOLDING YOURSELF AND OTHERS ACCOUNTABLE TO KEEP PROMISES AND COMMITMENTS

Have mercy on me, O God,
 according to your unfailing love;
 according to your great compassion
 blot out my transgressions.
Wash away all my iniquity
 and cleanse me from my sin.
For I know my transgressions,
 and my sin is always before me.
Against you, you only, have I sinned
 and done what is evil in your sight;
so you are right in your verdict
 and justified when you judge.

~ Psalm 51:1-4 NIV

Samuel said to Saul, "I am the one the Lord sent to anoint you king over his people Israel; so listen now to the message from the Lord. This is what the Lord Almighty says: 'I will punish the Amalekites for what they did to Israel when they waylaid them as they came up from Egypt. Now go, attack the Amalekites and totally destroy all that belongs to them. Do not spare them; put to death men and women, children and infants, cattle and sheep, camels and donkeys.'"

~ 1 Samuel 15:1-3 NIV

Then Saul attacked the Amalekites all the way from Havilah to Shur, near the eastern border of Egypt. He took Agag king of the Amalekites alive, and all his people he totally destroyed with the sword. But Saul and the army spared Agag and the best of the sheep and cattle, the fat calves and lambs—everything that was good. These they were unwilling to destroy completely, but everything that was despised and weak they totally destroyed.

MARCH—WEEK FOUR

> Then the word of the Lord came to Samuel: "I regret that I have made Saul king, because he has turned away from me and has not carried out my instructions." Samuel was angry, and he cried out to the Lord all that night.
> Early in the morning Samuel got up and went to meet Saul, but he was told, "Saul has gone to Carmel. There he has set up a monument in his own honor and has turned and gone on down to Gilgal."
> When Samuel reached him, Saul said, "The Lord bless you! I have carried out the Lord's instructions."
> But Samuel said, "What then is this bleating of sheep in my ears? What is this lowing of cattle that I hear?"
> ~ 1 Samuel 15:7–14 NIV

The Merriam-Webster's dictionary defines *accountability* as "the quality or state of being accountable; especially: an obligation or willingness to accept responsibility or to account for one's actions." It also defines the word "accountable" as being the one who must meet an obligation or suffer the consequences for failing to do so.

Accountability, as it is commonly used, seldom affects only one person. We can, of course, betray accountability to ourselves in broken commitments and promises, such as failing to follow a particular diet, failing to stop a particular bad habit we want to stop, or not getting the exercise we need. But more often, breaches of accountability affect two or more people. God, as Lord and Sovereign over all creation, cares about accountability. And whenever a breach in accountability occurs, there are consequences.

Because God is holy and righteous and sovereign over all of His creation, it does not matter if humanity acknowledges His authority or His power to judge and punish. When God chooses to act, He will act, and the outcome will be in accordance with His will. Genesis, the first book of the Bible, records a number of instances where God judged mankind:

- In Genesis 6 is the account of Noah and the Flood that destroyed all mankind but Noah's family.
- In Genesis 11 is the account of the Tower of Babel where God dispersed mankind and confused their language.

- Genesis 18 contains the story of the destruction of Sodom and Gomorrah: "Then the Lord said, 'The outcry against Sodom and Gomorrah is so great and their sin so grievous that I will go down and see if what they have done is as bad as the outcry that has reached me. If not, I will know'" (Genesis 18:20–21 NIV).

Throughout the Bible, God judged people and nations. Here are just a few other examples:

- God instructed Jonah to "Go to the great city of Nineveh and preach against it, because its wickedness has come up before me" (Jonah 1:2 NIV).
- When the prophet Habakkuk cried out to God to explain why God tolerated injustice and violence, God answered, "Look at the nations and watch—and be utterly amazed. For I am going to do something in your days that you would not believe, even if you were told. I am raising up the Babylonians, that ruthless and impetuous people, who sweep across the whole earth to seize dwellings not their own" (Habakkuk 1:5–6 NIV).
- God used the Assyrians to destroy the Northern Kingdom of Israel, and used the Babylonians to destroy Jerusalem and Judah and carry the people away to exile.
- God later judged the Babylonian King Belshazzar (Daniel 5:30), and he was slain.

In the selection from 1 Samuel that began this chapter, God had judged the Amalekites and decreed that Saul utterly destroy them. God's instructions were clear—everything was to be destroyed. Nothing was to be saved. This punishment seems harsh and particularly gruesome with the inclusion of women and children and livestock. But consider how Saul responded. Saul did not believe the judgment was too harsh. Rather, Saul believed the judgment was wasteful. So, acting just like any other heathen leader of the times, Saul destroyed most of the Amalekites and their possessions, but he kept trophies and tribute for himself and his people. He also kept the Amalekite king alive. And in these acts, Saul disgraced God.

Israel was a people chosen by God to be separate from the world. By choosing to spare Agag and the best livestock, Israel revealed its heart was no different from that of any conquering, warrior society. They destroyed the Amalekites for plunder. They showed mercy for livestock but not people. They acted in no way like messengers of God. As a result, God was mocked, his glory was impugned, and other nations did not see the Israelites as a people of the one true God. And Saul, as king, led the way in sin.

Even more about Saul was revealed in his act of establishing a monument for himself and his victory instead of acknowledging God's hand in the victory. Saul had become prideful and arrogant, caring more about what the people thought of him than what God thought. Because accountability includes a call to keep a promise, it also includes consequences when accountability is breached. Saul lost favor with God and eventually lost the kingdom from his family when Samuel anointed David king.

The Bible says, "There is no one righteous, not even one; there is no one who understands; there is no one who seeks God. All have turned away, they have together become worthless; there is no one who does good, not even one" (Romans 3:10–12 NIV).

As noted above, the Bible is replete with examples of broken promises, treachery, sinfulness, and breaches of accountability. But there is also a tremendous example of the appropriate response when accountability has been breached. In Psalm 51, David, writing about his sinful relationship with Bathsheba and the murder of her husband, acknowledged that his primary breach of accountability was against God. It was God who had selected David as king of Israel to replace Saul. Now, David had also stumbled and had committed the sins of murder and adultery. By breaking God's commandments, David had sinned against God.

When confronted by Nathan the prophet with his crimes and sins, David was ashamed and truly remorseful. David repented of his sins and cried out to God to restore him.

We do not know what would have been the outcome had Saul actually repented of his breach of promise to God. Saul did not repent, although he was "sorry" that God was angry with him. However, we do see that David, when he repented, was restored to God, and we have the beautiful and comforting testimony of Psalm 51 as a result.

As a leader, your team accomplishes tasks and objectives by being accountable to you, to each other, and to the company as a whole. Most organizations get more done by collaborative work than by individual performance. Nothing is sure in a work environment. Sometimes, things just go wrong. But when promises and commitments are not kept, it is very difficult for either an individual or the enterprise as a whole to achieve respective goals and objectives on time, on budget, and with the desired effects for the business.

Your role, as leader, is to keep your promises to the absolute best of your ability. Your role, as leader, is to demonstrate to your teams that a promise is important. If a promise is broken for whatever the reason, an explanation is required so that the culture of the business remains one of making and keeping promises. Biblically, the role of the leader in setting accountability for others is very clear.

REFLECTIONS FOR THE WEEK

1. When did your company last complete an employee survey that included subjective questions on trust, accountability, and integrity? What did the survey reveal about the level of accountability within the organization?

2. If you want to improve accountability in your organization, a good place to start is with yourself. Keep a list this week of promises and commitments, at home and work, and record how faithfully you kept them.

3. God gives wisdom to those who ask Him for it. Pray that God increases your wisdom in looking at yourself to enable you to grow as a person of accountability and leadership.

MARCH—WEEK FOUR

PRAYER

I am accountable to You, dear God, for the gifts You have given to me and for the commands You have ordained. I struggle, almost daily, to keep Your commands, and I fail in my accountability to others more than I care to admit. I also fail to be obedient to You. I am fully aware of Your righteous judgments of all of my actions, but I call upon Your mercy and grace to restore me to service and wholeness. Hear my cry for forgiveness. Through the power of Your Holy Spirit working within me, let me hear the cry of others, as well.

Amen

MARCH—WEEK FIVE

THE END OF THE FIRST QUARTER

DEFINING THE MISSION OF THE ORGANIZATION

The words of Nehemiah son of Hakaliah:
In the month of Kislev in the twentieth year, while I was in the citadel of Susa, Hanani, one of my brothers, came from Judah with some other men, and I questioned them about the Jewish remnant that had survived the exile, and also about Jerusalem.

They said to me, "Those who survived the exile and are back in the province are in great trouble and disgrace. The wall of Jerusalem is broken down, and its gates have been burned with fire."

When I heard these things, I sat down and wept. For some days I mourned and fasted and prayed before the God of heaven. Then I said:

"Lord, the God of heaven, the great and awesome God, who keeps his covenant of love with those who love him and keep his commandments, let your ear be attentive and your eyes open to hear the prayer your servant is praying before you day and night for your servants, the people of Israel. I confess the sins we Israelites, including myself and my father's family, have committed against you. We have acted very wickedly toward you. We have not obeyed the commands, decrees and laws you gave your servant Moses.

"Remember the instruction you gave your servant Moses, saying, 'If you are unfaithful, I will scatter you among the nations, if you return to me and obey my commands, then even if your exiled people are at the farthest horizon, I will gather them from there and bring them to the place I have chosen as a dwelling for my Name.'

"They are your servants and your people, whom you redeemed by your great strength and your mighty hand. Lord, let your ear be attentive to the prayer of this your servant and to the prayer of your servants who delight in revering your name. Give your servant success today by granting him favor in the presence of this man."

I was cupbearer to the king.

~ Nehemiah 1:1–11 NIV

I find the Old Testament story of Nehemiah engaging and relevant to leaders in any organization. Written in an autobiographical style, the book focuses on Nehemiah's role in rebuilding the walls of Jerusalem after the Jewish people had been allowed to return home. As revealed in the passage included above, Nehemiah was filled with a deep, burning desire to see Jerusalem restored. Upon hearing that the city still lay in ruins and the returning exiles still remained a broken people, Nehemiah was overcome with sorrow and petitioned the Lord to change the circumstances. Somewhere in that time of fasting and praying, Nehemiah must have said to God, "If you will use me, I will go." Nehemiah found his mission in life.

Against all odds, Nehemiah and the returning exiles overcame adversaries and obstacles and completed their work. Theirs is a story of faith, tenacity, courage, discipline, accountability, and leadership. And at its core is the mission that Nehemiah felt compelled to undertake: to restore the walls of Jerusalem. Accomplishing that task symbolized to the returning exiles and to the world the years of exile were completed and the Jewish people were again restored to community with each other and with God.

Mission statements provide the context in which we understand the guiding purpose of an enterprise. If you conduct a key-word search of "mission statements" on the Internet, you will be inundated with the available information on how to write them, what they should say, who should have them, what they are and are not—and pretty quickly you will be firmly grounded in a worldview of mission statements. All of the guidance on mission statements makes it clear they are important for an enterprise and deserve careful thought and deliberation as they are being crafted.

Similarly, God gave careful thought and deliberation when He created you; God has a specific and perfect mission for you. Consider these passages:

- So God said to Noah, "I am going to put an end to all people, for the earth is filled with violence because of them. I am surely going to destroy both them and the earth. So make yourself an ark of cypress wood; make rooms in it and coat it with pitch inside and out" (Genesis 6:13–14 NIV).
- The Lord had said to Abram, "Go from your country, your people and your father's household to the land I will show you" (Genesis 12:1 NIV).
- And now the cry of the Israelites has reached me, and I have seen the way the Egyptians are oppressing them. So now, go. I am sending you to Pharaoh to bring my people the Israelites out of Egypt (Exodus 3:9–10 NIV).
- I will give you every place where you set your foot, as I promised Moses. Your territory will extend from the desert to Lebanon, and from the great river, the Euphrates—all the Hittite country—to the Mediterranean Sea in the west. No one will be able to stand against you all the days of your life. As I was with Moses, so I will be with you; I will never leave you nor forsake you. Be strong and courageous, because you will lead these people to inherit the land I swore to their ancestors to give them (Joshua 1:3–6 NIV).
- One night Eli, whose eyes were becoming so weak that he could barely see, was lying down in his usual place. The lamp of God had not yet gone out, and Samuel was lying down in the house of the Lord, where the ark of God was. Then the Lord called Samuel. Samuel answered, "Here I am" (1 Samuel 3:2–4 NIV).
- Then I heard the voice of the Lord saying, "Whom shall I send? And who will go for us?" And I said, "Here am I. Send me!" (Isaiah 6:8 NIV).
- The word of the Lord came to me, saying, "Before I formed you in the womb I knew you, before you were born I set you apart; I appointed you as a prophet to the nations" (Jeremiah 1:4–5 NIV).

MARCH—WEEK FIVE

- As Jesus went on from there, he saw a man named Matthew sitting at the tax collector's booth. "Follow me," he told him, and Matthew got up and followed him (Matthew 9:9 NIV).
- He fell to the ground and heard a voice say to him, "Saul, Saul, why do you persecute me?" "Who are you, Lord?" Saul asked. "I am Jesus, whom you are persecuting," he replied. "Now get up and go into the city, and you will be told what you must do" (Acts 9:4–6 NIV).

This week I want you to think about the congruence you feel between the spiritual aspects of leadership and the importance of strengthening your spiritual relationship with God. I believe God has a plan for you and for your life. That plan includes your choice of occupation and your relationships with others.

Nehemiah never heard the audible voice of God, and God never speaks in the Book of Nehemiah. I like this aspect of the story because God does not audibly speak to us (He could, but I am unaware of any audible conversations in our time). Nonetheless, He strengthens us for our work, and He blesses our work when we pray and cry out to Him. And as marvelous as it is to contemplate, He reveals to us His hand moving in our lives! He wants us to know it is not random chance or fate or luck that affects us—it is God.

Like Nehemiah, we are instructed to make our prayers and requests known to God (Philippians 4:6). Because we are human and God is omniscient, He will not always give us what we ask for, but He will always give us what is best for us. Because God is sovereign, He can choose to withhold His blessing on particular prayers of ours where we are asking for things that are not ultimately going to serve His purposes or are not really wise or good for us. My personal experience has been that by prayer and supplication, over time, I either receive the blessing or answer that I seek, or my heart and mind are changed so that my prayers and petitions change too. Through time alone with God in prayer, meditating on who He is and acknowledging through faith His desire to have me come more and more to know Him, I find myself moving closer and closer to alignment with His will for my life.

Perhaps you have heard or read the passage of Scripture, "Truly, truly, I say to you, he who believes in Me, the works that I do, he will do also; and greater works than these he will do; because I go to the Father. Whatever you ask in My name, that will I do, so that the Father may be glorified in the Son. If you ask Me anything in My name, I will do it" (John 14:12–14 NASB). I know many people interpret this passage as a formulaic way to have God grant any and all petitions: have faith and ask in Jesus' name. Of course, if that is true, and we ask and do not receive, then by definition we must have not had faith, or enough faith. This seems to me to be a "friend of Job" argument where Job's friends counseled Job to acknowledge his sin before God (to agree that God had judged Job rightly). I do not share this philosophy. Faith is important, but God is divine.

As I wrote earlier, God is sovereign, and God knows what we need. I believe He always acts in our best interest and in the way that brings Him glory. Further, I believe that it is through times of testing that our faith is strengthened, that we come more and more to rely upon Him, that we learn more and more about His love and compassion and our place in His heart, and that we learn to have peace.

Mission statements for companies provide context in which to view the over-riding purpose of the enterprise. Most will include some statement asserting "beliefs" in how the enterprise will engage the world—employees, vendors, customers, society at large, community, and competitors. Mission statements for individuals also provide context in which to view the over-riding purpose of their lives. As you contemplate both your personal and your company's respective mission statements, I pray that God will use your time of reflection to call you to the purpose He had in mind for you.

The following Scripture helped me to frame my business life and my personal life. Perhaps it will speak to your heart also.

MARCH—WEEK FIVE

But godliness with contentment is great gain. For we brought nothing into the world, and we can take nothing out of it. But if we have food and clothing, we will be content with that. Those who want to get rich fall into temptation and a trap and into many foolish and harmful desires that plunge people into ruin and destruction. For the love of money is a root of all kinds of evil. Some people, eager for money, have wandered from the faith and pierced themselves with many griefs.

But you, man of God, flee from all this, and pursue righteousness, godliness, faith, love, endurance and gentleness. Fight the good fight of the faith. Take hold of the eternal life to which you were called when you made your good confession in the presence of many witnesses.

~ 1 Timothy 6:6–12 NIV

REFLECTIONS FOR THE WEEK

1. Consider how an obituary for your life would read. Would the writer depict you as a "man of God" or as someone who lived a life to be judged in the context of the world's view of success, influence, and importance? In your mind, are these two choices mutually exclusive?

2. If, in this time of reflection, you would like to confirm God's plans for you, consider Jesus' words in Matthew 7:7–8 (NASB). "Ask, and it will be given to you; seek, and you will find; knock, and it will be opened to you. For everyone who asks receives, and he who seeks finds, and to him who knocks it will be opened." As you pray, be confident and full of hope that God will reveal His will for your life. Frame your petitions with the following in mind:

- We are commanded to ask; we are not intruding on God.
- Be aware that God loves you.
- Acknowledge you do not control the circumstances of your life.
- Bend your will to obedience and to bring glory to God.
- Ask to deepen your love and relationship with Jesus.
- Ask knowing the Father hears your petitions.

- Ask expecting the Father to act.
- Be confident your petitions will deepen your trust in the Father.
- Allow the Father time to reveal the answer.
- Ask to learn from the answer more about the Father and Jesus.
- Ask without fear, aware that both Jesus and the Holy Spirit pray for you.
- Ask to bear fruit for Jesus and God.
- Ask what it is you should do?
- Ask for strength and power to accomplish the tasks assigned to you.

PRAYER

Almighty God, full of majesty and honor, all praise and glory are Yours. I thank You for creating me with a plan in mind for my life. I thank You for gifting me in unique and wonderful ways. I thank You for my circumstances, opportunities, hopes, desires, and dreams, and I pray that You bring my spirit and will into joyful obedience to Your will so that I bring glory to You and fulfill my mission.

Amen

APRIL
THE BEGINNING OF THE SECOND QUARTER

May God be gracious to us and bless us
and make his face shine on us—
so that your ways may be known on earth,
your salvation among all nations.
May the peoples praise you, God;
  may all the peoples praise you.
May the nations be glad and sing for joy,
  for you rule the peoples with equity
  and guide the nations of the earth.
May the peoples praise you, God;
  may all the peoples praise you.
The land yields its harvest;
  God, our God, blesses us.
May God bless us still,
  so that all the ends of the earth will fear him.

~ Psalm 67 NIV

April elicits a feeling of promise. The dark and cold days of winter are slipping away as the earth moves into spring. Surprising in the suddenness of their appearance are lilies that burst from the ground overnight. And equally teasing the spirit back to life are the chubby buds beginning to appear on twigs that had been stark and bleak just a few weeks earlier. Snow is mostly slush now, although a wintry blast is still possible, but such oddities of winter's fury can be endured because April will not allow winter to maintain its grasp for long.

In business, April is a very busy month. April not only marks the beginning of the second quarter, but it is also the time for reporting to interested outsiders and to us how close the enterprise came to its financial goals and objectives for the first quarter. April brings introspection into how well the business is doing—and how well we are doing. Regardless the level of success we or our businesses achieved in the past three months, April will be the point of departure for building on success, or regaining our footing. It is a time to reassess, and to celebrate or commiserate. Even the government is interested in April, with the deadlines for filing tax returns marking the mid-way point of the month.

The psalmist calls our attention to God's providence and to our proper response (praise) to the God who so richly provides our sustenance. The call to praise God is universal in the Psalm ("may all the peoples praise you" and "may the nations be glad and sing for joy"), because God's providence covers all mankind and God rules over all the earth. The psalmist observes from the very beginning that personal relationship with God is what brings forth God's bounty. The psalmist knows God in the sense of personal experience and relationship, and he is convinced God will bless those who love Him. There is both faith and hope at work in the Psalm.

The psalmist connects the acts of God's blessings with the praise of the people. By blessing the people, God will become known on the earth. Because of God's blessing, the people have an obligation to praise God, and in praising God, the world will come to know Him. God is not aloof. God has a desire to be known and to lavish blessings on the earth and on His creation. The psalmist knows, as do we, that man has nothing to do with the rotation of the earth, the times set for seasons, and whether or not the ground will yield a crop. We must conclude that the earth and all that is in it, and the universe and its laws and outcomes, are either chance, or Providence. The psalmist chooses to believe that God and not chance will direct the land to "yield its harvest."

April is (usually) also the time of Easter—the celebration of God's act of salvation that overcame death and conquered sin. Easter is the promise of resurrection, the hope of a future where God's blessings will rain down on the earth in never ending showers of love. Easter is our hope and confidence in the present time of waiting for God's will and kingdom to be fully present on earth.

> For God so loved the world that he gave his one and only Son, that whoever believes in him shall not perish but have eternal life. For God did not send his Son into the world to condemn the world, but to save the world through him. Whoever believes in him is not condemned, but whoever does not believe stands

condemned already because they have not believed in the name of God's one and only Son.

~ John 3:16–18 NIV

The importance of the second quarter to either ratify or rectify the results of the first quarter can bring a sense of urgency and even anxiety to leaders. April showers may bring May flowers, but April can also bring moments of tension and uncertainty. This is because results achieved in the second quarter will illuminate with more clarity the quality of the results achieved in the first quarter. Whatever causes and effects that led to the results of the first quarter, the second quarter must either build upon them or correct them. As a result, even amid the ever increasing evidence of renewal and the nearness of spring, there can still be anxiety associated with April. But let me remind you we stand strong when we stand in the love of God.

As you set your mind and your energies on achieving your goals and objectives, remember your personal relationship with the God of all blessings who cares for you and is always seeking the best for you.

And as you approach your tasks, consider the words of Paul when he said, "Finally, brothers and sisters, whatever is true, whatever is noble, whatever is right, whatever is pure, whatever is lovely, whatever is admirable—if anything is excellent or praiseworthy—think about such things" (Philippians 4:8 NIV). Gather your strength in confidence and find rest in the hope of spring, the assurance of Easter, and the love of God. Then, in confidence you can say, "I have learned the secret of being content in any and every situation, whether well fed or hungry, whether living in plenty or in want. I can do all this through him who gives me strength" (Philippians 4:12a, 13 NIV).

REFLECTIONS FOR APRIL

1. As you look back over the results of your enterprise in the first quarter, what can be truly celebrated? Where did you and your teams make the most positive contributions to the goals that had been set?

2. What areas of your personal growth or enterprise objectives did not meet with your expectations? If these are still important to you or to the enterprise, set down on paper what activities, energy, resources, collaboration, and attitudes would make their achievement more certain in the second quarter.

3. In your meditations and prayers, ask God to strengthen you to lead your teams in new ways that will build upon successes achieved. Pray also for guidance in choosing tactics to improve the enterprise and yourself where hoped for results were not achieved.

4. In all things, praise God for His care for you and your enterprise. Allow God the opportunity to reveal His love and His blessings to you.

PRAYER

Almighty God, and Jesus Christ, as winter now loosens its grip on the world, let me joyfully look forward to the promise of spring that April will reveal. I humbly ask for Your Spirit to illuminate my heart and mind so that I choose activities and courses of action in this month that uplift and encourage me and those around me. Recall to my mind the things that I do well and that are pleasing to You. Recall to my mind the many blessings You have poured out on me so that I rest in comfortable assurance that You are with me in all endeavors. Help me praise You for Your love and mighty acts in my life.

Amen

APRIL—WEEK ONE

RETAINING AND RECRUITING TALENTED EMPLOYEES

Jesus went through all the towns and villages, teaching in their synagogues, proclaiming the good news of the kingdom and healing every disease and sickness. When he saw the crowds, he had compassion on them, because they were harassed and helpless, like sheep without a shepherd. Then he said to his disciples, "The harvest is plentiful but the workers are few. Ask the Lord of the harvest, therefore, to send out workers into his harvest field."

~ Matthew 9:35–38 NIV

These twelve Jesus sent out with the following instructions: "Do not go among the Gentiles or enter any town of the Samaritans. Go rather to the lost sheep of Israel. As you go, proclaim this message: 'The kingdom of heaven has come near.' Heal the sick, raise the dead, cleanse those who have leprosy, drive out demons. Freely you have received; freely give.

"Do not get any gold or silver or copper to take with you in your belts— no bag for the journey or extra shirt or sandals or a staff, for the worker is worth his keep."

~ Matthew 10:5-10 NIV

On the day I called, you answered me; my strength of soul you increased.

~ Psalm 138:3 ESV

A business enterprise achieves its goals and objectives largely through the efforts of its employees who work together in a collaborative fashion for the common good. Without coordination among and between its employees, the enterprise will struggle to achieve its goals and objectives. However, consistently achieving coordination among and between employees is not an easy thing to accomplish. There can be a number of reasons for this. First, human nature is often self-centered, and compromise is never assured when pride, advancement, competition, compensation, and recognition are at stake. Self-centeredness and pride can create tension between employees, their coworkers, and even outsiders (customers, vendors, and suppliers). In such situations, conflicts will arise that will negatively affect the success of the enterprise.

Second, our inherent human differences can lead to misunderstandings between us that negatively affect our ability to work together. For example, some people are oriented more to be individual contributors rather than to work as part of teams, while other people are more productive when working in groups. Some people are introverted, while others are extroverted. Introverts and extroverts conduct interpersonal relationships in profoundly different ways. Some people learn in a sequential fashion with step one leading to step two and step two to step three; other people are intuitive and are not overly bothered by the sequence of events necessary to accomplish a task. Sequential versus intuitive styles of learning and completing tasks are so different that compromise and collaboration are difficult to achieve. Some people are oriented toward precision and not overly concerned with the time it takes to complete tasks—precision takes precedence over time constraints. Other people are more concerned about the time it takes to complete a task and are willing to sacrifice some precision for the sake of speed. Precision-oriented employees will experience tension when working on time-sensitive tasks, and time-oriented employees will experience tension when precision is the ultimate goal.

Many organizations seek to minimize problems associated with human dynamics and the incompatibility of employees by making hiring decisions using specialized tests of prospective employees to determine compatibility and fit for specific jobs and responsibilities. Nonetheless, our human individuality can be a roadblock preventing collaboration and compromise.

A third difficulty in leading a group of individuals to work collaboratively to achieve the common goals of the enterprise is the difference among individuals in faith and belief systems. These differences can strongly affect how individuals approach their jobs and each other, and how they choose among alternative courses of action, particularly when making moral choices.

APRIL—WEEK ONE

Customs born by religious beliefs can affect how people dress and groom themselves, what they eat, and the holidays they observe. These external points of difference can create tension and impede workplace collaboration. Within an organization, some employees may be Christians, and some will be of other faiths or of no faith at all. Even among Christians there will be interesting differences of opinion arising from denominationally specific matters of doctrine and belief, and these differences can influence personal relationships and boundaries.

Notwithstanding the difficulties of working collaboratively, God has called us to learn to live and work together in peace. Work is of God and is not to be considered a punishment.

> The Lord God took the man and put him in the Garden of Eden to work it and take care of it.
> ~ Genesis 2:15 NIV

> *Go to the ant, you sluggard;*
> *consider its ways and be wise!*
> *It has no commander,*
> *no overseer or ruler,*
> *yet it stores its provisions in summer*
> *and gathers its food at harvest.*
> *How long will you lie there, you sluggard?*
> *When will you get up from your sleep?*
> *A little sleep, a little slumber,*
> *a little folding of the hands to rest—*
> *and poverty will come on you like a thief*
> *and scarcity like an armed man.*
> ~ Proverbs 6:6–11 NIV

> Now when Jesus saw the crowds, he went up on a mountainside and sat down. His disciples came to him, and he began to teach them (saying) "Blessed are the peacemakers for they will be called children of God."
> ~ Matthew 5:1–2, 5:9 NIV

And make it your ambition to lead a quiet life: You should mind your own business and work with your hands, just as we told you, so that your daily life may win the respect of outsiders and so that you will not be dependent on anybody.

~ 1 Thessalonians 4:11–12 NIV

Whatever you do, work at it with all your heart, as working for the Lord, not for human masters, since you know that you will receive an inheritance from the Lord as a reward. It is the Lord Christ you are serving.

~ Colossians 3:23–24 NIV

As a Christian business leader, you are called to motivate your teams to accomplish common goals in spite of human differences. Jesus, as a leader, faced these same types of problems as He worked with His disciples to form them into a collaborative group that shared His vision and His mission. Jesus, as a leader, was able to transfer to these men the wisdom and lessons they needed to carry on His work after He ascended to heaven.

The accounts of Jesus in the Gospels reveal certain characteristics of leadership that Jesus displayed in His relationships with His disciples. Certainly He demonstrated love and compassion for them, and He enjoyed their companionship. In addition to caring for and about them, Jesus also demonstrated these key characteristics:

- Jesus was an active recruiter of His disciples.
- He was selective in His choice of disciples.
- He demonstrated for them the practices and the behaviors He wanted them to follow.
- Jesus invested time with them and taught them what they needed to know to be successful. And He corrected them when necessary in order that they not stray far off course.
- He allowed them to make mistakes and to fail, suffering the consequences of their actions. Nonetheless, time and time again He was willing to restore them to fellowship and service.
- Jesus prayed for His disciples and asked the Father to strengthen them for the tasks they would face.
- Best of all, He asked the Father to send the Holy Spirit to each disciple (and each believer thereafter, including you and me) to encourage

them in all things. "All this I have spoken while still with you. But the Advocate, the Holy Spirit, whom the Father will send in my name, will teach you all things and will remind you of everything I have said to you" (John 14:25–26 NIV).

By doing these things, Jesus was able to impart to His disciples everything they needed in order to successfully complete the mission He had called them to do after He ascended into heaven. Next week we will consider these attributes of Jesus in more detail.

REFLECTIONS FOR THE WEEK

1. Has your organization explored common personality traits and learning behaviors as it seeks to build teams to accomplish common goals and objectives? If so, take time to refresh your memory on the personality traits of your key employees or those who are responsible for a significant task right now. As a leader, how can you use this information to coach your team to more cooperation and better results?

2. If your organization has not identified common personality traits and learning behaviors of its employees, research for yourself how this information might be beneficial to your organization in gaining cooperation among employees.

PRAYER

Lord Jesus, You faced the same problems that I face in organizing teams to accomplish common goals and objectives. You overcame these problems and assembled a team of men that transformed the world through their belief in You and the power of the Holy Spirit working in their lives. God, You have called me to work. You have called me to live in harmony with others. Help me through Your power and strength to learn how to do these things in a godly way that is pleasing to You and brings You glory.

Amen

APRIL—WEEK TWO

RETAINING AND RECRUITING TALENTED EMPLOYEES

You have searched me, Lord,
 and you know me.
You know when I sit and when I rise;
 you perceive my thoughts from afar.
You discern my going out and my lying down;
 you are familiar with all my ways.
Before a word is on my tongue
 you, Lord, know it completely.
You hem me in behind and before,
 and you lay your hand upon me.
Such knowledge is too wonderful for me,
 too lofty for me to attain.
Where can I go from your Spirit?
 Where can I flee from your presence?
If I go up to the heavens, you are there;
 if I make my bed in the depths, you are there.
If I rise on the wings of the dawn,
 if I settle on the far side of the sea,
even there your hand will guide me,
 your right hand will hold me fast.
If I say, "Surely the darkness will hide me
 and the light become night around me,"
even the darkness will not be dark to you;
 the night will shine like the day,
for darkness is as light to you.
For you created my inmost being;
 you knit me together in my mother's womb.
I praise you because I am fearfully and wonderfully made;
 your works are wonderful,
 I know that full well.
My frame was not hidden from you
 when I was made in the secret place,

> *when I was woven together in the depths of the earth.*
> *Your eyes saw my unformed body;*
> *all the days ordained for me were written in your book*
> *before one of them came to be.*
>
> ~ Psalm 139:1–16 NIV

Last week, we considered that people often have trouble learning to work collaboratively together in a business environment. As a leader, you are charged with overcoming those obstacles and leading your teams toward achieving the goals of the organization in spite of individual differences. A leader who learns something about the people working under him or her—what motivates them to succeed, what do they fear or resent, and what resources (for example time, training, coaching, assistance) they are in need of to complete their assignments in a satisfactory way—increases his probability of successfully achieving assigned goals and objectives.

In the passage of Scripture from Psalm 139, the psalmist recounts in awestruck wonder how fully, how completely, God knew and understood him. The knowledge of God included a full understanding of the author's weaknesses as well as his strengths. Jesus, too, demonstrated a complete understanding of everyone with whom He came in contact, including His twelve chosen disciples. While we will never obtain such an understanding of the people we work with every day, we can increase our likelihood of successfully achieving goals and objectives when we emulate God and spend time and energy getting to know the people in our care and actively seeking after their welfare.

Jesus always demonstrated His love and compassion for His disciples. He displayed His love and compassion by investing time with them, by praying for them, and by serving them. A Christian leader should do likewise. These three actions alone would go a long way toward helping you and your teams achieve the organization's goals and objectives.

In addition, Jesus demonstrated other characteristics that we would be wise to imitate in guiding our relationships with coworkers. Those characteristics are: actively recruiting coworkers, being selective in accepting coworkers on the team, leading by example, teaching and correcting mistakes, being willing to accept that mistakes will occur, and restoring those who make mistakes to fellowship.

RECRUITING COWORKERS

It is clear Jesus **chose** His disciples with care and specificity. Here are some examples of Jesus choosing His coworkers.

> The next day Jesus decided to leave for Galilee. Finding Philip, he said to him, "Follow me."
>
> ~ John 1:43 NIV

> As Jesus went on from there, he saw a man named Matthew sitting at the tax collector's booth. "Follow me," he told him, and Matthew got up and followed him.
>
> ~ Matthew 9:9 NIV

> Meanwhile, Saul was still breathing out murderous threats against the Lord's disciples. He went to the high priest and asked him for letters to the synagogues in Damascus, so that if he found any there who belonged to the Way, whether men or women, he might take them as prisoners to Jerusalem. As he neared Damascus on his journey, suddenly a light from heaven flashed around him. He fell to the ground and heard a voice say to him, "Saul, Saul, why do you persecute me?"
>
> "Who are you, Lord?" Saul asked.
> "I am Jesus, whom you are persecuting," he replied. "Now get up and go into the city, and you will be told what you must do."
>
> ~ Acts 9:1–6 NIV

Leaders have a responsibility to actively seek out coworkers who can assist them in carrying out their missions.

BEING SELECTIVE IN CHOOSING COWORKERS

Not everyone who wanted to be part of Jesus' group of followers was selected. It follows that Christian leaders are also expected to be selective in their choices of coworkers.

> When Jesus saw the crowd around him, he gave orders to cross to the other side of the lake. Then a teacher of the law came to him and said, "Teacher, I will follow you wherever you go."

Jesus replied, "Foxes have dens and birds have nests, but the Son of Man has no place to lay his head."

Another disciple said to him, "Lord, first let me go and bury my father."

But Jesus told him, "Follow me, and let the dead bury their own dead."

~ Matthew 8:18–22 NIV

Then they prayed, "Lord, you know everyone's heart. Show us which of these two you have chosen to take over this apostolic ministry, which Judas left to go where he belongs."

~ Acts 1:24–25 NIV

So the Twelve gathered all the disciples together and said, "It would not be right for us to neglect the ministry of the word of God in order to wait on tables. Brothers and sisters, choose seven men from among you who are known to be full of the Spirit and wisdom. We will turn this responsibility over to them and will give our attention to prayer and the ministry of the word."

This proposal pleased the whole group. They chose Stephen, a man full of faith and of the Holy Spirit; also Philip, Procorus, Nicanor, Timon, Parmenas, and Nicolas from Antioch, a convert to Judaism. They presented these men to the apostles, who prayed and laid their hands on them.

~ Acts 6:2–6 NIV

LEADING BY EXAMPLE

The Gospel accounts of Jesus make it clear that many Jews were praying and seeking for the Messiah. Roman occupation of Israel made their lives very difficult and hard. The Scriptures and the prophets pointed to a coming Messiah who would restore the people and the land. Jesus' ability to preach God's Word, to heal the sick, raise the dead, feed the multitudes and confront His critics led many to hope that He was the promised Messiah. However, Jesus did not conform to the worldview of the Messiah, and as He continued his ministry, it became increasingly clear that He was not what the people expected. Jesus' disciples (the twelve and the entire group of other followers) had to come to grips with Jesus' mission contrasted with that of Jewish expectations, and Jesus accomplished this by leading them by example.

> Just then his disciples returned and were surprised to find him talking with a woman. But no one asked, "What do you want?" or "Why are you talking with her?"
> Then, leaving her water jar, the woman went back to the town and said to the people, "Come, see a man who told me everything I ever did. Could this be the Messiah?" They came out of the town and made their way toward him.
> ~ John 4:27–30 NIV
> People were bringing little children to Jesus for him to place his hands on them, but the disciples rebuked them. When Jesus saw this, he was indignant. He said to them, "Let the little children come to me, and do not hinder them, for the kingdom of God belongs to such as these."
> ~ Mark 10:13–14 NIV

> On reaching Jerusalem, Jesus entered the temple courts and began driving out those who were buying and selling there. He overturned the tables of the money changers and the benches of those selling doves, and would not allow anyone to carry merchandise through the temple courts.
> ~ Mark 11:15–16 NIV

JESUS TAUGHT THEM AND CORRECTED THEM WHEN NECESSARY

In addition to leading by example, Jesus also spent time teaching His disciples about who He was, His mission, and what they could expect from the world because of being His followers. He also rebuked them and corrected them when they erred in their knowledge or actions.

> Now when Jesus saw the crowds, he went up on a mountainside and sat down. His disciples came to him, and he began to teach them.
> ~ Matthew 5:1–2 NIV

> The disciples came to him and asked, "Why do you speak to the people in parables?"

APRIL—WEEK TWO

He replied, "Because the knowledge of the secrets of the kingdom of heaven has been given to you, but not to them. Whoever has will be given more, and they will have an abundance. Whoever does not have, even what they have will be taken from them."

~ Matthew 13:10–12 NIV

"Have you understood all these things?" Jesus asked.
"Yes," they replied.
He said to them, "Therefore every teacher of the law who has become a disciple in the kingdom of heaven is like the owner of a house who brings out of his storeroom new treasures as well as old."

~ Matthew 13:51–52 NIV

Jesus was in the stern, sleeping on a cushion. The disciples woke him and said to him, "Teacher, don't you care if we drown?"
He got up, rebuked the wind and said to the waves, "Quiet! Be still!" Then the wind died down and it was completely calm.
He said to his disciples, "Why are you so afraid? Do you still have no faith?"

~ Mark 4:38–40 NIV

And he sent messengers on ahead, who went into a Samaritan village to get things ready for him; but the people there did not welcome him, because he was heading for Jerusalem. When the disciples James and John saw this, they asked, "Lord, do you want us to call fire down from heaven to destroy them?" But Jesus turned and rebuked them. Then he and his disciples went to another village.

~ Luke 9:52–56 NIV

While everyone was marveling at all that Jesus did, he said to his disciples, "Listen carefully to what I am about to tell you: The Son of Man is going to be delivered into the hands of men." But they did not understand what this meant. It was hidden from them, so that they did not grasp it, and they were afraid to ask him about it.

~ Luke 9:43b–45 NIV

Peter took him aside and began to rebuke him. "Never, Lord!" he said. "This shall never happen to you!"

> Jesus turned and said to Peter, "Get behind me, Satan! You are a stumbling block to me; you do not have in mind the concerns of God, but merely human concerns."
> ~ Matthew 16:22–23 NIV

JESUS ALLOWED HIS DISCIPLES TO FAIL AND SUFFER THE CONSEQUENCES OF THEIR ACTIONS

Even though Jesus led by example and spent many hours in dialogue with His disciples to teach them how to obey and follow His example, each of them was ultimately responsible for their own actions. Jesus always gave His disciples the freedom to choose and to suffer the consequences of their own actions.

> Peter replied, "Even if all fall away on account of you, I never will."
> "Truly I tell you," Jesus answered, "this very night, before the rooster crows, you will disown me three times."
> But Peter declared, "Even if I have to die with you, I will never disown you." And all the other disciples said the same.
> ~ Matthew 26:33–35 NIV

> As soon as Judas took the bread, Satan entered into him. So Jesus told him, "What you are about to do, do quickly."
> ~ John 13:27 NIV

JESUS RESTORED HIS DISCIPLES TO FELLOWSHIP

As a leader, Jesus was willing to restore His disciples to fellowship when they acknowledged their errors. Jesus judged the heart and was willing to forgive.

> While they were still talking about this, Jesus himself stood among them and said to them, "Peace be with you."
> They were startled and frightened, thinking they saw a ghost. He said to them, "Why are you troubled, and why do doubts rise in your minds? Look at my hands and my feet. It is I myself! Touch me and see; a ghost does not have flesh and bones, as you see I have."
> ~ Luke 24:36–39 NIV

A week later his disciples were in the house again, and Thomas was with them. Though the doors were locked, Jesus came and stood among them and said, "Peace be with you!" Then he said to Thomas, "Put your finger here; see my hands. Reach out your hand and put it into my side. Stop doubting and believe."

~ John 20:26-27 NIV

When they had finished eating, Jesus said to Simon Peter, "Simon son of John, do you love me more than these?"
"Yes, Lord," he said, "you know that I love you."
Jesus said, "Feed my lambs."
Again Jesus said, "Simon son of John, do you love me?"
He answered, "Yes, Lord, you know that I love you."
Jesus said, "Take care of my sheep."
The third time he said to him, "Simon son of John, do you love me?" Peter was hurt because Jesus asked him the third time, "Do you love me?" He said, "Lord, you know all things; you know that I love you."
Jesus said, "Feed my sheep. Very truly I tell you, when you were younger you dressed yourself and went where you wanted; but when you are old you will stretch out your hands, and someone else will dress you and lead you where you do not want to go." Jesus said this to indicate the kind of death by which Peter would glorify God. Then he said to him, "Follow me!"

~ John 21:15-19 NIV

As a leader, your ability to recruit, retain, and train talented coworkers will be vital to your ability to reach your enterprise's goals and objectives. You can assist your teams in reaching their goals by modeling the leadership principles of Jesus. Your ability to do these things will be greatly enhanced if you approach these tasks with prayer. And, just as Jesus did, continue to pray for your existing employees that they may be fruitful in their work, growing and learning how to live in harmony with one another and to fulfill God's purpose for their lives.

As the author of Psalm 139 discovered, God cares for you. He wants to bless your life, and in turn, He wants you to be a blessing to others. Whether at work, at play, or at home, God has called the Christian to live a life that is full of recognition of the gift of salvation, and to live a life that is pleasing to Him. "Let us not become weary in doing good, for at the proper time we will reap a harvest if we do not give up. Therefore, as we have opportunity, let us do good to all people, especially to those who belong to the family of believers" (Galatians 6:9–10 NIV).

REFLECTIONS FOR THE WEEK

1. Record in a journal a record of your prayers offered on behalf of your teams. Pray as specifically as possible how God can help your coworkers be successful in their work.

2. Recall that God uses both successes and failures to shape our character and to mold us more and more into the likeness of His Son. Recall a time when a group task was not as successful as you would have liked. How did you respond to the team and/or individuals whose performance was not what was hoped for or expected? How might you respond to the next situation so that Jesus is seen to be growing in your life?

PRAYER

Father, I thank You for giving me a new life as a Christian. I thank You for illuminating my life with the knowledge of Jesus, and I ask that You continue to reveal Jesus to me so that I grow in His likeness. I ask that You give me words to say when opportunities arise for me to comfort others with the hope and peace I possess. I ask for the courage to live my faith in a quiet way, but in a way that is unmistakable to those who need to know more about You. Guide and protect my thoughts at work so that I can be a blessing to those who work with me and who count on me.

Amen

APRIL—WEEK THREE

INCREASING SALES AND REVENUES

If the Lord had not been on our side—
let Israel say—
if the Lord had not been on our side
when people attacked us,
they would have swallowed us alive
when their anger flared against us;
the flood would have engulfed us,
the torrent would have swept over us, the raging waters
would have swept us away.
Praise be to the Lord,
who has not let us be torn by their teeth.
We have escaped like a bird
from the fowler's snare;
the snare has been broken,
and we have escaped.
Our help is in the name of the Lord,
the Maker of heaven and earth.

~ Psalm 124 NIV

Do not love the world or anything in the world. If anyone loves the world, love for the Father is not in them. For everything in the world—the lust of the flesh, the lust of the eyes, and the pride of life—comes not from the Father but from the world. The world and its desires pass away, but whoever does the will of God lives forever.

~ 1 John 2:15–17 NIV

Though the fig tree does not bud
and there are no grapes on the vines,
though the olive crop fails
and the fields produce no food,
though there are no sheep in the pen
and no cattle in the stalls,
yet I will rejoice in the Lord,

> *I will be joyful in God my Savior.*
> *The Sovereign Lord is my strength;*
> *he makes my feet like the feet of a deer,*
> *he enables me to tread on the heights.*
> ~ Habakkuk 3:17–19 NIV

One of the most important objectives of any enterprise is to generate sales or revenues in sufficient amount to keep the enterprise operating, enabling it to pay its bills, pay its employees, invest in its infrastructure, pay its taxes, and earn a profit. Achieving sales and revenue goals is so important that all leaders within an organization spend significant time and energy in monitoring actual results versus forecasted sales and revenues and the methods that might be employed to attain goals, maintain existing revenues, and open avenues for revenue growth.

Have you contemplated in a serious way the possibility that sales and revenue goals and requirements will not be met and the implications such an event would have on your enterprise? As Christians, we are not to be anxious about unforeseen circumstances that may arise in the future. For that matter, Christians are not to "be anxious about anything, but in every situation, by prayer and petition, with thanksgiving, present your requests to God" (Philippians 4:6 NIV). Yet, we all understand that the unthinkable can happen and that events and circumstances may turn against our hopes and dreams.

As an example of the uncertainty of our times, you will certainly recall the following events. In 2001, terrorists attacked the World Trade Center and the Pentagon, and our economy was thrust into uncertainty. In 2005, Louisiana and Mississippi suffered significant economic distress when Hurricane Katrina made landfall. The devastation was non-discriminate and substantial. In 2010, the Gulf South was again rocked by the explosion and sinking of the oil rig Deep Water Horizon and the resulting oil spill that lasted from April 20, 2010 until September 19, 2010. Finally, economists tell us that in 2007 the United States entered into the most significant recession it had experienced since the Great Depression. As a result of the recession, businesses were lost, jobs were lost, and lives were changed.

In the face of these examples, and many others that you might recall for yourselves, prudence dictates leaders would be wise to anticipate what courses of action they will take should a catastrophe strike or an enterprise become faced with a significant revenue shortfall.

While specific courses of action to take will vary enterprise to enterprise and situation to situation, it is still possible to contemplate your individual approach to trouble and difficult circumstances. As a leader, those you lead will look to you for wisdom, guidance, and confidence.

Here are eight steps to take that will equip you for the challenges you will face when disaster strikes.

- **Begin with God** and acknowledge that He is in the midst of your trouble, aware of your concerns, and "that in all things God works for the good of those who love Him, who have been called according to His purpose" (Romans 8:28 NIV). The Psalms are a wonderful place to begin a time of reflection in the face of troubled times. The Psalms reveal the power and the hope that can be yours when you seek God's guiding and loving hand. The Psalms remind us that God is concerned for us and that He is a shelter and a refuge for His children in their time of need. Here are some suggested readings from the book of Psalms: Psalm 20, Psalm 25, Psalm 56, Psalm 73, Psalm 91, and Psalm 92.
- **Ask God to prepare you for the tasks that will lie ahead**. Make your requests with confidence, and ask God to strengthen you and to sharpen your mind to be aware of the possibilities He brings to you and your circumstances.
- **Be alert to God's will for you.** Ask God to reveal to you what He wants you to see and learn during the time of testing. Knowing that God is always working to shape you into the person He wants you to be can provide comfort in times of testing. Nothing is wasted by our God—not even times of testing and difficulty.
- **Be courageous**. Act with godly speed to begin addressing problems. However, be careful to take all of your decisions and strategies to God in prayer before you irrevocably commit to completing them. Pray

earnestly and specifically about your plans and pray that God grant you success. As noted later, the Bible teaches that we are not to rush into things but are to wait patiently for the Lord to act. Godly speed is acting within the time frame that God through the Holy Spirit brings to your consciousness. Not all problems are the same. Some problems and circumstances are more urgent from a time perspective than others. But if you have diligently sought the Lord's counsel through prayer and meditation at each step along the way, you will guard against taking actions precipitously.

- **Be patient and be willing to wait on the Lord to act.** God's timing is always perfect. Judge carefully the time pressures in which you are operating so that you do not hinder your own success by acting too quickly.
- **Seek godly wisdom.** Pray for God to bring to you godly counselors to help you discern among possible courses of action. Remember that God does not operate along the standards of the world. As a result, worldly advice and counsel will not often coincide with godly counsel. When confronted with alternative choices, remember what God requires of you: "To act justly and to love mercy and to walk humbly with your God" (Micah 6:8b).
- **Maintain a godly perspective.** Remember that there is a season for everything. Difficult times will not last always. Whatever the outcome, God will stand with you to see it through.
- **Rejoice and give thanks.** Always be thankful, regardless the circumstances. As a Christian it is important to remember that this age and everything in it is passing away. Christians view time through the perspective of eternity versus vanity. No matter how bad a circumstance is now, the result will not be your destruction. Jesus said to His disciples, "I have told you these things, so that in me you may have peace. In this world you will have trouble. But take heart! I have overcome the world" (John 16:33 NIV).

Oswald Chambers wrote that God is more likely to be found when one is in the midst of turmoil than when the turmoil is concluded. This insight has helped me during times of testing—both at work and at home. If things do not work out as you hope, remember those circumstances do not necessarily mean that God has not blessed you or that you are in His disfavor. Ultimately, your attitude about God's role in your life and your sincere desire to walk according to His way will dictate the conclusions you are able to draw as your time and history unfolds. I pray that you will allow God to reveal to you His purposes, His presence, and His mercy and grace at work in your life.

REFLECTIONS FOR THE WEEK

1. As a leader, reflect upon what circumstances might occur that would jeopardize your personal or business goals and objectives. List as many events as you can imagine before you attempt to rationalize them or discount them as improbable.

2. In your mind, role play how you would react to these circumstances. Make an initial list of actions you might take to respond to these circumstances.

3. Pray that God protect you and your business from any of the events you have briefly imagined. Present to God your hopes and dreams for your business and for your family. Thank God for all He has done and is doing in your life.

PRAYER

Almighty God, You hold my hopes and dreams in Your hands. You gave me my desires and passions, and I thank You for them. I live in an uncertain world. Lord, help me to value the blessings You provide to me every day. Help me to stand firm when troubles come, relying on Your strength in confidence. Let me say as Paul, "Let love be sincere (in our lives), (let me) hate what is evil, cling to what is good; be devoted to one another in love; (and) honor one another above yourselves. (Let me) never be lacking in zeal, but keep (my) spiritual fervor, (and) serve the Lord. (Let me) rejoice in hope, (be) patient in affliction, (and) faithful in prayer" (Romans 12:9-12 NIV).

Amen

APRIL—WEEK FOUR

MANAGING THE BALANCE SHEET AND ANTICIPATING TROUBLE

Now these are the last words of David:
The oracle of David, the son of Jesse,
the oracle of the man who was raised on high,
the anointed of the God of Jacob,
the sweet psalmist of Israel:
"The Spirit of the Lord speaks by me;
his word is on my tongue.
The God of Israel has spoken;
the Rock of Israel has said to me:
When one rules justly over men,
ruling in the fear of God,
he dawns on them like the morning light,
like the sun shining forth on a cloudless morning,
like rain that makes grass to sprout from the earth.
"For does not my house stand so with God?
For he has made with me an everlasting covenant,
ordered in all things and secure.
For will he not cause to prosper
all my help and my desire?
But worthless men are all like thorns that are thrown away,
for they cannot be taken with the hand;
but the man who touches them
arms himself with iron and the shaft of a spear,
and they are utterly consumed with fire."
~ 2 Samuel 23:1–7 NIV

May God be gracious to us and bless us
and make his face to shine upon us, Selah
that your way may be known on earth,
your saving power among all nations.
Let the peoples praise you, O God;
let all the peoples praise you!
Let the nations be glad and sing for joy,

> *for you judge the peoples with equity*
> *and guide the nations upon earth. Selah*
> *Let the peoples praise you, O God;*
> *let all the peoples praise you!*
> *The earth has yielded its increase;*
> *God, our God, shall bless us.*
> *God shall bless us;*
> *let all the ends of the earth fear him!*
>
> ~ Psalm 67 ESV

Two familiar colloquialisms used to describe troubling situations are to say the situation is "out of balance" and that "things just don't add up." A person who keeps things in "balance" discovers a clear perspective to evaluate proper courses of action. Conversely, a person who is "out of balance" experiences feelings of loss of control and the intrusion of chaos in their lives. The concept of being in balance or out of balance therefore describes and colors our view of our work, our relationships, and our personal growth (spiritual, mental and physical).

Maintaining a sense of balance in our work, in our relationships, and in ourselves is difficult to do because each of these is susceptible to change at any moment, and change is what disrupts balance. Becoming out of balance can seriously impair judgment just when sound judgment is desperately needed. Maintaining a sense of balance, on the other hand, provides an opportunity to plan and execute strategies and activities to achieve goals and objectives even in times of change. And practicing moving in and out of balance improves an individual's ability to return to balance more quickly when disequilibrium occurs.

A Christian's sense of balance is best measured when our scale measurements are attuned to God's call on our lives. Here are some scriptural examples of godly balance:

> *Two things I ask of you, Lord;*
> *do not refuse me before I die:*
> *Keep falsehood and lies far from me;*
> *give me neither poverty nor riches,*
> *but give me only my daily bread.*

> *Otherwise, I may have too much and disown you*
> *and say, "Who is the Lord?"*
> *Or I may become poor and steal,*
> *and so dishonor the name of my God.*
>
> ~ Proverbs 30:7-9 NIV

So do not worry, saying, "What shall we eat?" or "What shall we drink?" or "What shall we wear?" For the pagans run after all these things, and your heavenly Father knows that you need them. But seek first his kingdom and his righteousness, and all these things will be given to you as well. Therefore do not worry about tomorrow, for tomorrow will worry about itself. Each day has enough trouble of its own.

~ Matthew 6:31-34 NIV

Therefore everyone who hears these words of mine and puts them into practice is like a wise man who built his house on the rock. The rain came down, the streams rose, and the winds blew and beat against that house; yet it did not fall, because it had its foundation on the rock.

~ Matthew 7:24-25 NIV

For the entire law is fulfilled in keeping this one command: Love your neighbor as yourself.

~ Galatians 6:14 NIV

For he himself is our peace, who has made the two groups one and has destroyed the barrier, the dividing wall of hostility, by setting aside in his flesh the law with its commands and regulations. His purpose was to create in himself one new humanity out of the two, thus making peace, and in one body to reconcile both of them to God through the cross, by which he put to death their hostility.

~ Ephesians 2:14-16 NIV

You were taught, with regard to your former way of life, to put off your old self, which is being corrupted by its deceitful desires; to be made new in the attitude of your minds; and to put on the new self, created to be like God in true righteousness and holiness.

~ Ephesians 4:22-24 NIV

The importance of maintaining balance is also applicable to your organization and the people you lead, particularly in the context of achieving the mission of the enterprise. A leader's personal equilibrium plays an important part in the equilibrium of the people they lead.

Where one stands, either in balance or out of balance, is discerned through introspection, prayer, and feedback from trusted counselors. A leader feeling out of balance will struggle with identifying and properly responding to areas of difficulty within their organization. And a leader who is in balance or regains their balance quickly will more ably look outward to the organization and judge rightly the areas of disequilibrium affecting the enterprise. Quickly identifying the internal and external factors that threaten disequilibrium provides the opportunity to take corrective actions.

The Bible provides excellent examples of the importance of balance in the life of a leader. In the following examples, notice how David, Solomon, and Rehoboam responded to situations of great significance in the lives of the people they led. In two cases, the leaders sought personal balance and alignment with God's will. In two other examples, the leaders disregarded their own disequilibrium to the detriment of themselves and their followers.

DAVID SHARES THE WEALTH

This story (found in 1 Samuel 30) concerns David shortly before he became king of Israel. In the story, David and his men return home from other adventures and discover their village plundered and all of their wives and children taken as captives. The event so shocks and saddens the men that they become angry at David (verse 6). But David takes heart, praying to God for guidance. God tells David to pursue the enemy and assures him of victory.

After consulting with God, David and 600 of his men begin the arduous process of tracking the enemy. At a place called the Besor Ravine, two hundred of David's men are too exhausted to continue on. Leaving those men behind to watch the supplies, the four hundred proceed and overtake the enemy and, as God had promised, win a great victory. To their joy, they discover all the captives are alive. All of the spoils taken by the enemy in their raids of other villages are also seized by David and his men.

Returning victorious to the Besor Ravine, David greets the men who had been left behind, but not all the fighting men were interested in sharing with the men left behind.

> But all the evil men and troublemakers among David's followers said, "Because they did not go out with us, we will not share with them the plunder we recovered. However, each man may take his wife and children and go."
>
> David replied, "No, my brothers, you must not do that with what the Lord has given us. He has protected us and delivered into our hands the raiding party that came against us. Who will listen to what you say? The share of the man who stayed with the supplies is to be the same as that of him who went down to the battle. All will share alike." David made this a statute and ordinance for Israel from that day to this.
>
> ~ 1 Samuel 30:23–25 NIV

Although not yet king, David was still a leader in tune with God and his people. At the onset of trouble and change, he had taken stock of his personal situation and relied on God to provide guidance. He was then able to lead his people to victory. Along the way, he had correctly assessed the need of the two hundred to rest, and at the end he had correctly ascribed the subsequent victory over the enemy to God. The idea of not sharing was then properly seen as unrighteous. In the end, all the men shared in the victory and the spoils of victory.

SOLOMON SEEKS WISDOM

The second example (found in 1 Kings 3) concerns Solomon after he had assumed the throne of his father, David. Solomon was concerned about his ability to govern. Considering how to lead his people, he decided to strengthen his kingdom by establishing alliances with another powerful nation (Egypt) through marriage. But Solomon also decided to make a sacrifice to God and seek God's guidance for himself. God appears to Solomon in a dream and says, "Ask for whatever you want me to give you" (1 Kings 3:5b NIV).

Solomon responded,

> "You have shown great kindness to your servant, my father David, because he was faithful to you and righteous and upright in heart. You have continued this great kindness to him and have given him a son to sit on his throne this very day.
>
> "Now, Lord my God, you have made your servant king in place of my father David. But I am only a little child and do not know how to carry out my duties. Your servant is here among the people you have chosen, a great people, too numerous to count or number. So give your servant a discerning heart to govern your people and to distinguish between right and wrong. For who is able to govern this great people of yours?"
>
> ~ 1 Kings 3:6–9 NIV

Pleased with Solomon's request, God granted it, giving Solomon greater wisdom than any man ever had before. God also granted Solomon a number of things he did not ask for—wealth, power, peace, and a long life. During his life, Solomon extended the size of the kingdom, built the Lord's Temple, and brought peace and prosperity to Israel that was never matched again. Solomon's self-awareness and reliance on God provided him with wisdom and blessings that also overflowed to his people.

In contrast to these examples of godly leadership and balance, two other stories demonstrate the consequences when leaders become out of balance with themselves and with God.

DAVID CONDUCTS A CENSUS

One of David's notable lapses in character and balance was his adulterous relationship with Bathsheba. But during David's reign, there was another notable lapse in his character and balance that is recorded in the 24th chapter of 2 Samuel. It concerns David's decision to take a census of his fighting men. David's desire to know the size of his army was not good; it implied at least two evils. First, his desire to know the size of his army implies David had grown self-reliant, placing his hope in himself rather than relying on God. Second, in addition to self-reliance, David has grown prideful about the success rightly attributable to God alone. The census will reaffirm the lofty position he has attained. God hates pride and self-reliance.

One of David's advisors, a general named Joab, strongly cautions David against taking the census, saying, "May the Lord your God multiply the troops a hundred times over, and may the eyes of my lord the king see it. But why does my lord the king want to do such a thing?" (2 Samuel 24:3 NIV). Unfortunately, David ignored Joab and carried out the census.

Immediately upon hearing the report of the census and the number of fighting men, David is "conscience-stricken after he had counted the fighting men, and he said to the Lord, 'I have sinned greatly in what I have done. Now, Lord, I beg you, take away the guilt of your servant. I have done a very foolish thing'" (2 Samuel 24:10 NIV).

David's self-assessment was confirmed by Gad, a prophet of God, who pronounced God's judgment: David had to choose between three years of famine, or three months fleeing for his life from his enemies, or three days of plague in Israel. "David said to Gad, 'I am in deep distress. Let us fall into the hands of the Lord, for his mercy is great; but do not let me fall into human hands'" (2 Samuel 24:14 NIV).

The plague that fell on the land was horrendous—70,000 people died. (It's ironic the exact number of the dead is given since the punishment followed a foolish census, isn't it?) During the plague, David saw an angel of the Lord about to strike Jerusalem, and he cried out to God for mercy. In anguish, David confessed the sin as his alone and that God's anger should fall on him, not the people. God instructs David to build an altar at a certain place and make a sacrifice there. The owner of the land offered to give it and everything else needed for the sacrifice to David for free. But David realized that a sacrifice that costs nothing is no sacrifice, so he bought the land and the animals for the sacrifice, built the altar, and made the sacrifice. God stopped the plague on Israel.

When David allowed himself to fall out of balance with God, the results were terrible for his people. Rather than consult the Lord about whatever was on his mind leading to the census, David remained silent, choosing to go his own way. David also ignored words of wisdom from another leader of Israel—a general in his army. In the end, David remembered that his balance was to be found in God and God alone. Working from a position of balance, David made the intercession and the sacrifice acceptable to God, and God restored the people.

REHOBOAM AND THE LOST KINGDOM

Rehoboam was a son of Solomon who succeeded to Solomon's throne. His first acts as king (recorded in 1 Kings 12:1-9) led to civil war between the Northern Kingdom (thereafter called Israel) and the Southern Kingdom (thereafter called Judah). Rehoboam's lack of balance and his reckless behavior sundered the kingdom.

This is the story. After Solomon's death, Rehoboam journeys to Shechem, a city in Israel, to meet with all the Israelites to be confirmed as king. But a rival, Jeroboam son of Nebat, has returned from hiding in Egypt and confronts Rehoboam over some of the past practices of Solomon. According to Jeroboam, King Solomon had conscripted labor and imposed heavy taxes on the people during his reign. Now the people, represented by Jeroboam, ask Rehoboam to relax some of these previous policies. Rehoboam sends the people away for three days while he consults with his advisors.

Rehoboam first consulted with "elders" who had served his father. Their advice was to concede and restore Rehoboam's relationship with the people. Rehoboam next consulted the "young men" who had grown up with him. Their advice was to taunt the people and threaten them with policies worse than those they had complained about. Rehoboam unwisely chose to accept the advice of the young men.

Upon hearing Rehoboam's answer, the people of the northern part of Israel said,

> *"What share do we have in David,*
> *what part in Jesse's son?*
> *To your tents, Israel!*
> *Look after your own house, David!"*
> *So the Israelites went home.*
>
> ~ 1 Kings 12:16 NIV

With that, the kingdom entered a period of civil war and was torn apart forever.

There are important contrasts of Rehoboam and Solomon in their first acts as king. Rehoboam was reckless and full of himself. Although he surrounded himself with both wise and foolish advisors, he chose to listen only to those who supported his own view. Rehoboam was clearly out of balance with himself (arrogant and prideful), and he was out of balance with his people. Nowhere in the narrative does Rehoboam consider or approach God for advice and counsel. Solomon, on the other hand, approached being king with humility and fear. Solomon remembered God had been responsible for the success of David's kingdom. The result: Solomon ruled a growing and prosperous kingdom. Rehoboam, on the other hand, saw the separation of his father's kingdom, and it was never restored.

REFLECTIONS FOR THE WEEK

1. How would you describe your personal balance at this time? Are there aspects of your life that you would balance differently if you could do so?

2. Balance can be lost due to time constraints placing difficult and unusual pressure on our lives. Balance can also be lost when unforeseen circumstances suddenly and significantly change our lives. Personal balance and godly perspective can be regained by seeking the guidance of trusted friends and advisors. Who would be on your list of trusted friends and advisors? On whose list would you be on?

3. Are there aspects of your business that seem to be out of balance or moving out of balance? Prayerfully consider what steps and actions would be godly and wise to take in response.

PRAYER

Lord, I thank You for the stories in the Bible that speak great truths about humans and our weaknesses, including me and my own. Through Your Scriptures I see myself in the lives of saints and sinners. I know I am prone to becoming out of balance and losing my way. Call such times to my attention, Lord. Give me the wisdom to call upon You and Jesus to strengthen me when I falter or fall, and to hold me until I once again regain my footing. I rely in confidence on Your great mercy and love through the redeeming love of Jesus, our Lord.

Amen

MAY

How lovely is your dwelling place,
 O Lord of hosts!
My soul longs, yes, faints
 for the courts of the Lord;
my heart and flesh sing for joy
 to the living God.
Even the sparrow finds a home,
 and the swallow a nest for herself,
 where she may lay her young,
at your altars, O Lord of hosts,
 my King and my God.
Blessed are those who dwell in your house,
 ever singing your praise! Selah
Blessed are those whose strength is in you,
 in whose heart are the highways to Zion.
As they go through the Valley of Baca
 they make it a place of springs;
 the early rain also covers it with pools.
They go from strength to strength;
 each one appears before God in Zion.
 O Lord God of hosts, hear my prayer;
 give ear, O God of Jacob! Selah
Behold our shield, O God;
 look on the face of your anointed!
For a day in your courts is better
 than a thousand elsewhere.
I would rather be a doorkeeper in the house of my God
 than dwell in the tents of wickedness.
 For the Lord God is a sun and shield;
 the Lord bestows favor and honor.
No good thing does he withhold
 from those who walk uprightly.

O Lord of hosts,
blessed is the one who trusts in you!
                                    ~ Psalm 84 ESV

For me, the month of May is a month filled with momentum. Winter has fully lost its grasp, spring is in full bloom, and May brings a promise of success to businesses and relationships. After all, as children we learned April showers bring May flowers. In 1600, Thomas Decker's poem, "The Merry Month of May," gave us a phrase that still encourages us to look forward to a month of good tidings. Lewis and Clark's expedition began in May 1804. And May is filled with holidays and festivals that are upbeat, optimistic, and fun. Here are just a few of them:

- The Kentucky Derby (first Saturday in May)
- The Indianapolis 500
- The Daytona 500
- Mother's Day
- Cinco de Mayo
- American bike month
- National barbecue month
- National strawberry month

Psalm 84 has a month of May feel to me. The author, cognizant that God refreshes everything, is filled with awe and respect, and acknowledges that nothing is as significant as spending time with God, residing under His care and protection. Even though the earth and its pleasures offer many delights, the author affirms only the Lord is permanent and trustworthy. The psalmist desires to pursue the Lord and appropriate His message into his life. The result: barren places will be made to feel like springtime; strength will be granted for the pilgrim's journey.

A pilgrimage is a journey to a religious place or a place with significance to the pilgrim. The implication is the journey will be long and difficult. The effort and diligence required to reach the goal often make the journey and its relevance take on deeper meaning. Lately, I have come to think of my years as a business leader as a pilgrimage. Looking back across the years in retrospection, I see goals or dreams or desires, once pursued by diligent and purposeful activities, differently than before. With a pilgrim's keen insight, the goals or dreams or desires that before had seemed so important now seem less important. Leadership and the journey have given me perspective.

The month of May provides excellent opportunity to instill a spirit of optimism in your teams by building on the natural experience of renewal and life that spring restores. The results of all the activities of the first four months provide the necessary raw ingredients to inspire, invigorate, challenge, and motivate teams to strive for the desired outcomes, goals, and objectives of the enterprise. Where the enterprise is making sound progress against goals and objectives, May provides the opportunity to assess if targets can be stretched higher. On the other hand, if the results of activities for the first four months have been disappointing, May is a pivotal month to restore confidence and make necessary corrections in actions and expectations.

May is therefore a significant month for judging how successful the year will be in the enterprise's efforts to achieve its annual goals and objectives. As we enter the month of May, it is my hope that God will lead you in wisdom and sound judgment, enabling you to lead your teams successfully toward common goals and objectives.

REFLECTIONS FOR MAY

1. What does the phrase "they go from strength to strength" evoke in you? Do you find yourself moving from strength to strength as you lead your teams and organizations? What would it be like to know that each problem, each obstacle could be encountered with the assurance of strength sufficient to overcome?

2. Who do you know that demonstrates the ability to move from strength to strength no matter the difficulty? What is the source of their strength?

PRAYER

Father, I thank You for creating time so that our future is always open to new possibilities. Times of difficulty will give sway to better times; times of peace will move into times of unease or discord. I acknowledge that the uncertainty of life can at different times bring hope and tension, but through all circumstances, You remain steadfast and true. You control all aspects of time. You are never uncertain. And You always seek after the good of Your children. Bless me, my family, and my business as we move into the month of May with a sense of continuing pilgrimage to a greater awareness of Your majestic presence in our lives.

Amen

MAY—WEEK ONE

DETERMINING PRIORITIES, SETTING GOALS, AND COMMUNICATING THEM TO OTHERS

In the second year of Darius the king, in the sixth month, on the first day of the month, the word of the Lord came by the hand of Haggai the prophet to Zerubbabel the son of Shealtiel, governor of Judah, and to Joshua the son of Jehozadak, the high priest: "Thus says the Lord of hosts: These people say the time has not yet come to rebuild the house of the Lord." Then the word of the Lord came by the hand of Haggai the prophet, "Is it a time for you yourselves to dwell in your paneled houses, while this house lies in ruins? Now, therefore, thus says the Lord of hosts: Consider your ways. You have sown much, and harvested little. You eat, but you never have enough; you drink, but you never have your fill. You clothe yourselves, but no one is warm. And he who earns wages does so to put them into a bag with holes.

"Thus says the Lord of hosts: Consider your ways. Go up to the hills and bring wood and build the house, that I may take pleasure in it and that I may be glorified, says the Lord. You looked for much, and behold, it came to little. And when you brought it home, I blew it away. Why? declares the Lord of hosts. Because of my house that lies in ruins, while each of you busies himself with his own house. Therefore the heavens above you have withheld the dew, and the earth has withheld its produce. And I have called for a drought on the land and the hills, on the grain, the new wine, the oil, on what the ground brings forth, on man and beast, and on all their labors."

~ Haggai 1:1–11 ESV

In approximately 587 BCE (some disputes exist over the exact date), the Babylonian king Nebuchadnezzar's armies destroyed Jerusalem and the Temple of the Lord. Most of the population left in Jerusalem—after the devastating effects of a long siege and a raging army—were deported to Babylon. The nation of Israel was demoralized, downtrodden, and baffled by the magnitude of the decimation of their land. Prior to suffering defeat at the hands of the Babylonians, most of the Jewish people, as well as the king, his court, and his paid prophets, had refused to believe that God would allow His Temple or His people to be destroyed. Some true prophets had seen the disaster coming. A number of them had proclaimed the truth about the people's sins and the coming wrath and the judgment of God. Chief among the people's sins was "apostasy" (renouncing their faith in God alone).

The destruction of the Temple and the fall of Jerusalem overturned and eliminated the priorities and goals of the Jewish people. Whatever they had thought to be important was important no longer. In the sudden and stark abandonment, loneliness, and grief that follow disaster, they had to reflect on their responsibility in causing the disaster. They had to consider anew the righteousness of God in executing judgment and what they might expect in the future now that God had punished them so severely.

At first, the Jewish people prayed for a quick release and return to their homeland. Their hopes were fanned by false prophets who prophesied God would punish the Babylonians and quickly save His people. However, the prophet Jeremiah, speaking God's words, wrote to the people held in captivity saying their captivity would be long (seventy years) and advising them not to rebel against God's judgment that had brought them to Babylon. Rather, Jeremiah said it was God's will for the people to remain absent from Jerusalem and Judah for many years. Jeremiah, still living in Jerusalem after the destruction of the Temple, wrote the following to the captives in Babylon:

> Thus says the Lord of hosts, the God of Israel, to all the exiles whom I have sent into exile from Jerusalem to Babylon: Build houses and live in them; plant gardens and eat their produce. Take wives and have sons and daughters; take wives for your sons, and give your daughters in marriage, that they may bear sons and daughters; multiply there, and do not decrease. But seek the welfare of the city where I have sent you into exile, and pray to the Lord on its behalf, for in its welfare you will find your welfare.
>
> ~ Jeremiah 29:4–7 ESV

MAY—WEEK ONE

Through retrospection and reflection, and the guidance of prophets like Jeremiah and other leaders, the years in captivity brought the Jewish people new insights about God and His promises to restore the people in spite of their falling away. The years in captivity led the people into a richer and deeper understanding of God's laws and His sovereignty over all nations and all peoples.

The books of Ezra and Nehemiah tell the story of the return of the Jewish people to Jerusalem from captivity. The returning people were poorly prepared for the ruins that had once been a strong and prosperous city. They were also unprepared for the conflicts that were part of the process of rebuilding; from defending against new adversaries who had entered the land and settled there, to pragmatic concerns of how to live and make a living, the people faced severe hardships. In this time of uncertainty, priorities were difficult to make and to keep.

God used the prophet Haggai to shake the people out of their everyday sameness and to call them again to the greater purpose of relationship with Him. God wanted His people to get their priorities straight—saying, in essence, that **nothing matters if God is not first in your hearts and minds**; nothing will satisfy you, though you work hard for it. The words of the prophet reminded them God's desire was to bless them in surprising ways, but their distance and aloofness prevented that from happening. The prophet called out, "give careful consideration to your ways." Then God would bless the work of their hands.

I believe the Jewish people returning from exile arrived in Jerusalem with joy, thinking thoughts of victory and hope, expectantly looking toward the realization and fulfillment of the blessings and promises of God. I believe their priorities were aligned with God's priorities for their lives. But soon, their struggles to merely eke out an existence began to reshape their priorities. And their efforts to restore the Temple to the glory it once had were failing. Materials and laborers were hard to come by; disheartened and impatient, they soon found other priorities.

Has that ever happened to you? Have you found your once important priorities slip because of too much of the day-to-day small crises and obligations?

The prophet Haggai (the name means "encourager"), speaking on behalf of God, called the people to return their focus to God. God's assessment of their falling away due to tough circumstances was accurate. But even though the people had (once again) assigned God a lesser role in their lives, God did not rebuke them severely. Rather, God's message through Haggai offered the answer of why their lives were unproductive and offered the solution to their problems. God called the people to look at their lives from His perspective.

As a leader, it is important to seek God's affirmation of your priorities and those of the groups you lead. Seeking God's affirmation often requires a different paradigm—using a different perspective than the one afforded by the actual circumstances. After all, days tend to run together, and soon projects and activities also run together. What we do each day tends to become what we do every day. Isn't that what happened to the returning Jewish exiles? But God called them, and He calls us, to periodically stop whatever it is we are so purposefully doing and consider our work and our lives in relation to Him. He calls us to stop and listen for His purpose, His plan, and His blessing. Consider these passages of Scripture:

> All the ways of a man are pure in his own eyes, but the Lord weighs the spirit. Commit your work to the Lord, and your plans will be established.
> ~ Proverbs 16:2–3 ESV

> I will instruct you and teach you in the way you should go; I will counsel you with my eye upon you. Be not like a horse or a mule, without understanding, which must be curbed with bit and bridle, or it will not stay near you.
> ~ Psalm 32:8–9 ESV

> The Lord will fulfill his purpose for me; your steadfast love, O Lord, endures forever. Do not forsake the work of your hands.
> ~ Psalm 138:8 ESV

> Delight yourself in the Lord, and he will give you the desires of your heart.
> ~ Psalm 37:4 ESV

> If any of you lacks wisdom, let him ask God, who gives generously to all without reproach, and it will be given him.
>
> ~ James 1:5 ESV

> With my whole heart I cry; answer me, O Lord! I will keep your statutes. I call to you; save me, that I may observe your testimonies.
>
> ~ Psalm 119:145–146 ESV

> O Lord, you have searched me and known me! You know when I sit down and when I rise up; you discern my thoughts from afar. You search out my path and my lying down and are acquainted with all my ways. Even before a word is on my tongue, behold, O Lord, you know it altogether.
>
> ~ Psalm 139:1–4 ESV

Benefits will inure to all who seek the will of the Lord and His wisdom in setting or recalibrating priorities. If God is aware of all outcomes before they happen, if God loves His children and wants to bless them so they are fruitful, is there any reason not to bring God your plans, priorities, and ambitions and to seek His guidance and wisdom? Our God is with us every moment of every day—at work, at home, and anywhere else.

In this first week of May, take some time to pray and reflect on the important priorities you have set for yourself and your teams. Ask God to illuminate your mind to His plans for you in your role as a leader.

REFLECTIONS FOR THE WEEK

1. Haggai pointed out to the people that God expected action to follow their deliberations of His call to re-prioritize their lives. God said, "Be strong, all you people of the land, declares the Lord. Work, for I am with you, declares the Lord of hosts, according to the covenant that I made with you when you came out of Egypt. My Spirit remains in your midst. Fear not" (Haggai 2:4b–5 ESV). Is there anything that you fear when you consider changing some of your priorities at work or at home?

2. How does it make you feel to read passages of Scripture where God actually says He withholds blessings from people when they do not put Him first in their lives?

3. If this thought creates fear or mistrust of God in your mind, make time to actively research and contemplate such events as they are set out in the Bible. Use this research to pray that God reveal to you more of His character and His love, even in difficult circumstances.

4. When describing the Temple being reconstructed by the people, God points out that its magnificence was nothing like the glory it had before the exile to Babylon. Nonetheless, God assured the people He was involved in the work, and only He had the proper vantage point to evaluate the worth of the project. Apply this insight to yourself. If you are struggling to achieve your priorities, it does not necessarily mean God is against them. What might God be communicating to you if things are not going as well as you would like, yet you believe you are following God's will?

PRAYER

Almighty God, who knows me better than I know myself, who uses the events and circumstances of my life to shape me into the image of Your son so that I can be of use in His kingdom, and who will not forsake me or leave me under any circumstances, guide my thoughts and mind as I set priorities for myself and for my team. Then, God, guide our thoughts and meditations so that Your will is made manifest to us and together we accomplish much. Give us the courage to follow Your path and to leave the results of obedience in Your hands.

Amen

MAY—WEEK TWO

HOLDING YOURSELF AND OTHERS ACCOUNTABLE TO KEEP PROMISES AND COMMITMENTS

People of Israel, the Lord's arm is not too weak to save you.
His ears aren't too deaf to hear your cry for help.
But your sins have separated you from your God.
They have caused him to turn his face away from you.
So he won't listen to you.
Your hands and fingers are stained with blood.
You are guilty of committing murder.
Your mouth has told lies.
Your tongue says evil things.
People aren't fair when they present their cases in court.
They aren't honest when they state their case.
They depend on weak arguments. They tell lies.
They plan to make trouble.
Then they carry it out.
The plans they make are like the eggs of poisonous snakes.
Anyone who eats those eggs will die.
When one of them is broken, a snake comes out.
Those people weave their evil plans together like a spider's web.
But the webs they make can't be used as clothes.
They can't cover themselves with what they make.
Their acts are evil.
They do things to harm others.
They are always in a hurry to sin.
They run quickly to murder those who aren't guilty.
Their thoughts are evil.
They leave a trail of suffering and pain.
They don't know how to live at peace with others.
What they do isn't fair.
They lead twisted lives.
No one who lives like that will enjoy peace and rest.
We aren't being treated fairly.

We haven't been set free yet.
The God who always does what is right
hasn't come to help us.
We look for light. But we see nothing but darkness.
We look for brightness. But we walk in deep shadows.
Like blind people we feel our way along the wall.
We are like those who can't see.
At noon we trip and fall as if the sun had already set.
Compared to those who are healthy, we are like dead people.
All of us growl like hungry bears.
We cry like sad doves.
We want the Lord to do what is fair and save us.
But he doesn't do it.
We long for him to set us free.
But the time for that seems far away.
~ Isaiah 59:1–11 NIRV

The Lord sees that people aren't treating others fairly.
That makes him unhappy.
He sees that there is no one who helps his people.
He is shocked that no one stands up for them.
So he will use his own powerful arm to save them.
He has the strength to do it because he is holy.
He will put the armor of holiness on his chest.
He'll put the helmet of salvation on his head.
He'll pay people back for the wrong things they do.
He'll wrap himself in anger as if it were a coat.
~ Isaiah 59:15b–17 NIRV

The United States Air Force defines leadership as the art of influencing and directing people in such a way that wins their obedience, respect, and loyal cooperation in achieving common objectives (AFP 35-49). The Air Force definition includes two important elements: the mission, and the people through which the mission is accomplished. Effective leadership completes the mission. And because people are directly involved in completing a mission, leaders must take care of the people resources entrusted to them.

The art of influencing and directing people in a way that wins their obedience, respect, and loyal cooperation includes, at a minimum, the practices of holding yourself and others accountable (responsible) for assigned activities and following through on commitments. Execution, or achievement of the mission, depends on a leader who gives clear instructions, obtains clear commitments from subordinates, and diligently follows up with them on progress of those commitments. These activities honor the work of subordinates and demonstrate the leader's faith and trust in them while nonetheless holding them accountable for their obligations.

There are two certainties in life—death and taxes. I submit there are two other things equally as certain: promises will be made, and promises will be broken. We live in a fallen world. It is also a complicated world. A complicated, fallen world is one where promises are hard to keep.

Perhaps in recognition of our innate ability to make and break promises, modern society has adopted the use of the word "maybe" to hedge against broken promises. In her article "The Many Powers of Maybe: Refusing to Commit Has Never Been Easier, and It Says a Lot About Us" (Wall Street Journal November 1, 2010), Elizabeth Bernstein notes the use of the simple word "maybe" provides a form of power and boundary between people because "maybe" entails no commitment and no consequences to the giver. According to Bernstein, "maybe" means different things to different people; its very ambiguity makes it commitment free. Bernstein does not like the ambiguity. She goes on to poke a little fun at the increasing use of the word "maybe" by inserting it as the answer to the following questions:

- "Will you marry me?"
- "Will I get to heaven?"
- "Am I pregnant?"

Not every communication between people can be prefaced or answered with "maybe." We want commitments from others even if we personally hope to avoid making them. God cares about commitments; keeping promises is a godly characteristic. Although not one of the Ten Commandments, we can hear the importance of keeping promises in Jesus' assertion of the greatest commandment—"You shall love the Lord your God with all your heart and with all your soul and with all your strength and with all your mind, and your neighbor as yourself" (Luke 10:27 ESV). No one would believe a promise breaker's declaration of love.

As the passage from Isaiah 59 above points out, God is deeply concerned about accountability for one's actions and keeping promises and commitments. God's observations indict everyone—no person in the passage exemplified integrity. The passage goes on to link outcomes with behaviors. Here are some of the outcomes from breaking promises:

- No peace
- No justice
- Confusion
- Unanswered prayers
- Sorrow
- Anxiety

Only God is unchanging. Only God keeps every promise. Therefore, we can rely only on Him to guide our lives. Our ability to trust God is a source of great hope and comfort, incomparable really to any other thing we might try to cling to when trouble besets us. After listing the indictments against man in the passages from Isaiah above, God affirms His integrity in the following Scripture:

> "And as for me, this is my covenant with them," says the Lord: "My Spirit that is upon you, and my words that I have put in your mouth, shall not depart out of your mouth, or out of the mouth of your offspring, or out of the mouth of your children's offspring," says the Lord, "from this time forth and forevermore."
>
> Isaiah 59:21 ESV

Breaking promises to God or anyone else is considered a sin by God. Because you are a leader, people will watch you to see if you keep your promises. They will also observe and be interested in how you lead others. They will be alert to see whether or not you hold others similarly accountable for keeping their promises. Strive to keep your promises.

Strive to hold others accountable for their promises. Seek to have clarity in instructions and agreement on promises made.

When you fail or others let you down, remain close to God. God has promised He will forgive our sins through Jesus Christ if we confess them and repent of them. Be accountable to God for what you say, and trust God to help you become more trustworthy as you seek to imitate Jesus. Be compassionate with others who let you down, but speak the truth in love so that they are also made to understand that promises matter.

REFLECTIONS FOR THE WEEK

1. Keep a record of the number of times this week you use the word "maybe" or the word "maybe" is used on you. Consider how the use of the word felt to you as giver and receiver.

2. The Bible has a number of passages regarding the implications of making a promise to God. Here are some of them: Numbers 30:2; Ecclesiastes 5:2–5; Deuteronomy 23:23; Joshua 9:19; and Psalm 34:12-13. Read these passages and consider their implications.

3. Have you ever broken a specific promise to God? If so, read 1 John 3:4-6 and 1 John 3:16-24. Then consider again the wonderful, unsurpassable, absolutely undeserved but magnificent promise of Jesus to wash away all of your sins—even broken promises. Do not be bowed down, but rejoice!

PRAYER

Lord God, You alone are trustworthy and true. You alone are righteous. When I consider how often I fail to keep my promises to You and to others, I am embarrassed and ashamed. I humbly ask You to forgive me for these shortcomings. Remember Your promise of mercy, O God, and let me rely upon Your promises and integrity to forgive me. Help me in turn to forgive others who break their promises to me. Remind me that the gift of forgiveness You gave is to be shared with others. Then grant me wisdom to respond in love while being accountable for my own actions and for others as a leader.

Amen

MAY—WEEK THREE

ACCUMULATING SUFFICIENT RESOURCES TO ACHIEVE THE GOALS AND OBJECTIVES OF THE ORGANIZATION

Sing to God, sing praises to his name;
lift up a song to him who rides through the deserts;
his name is the Lord;
exult before him!
Father of the fatherless and protector of widows
is God in his holy habitation.
God settles the solitary in a home;
he leads out the prisoners to prosperity,
but the rebellious dwell in a parched land.
O God, when you went out before your people,
when you marched through the wilderness, Selah
the earth quaked, the heavens poured down rain,
before God, the One of Sinai,
before God, the God of Israel.
Rain in abundance, O God, you shed abroad;
you restored your inheritance as it languished;
your flock found a dwelling in it;
in your goodness, O God, you provided for the needy.
~ Psalm 68:4–10 ESV

What man of you, having a hundred sheep, if he has lost one of them, does not leave the ninety-nine in the open country, and go after the one that is lost, until he finds it? And when he has found it, he lays it on his shoulders, rejoicing. And when he comes home, he calls together his friends and his neighbors, saying to them, "Rejoice with me, for I have found my sheep that was lost." Just so, I tell you, there will be more joy in heaven over one sinner who repents than over ninety-nine righteous persons who need no repentance.
~ Luke 15:4–7 ESV

Let me ask you a serious, soul-searching question. When did we stop relying on God? When did we lose confidence in God to save us from our enemies? When did we lose confidence in God to guide us in paths of righteousness?

"We did not do any of these things!" some of you might be thinking. Perhaps you are different from me, but I confess I *do* allow some events and decisions to pass only before my judgment—times where I seek to guide my life and the events in it by my own hand. In spite of my confession of Jesus Christ as the Son of God, Savior of my soul, in whom I place all my trust for salvation, I still move through much of my day on my own recognizance.

This is not to say that I spend any day without prayer or conscious yearning for understanding and communion with my God. That is not true. But to say that I bring every decision to the Lord in prayer is also not true. If you find yourself to be in similar straits as I, what can we learn from Scripture regarding possible consequences?

One of the clearest examples is the compelling story of Abraham contained in the book of Genesis. If you have not read Abraham's story in a while, here is a summary.

Abram (his name before God renamed him Abraham) was a direct descendant of Noah's son Shem, and Noah was still alive when Abram was born. When Abram was 99 years old and childless, he received a unique summons from God to take his wife Sarah and their possessions, leave his father and his home, and go to a country that God would show him. God told Abraham, "And I will make of you a great nation, and I will bless you and make your name great, so that you will be a blessing. I will bless those who bless you, and him who dishonors you I will curse, and in you all the families of the earth shall be blessed" (Genesis 12:2–3 ESV).

Abram believed God and, taking his wife, his possessions, and his nephew Lot, left his father and made his way into Canaan.

In a broad sense, the story of Abraham is about a man who heard a call from God and then spent the rest of his life learning how to nurture his faith. In the process, he had to learn to wait patiently on God's timing and not to take matters into his own hands. Abram was not always perfect. For example, on more than one occasion he lied about Sarah being his wife, claiming instead she was his sister because he feared powerful men, desiring her, were going to kill him. This in spite of God's promise that he was to be a father and that God would bless anyone who blessed Abraham. In both circumstances, Sarah was taken into another's harem and only God was able to bring her out safely. Abraham's self-reliance did not work very well in these instances.

Another time, and perhaps the worst instance of Abraham not waiting on God's timing, was the decision, concocted by Sarah but agreed to by Abraham, for him to sleep with Sarah's maid, Hagar. Out that union a son, Ishmael, was born. Abraham, then 86 years old, had fathered a son at long last. But their plan was not God's plan. Ishmael was not destined to be the son of the promise, and Abraham's home life suffered significantly because of his actions.

When he was 125 years old, Abraham and Sarah received visitors—three *men* appeared who turn out to be God and two angels. God was going down to Sodom and Gomorrah to examine the sin in that wicked city and to bring judgment upon it. As the heavenly visitors tarried with Abraham, God assured Abraham that one year later he and Sarah would have a son. Sarah, eavesdropping, experienced disbelief given her age (she was now very old), and laughed at the thought. God heard her laugh and chided her disbelief, but He kept His promise. One year later, Sarah and Abraham received with joy the birth of their son, Isaac.

When Isaac was still a boy, God tested Abraham's faith by telling him to take Isaac and offer him to God as a burnt sacrifice. After twenty-five years of listening to God and reflecting on all he had been through, Abraham chose to obey. He got up early the next morning and went to the mountain God showed him. There, he bound Isaac on the altar and was poised to kill his beloved son when God cried out for him to stop. Abraham was willing to place his son on the altar because he had learned that God was trustworthy to keep His promises.

Abraham's times of self-reliance did not go as he had hoped. Nevertheless, God continued to work in Abraham's life, and ultimately

God's promises were fulfilled. Out of Abraham and Isaac came Jacob, renamed Israel, the father of the Jewish people.

The story of Abraham and the story of his progeny, the Jewish people, reveal a difficult truth for a modern leader to grasp: **God does not glorify self-sufficiency and does not hold it in high regard.** The history of Abraham and the Jewish people is not about how they were able to pull themselves up by their bootstraps and make their circumstances better. Rather, their history clearly reveals their success came only when they gave up their self-sufficiency and literally fell at the feet of God, imploring Him to bless them, forgive them, heal them, and save them.

This theme is certainly carried forward to Christians in the New Testament. Consider what Paul says of Jesus in Philippians:

> *Have among yourselves the same attitude that is also yours in Christ Jesus,*
> *Who, though he was in the form of God,*
> *did not regard equality with God something to be grasped.*
> *Rather, he emptied himself,*
> *taking the form of a slave,*
> *coming in human likeness;*
> *and found human in appearance,*
> *he humbled himself,*
> *becoming obedient to death,*
> *even death on a cross.*
> *Because of this, God greatly exalted him*
> *and bestowed on him the name*
> *that is above every name,*
> *that at the name of Jesus*
> *every knee should bend,*
> *of those in heaven and on earth and under the earth,*
> *and every tongue confess that*
> *Jesus Christ is Lord,*
> *to the glory of God the Father.*
> ~ Philippians 2:5–11 NASB

Consider also what Paul says about his own circumstances:

> Therefore, that I might not become too elated, a thorn in the flesh was given to me, an angel of Satan, to beat me, to keep me from being too elated. Three times I begged the Lord about this, that it might leave me, but he said to me, "My grace is sufficient for you, for power is made perfect in weakness." I will rather boast most gladly of my weaknesses, in order that the power of Christ may dwell with me. Therefore, I am content with weaknesses, insults, hardships, persecutions, and constraints, for the sake of Christ; for when I am weak, then I am strong
> ~ 2 Corinthians 12:7–10 NASB

There is a saying that circulates among Christians—"let go and let God." Yet, in spite of the testimony of the witnesses in the Old and New Testament, in spite of the witnesses of people we know, and even in spite of our own personal testimony that God is faithful and trustworthy to take care of us in any circumstance, we struggle to let go. We choose to ignore the riches of God's providential hand that is readily available for us in the everyday work of our lives. In the words of the old hymn by Robert Robinson, "Come Thou Fount of Every Blessing"—*Prone to wander, Lord, I feel it, Prone to leave the God I love*—we forget God's promises and strike out on our own.

America encourages a "bootstrap" culture: Americans honor those who take care of themselves and look out for themselves, who pick themselves up when they are down and find the will to move on, or who start from nothing yet succeed against all odds. But there is a profound difference in picking yourself up and moving on under your own steam and picking yourself up and moving on under the guiding and uplifting hand of God. There is a profound difference between going your own way and finding the way that God wants you to go. God knows we strike out on our own. He knows we are impatient. He knows we value self-reliance. Thank God He is gracious, patient, and trustworthy.

How great a story Jesus told in the Scripture quoted above (Luke 15:4–7)! I don't know about you, but I would not leave the ninety-nine alone and go in search of the one. That would be a risky proposition and one with the potential for even greater loss. But God will search for the one. God will not abandon the one who strikes out on his own in folly. For God knows our human condition and loves us anyway. God will seek the lost. I know it to be true from firsthand experience: Jesus came looking for me!

Just as Abraham, I am a man who heard a call from God. Perhaps you are too. My call was not to move somewhere and become a patriarch of nations; my call was the conviction of the Holy Spirit that Jesus Christ is Lord and that He loves me. He alone is my hope of salvation.

Each of us, like Abraham, must work out the implications of God's call in our lives. Slowly, ever so slowly, I am learning to trust God with everything in my life—whether at work or at home. In so doing, I am connecting in a powerful and mysterious way with the Sovereign God of the universe who wants to bless me so that I may be a blessing to others. In looking to find resources sufficient to achieve my goals and objectives, there is no resource comparable on any level to the faithfulness and love of Almighty God.

The record in the Bible is very clear: God cares deeply about every aspect of our lives and has a plan for us. God will guide us when we seek to align our purposes and plans with His.

The Bible is equally clear that when we seek to impose our will on God, our will may prevail, but the results will not be in our favor. As you respond to the call of God in your life, prayerfully ask God to enlighten you to those times you have gone your own way, and in gentleness, bring you back to the path He has set before you.

REFLECTIONS FOR THE WEEK

1. How do you approach the biblical theme of humility in light of today's society that celebrates the "self-made" man?

2. Quietly reflect on one aspect of your business life where you are working to solve a problem or complete an assignment and have not asked God to guide you and to bless your effort. What might be keeping you from including such a problem or assignment in your prayers?

3. How do you respond to the idea that we are to "work out (our) own salvation with fear and trembling?" (Philippians 2:12b NRSV).

PRAYER

Almighty God, thank You for Your promises and Your patience with me. I acknowledge I often exclude You from my life, particularly my work life, and I ask that You continue to enlighten me so that I learn to put my trust in You daily. Remind me, and then encourage me, that You are pleased with boldness in Christ. Through Your power and love, continue to demonstrate to me Your desire to participate in my daily life and continue to search for me if I move off in my own wisdom. Find me, Lord, and return me to Your safety and rest.

Amen

MAY—WEEK FOUR

MANAGING THE BALANCE SHEET AND ANTICIPATING TROUBLE

Finally, draw your strength from the Lord and from his mighty power. Put on the armor of God so that you may be able to stand firm against the tactics of the devil. For our struggle is not with flesh and blood but with the principalities, with the powers, with the world rulers of this present darkness, with the evil spirits in the heavens. Therefore, put on the armor of God, that you may be able to resist on the evil day and, having done everything, to hold your ground. So stand fast with your loins girded in truth, clothed with righteousness as a breastplate, and your feet shod in readiness for the gospel of peace. In all circumstances, hold faith as a shield, to quench all [the] flaming arrows of the evil one. And take the helmet of salvation and the sword of the Spirit, which is the word of God. With all prayer and supplication, pray at every opportunity in the Spirit. To that end, be watchful with all perseverance and supplication for all the holy ones and also for me, that speech may be given me to open my mouth, to make known with boldness the mystery of the gospel.

~ Ephesians 6:10-19 NASB

Then the disciples came to Jesus privately and said, "Why could we not drive it out?" And He said to them, "Because of the littleness of your faith; for truly I say to you, if you have faith the size of a mustard seed, you will say to this mountain, 'Move from here to there,' and it will move; and nothing will be impossible to you."

~ Matthew 17:19-20 NASB

Does your place of employment have a dress code or a uniform policy? Many places of employment do. From protective eyewear, ear plugs, masks, gloves, hair nets, coveralls and boots, to suits, sport coats, lab coats, dresses, slacks, ties, scarves, and closed toe or open toed shoes, employers often specify what clothing employees must wear on the job. Clothing standards are usually the result of the type of work itself, the nature of the work environment, or the image that an employer desires to present to others.

What employees wear at work can protect them from harm and at the same time support or further the business's purposes. And just like employees who often need protective clothing to keep them from harm, an enterprise needs protective mechanisms to reduce its risks and to support its purposes. Consider these types of events that can bring harm to an organization:

- Its assets can be (and often are) misappropriated.
- Its assets can be lost or destroyed due to unexpected events of nature, fire, or other calamity.
- Computer systems can fail or be subject to attack by hackers and viruses.
- Key employees can die, quit, or become disabled, depriving the enterprise of their services.
- Market position can be lost due to competition, innovation, or a calamitous event that turns its customers away.
- The business may be subject to litigation and damages due to injury sustained by an employee, caused by an employee or caused by its products or operations.
- Government regulations affect businesses with new rules and regulations, many of which carry a significant cost.

Business leaders are charged with actively considering these types of risks, the probabilities of their occurrence, and establishing contingency plans to deal with them as they arise. A number of methods can be employed to defend and protect the business from such circumstances include: physical safeguards (locks, restricted access, security guards, and cameras), internal controls specifying who can do what and with what authority, written policies governing codes of conduct and how transactions are approved and documented, retaining adequate cash reserves (rainy day funds), making redundancy plans, keeping an eye on the world and particular market segment, establishing and monitoring internal performance measures, insurance, establishing training programs, and performing drug and background checks on key employees.

However, in spite of protective measures such as those listed above, and even in spite of outstanding leadership, things can, do, and will go wrong. Consider this passage from Ecclesiastes:

> I again saw under the sun that the race is not to the swift and the battle is not to the warriors, and neither is bread to the wise nor wealth to the discerning nor favor to men of ability; for time and chance overtake them all. Moreover, man does not know his time: like fish caught in a treacherous net and birds trapped in a snare, so the sons of men are ensnared at an evil time when it suddenly falls on them.
>
> ~ Ecclesiastes 9:11–12 NASB

A leader seeks to protect their enterprise to the best of their abilities. But when things do not go well, when trouble comes to call, what then? Have you considered how prepared you are to deal with problems from a personal capacity and strength perspective? As a leader, you are expected to lead in times of difficulty, too. In times of stress and travail, your teams will look to you for guidance, leadership, solutions, and hope.

Earlier in this book, we listed eight steps to follow when challenges come or disaster strikes:

- Start with God and acknowledge that He is in the midst of your trouble.
- Ask God to prepare you for what lies ahead.
- Ask God to reveal to you what He wants you to see and learn.
- Act with godly speed.
- Be patient and willing to wait upon the Lord to act.
- Pray that God will send you godly counselors for encouragement and advice.
- Remember there is a season for everything, and all things will pass.
- Always be thankful, regardless the circumstances.

These eight steps will help you through times of trouble when you find yourself in the midst of difficult times. But there is something you can do now to prepare yourself before trouble comes. That something is a type of "preventive maintenance" you can do, every day, to put yourself in a mindset of preparedness, able to withstand the first wave of difficulty.

Simply put, you can put on your Christian protective clothing. It will protect your spirit so that you can face difficulties and stressful times with God's power and not your own. In the passage of Scripture above, Paul advises each of us to put on the armor of God, every day.

In the modern world, conversations about Satan and demons (fallen angels) and their intent toward evil can be difficult to have. *Saturday Night Live*, the much acclaimed comedy show, had a long-running skit starring Dana Carvey as the "church lady" who poked fun at everything "bad" as coming from Satan. In the face of such mockery from such a wildly popular show, it is not surprising that conversations about the devil expose one to ridicule. But whether or not you believe Satan exists and is working evil in the world, and specifically working to harm Christians, the armor of God nonetheless provides significant resources for dealing with trouble, no matter where or what you ascribe as its source. To understand how this is so, consider each piece of armor for the benefit it provides rather than the specific point of attack it protects against.

The **belt of truth**, when contemplated daily, requires the Christian to acknowledge God as the source of truth. The belt of truth therefore girds the Christian with the overwhelming sense of security that God's goodness, His mercy, His righteousness, His love, His omnipotence, His power, and His plan will prevail against all challenges. The act of mentally putting on the belt of truth prepares the mind for difficulties.

Aware of the truth of God, the Christian can **stand in peace** in all circumstances. Jesus said, "Peace I leave with you; My peace I give to you; not as the world gives do I give to you. Do not let your heart be troubled, nor let it be fearful" (John 14:27 NASB). The mental image of donning shoes made from the peace of Jesus will enable you to have calm in the midst of struggles.

Your heart may experience moments of conflict and grief during the course of a day. Injuries to your sense of justice, fairness, respect, and character all affect the heart. Clothed with the **breastplate of God's righteousness,** you can discipline your heart and subject the human inclinations of pride and self-righteousness to the gentle self-awareness that "all that you have you received" (1 Corinthians 4:7). And if everything you have is what you received, defending your rights or claiming your rights over others will seem less important or necessary. Operating out of God's righteousness and not out of prideful emotions will leave you open to consider alternatives that are godly and full of wisdom and peace.

Finding the way to be an encourager, even in the midst of troubles, is a key characteristic for a leader. Often, a leader's most important encouragement is directed at themselves. It truly is lonely at the top. **Protecting your mind** with the knowledge of Jesus' act of salvation can free your mind to find words of encouragement for yourself and for others. Clothing your mind with the helmet of salvation and the image of Jesus' sacrificial love will equip you to contemplate positive things—things that uplift the spirit. You will have the power and the desire to focus your thoughts on the noble and not the ignoble.

God's armor provides a weapon, as well. **The sword is the Word of God**—living and alive. God's Word is powerful and available to both defend and to attack strongholds in the life of the Christian. Scripture says, "For the word of God is living and active and sharper than any two-edged sword, and piercing as far as the division of soul and spirit, of both joints and marrow, and able to judge the thoughts and intentions of the heart. And there is no creature hidden from His sight, but all things are open and laid bare to the eyes of Him with whom we have to do" (Hebrews 4:12–13 NASB).

And concerning the power of the Word of God, Scripture also says,
For as the rain and the snow come down from heaven,
And do not return there without watering the earth
And making it bear and sprout,
And furnishing seed to the sower and bread to the eater;
So will My word be which goes forth from My mouth;

> *It will not return to Me empty,*
> *Without accomplishing what I desire,*
> *And without succeeding in the matter for which I sent it.*
> ~ Isaiah 55:10–11 NASB

The remaining article of protective clothing is one I use most often in my life—**the shield of faith.** Attacks on our lives as Christians—at home, at work or at play, come without warning. I find great comfort in the mental image of a shield able to accept the attacks and ward them off. It seems that I am most susceptible to doubts, stress, and anxiety at night, just as I am drifting off to sleep. When such events overtake me, I mentally draw the image of the shield of faith and crawl under it to sleep, as if it were a blanket. I pray and thank God for the shield of faith to cover me. It has never failed me yet.

The shield of faith is important. Without faith, the mental imagery of donning armor can seem silly. You may begin to question the power of your faith and fear your lack of faith renders useless the armor of God. There are two things to point out with respect to such thoughts. First, the armor will absolutely be of no use to you at home in the closet. Practicing putting it on, contemplating with each article of clothing the symbolism of God's strength in all circumstances, and the promises of God in Jesus will be beneficial. Wearing it daily will allow you the opportunity to test its strength and to gain confidence and courage. Second, Jesus said you need have faith only the size of a mustard seed to accomplish the things that God wants you to accomplish. In some respects, growing faith requires taking small steps—literally "fake it until you make it." Take confidence that you can demonstrate a mustard seed sized faith, and see the miracles God will work in your regard.

The Apostle Paul was convinced that Christians were going to face persecution for their belief that Jesus was the Son of God. He formed his opinion on good authority—he, himself, had persecuted the Christian church before his conversion by Jesus on the road to Damascus. Moreover, his life as an apostle of the Lord Jesus Christ was thereafter filled with persecution and mistreatment at the hands of many.

Jesus also warned His original disciples that they would be subject to mistreatment and abuse because of their allegiance to Him. And this warning continues to Christians today. Pray about the armor of God and begin to use it in advance of the day of trouble that will inevitably come your way.

REFLECTIONS FOR THE WEEK

1. Is it possible for you as a learned person in a modern society to believe that Satan is a real force of evil in this world? If it is difficult for you to believe that God has an enemy who is at work in the world, how do you account for evil?

2. Jesus said, in the Sermon on the Mount, that *peacemakers* are blessed by God (Matthew 5:9). What circumstances are in effect right now for you that are threatening to rob you or others of peace? What can you do to bring peace to a difficult situation?

PRAYER

Almighty God, Your love provides me with the capacity to persevere in difficult times. Your promises of deliverance provide me with the strength to bear under the weight of troubles. Your word of hope rings true through the pages of Scripture. Strengthen me when I wear Your armor. Tailor it to fit my needs and enable me to wear it, secure not in my strength but in the strength of the Lord who forged the armor with power and might.

Amen

JUNE

Dear friends, this is now my second letter to you. I have written both of them as reminders to stimulate you to wholesome thinking. I want you to recall the words spoken in the past by the holy prophets and the command given by our Lord and Savior through your apostles.

~ 2 Peter 3:1–2 NIV

What kind of people ought you to be? You ought to live holy and godly lives as you look forward to the day of God and speed its coming. That day will bring about the destruction of the heavens by fire, and the elements will melt in the heat. But in keeping with his promise we are looking forward to a new heaven and a new earth, where righteousness dwells.

So then, dear friends, since you are looking forward to this, make every effort to be found spotless, blameless and at peace with him.

~ 2 Peter 3:11b–14 NIV

My heart, O God, is steadfast;
I will sing and make music with all my soul.
Awake, harp and lyre!
I will awaken the dawn.
I will praise you, Lord, among the nations;
I will sing of you among the peoples.
For great is your love, higher than the heavens;
your faithfulness reaches to the skies.
Be exalted, O God, above the heavens;
let your glory be over all the earth.

~ Psalm 108:1–5 NIV

Does your soul sing with joy now that it is finally June?

I think June has to be one of my favorite months; June has long infused my subconscious with pleasant and joyful memories. As a child, June was the month when summer vacation began in earnest. It was in the month of June I first saw and marveled at a color television set at a friend's house. There were no computers and no computer games, so outside was where play took place. Near my house was a creek bed full of minnows and crawfish we would catch, and hanging down over the middle of the creek from an old and oft-climbed tree was a rope (the "Tarzan rope") that would occupy us for hours, leaving our hands callused but our spirits soaring! Away from the creek, my parents would sometimes take us to a local miniature golf course or the skating rink, and we would revel in these activities and the snack stands. And with friends, there were pick-up games of baseball and hide-and-seek when evening came.

My fascination with June has not abated. I still recall June with a child's eye, keeping the wonder and newness of those days in my heart even now. In June, the wilting heat of summer is not yet upon us. It is enjoyable to have the days lengthen so that outside activities can extend beyond the work day. The smell of a fresh mown lawn, the sound of birds, and the rustle of a gentle breeze in the trees all contribute to a sense of life and the wonder of it. Now that I am a parent, June brings thoughts of family vacation with my own children and creating for them memories that will last and refresh their spirits when they are grown.

June is also a time to again take stock of progress against goals and objectives—at home and at work. The year is now almost half gone. It is with a feeling of incredulity that my reflections on accomplishments sadly acknowledge more was planned than done, more was hoped for than accomplished, and more is still required. I am not being overly critical in this assessment. I judge my time and accomplishments strictly, but I am not a defeatist, and I possess a healthy self-respect. June, I believe, provides a perfect time to make course adjustments where called for and to re-establish the pace at which goals and objectives need to progress if they are to be achieved.

As you enter June, amid the newness of summer and the memories of pleasant summers long past, refresh your spirit and rejoice that God gave us seasons to enjoy. More importantly, remember that God is at work in your life. God is at work in the lives of everyone you know and everyone you do not know. God is at work in the month of June to bring about His plans on the earth, and the thought of this leaves us in wonder at the scope and the beauty of His efforts to bring us into right relationship with Him. As we consider the devotions this month, let us not lose sight that God sees your true self. God loves your true self. God will cause every day in your life to shine with the joy and wonder of June, even when you do not look for it and do not think you deserve any of it. It's June!

The psalmist shouts, "Awake, harp and lyre!" Sing out for joy and let God know your happiness in His marvelous works of creation! O, Lord, thank you for giving us hearts capable of joy and rejoicing!

REFLECTIONS FOR JUNE

1. Looking back over your life, is there something that you left behind that once brought you great joy? Allow yourself the opportunity to again take a stroll down memory lane and experience anew the wonder and joy you felt in that activity.

2. Make it a goal in June (through careful observation and genuine interest) to identify in another (child, spouse, friend, or coworker) what may become for them a future cherished memory. Through genuine care and interest, allow them to share that joy with you. Be interested in their joys, and let them build an even deeper memory connection by sharing their passion and joy with you.

PRAYER

Lord, as Christians we live in the love of Christ. We feel Your presence in our daily lives. We marvel at the gift of life, the struggles of life, the accomplishments of life, and the beauty of life. Fill our hearts with child-like wonder at this season of life and renewal in the world around us. Let us sing in our hearts praises to You and be aware of the grace You bestow upon us.

Amen

JUNE—WEEK ONE

DEFINING THE MISSION OF THE ORGANIZATION

Then we turned back and set out toward the wilderness along the route to the Red Sea, as the Lord had directed me. For a long time we made our way around the hill country of Seir.

Then the Lord said to me, "You have made your way around this hill country long enough; now turn north. Give the people these orders: 'You are about to pass through the territory of your relatives the descendants of Esau, who live in Seir. They will be afraid of you, but be very careful. Do not provoke them to war, for I will not give you any of their land, not even enough to put your foot on. I have given Esau the hill country of Seir as his own. You are to pay them in silver for the food you eat and the water you drink.'"

The Lord your God has blessed you in all the work of your hands. He has watched over your journey through this vast wilderness. These forty years the Lord your God has been with you, and you have not lacked anything.

~ Deuteronomy 2:1–7 NIV

The third time he said to him, "Simon son of John, do you love me?"

Peter was hurt because Jesus asked him the third time, "Do you love me?" He said, "Lord, you know all things; you know that I love you."

Jesus said, "Feed my sheep. Very truly I tell you, when you were younger you dressed yourself and went where you wanted; but when you are old you will stretch out your hands, and someone else will dress you and lead you where you do not want to go." Jesus said this to indicate the kind of death by which Peter would glorify God. Then he said to him, "Follow me!"

~ John 21:17–19 NIV

Then he said to Thomas, "Put your finger here; see my hands. Reach out your hand and put it into my side. Stop doubting and believe." Thomas said to him, "My Lord and my God!"

JUNE—WEEK ONE

Then Jesus told him, "Because you have seen me, you have believed; blessed are those who have not seen and yet have believed."
~ John 20:27–29 NIV

Certainly one of the most significant and fundamental roles a leader has is to establish the mission of the enterprise—its reason and its purpose for being in existence. The significance of any "mission" is such that it is not likely to be developed with a short-lived perspective. Rather, the mission is more likely established possessing some sense of perpetuity. As time moves forward, the mission will be judged against changing environments and changing circumstances.

In addition, the mission of a person or an enterprise is also likely to represent the vision of just one person rather than the consensus of a group of people, although others may and usually do serve important roles in developing ideas, providing insights and suggestions, gathering and interpreting information, and helping to craft the words that define the mission. A mission statement, even carefully crafted, is not immune to criticism and attack as time passes, and its certainty of purpose may become doubtful. Since the mission is closely aligned with the heart and the inner calling of the leader, such times of challenge and difficulty can bring a personal discomfort to a leader.

In the Scripture passages above, the mission of Moses (to bring the people out of bondage and into the Promised Land) and the mission of Peter (to evangelize the message of salvation in Jesus Christ) had not gone smoothly. Nonetheless, in both instances, God was working to graciously restore Moses and Peter to their original mission, in spite of their previously experienced setbacks.

In the case of Moses, with respect to the people of Israel (called out of slavery in Egypt to possess the "promised land"), the people had shrunk back in disbelief just as they had been on the verge of taking possession of it. As a result, God decreed they would wander in the desert until that generation of unbelievers had passed away. In the Scripture from Deuteronomy above, the time of punishment had passed, and God was calling the people to journey again to the Promised Land.

Peter, that bold and impulsive disciple, had denied Christ three times in the hours before the crucifixion. Even though he was aware of Christ's resurrection, we find him in the passage above back in his home town fishing—and he had taken with him a number of the disciples. In this story, Peter seems to be on the verge of returning to a life of fishing for fish and not for men. When Peter needed the Lord the most, Jesus appeared and graciously restored to Peter love, respect, and mission.

Our missions, too, will come into times of confusion and difficulty. For example, in a closely held business, it is very difficult for the founder's vision and mission to survive the second generation. And it is not just the "changing of the guard" that can be disruptive to missions. Society, competitors, laws, inventions, science, ethics, fashions, fads, innovations, and general economic circumstances can wreak havoc on any enterprise's mission. While the mission is fundamental to everything an enterprise is about, it cannot be expected to stand forever without periodic scrutiny or thoughtful re-examination.

A leader is responsible for setting the mission, monitoring the progress toward attaining its goals, and taking the steps necessary to respond to difficulties and circumstances that have thrown up roadblocks to the success of achieving the mission. External forces are the usual reasons for re-evaluation of a specific mission. In dealing with these types of circumstances, the achievement of the mission is in doubt, but the mission itself (the purpose) remains sound. This would seem to fit the case of Moses and the people who at first refused to enter the Promised Land. But, sometimes, circumstances occur that actually call the leader to doubt the mission itself. This seems to be the case with Peter. What happens when a leader begins to have doubts about a mission apart from external circumstances calling for retrospection? What is a leader to do with doubt about the mission of their enterprise and even the calling of their own lives?

Most often, the characteristic of doubt is not viewed in a positive light. Biblically, there are many examples of doubt casting the "doubter" in a negative light.

- We have the "doubting Thomas" saying because of the disciple Thomas's stubborn refusal to believe Jesus had been resurrected until he had seen it with his own eyes.
- The four Gospels (Matthew, Mark, Luke, and John) depict Jesus chastising the disciples when they demonstrate repeatedly their lack of faith in Him (cf. Matthew 16:8, 21:21).
- The two disciples walking away from Jerusalem to Emmaus (Luke 24:13) after the resurrection fail to recognize Jesus until He had spoken to them about why the Christ had to die, the basis for Christ found in the Scriptures, and had even broken bread with them!
- And we have the doubt of John the Baptist's father (Luke 1:18) who fails to believe the announcement of the birth of John the Baptist delivered to him by the angel Gabriel, in spite of his role as priest and his awareness of the miraculous stories in the Bible and God's promises of sending a Savior into the world who would be preceded by a forerunner.

Doubt can be a negative emotion.

On the other hand, doubt about mission can have positive effects, as well. Some positive outcomes associated with doubt include:

- A struggle with doubt may represent a test of will and become the necessary ingredient to restore the mission to a more secure position in the mind of the leader.
- Doubt may represent a time of preparation before God acts in your life. Doubt can lead you to reflect upon your mission so that you are receptive to His call.
- Doubt may provide the leader with the time and the opportunity to choose a different and perhaps more appropriate path rather than staying blindly loyal to the original one.
- Doubt may also signal the ultimate answer to prayer is near at hand. Doubt in this case represents the initial response to the last attack of Satan upon a person who has persevered and struggled to stay true to mission in spite of setbacks.

Doubt, where it is centered upon a lack of faith and trust in God, is not good, and it is not likely that good will come from it. However, where the "doubter" is crying out to God for clarity, for leading, for strength, for wisdom, for discernment, and for courage, doubt is not evil. Such doubt is rooted in the faith and trust in God to answer prayer and to be working in the life of the Christian to shape and mold him or her into the very image of Jesus. Such doubt does not call into question God, but rather highlights the profound need of the servant to hear and know the will of the Master. When you doubt that you are doing everything you can to be inside the will and the blessing of God, introspection will lead to stronger faith, greater courage, and deeper conviction.

REFLECTIONS FOR THE WEEK

1. Read the story of Gideon (Judges, chapter six). Look for instances of godly doubt and instances of Gideon doubting God. How would you act toward someone who needed the coaching that Gideon needed before he would assume the mission?

2. Read the story of Shadrach, Meshach, and Abednego in Daniel, chapter three. Consider their faith in the face of severe danger. As you read the story, can you imagine their thoughts as they came to grips with their fate? Can you imagine a "doubt" struggle that ultimately led to even stronger faith?

3. Are you experiencing doubts about a mission or a call in your life? How can you use this time of doubt to better prepare you for what lies ahead? How can you use this time to grow in confidence toward God?

PRAYER

Almighty God, doubt assails me and I wish it were not so. Throughout the Scriptures I read testimony of Your love and faithfulness, even when all others, like me, fall away. Still I confess my hope is with You. Forgive me for times of doubting where my misgivings really reflect a lack of trust in You. I ask that You, in Your infinite mercy, continue to work Your love and will toward me in spite of my failings, and to use the doubts in my life to strengthen my faith and hope.

Amen

JUNE—WEEK TWO

ACCUMULATING SUFFICIENT RESOURCES TO ACHIEVE THE GOALS AND OBJECTIVES OF THE ORGANIZATION

Hear my cry, O God;
listen to my prayer.
From the ends of the earth I call to you,
I call as my heart grows faint;
lead me to the rock that is higher than I.
For you have been my refuge,
a strong tower against the foe.

~ Psalm 61:1–3 NIV

Come, all you who are thirsty,
come to the waters;
and you who have no money,
come, buy and eat!
Come, buy wine and milk
without money and without cost.
Why spend money on what is not bread,
and your labor on what does not satisfy?
Listen, listen to me, and eat what is good,
and you will delight in the richest of fare.
Give ear and come to me;
listen, that you may live.

~ Isaiah 55:1–3a NIV

For this reason, since the day we heard about you, we have not stopped praying for you. We continually ask God to fill you with the knowledge of his will through all the wisdom and understanding that the Spirit gives, so that you may live a life worthy of the Lord and please him in every way: bearing fruit in every good work, growing in the knowledge of God, being strengthened with all power according to his glorious might so that you may have great endurance and patience, and giving joyful thanks to the

Father, who has qualified you to share in the inheritance of his holy people in the kingdom of light.

~ Colossians 1:9–12 NIV

An enterprise needs resources in order to complete its mission. Thus, ensuring that sufficient resources are obtained for that purpose is an important task of the leader. In completing that task, a leader must consider a number of related objectives, among which are:

- Determining the types, quality, and quantity of the resources needed
- Ensuring needed resources are where they are needed when they are needed
- Making judgments to allocate scarce resources among different projects and missions to achieve the most good
- Assessing the effects changes in circumstances have on the needs of the enterprise or the source(s) of the resources and reacting to them

Resources are needed by everyone—leaders and workers alike. But a key role of leadership is to ensure whatever resources are needed are made available in sufficient quantities and quality at the right time. Jesus displayed this key role of leadership as He carried out His mission on earth. He looked after His own needs, and He accepted the responsibility to provide His followers with the resources they needed to be successful.

JESUS OBTAINED RESOURCES FOR HIMSELF

1. We can trace back to His childhood Jesus obtaining resources necessary to prepare Him for His work and mission. For example, as a twelve-year-old child, Jesus goes to the temple and questions the teachers and authorities on the interpretation of Scriptures. "After three days they found him in the temple courts, sitting among the teachers, listening to them and asking them questions. Everyone who heard him was amazed at his understanding and his answers" (Luke 2:46–47 NIV). Jesus developed spiritual discernment and spiritual wisdom about the beliefs of the religious leaders of Israel at an early age. As an adult, Jesus' ministry and message would stand in stark contrast with the established wisdom of the leaders of His day.

2. When He was about thirty years of age, Jesus began His ministry and His mission. All of the Gospel accounts link the beginning of His ministry with the work of John the Baptist, the forerunner of Jesus, who was sent by God to prepare the people to receive the good news of God's redemptive work in Jesus. As the time of His earthly ministry approached, Jesus went to be baptized by John the Baptist in the Jordan River. The disciple John records the following:

> The next day John saw Jesus coming toward him and said, "Look, the Lamb of God, who takes away the sin of the world! This is the one I meant when I said, 'A man who comes after me has surpassed me because he was before me.' I myself did not know him, but the reason I came baptizing with water was that he might be revealed to Israel."
>
> Then John gave this testimony: "I saw the Spirit come down from heaven as a dove and remain on him. And I myself did not know him, but the one who sent me to baptize with water told me, 'The man on whom you see the Spirit come down and remain is the one who will baptize with the Holy Spirit.' I have seen and I testify that this is God's Chosen One."
>
> ~ John 1:29–34 NIV

As the passages show, Jesus was fully aware of the purpose and role of John the Baptist; John the Baptist was a resource integral to Jesus' mission. The act of baptism enabled John to identify and testify to others that Jesus was the Christ. And through the act of baptism, Jesus received the anointing power of the Holy Spirit (an unlimited resource) to sustain Him and empower Him as He carried out His mission. Jesus was aware of what was needed to set into motion His earthly ministry, and He diligently sought and obtained them.

3. Jesus knew His mission required others to ensure it would continue after He was gone. Therefore, Jesus identified, sought after, and obtained the people resources He needed—some were disciples, some were followers, some were financial supporters, and some were friends. With respect to the twelve disciples, Mark records the following:

> After John was put in prison, Jesus went into Galilee, proclaiming the good news of God. "The time has come," he said. "The kingdom of God has come near. Repent and believe the good news!"
>
> As Jesus walked beside the Sea of Galilee, he saw Simon and his brother Andrew casting a net into the lake, for they were fishermen. "Come, follow me," Jesus said, "and I will send you out to fish for people." At once they left their nets and followed him.
>
> When he had gone a little farther, he saw James son of Zebedee and his brother John in a boat, preparing their nets. Without delay he called them, and they left their father Zebedee in the boat with the hired men and followed him.
>
> ~ Mark 1:14–20 NIV

Jesus identified, sought after, and obtained the human resources necessary to help him achieve his mission. And knowing the cross was His ultimate destiny, Jesus even chose the one who would betray Him.

4. The accounts of Jesus' activities in the four Gospels reveal Jesus used prayer as a great personal resource. Here are examples of His use of prayer:

> a. Jesus prayed before selecting the twelve disciples (Luke 6:12–16).
>
> b. Jesus prayed when He was "transfigured," and He received encouragement to go to Jerusalem where He would be crucified (Luke 9:28–36). By bringing with Him Peter, John, and James, Jesus allowed them to see His Deity. This gave them the resource of personal experience, a resource that would encourage and embolden them in their future work.
>
> c. Jesus prayed for Himself and for His disciples and all future believers in the hours before His arrest and crucifixion (John 17).
>
> d. Jesus prayed to the Father for the "workers" who were needed for the harvest as He continued His ministry of healing and preaching the message of the kingdom of God coming upon Israel (Luke 10:2b). He also prayed to the Father for the same type of work to be performed by the disciples as they went out for a "training mission" of what would become their life-long vocation (Matthew 9:37–38).

JESUS OBTAINED RESOURCES FOR OTHERS

Jesus was also aware of the needs of His followers for resources sufficient for them to complete their tasks. Sometimes the disciples asked for specific resources, but most often Jesus was the one who made the determination and provided His followers with the resources they needed.

1. An example of Jesus providing specific resources is found in Matthew 10 where Jesus sends the disciples to go alone into Israel and preach the good news and heal the sick. Before they go, Jesus gives them specific and detailed instructions about why they were being sent, where they were to go and not go, what they were to take on the journey, where they were to stay, how they were to behave, what they were to say, what response they would receive from others, how they were to sustain themselves on the journey, and what dangers lurked along the way. These clear instructions provided the training they needed to embark upon their mission with confidence.

2. An example of Jesus responding to a specific request by His disciples is found in Luke 11:1–13, where Jesus taught the disciples (and us) how to pray. Another example is found in Jesus' response to the disciples' request for Jesus to "increase their faith" (Luke 17:5). In their request, the disciples reveal they believe faith to be a valuable resource they needed in greater supply. In responding to them, Jesus did not increase their faith. Rather, He teaches them faith the size of a mustard seed is sufficient to accomplish their appointed tasks. Immediately after making this comment, Jesus tells them the following parable.

> Suppose one of you has a servant plowing or looking after the sheep. Will he say to the servant when he comes in from the field, "Come along now and sit down to eat"? Won't he rather say, "Prepare my supper, get yourself ready and wait on me while I eat and drink; after that you may eat and drink"? Will he thank the servant because he did what he was told to do? So you also, when you have done everything you were told to do, should say, "We are unworthy servants; we have only done our duty."
>
> ~ Luke 17:7–10 NIV

This parable, given in response to a request for greater faith, is both difficult and interesting to consider. Joh. Ylvisaker, a Lutheran theologian in the early 1900s, explained the parable as Jesus' response to the disciples asking for the wrong type of faith. According to Ylvisaker, the disciples were asking for wonder-working, miracle-working faith; that kind of faith was not in keeping with the servant-oriented faith required of the servants of God. Ylvisaker's conclusion asserts God cares about our motives when answering requests for resources.

Taking a different tack, Marcia Greenwood, in an article entitled "Mustard Seed Faith," used the disciples' request for more faith to rhetorically ask, isn't it the same size faith that allows us to pray, that allows us to believe Jesus saves us, that allows us believe we have been indwelt by the Holy Spirit, that informs us that God will grant us wisdom and discernment when we ask for it, or that allows us to believe that God is the Creator of everything? Her observations also seem reasonable to me. It is hard to imagine there are varying degrees of faith—what we are really asserting when we doubt our faith is sufficient is there are varying degrees of trust and mistrust. Dovetailing this point, in the November 17, 2009 entry from Daily Exegesis, the author notes that faith is always both a belief and a trust. The disciples request for more faith was really an admission of their failure to trust, and it was trust that was needed.

Still another view of the parable was offered to me by my wife. She believes Jesus used the parable to point out to them that they were really asking Him to make their path easier than it was going to be. According to her, the parable points out to them their jobs are to serve and not to be served. The level of difficulty associated with the servant's task is not to be their concern—that is solely the concern of Jesus. Faith ultimately would be sufficient to allow them to carry out the task at hand and provide the strength necessary to complete the work. This also seems reasonable to me.

Jesus' example as a leader seeking and obtaining resources is important to us. His example shows us that a Christian leader anticipates needs and obtains the resources needed to complete the mission. A Christian leader uses discernment to determine what is truly needed. Prayer provides strength and wisdom to a Christian leader in search of necessary resources. And a Christian leader approaches their responsibility to gather resources with confidence, aware that God will never desert them and will always supply what is needed to complete a mission that is consistent with God's will in their life.

REFLECTIONS FOR THE WEEK

1. Prayer is a powerful resource that is readily available to the believer. Read Luke 11:1–13 and Matthew 7:7–12 for Jesus' admonition for the believer to ask, seek, and knock. Consider how this advice might change whatever tasks, trials, concerns, or uncertainties you may be presently facing.

2. How does the idea that faith is both a belief and a trust enlighten a current problem or opportunity in which you have doubted your faith was sufficient?

PRAYER

Almighty God, I am prone to worry. I know that worry is part of the human condition—I have a mind and experiences that have proven things do not always work out as I had hoped. But looking back, I see Your guiding hand and Spirit at work in my life to bring good out of difficulty, hope out of hopelessness, and faith through perseverance. Lord, of the very many things that I have contemplated as needs and wants in just the last week, one thing I desperately need: Your will fulfilled in my life. You know all that I truly need. Guide me to pray rightly for the things I should. Pray for me when I miss the mark. Be thou my Vision, O Lord of my heart![2]

Amen

---

[2] From the hymn "Be Thou My Vision," public domain.

JUNE—WEEK THREE

PRACTICING GOOD STEWARDSHIP THROUGH THE DILIGENT MANAGEMENT AND ALLOCATION OF RESOURCES

King Solomon was greater in riches and wisdom than all the other kings of the earth. The whole world sought audience with Solomon to hear the wisdom God had put in his heart. Year after year, everyone who came brought a gift—articles of silver and gold, robes, weapons and spices, and horses and mules.

~ 1 Kings 10:23–25 NIV

King Solomon, however, loved many foreign women besides Pharaoh's daughter—Moabites, Ammonites, Edomites, Sidonians and Hittites. They were from nations about which the Lord had told the Israelites, "You must not intermarry with them, because they will surely turn your hearts after their gods." Nevertheless, Solomon held fast to them in love.

~ 1 Kings 11:1–2 NIV

The Lord became angry with Solomon because his heart had turned away from the Lord, the God of Israel, who had appeared to him twice. Although he had forbidden Solomon to follow other gods, Solomon did not keep the Lord's command. So the Lord said to Solomon, "Since this is your attitude and you have not kept my covenant and my decrees, which I commanded you, I will most certainly tear the kingdom away from you and give it to one of your subordinates. Nevertheless, for the sake of David your father, I will not do it during your lifetime. I will tear it out of the hand of your son.

~ 1 Kings 11:9–12 NIV

Two things I ask of you, Lord;
do not refuse me before I die:
Keep falsehood and lies far from me;
give me neither poverty nor riches,
but give me only my daily bread.

> *Otherwise, I may have too much and disown you*
> *and say, "Who is the Lord?"*
> *Or I may become poor and steal,*
> *and so dishonor the name of my God.*
> ~ Proverbs 30: 7–9 NIV

One of my primary motives in writing this book is to provide Christian leaders in a work-setting with devotionals that will inspire, uplift, motivate, encourage, engage, and enrich their work-lives. Additionally, in so doing, my hope is that readers will gain greater congruence in their spiritual life at home, at church, or at work. In order to illustrate how Christ and His call on a Christian runs even through work activities, I have chosen to center the devotionals on common tasks that generally fall to the leader in a business setting. Except for the first task—defining the mission of the enterprise—most of the tasks occur throughout all levels of an organization, affecting every leader in it. Practicing good stewardship is one such task that is a responsibility of every leader in an organization.

The Merriam-Webster dictionary defines *stewardship* as "the conducting, supervising, or managing of something, **especially**: the careful and responsible management of something entrusted to one's care." Stewardship is a concept and obligation applicable to everyone at work, not just the leader. This can be demonstrated by two examples. First, every employee is responsible for using their time and effort productively in exchange for wages. Employees are paid to be productive, not to be slackers. Second, many employees are entrusted with assets (tangible or intangible) of considerable value to the enterprise and are expected to use and maintain them with care.

The Bible is clear that God takes the idea of stewardship seriously. The story of Solomon summarized in the Scripture passage above provides a clear example of God's judgment on Solomon's poor stewardship of the wealth granted to him and his poor stewardship of the spiritual lives of his people. The book of Ecclesiastes discusses in great detail the excesses experienced by its author in his pursuit of understanding the meaning and purpose of life.

Solomon is attributed by many to be the author of Ecclesiastes. Ecclesiastes makes clear God is not pleased by wanton living.

Jesus also spoke on certain occasions about stewardship. In one instance, Jesus said, "Watch out! Be on your guard against all kinds of greed; life does not consist in an abundance of possessions" (Luke 12:15 NIV). Jesus then told the following parable:

> The ground of a certain rich man yielded an abundant harvest. He thought to himself, "What shall I do? I have no place to store my crops."
>
> Then he said, "This is what I'll do. I will tear down my barns and build bigger ones, and there I will store my surplus grain. And I'll say to myself, 'You have plenty of grain laid up for many years. Take life easy; eat, drink and be merry.'"
>
> But God said to him, "You fool! This very night your life will be demanded from you. Then who will get what you have prepared for yourself?"
>
> This is how it will be with whoever stores up things for themselves but is not rich toward God.
>
> ~ Luke 12:16-21 NIV

On the one hand, the man in the parable was a good steward of the land because it produced a very good crop for him. On the other hand, the man hoarded his providence and was unconcerned about the needs of others whom he clearly was in a position to help with his bounty. He was a miserable steward of his relationships with others and was irresponsible with the wealth entrusted to him. Luke implies that the man's greediness was due in part to a lack of trust in anything other than his riches because Jesus immediately tells His disciples "do not worry about your life, what you will eat; or about your body, what you will wear. For life is more than food, and the body more than clothes" (Luke 12:22-23 NIV). In this way, Jesus reminds His disciples that they have a greater responsibility than the accumulation of wealth. God is fully aware of our physical needs and is both capable and willing to provide for them if our hope and faith and trust are placed in Him.

Again in Luke, Jesus says, "Who then is the faithful and wise manager, whom the master puts in charge of his servants to give them their food allowance at the proper time? It will be good for that servant whom the master finds doing so when he returns. Truly I tell you, he will put him in charge of all his possessions. But suppose the servant says to himself, 'My master is taking a long time in coming,' and he then begins to beat the other servants, both men and women, and to eat and drink and get drunk. The master of that servant will come on a day when he does not expect him and at an hour he is not aware of. He will cut him to pieces and assign him a place with the unbelievers" (Luke 12:42–46 NIV).

Clearly, Jesus was calling His disciples to work toward good stewardship.

Another time Jesus said, "Whoever can be trusted with very little can also be trusted with much, and whoever is dishonest with very little will also be dishonest with much. So if you have not been trustworthy in handling worldly wealth, who will trust you with true riches? And if you have not been trustworthy with someone else's property, who will give you property of your own?" (Luke 16:10–12 NIV).

The importance of good stewardship is also evident in the story of Zacchaeus the tax collector. Here is what Luke records:

> Jesus entered Jericho and was passing through. A man was there by the name of Zacchaeus; he was a chief tax collector and was wealthy. He wanted to see who Jesus was, but because he was short he could not see over the crowd. So he ran ahead and climbed a sycamore-fig tree to see him, since Jesus was coming that way.
>
> When Jesus reached the spot, he looked up and said to him, "Zacchaeus, come down immediately. I must stay at your house today." So he came down at once and welcomed him gladly.
>
> All the people saw this and began to mutter, "He has gone to be the guest of a sinner."
>
> But Zacchaeus stood up and said to the Lord, "Look, Lord! Here and now I give half of my possessions to the poor, and if I have cheated anybody out of anything, I will pay back four times the amount."

Jesus said to him, "Today salvation has come to this house, because this man, too, is a son of Abraham. For the Son of Man came to seek and to save the lost."

~ Luke 19:1–10 NIV

The story of Zacchaeus does not imply that Zacchaeus was honest and merely misunderstood by the people. He was rich and a tax collector—and in Palestine under Roman occupation, that meant he had obtained his fortune by taxing the people more than he was required to collect for Rome. In that fashion, he made his living. Tax collecting in that time was notoriously corrupt. But in the story, somehow Zacchaeus comes to his senses and repents of his greed and poor stewardship of the job entrusted to him. Zacchaeus seeks forgiveness, and Jesus graciously grants his request. Joyfully and in response to his newfound salvation, Zacchaeus gives up his former ways. In this story Jesus again judges the stewardship of man as being either good or evil.

In contrast to stories of poor stewardship, there are also stories demonstrating good stewardship. Sometimes stewardship that is pleasing and acceptable to God can be found in **extravagance** when directed toward the worship of God as opposed to restraint or conservation, concepts more typically associated with stewardship. Two stories demonstrate extravagant stewardship.

The first takes place as Jesus is nearing the time of His arrest and crucifixion. During a meal at the home of Lazarus, the man that Jesus had raised from the dead, John records:

> Then Mary took about a pint of pure nard, an expensive perfume; she poured it on Jesus' feet and wiped his feet with her hair. And the house was filled with the fragrance of the perfume.
>
> But one of his disciples, Judas Iscariot, who was later to betray him, objected, "Why wasn't this perfume sold and the money given to the poor? It was worth a year's wages." He did not say this because he cared about the poor but because he was a thief; as keeper of the money bag, he used to help himself to what was put into it.

> "Leave her alone," Jesus replied. "It was intended that she should save this perfume for the day of my burial. You will always have the poor among you, but you will not always have me."
>
> ~ John 12:3–8 NIV

The second story occurs as Jesus observes people making offerings at the Temple in Jerusalem. "As Jesus looked up, he saw the rich putting their gifts into the temple treasury. He also saw a poor widow put in two very small copper coins. 'Truly I tell you,' he said, 'this poor widow has put in more than all the others. All these people gave their gifts out of their wealth; but she out of her poverty put in all she had to live on'" (Luke 21:1–4 NIV).

These stories provide examples of people using their gifts and blessings, however meager or profound, to bring honor and glory to God. The intentions of the givers were recognized by Jesus as honorable and directed in worship toward God, and they were not rebuked for poor use of their assets even though the extravagance was extreme.

God is aware of our actions and expects us to behave as good stewards of all that has been entrusted to us. God will judge motives in the stewardship of money and other blessings entrusted to us. We are personally accountable for our own actions in matters of stewardship. However, our accountability does not end with ourselves. As a leader, you influence the actions of those you lead by your words and your actions. If those you lead see you demonstrate good stewardship practices at work, they will be more likely to imitate your behavior. On the other hand, if your actions demonstrate poor stewardship, they will likely imitate that behavior in spite of any words you speak about behaving differently.

We know that actions speak louder than words. Remember, you cast a long shadow over those who follow you. Consequently, you bear some responsibility in leading or enticing others to behavior inconsistent with the will of God. Accordingly, it is important to remember what Jesus had to say about this too.

> Woe to the world because of the things that cause people to stumble! Such things must come, but woe to the person through whom they come! If your hand or your foot causes you to stumble, cut it off and throw it away. It is better for you to enter life maimed or crippled than to have two hands or two feet and be thrown into eternal fire. And if your eye causes you to stumble, gouge it out and throw it away. It is better for you to enter life with one eye than to have two eyes and be thrown into the fire of hell.
>
> ~ Matthew 18:7–9 NIV

REFLECTIONS FOR THE WEEK

1. This week, thoughtfully consider how you came to be in your present position as a leader. It is likely some of the events that occurred as you became a leader can be attributed to your own unique abilities—for example talent, training, experience, effort, willpower, desire, the ability to obtain targeted results, or patience when dealing with uncertain times. Accept this at face value as true. However, consider how some of the "circumstances" that presented themselves to you (from which you acted or behaved in certain ways and that ultimately led to your position) happened to come your way in the first place. The world will say luck or random chance brought such circumstances to you. But what do you say? As a Christian, can you acknowledge that God played a significant (leading) part in each and every event associated with bringing the circumstances to you, and your role was to "act" upon those circumstances? If you acknowledge that God was involved, does God deserve to have a say in your stewardship?

2. Stewardship is often thought of in terms of money. Are there other areas of your life and work, besides money, in which you are demonstrating Christian stewardship principles? Are there areas in which you feel you need to devote more time and energy?

PRAYER

Lord, it is just too easy to think of personal possessions, money, and wealth as being my own. I confess I do not always consider the stewardship of resources as something that interests You. Nor do I always consider that my actions can influence the behaviors of others. Forgive me when I am ignorant of my behaviors that are displeasing to You and harmful to others. By the convicting and uplifting power of the Holy Spirit, guide my thinking so that I become more and more aware of godly stewardship of the blessings You have so graciously and wonderfully granted to me.

Amen

JUNE—WEEK FOUR

PRACTICING GOOD STEWARDSHIP THROUGH THE DILIGENT MANAGEMENT AND ALLOCATION OF RESOURCES

The blessing of the Lord makes rich,
and he adds no sorrow with it.
~ Proverbs 10:22 ESV

A rich man's wealth is his strong city;
the poverty of the poor is their ruin.
~ Proverbs 10:15 ESV

Riches do not profit in the day of wrath,
but righteousness delivers from death.
~ Proverbs 11:4 ESV

Honor the Lord with your wealth
and with the firstfruits of all your produce;
then your barns will be filled with plenty,
and your vats will be bursting with wine.
~ Proverbs 3:9–10 ESV

Your word is a lamp to my feet
and a light to my path.
~ Psalm 119:105

Practicing good stewardship of the monetary and other resources entrusted to you, both at home and at work, pleases God. In an earlier chapter, we considered some aspects of godly stewardship at work. But what about stewardship as it pertains to a Christian outside of the workplace? How should a Christian approach stewardship at home?

Conversations about stewardship can be very touchy. Before you erect walls of defense on this subject, let me assure you my purpose is not to lecture you about stewardship of the money and other blessings God has given you. Neither is it my purpose to criticize you on your current behaviors, no matter what they are. You may tithe to your church, or maybe you do not. OK. You may live in a big house and drive a very nice car, or maybe you do not have a big house or nice car. OK. You may be able to afford nice things (the world speaking) and choose to buy them, or you may willingly choose a more frugal lifestyle. OK. For me, offering advice on good stewardship brings us perilously close to the teaching of Jesus to first remove the plank from your own eye before you assist a brother in removing a splinter from his eye. We all live in glass houses with respect to stewardship, I think.

So, I will not preach to you about stewardship at home. Rather, let's consider what the Bible teaches about wealth, resources, and the type of stewardship God approves of. This approach—considering what Scripture reveals about a topic—is a godly and wise way to discern and appropriate what God's will is for His children. It works for all aspects of daily living, and it works just as well for gaining wisdom with respect to stewardship. After all, how are we to know what Jesus wants and God finds pleasing if we do not study the Scriptures, reflect and pray about what we have read, mentally wrestle with the implications the Scriptures have on our lives, and will ourselves, with God's help, to become more and more like Jesus?

At the outset, and as a starting point for our discussion of Christian stewardship, let's be clear the Bible does not say money is evil. In fact, consider the following list of notable biblical figures, all of whom possessed great wealth:

Job—"There was a man in the land of Uz whose name was Job, and that man was blameless and upright, one who feared God and turned away from evil. There were born to him seven sons and three daughters. He possessed 7,000 sheep, 3,000 camels, 500 yoke of oxen, and 500 female donkeys, and very many servants, so that this man was the greatest of all the people of the east" (Job 1:1–3 ESV).

Abraham—"Now Abram was very rich in livestock, in silver, and in gold" (Genesis 13:2 ESV).

Jacob (Israel)— "Thus the man (Jacob) increased greatly and had large flocks, female servants and male servants, and camels and donkeys" (Genesis 30:43 ESV).

Joseph—"And Pharaoh said to Joseph, 'See, I have set you over all the land of Egypt.' Then Pharaoh took his signet ring from his hand and put it on Joseph's hand, and clothed him in garments of fine linen and put a gold chain about his neck. And he made him ride in his second chariot. And they called out before him, 'Bow the knee!' Thus he set him over all the land of Egypt" (Genesis 41:41–43 ESV).

David—"And David the king said to all the assembly, 'Solomon my son, whom alone God has chosen, is young and inexperienced, and the work is great, for the palace will not be for man but for the Lord God. So I have provided for the house of my God, so far as I was able, the gold for the things of gold, the silver for the things of silver, and the bronze for the things of bronze, the iron for the things of iron, and wood for the things of wood, besides great quantities of onyx and stones for setting, antimony, colored stones, all sorts of precious stones and marble. Moreover, in addition to all that I have provided for the holy house, I have a treasure of my own of gold and silver, and because of my devotion to the house of my God I give it to the house of my God: 3,000 talents of gold, of the gold of Ophir, and 7,000 talents of refined silver, for overlaying the walls of the house, and for all the work to be done by craftsmen, gold for the things of gold and silver for the things of silver'" (1 Chronicles 29:1–5a ESV).

Solomon—"Thus King Solomon excelled all the kings of the earth in riches and in wisdom" (1 Kings 10:23 ESV).

Daniel—"Then Belshazzar gave the command, and Daniel was clothed with purple, a chain of gold was put around his neck, and a proclamation was made about him, that he should be the third ruler in the kingdom" (Daniel 5:29 ESV).

Mordecai—"For Mordecai the Jew was second in rank to King Ahasuerus, and he was great among the Jews and popular with the multitude of his brothers, for he sought the welfare of his people and spoke peace to all his people" (Esther 10:3 ESV).

Boaz (grandfather of David)—"Now Naomi had a kinsman of her husband, a man of great wealth, of the family of Elimelech, whose name was Boaz" (Ruth 2:1 NASB).

All these men were wealthy—fabulously wealthy. Yet their positive or negative character attributes and their standing before God had nothing to do with their wealth. Let's be clear about this: wealth did not curry the favor of God, did not insure the favor of God, and was not a reward from God for their "behavior."

God does not consider "possessions" as demonstrating preference or superiority among men or with him. God examines the heart and the motives of people. He lays bare the trappings of the world to see us as we truly are. Even though money possesses no intrinsic goodness or evil, the Bible reveals it can be a stumbling block to a person's relationship with God. Money can be the "thing" that people rely upon instead of relying on God and His sovereign role as Lord. If that occurs, then wealth is a curse and not a blessing.

Consider the effect of wealth and power on Solomon, one of the men listed in the examples above. Solomon was successor to King David, and after he became king, God appeared to him. The Bible records the following:

> In Gibeon the Lord appeared to Solomon in a dream at night; and God said, "Ask what you wish Me to give you."
> Then Solomon said, "You have shown great lovingkindness to Your servant David my father, according as he walked before You in truth and righteousness and uprightness of heart toward You; and You have reserved for him this great lovingkindness, that You have given him a son to sit on his throne, as it is this day. Now, O Lord my God, You have made Your servant king in place of my father David, yet I am but a little child; I do not know how to go out or come in. Your servant is in the midst of Your people which You have chosen, a great people who are too many to be numbered or counted. So give Your servant an understanding

heart to judge Your people to discern between good and evil. For who is able to judge this great people of Yours?"

~ 1 Kings 3:5–9 NASB

God was pleased with Solomon's request for wisdom. God then said, "I have also given you what you have not asked, both riches and honor, so that there will not be any among the kings like you all your days. If you walk in My ways, keeping My statutes and commandments, as your father David walked, then I will prolong your days."

~ 1 Kings 3:13–14 NASB

It is possible to view God's added gifts as rewards for Solomon's behavior. But it is more likely that God was blessing Solomon for other reasons. For example, Solomon was David's son, and God had loved David and promised him that his offspring would rule the kingdom and God Himself would establish that kingdom (2 Samuel 7:12–16). Wealth and power would thus be visible displays of God's favor. And do not overlook how God was going to hold Solomon to a higher standard, as the closing admonition above indicates. What better example for the people and for us than to see that wealth and power do not make one's life perfect or pleasing to God? In Solomon's case, unfortunately, wealth and power became his snare. In the end, he led his people into the worship of many foreign gods. At the end of his reign, God tore the kingdom from the hands of his son Rehoboam and Israel was divided into two countries.

Solomon's first request was pure and pleasing to God and initially, Solomon used his wisdom to govern wisely. He wrote many of the wisdom proverbs and is attributed to be the author of the book of Ecclesiastes. Ecclesiastes probes many important questions of life, such as what is the purpose of life, of what value is wealth or of what penalty is poverty, of what value is wisdom or of what penalty is foolishness, is it better to exhibit godly behavior or ungodliness, and is justice better than injustice.

In spite of his wisdom, at some point Solomon stopped following God. His wealth and power corrupted him, and he abandoned his early faith and reliance upon God. As a result, Solomon provides an example of what wealth and power can do to corrupt us. If someone like Solomon, who was extremely wise, who had direct communication with God, who was witness to God's miracles in the life of his family, who heard the praises of worship and the love of God that came from the lips of his father, who wanted for nothing money could buy, and who knew firsthand that wealth does not bring happiness, if he can succumb to living an ungodly life, can we expect to fare any better?

One of the snares that trapped Solomon and continues to trap people today is the belief this world is all that there is. Solomon probed deeply the meaning of life. At the time of Solomon's reign, there was no accepted belief system about what happens when we die. There was no common belief about an afterlife or heaven. Absent a "heaven" to look forward to, the finality and universality of death made Solomon feel bitter and angry. Solomon observed the good die, the frugal die, the profligate die, the godly die, the sinners die, the wise die, and the foolish die. Following this view, since all men suffer the same fate, an obvious conclusion is the best one can do is to "eat, drink and be merry" while living. This belief obviates a need for stewardship of any kind.

Nonetheless, Solomon believed God cared how a person behaved in life and God would judge actions. According to Solomon, a person's best hope in life was to do what God called him or her to do.

The revelation of Jesus Christ enables us to look past this world and into eternity. With the revelation of Jesus Christ, we see the depth of the love of God for us, that He has reached down into our fallen world to save us while we were still sinners and incapable of doing anything in our own behalf.

And with the revelation of Jesus Christ, we have a number of reasons to want to please God.

We are already blessed by God with everything.
> Blessed be the God and Father of our Lord Jesus Christ, who has blessed us with every spiritual blessing in the heavenly places in Christ.
>
> ~ Ephesians 1:3 NASB

JUNE—WEEK FOUR

We did not deserve to be blessed. We were sinners.
> And you were dead in your trespasses and sins, in which you formerly walked according to the course of this world, according to the prince of the power of the air, of the spirit that is now working in the sons of disobedience. Among them we too all formerly lived in the lusts of our flesh, indulging the desires of the flesh and of the mind, and were by nature children of wrath, even as the rest."
>
> ~ Ephesians 2:1–3 NASB

God continues to reveal His love for us.
> For this reason I bow my knees before the Father, from whom every family in heaven and on earth derives its name, that He would grant you, according to the riches of His glory, to be strengthened with power through His Spirit in the inner man, so that Christ may dwell in your hearts through faith; and that you, being rooted and grounded in love, may be able to comprehend with all the saints what is the breadth and length and height and depth, and to know the love of Christ which surpasses knowledge, that you may be filled up to all the fullness of God."
>
> ~ Ephesians 3:14–19 NASB

Our grateful response to all we have received is to live lives acceptable to God.
> Therefore I, the prisoner of the Lord, implore you to walk in a manner worthy of the calling with which you have been called, with all humility and gentleness, with patience, showing tolerance for one another in love, being diligent to preserve the unity of the Spirit in the bond of peace.
>
> ~ Ephesians 4:1–3 NASB

We are different from others who do not know Christ. Our behavior will be noticed by them.
> For you were formerly darkness, but now you are Light in the Lord; walk as children of Light (for the fruit of the Light

consists in all goodness and righteousness and truth), trying to learn what is pleasing to the Lord."

~ Ephesians 5:8–10 NASB

We are different from non-Christians; at least we are supposed to be. We know there is more to life than to eat, drink, and be merry.

Working out the practical application of God's teaching and His will for our lives about stewardship of the monetary and other blessings He has provided is . . . well, work. It requires deep thought, spiritual wisdom, and spiritual maturity. We help ourselves gain wisdom when we worship God in fellowship with other Christians and when we study His Word in a contemplative and respectful way. We help ourselves gain wisdom when we believe His promises to us and when we make a habit of prayer, tuning our minds to listen for His wisdom in our lives. We help ourselves gain wisdom when we exercise our faith through our works (what we do), and when we use times of error to learn, turning away from practices that are not pleasing to Him.

John Wesley (the founder of the Methodist church) had a lot to say about stewardship. In an article entitled "What Wesley Practiced and Preached about Money," (http://www.christianitytoday.com/le/1987/winter/87l1027.html?start=1) Charles Edward White recounted Wesley's advice to Christians: "gain all you can, save all you can, and share all you can." White noted that Wesley lived a life consistent with his message. According to White, Wesley believed an increasing level of income should not correspond to an increasing standard of living. Rather, increasing income should correspond to an increasing standard of **_giving._** Consistent with the message of Ecclesiastes, Wesley believed that spending more does not satisfy desires but only increases them.

Wesley looked at stewardship of money in regards to three distinct areas of our lives: home (family), business (work), and community (neighbors). Wesley believed Christians were to first take care of their families with their earnings from their work. Next, they were to take care of their businesses so that their businesses could in turn take care of creditors and employees. Finally, through savings, the Christian would be able to take care of their neighbor's needs.

Wesley's views seem reasonable to me, but a few years ago I read a book a friend gave to me entitled *Riches: A Biblical Perspective (Ministry in the Marketplace)* (published by Vision Foundation, Inc., 1994) that pointed out God also gives us material blessings for our enjoyment of life. I agree with that viewpoint as well. From what I know of Wesley, he never increased his standard of living, even though he made a large amount of money. Fine; that worked for him. I happen to enjoy football games and nice cars.

And here is one of the primary rubs in discerning stewardship from a godly perspective: The difficulty in applying principles of stewardship is in discerning "what is enough" for us, our families, our businesses, and our neighbor's needs and our own enjoyment of life.

Assessing what are our true needs is difficult because needs change over time. Stewardship should therefore be evaluated periodically in the life of a Christian. I know God loves a cheerful giver and does not want His children to give out of guilt or compulsion. Neither does God want us to give to receive the award of man's approval. As a result, I want to check my "giving" from time to time to see if I am giving out of pure motives. Similarly, I want to inspect my spending and my saving habits from time to time, because they change over time and I am prone to being susceptible to excess in one or the other.

Nonetheless, because we are each of us in different circumstances economically, and in our degrees of faith and Christian maturity, I do not think there is a formulaic method or series of boxes to check off that proves our stewardship is right with God. As a result, I do not think we should sell our homes (regardless of their size) and give to the poor and take up a life of meager living **UNLESS** God has placed that urging on our hearts. God placed such an urging on the heart of John Wesley, but he does not place it on us all.

What then? In my view, here are some truths: We are called to lead quiet lives; to live lives that bring glory to God; to care about the needs of others; and to be examples to the unbelieving world that God exists and has a plan of salvation for them. In doing this the true meaning of life is revealed to them and lived out in us. Never forget that God has the right to call you into stewardship different from what you are currently practicing or experiencing. When God leads you, follow Him and go where He points you to go.

REFLECTIONS FOR WEEK

1. Set aside some time this week to prayerfully consider what God has to say to you about your current practices of stewardship. If in your meditations you reach areas of difficulty or uneasiness, probe even harder to ask God to reveal to you why the area is one in which you struggle.

2. Although wealth can lead to idolatry, arrogance, self-sufficiency, and other ungodly traits, it is not in and of itself a determinative feature of a person's standing before God. We looked at some passages in the previous week's devotional that demonstrate this conclusion. For further guidance, consider Luke 9:46–48, Luke 16:14–15, the story of the rich ruler found in Luke 18:18–29, 1 Timothy 6:17–19, and James 2:5–13.

PRAYER

Lord, You are the Sovereign Lord of my life, and all things in the world are Yours. While I acknowledge this is true, I still struggle with the day-to-day business of living in the world. I have desires. I have needs. I have to pay my bills, provide food and shelter for myself and my family, set aside money for times of difficulty and retirement, and return some of the blessings You have provided to me to You for use in Your kingdom. Let me not be an unwise steward, but teach me to please You in this area of my life. Gently inform me of what is pleasing to You through the convicting, uplifting, encouraging, and strengthening work of the Holy Spirit.

Amen

JUNE—WEEK FIVE

THE END OF THE SECOND QUARTER

HARVESTING AND PRUNING THE ORGANIZATION

I am the true vine, and my Father is the vinedresser. Every branch in me that does not bear fruit he takes away, and every branch that does bear fruit he prunes, that it may bear more fruit.

~ John 15:1–2 ESV

For everything there is a season, and a time for every matter under heaven:
a time to be born, and a time to die;
a time to plant, and a time to pluck up what is planted;
a time to kill, and a time to heal;
a time to break down, and a time to build up;
a time to weep, and a time to laugh;
a time to mourn, and a time to dance;
a time to cast away stones, and a time to gather stones together;
a time to embrace, and a time to refrain from embracing;
a time to seek, and a time to lose;
a time to keep, and a time to cast away;
a time to tear, and a time to sew;
a time to keep silence, and a time to speak;
a time to love, and a time to hate;
a time for war, and a time for peace.

~ Ecclesiastes 3:1–8 ESV

He who gathers in summer is a prudent son,
 but he who sleeps in harvest is a son who brings shame.

~ Proverbs 10:5 ESV

We get very caught up in the present, yet our lives are always changing. Sometimes the movement is very hard to detect, but as I write this I remember my grown son as he was thirty years ago—a newborn baby boy in my arms. What a day! I remember feeling a variety of emotions, one upon another—wonder, fear, joy, befuddlement, amazement, helplessness, newness, purpose, and love. Clearly love stood out in a new and exciting way. And there was ample anxiety as I stared at the little boy that I would soon take home without an owner's manual. Praying that I would be a good father, I looked forward to watching him grow and learn and to become his own person.

Looking back, I do not remember sensing that the years were building and flowing past quickly, but it is now thirty years later, and the passage of the time can only be described as breathtaking. We lived daily in the present, but there was a pace, an altogether too rapid pace, to the movement of years. Children provide an inescapable but gentle reminder that our lives change, and that is part of God's plan.

Things change in our lives at work too. There is seasonality to our work years, just as there is a natural maturing of our human lives. Even if you work for an enterprise that is old, and even if you work for an enterprise that legally goes on forever because of the manner in which it was formed, you will not. Your productive years will slowly move behind you, and another will be groomed or located to take your place. I hope this does not disturb you, because it is a natural part of our lives. In my view, knowing our time with a child, a business, an organization, a family, or a calling is brief just helps us celebrate the times we have with those things and people while we (and they) are with us. And, the inexorable passage of time calls us to pay attention to the details.

Here at the end of the second quarter, you may find it beneficial to take stock of the enterprise that has been entrusted to your care. Is it being fruitful? Is it making good progress toward achieving its mission, living up to its values, and serving the purpose for which it was intended? Or do some aspects of your work need attending to? Our work should serve a purpose beyond merely being "what we do." From a Christian viewpoint, our work should bring glory to God and should include elements of joy, service, and fulfillment.

Anticipating the time and ways of harvesting and pruning the business are important responsibilities of the leaders in an organization. This aspect of leadership directly impacts the activities of defining the mission; determining priorities and setting goals and objectives; accumulating and allocating scarce resources; managing the balance sheet and anticipating trouble; recognizing when change is necessary; and practicing good stewardship. Harvesting and pruning the business is an integral part of leadership. Jesus said that God acts to prune our lives in order to make them more fruitful. We are wise to be aware of the need to do the same with our businesses.

Biblically, there are some important things to consider as you approach the idea of pruning and/or harvesting the business.

First, as Christians we serve the Lord in everything we do. Because we serve Jesus, we are open and willing to hear His call for change in our lives. We do not cling to things. We cling to Jesus. We do not chase after fantasies of our own imagination, but we are willing to listen to the guidance of our hearts, our minds, and godly counselors so that we respond to the prompting of the Lord to make changes in our lives at work and at home.

> Whoever works his land will have plenty of bread,
> but he who follows worthless pursuits lacks sense.
> ~ Proverbs 12:11 ESV

> The people curse him who holds back grain,
> but a blessing is on the head of him who sells it.
> ~ Proverbs 11:26 ESV

> Come now, you who say, "Today or tomorrow we will go into such and such a town and spend a year there and trade and make a profit"— yet you do not know what tomorrow will bring. What is your life? For you are a mist that appears for a little time and then vanishes. Instead you ought to say, "If the Lord wills, we will live and do this or that." As it is, you boast in your arrogance. All such boasting is evil. So whoever knows the right thing to do and fails to do it, for him it is sin.
> ~ James 4:13–17 ESV

Second, we are aware that success can become an idol, alienating us from God's will for our lives. Sometimes we will cling to what we have and ignore God prompting us to change in some way. But when we accepted Christ as Lord, we agreed that we would follow the Lord as obedient children. We also agreed that God has the right to discipline us as His children when we disobey. Sometimes that discipline comes in the form of hardship.

> Endure trials for the sake of discipline. God is treating you as children; for what child is there whom a parent does not discipline? If you do not have that discipline in which all children share, then you are illegitimate and not his children. Moreover, we had human parents to discipline us, and we respected them. Should we not be even more willing to be subject to the Father of spirits and live? For they disciplined us for a short time as seemed best to them, but he disciplines us for our good, in order that we may share his holiness.
> ~ Hebrews 12:7-10 NRSV

Whether your choice or not, it is possible that God will prune your business as a means of discipline—not to punish you but to call you to closer fellowship with Him.

Third, when we are blessed, we are expected to share our blessings with others. Importantly, our first fruits are to be shared with the Lord.

> *Honor the Lord with your wealth,*
> *with first fruits of all your produce;*
> *Then will your barns be filled with plenty,*
> *with new wine your vats will overflow.*
> ~ Proverbs 3:9-10 NASB

To do otherwise is a sign of greediness. Jesus condemned the person in the parable of the farmer who had a bumper crop and chose to build more barns to house his produce rather than share it with others (Luke 12:13-21). However, Jesus said that God is pleased when we are fruitful, and God will work in our lives to makes us even more fruitful (John 15:8). Harvesting and pruning the business may provide the means to share the blessings that God has provided.

Fourth, contemplating pruning or harvesting different aspects of our work helps us to avoid falling into complacency and stagnating. Sometimes, when things are going well, we tend to want them to stay that way for a long while. When we become lazy, however, we open ourselves to danger. Consider the genesis of the story of David and Bathsheba:

> At the turn of the year, the time when kings go to war, David sent out Joab along with his officers and all Israel, and they laid waste the Ammonites and besieged Rabbah. David himself remained in Jerusalem.
>
> ~ 2 Samuel 11:1 NASB

Something made David decide to stay behind and not accompany his troops as was his habit. Perhaps he had grown complacent, or he was just tired of joining his troops in battle. Whatever the reason, by remaining behind and being bored, David spied Bathsheba bathing on a neighboring rooftop, desired her, seduced her, and when he found out she was pregnant, made plans to murder her husband (who had gone out to war with the rest of the Israelite army). We must remain vigilant that our work effort remains strong and consistent with the call that God has made on our lives. Consideration of pruning certain aspects of our business, or harvesting others, opens us to the possibility of other work and defends against complacency.

Fifth, awareness of our mortality will help us identify and groom successors. This may include selling a business to another who can provide the resources and leadership that are necessary but that we no longer have available to provide. Or it can mean identifying and mentoring a next generation of leaders to succeed us. Moses groomed Joshua. Paul groomed Timothy and Titus. Jesus groomed the disciples. Since we will all die, the only time to really influence what will be done with accumulated wealth and knowledge is to do it now. Awareness of our own mortality may prompt us to harvest and prune our businesses in order to pass along our legacy in a manner consistent with our belief system and provide a legacy to others that is greater than our wealth.

Sixth, there is a risk in humans to associate too much of ourselves in what we do at work. When this happens, the thought of harvesting or pruning the business may be frightening to consider. God does not want you to become what you do; He wants you to become like Jesus. God wants you to do something that allows you to learn more about Jesus and to live a life that is pleasing to Him.

> As they continued their journey he entered a village where a woman whose name was Martha welcomed him. She had a sister named Mary [who] sat beside the Lord at his feet listening to him speak. Martha, burdened with much serving, came to him and said, "Lord, do you not care that my sister has left me by myself to do the serving? Tell her to help me." The Lord said to her in reply, "Martha, Martha, you are anxious and worried about many things. There is need of only one thing. Mary has chosen the better part and it will not be taken from her."
> ~ Luke 10:38–42 NASB

Here at the end of the second quarter, spend time reflecting on how your business is bearing fruit for the kingdom of God. If your business is not bearing fruit, perhaps some pruning is in order. Consider the following parable:

> And he told them this parable: "There once was a person who had a fig tree planted in his orchard, and when he came in search of fruit on it but found none, he said to the gardener, 'For three years now I have come in search of fruit on this fig tree but have found none. [So] cut it down. Why should it exhaust the soil?' He said to him in reply, 'Sir, leave it for this year also, and I shall cultivate the ground around it and fertilize it; it may bear fruit in the future. If not you can cut it down.'"
> ~ Luke 13:6–9 NASB

Christians are expected to bear fruit. As Christian leaders, our work is expected to bear fruit too. If what we do is not bearing fruit, it is using up soil that could be used by other plants that will bear fruit. Even though we are given the time and the opportunity to grow and thrive, often at the hand of a loving and patient gardener, we do not have unlimited time to respond to the urging to be fruitful. Time is moving forward as it always does. What we do with our lives and our time matters to God. Be alert and attentive to His guidance in managing your garden.

REFLECTIONS FOR THE WEEK

1. This week, reflect upon your career—how you came to do what you do now and all of the milestones along the way. Make a list of the times in which what you do (your work) took a different direction than you had expected. Can you see in those times of change a movement more toward bearing spiritual fruit, or away?

2. If God were prompting you to move in a different direction, how do you think He might accomplish that? What methods do you employ to insure you hear clearly God's call on your life?

3. Consider your workplace as a garden and you, as leader, are the gardener. Where is the soil rich and yielding good fruit? Where is the soil in need of fertilizing? Is it planting season or harvest?

PRAYER

Lord, what I do matters because it matters to You. You promised to be with us always and to work with us so that our lives become rich in the knowledge of Christ. You promised that Your work in our lives would bring us to an abundant life filled with the fruit of the Holy Spirit. Accomplish that work in my life, O God! Do not abandon me to the pursuit of things that do not last. Call me, as the psalmist does, to count my days correctly so that what I do is exactly what You would have me do. By Your loving, renewing, restraining, and encouraging hand, lead me to recognize the times of harvest.

Amen

JULY

THE BEGINNING OF THE THIRD QUARTER

Sing joyfully to the Lord, you righteous;
  it is fitting for the upright to praise him.
Praise the Lord with the harp;
  make music to him on the ten-stringed lyre.
Sing to him a new song;
  play skillfully, and shout for joy.
For the word of the Lord is right and true;
  he is faithful in all he does.
The Lord loves righteousness and justice;
  the earth is full of his unfailing love.
By the word of the Lord the heavens were made,
  their starry host by the breath of his mouth.
He gathers the waters of the sea into jars;
  he puts the deep into storehouses.
Let all the earth fear the Lord;
  let all the people of the world revere him.
For he spoke, and it came to be;
  he commanded, and it stood firm.
The Lord foils the plans of the nations;
  he thwarts the purposes of the peoples.
But the plans of the Lord stand firm forever,
  the purposes of his heart through all generations.
Blessed is the nation whose God is the Lord,
  the people he chose for his inheritance.
From heaven the Lord looks down
  and sees all mankind;
from his dwelling place he watches
  all who live on earth—
he who forms the hearts of all,
  who considers everything they do.
No king is saved by the size of his army;
  no warrior escapes by his great strength.
A horse is a vain hope for deliverance;

> *despite all its great strength it cannot save.*
> *But the eyes of the Lord are on those who fear him,*
> *on those whose hope is in his unfailing love,*
> *to deliver them from death*
> *and keep them alive in famine.*
> *We wait in hope for the Lord;*
> *he is our help and our shield.*
> *In him our hearts rejoice,*
> *for we trust in his holy name.*
> *May your unfailing love be with us, Lord,*
> *even as we put our hope in you.*
>
> ~ Psalm 33 NIV

Music is a very important ingredient of worship. Sometimes the people of God just can't help themselves and break out into joyful singing! David, the second king of Israel, and from whom the lineage of Israel's kings is traced all the way to Jesus, was a prolific musician, composer, and poet/songwriter. David was known as a man who pleased God, a man after God's own heart (1 Samuel 13:13).

David is first introduced to us in the Bible as a boy in charge of his father's sheep. He had done nothing that would have qualified him for a lofty appraisal by God and his destiny to assume the role of king. Even Samuel, the prophet of God tasked with anointing the future king of Israel, struggled to identify the one chosen by God. Samuel, looking on the outward appearance, thought Jesse's first son, Eliab, was the one God had sent him to find. But God said, "Do not look on his appearance or on the height of his stature, because I have rejected him. For the Lord sees not as man sees: man looks on the outward appearance, but the Lord looks on the heart" (1 Samuel 16:7 ESV).

Because Samuel knew one of Jesse's sons was to be anointed king of Israel, he asked Jesse to present each of his sons to him one at a time. But as each son came forward, the Lord remained silent. Seven sons, yet no word came from God. Samuel asked if there were no others. Jesse said there was one more, the youngest, out in the fields tending the sheep. Even Jesse could not see the future king in his youngest son, David.

At Samuel's command, David was brought in and God told Samuel David was to be king. God saw something pleasing in David. What we know about David is that he unashamedly and unabashedly worshiped God all of his life. David also made mistakes, some really big ones (murder and adultery), but he would earnestly repent (acknowledge the sin and turn away from it) rather than just suffer remorse over being caught in wrongdoing. David's contrition allowed God to forgive his sins, showing us in the process just how forgiving and loving is our God. David developed a good understanding of God and himself, and joyfully entered into fellowship and relationship with the Creator of the universe.

And God gave David the ability to write songs and poems of praise and worship that would encourage and heal broken hearts for generations to come.

The stories of David and the content of the Psalms teach us many important things about God and our relationship with God. Perhaps one of the most important is God is never far from us if we search for Him diligently with a pure heart. Reading the Psalms brings relationship with God into clear focus for us. We cry out to God when we are frightened, and we know He hears us. We sing out when we are joyful because we know God hears us. We plead with Him to make us well, to heal our sin-sick selves and to restore our fellowship with Him, and we know our pleas are heard. We come to God naked because He knows all there is to know about us, yet He does not reject the penitent heart. God welcomes us home, time and time and time again. David knew this about God, and he worshiped God with abandon.

We learn a great deal about God when we are challenged, facing struggles, or falling short of our hopes, goals, and dreams. Such times cause our minds to turn inward, and we are receptive to the quiet voice of God calling us to an undeniable self-appraisal.

As we mature as Christians, we do well to remember God also in times when things are going well. The Psalms show us who we are because they give brilliant voice to our lives—those times of fear and uncertainty and those times of joy and peace. We become one with the psalmist in times of sorrow and anxiety as well as times of joy and celebration. When we struggle to find the words to say, the psalmist gives voice to our feelings, and the words have even more power when we recite them out loud. There is just something about the spoken word that brings forth power—it helps our memory, and it engages more of our senses.

It's July in America, and somewhere a band is playing, a parade is marching, and soon fireworks will be exploding into joyful color as we celebrate the anniversary of our nation. Backyard grills are being used to cook hamburgers, steaks, chicken, and hot dogs. Ice cream is being consumed by young and old alike. Days are hot and long, but it is a time of vacation, a time of celebration, and I pray that you will be able to enjoy time off with your family and loved ones.

We all need to enjoy life—it is a gift of God. Allow yourself the opportunity to break out into joyful song over lightning bugs, the unmistakable smells of freshly mown yards or rain on hot pavements, the sounds of children playing outside, the chirping of birds in the morning, and the absolutely unfathomable but nonetheless true revelation that you too are a person "after God's own heart." Just as God saw much in David, He sees much in you. God says, "Before I formed you in the womb I knew you" (Jeremiah 1:5a ESV). Now there is a reason for breaking out into song!

REFLECTIONS FOR JULY

1. Read Psalm 8 aloud. Reflect upon its meaning for you.

2. Read Psalm 34 aloud. When have you "tasted and seen that the Lord is good"?

3. For a breathtaking image of heaven, read Revelation 4 and 5 aloud (the book of Revelation is to be read out loud). Armed now

with the Psalms and the vision of the glory of heaven, praise your God as you move joyously into July.

PRAYER

Almighty God, when I really think about it, I wonder what makes me so valuable to You. My close friends, my family, they love me, but there are parts of me that are unloving that they do not know. Yet You know, and You love me anyway. I am amazed that You care about me. I am rendered speechless when I think of Your redeeming love through Jesus. Spellbound, I remember that I am considered Your child —an inheritor of life eternal and heaven, and all of this given to me freely by grace. Grace is free, but it is not cheap. Your grace is a gift I do not deserve, but one that I am so thankful for. Help me to celebrate joyfully this summer and to keep a song of thankfulness in my heart. Stay near to me, O God.

Amen

JULY—WEEK ONE

ESTABLISHING THE VALUES AND THE CULTURE OF THE ORGANIZATION

On the third day there was a wedding in Cana of Galilee, and the mother of Jesus was there; and both Jesus and His disciples were invited to the wedding. When the wine ran out, the mother of Jesus said to Him, "They have no wine." And Jesus said to her, "Woman, what does that have to do with us? My hour has not yet come." His mother said to the servants, "Whatever He says to you, do it." Now there were six stone waterpots set there for the Jewish custom of purification, containing twenty or thirty gallons each. Jesus said to them, "Fill the waterpots with water." So they filled them up to the brim. And He said to them, "Draw some out now and take it to the headwaiter." So they took it to him. When the headwaiter tasted the water which had become wine, and did not know where it came from (but the servants who had drawn the water knew), the headwaiter called the bridegroom, and said to him, "Every man serves the good wine first, and when the people have drunk freely, then he serves the poorer wine; but you have kept the good wine until now." This beginning of His signs Jesus did in Cana of Galilee, and manifested His glory, and His disciples believed in Him.

~ John 2:1–11 NASB

Therefore many other signs Jesus also performed in the presence of the disciples, which are not written in this book; but these have been written so that you may believe that Jesus is the Christ, the Son of God; and that believing you may have life in His name.

~ John 20:30–31 NASB

Conversations about values, principles, and the "culture" of a business can be disagreeable, particularly when discussing those dealing with ethics and morality. Some behaviors and actions, like murder, adultery, and lying, are generally disdained and condemned by all people. But many other values and principles dealing with ethical and moral behavior seem to require "context" before judgment can be rendered on their appropriateness and acceptability. What behavior is ethical and moral, or unethical and immoral, seems to fall along a continuum between extremes. People draw a line somewhere on that continuum and believe another inch in either direction separates moral and immoral, ethical and unethical.

But where, exactly, to draw that line is always a matter of personal choice. For example, we value a competitive spirit in ourselves and in others, but the desire to win can cause us to cross an imaginary (but nonetheless real) line of fairness. During the Cold War, in the United States in particular, the Soviet bloc Olympic athletes were commonly believed to be professionals, not amateurs. When our amateur athletes would lose to them, we felt cheated. My guess is the Soviets did not feel the same way we did. Professional athletes in the United States are prohibited from using performance enhancing drugs to help them heal faster and get stronger, yet some athletes use them anyway. Cheating may be wrong, but agreeing on what exactly is cheating is difficult.

So, writing a devotional about a leader's responsibility to establish the values and principles of their organization could be controversial. For now, though, let's not go there. It's not that I want to avoid having a conflict about what is right or wrong behavior—after all, I am writing a Christian devotional; but my preference for now is to focus on the leader's role in establishing the values and principles they believe are appropriate, and on how their behaviors will either enforce or erode the application of those values and principles in their organizations.

Having a comprehensive set of values and principles and fostering a culture to shape and guide behaviors within an organization is important. Why? Consider two environmental extremes: order and chaos. An orderly environment stands a better chance of meeting goals and objectives and producing results efficiently and harmoniously than an environment of chaos. Values, principles, and culture are designed to promote order within the organization.

Since values, principles, and culture help an enterprise achieve its goals and objectives, two of the most important responsibilities of leadership are to (1) ensure that the core values, principles, and culture of the enterprise are communicated to employees and other interested parties and, (2) ensure employees adhere to them. When values, principles, and culture are written, they stand a greater chance of being consistently implemented. Such writings assist leaders in broadly disseminating information to multiple users while simultaneously ensuring a consistent message is received by everyone. Written core values, principles, and cultural statements reduce the risks of misunderstanding or miscommunication.

While the importance of having written core values, principles, and cultural statements cannot be ignored, a leader's actions will speak louder than words ever will about them. If a core value is fairness, the leader needs to demonstrate fairness if fairness is to be woven into the fabric of the enterprise. If a core value is honesty, the leader needs to demonstrate honesty in all dealings with employees and customers, or honesty will not become a core value of the enterprise. If a core value is hard work, the leader needs to work hard too. The leader's actions and behaviors are always under scrutiny and become a living testimony of his or her core values regardless of any written statements to the contrary. This is true over the long-term and is also true for first impressions a leader makes on anyone coming into first contact with them or their enterprise.

Organizations are not static; they behave a lot like people behave—there is an ebb and flow to their activities, and they undergo a variety of changes akin to human lifestyles. Start-ups face different challenges than established organizations and solve their problems differently. Large organizations have different resources at their disposal than small organizations. Some organizations have bright futures; others are in the process of winding down. These life cycles affect values, principles, and culture.

And organizations, like people, are constantly "meeting" strangers—some are new employees and some are new customers, vendors, or other interested parties. When strangers meet, first impressions are formed. New employees and other interested parties are suspicious and want to validate their decision to associate with an enterprise.

A new employee wants to fit in and to be accepted, so the core values, principles, and culture of the enterprise are important to understand. A new employee hopes to affirm their compatibility with the core values, principles, and culture of their new employer, and they hope the organization maintains them with integrity so they can be assured of fair treatment. The written core values, principles, and statements of culture give them a starting point to make their assessment.

Other interested parties, such as customers or vendors, want to justify their decisions to enter into a relationship with the enterprise—they want to prove the risk they took in selecting a particular enterprise over competing alternatives was worthwhile. The integrity of the core values, principles, and culture of the enterprise will directly affect how they will be treated in their dealings with the enterprise.

The first impression of the leader (and the corresponding inference of the enterprise's and the leader's core values, principles, and cultural environment) will therefore be remembered by new employees and other interested parties and will be highly influential in their ultimate acceptance or rejection of those values and principles. Over time, first impressions will either be further validated or contradicted.

So whether as a first impression or as a continuing role model, a leader bears great responsibility for modeling the core values, principles, and culture of the enterprise. If a leader's behavior is consistent, the core values, principles, and culture will be strengthened for the entire organization. On the other hand, if the leader behaves in a manner inconsistent with such values, principles, and culture, they will be weakened for the entire organization.

Now comes the disagreeable part: **As Christians, we know there is a right and wrong.**

To be certain, Christians can and do disagree about right and wrong behavior, but they should not (cannot) disagree that God alone truly determines right and wrong. He is the only holy, honest, and just judge. As Christian leaders, the source of our core values, principles, and the culture by which we want to live must come from Jesus.

Our direct guidance on what Jesus taught and believed is primarily contained within the four Gospels (Matthew, Mark, Luke, and John). Three of the books (Matthew, Mark, and Luke) are remarkably similar to each other. As a result, these three books are referred to as the "Synoptic Gospels." The book of John, on the other hand, is different in many respects from the Synoptic Gospels. Each of the Gospel writers wrote their books with a particular purpose and audience in mind. Their choice of particular events, sayings, teachings, and personal interactions of Jesus give us slightly different and distinct impressions of Jesus and the values that He lived and imparted to His followers. When all four Gospels are taken together, however, we gain a more complete understanding of Jesus and His call upon our lives.

The Gospel of John provides excellent examples for Christian leaders of the importance of "first impressions" in setting forth clearly the values, principles, and culture of the leader.

John's Gospel begins with an amazing and astounding first impression of Jesus to His readers:

> In the beginning was the Word, and the Word was with God, and the Word was God. He was in the beginning with God. All things came into being through Him, and apart from Him nothing came into being that has come into being. In Him was life, and the life was the Light of men. The Light shines in the darkness, and the darkness did not comprehend it.
>
> ~ John 1:1–5 NASB

No pun intended, but Jesus was truly the "first" first impression in the universe and in our created world. Jesus was one with the Father, has always existed, and is the co-Creator of everything that has been created with the Father. The opening lines of John give us Jesus' credentials. John also foretells that Jesus will not be recognized or well received by His creation, but in spite of opposition, He nonetheless overcomes.

Since John declares from the outset Jesus is one with God and Deity incarnate, it is easy to believe Jesus' early followers were somehow so overwhelmed by their first impressions that His true identity was evident. But not everyone was impressed with Jesus, nor did everyone believe He was

God. The next two stories in the book of John begin to paint for us a picture of Jesus and how He chose to interact with the world.

The passage of Scripture of the wedding in Cana (John 2:1-11) is chronologically the next story John presents. In it, John introduces us to Jesus in a normal earthly setting with His early followers, His mother, and with a group of people celebrating a wedding. At the request of His mother, Jesus performs a miracle that John says is His first miracle—turning water into wine. For some of those present, Jesus has provided a "first impression" that He was not just an ordinary person. What did they (and we) learn?

For one thing, Jesus was particular about displaying His power and to whom. Jesus was also approachable; He associated completely and fully with people and enjoyed their company. And we begin to see that He used His power to cause others to see and to believe that He had a unique relationship with God the Father.

To highlight these impressions, John next takes us to the Temple, the place of holy worship in Israel, where Jesus overturns tables and clears the temple of animals being bought and sold (John 2:13-22)—another unforgettable "first impression."

> The Jews then said to Him, "What sign do You show us as your authority for doing these things?"
>
> ~ John 2:18 NASB

Unlike at the wedding in Cana, Jesus refused to perform any "sign" for them. Thus John presents the inevitable conflict Jesus would face with the traditional leaders and powerful elite of Israel. Jesus would not "perform" signs for those who would not believe, but most particularly He would not perform signs for those He expected should have believed because of their religious training. Jesus instead would confront such people with reasoning, showing them their beliefs had become corrupted, but He would not use signs and wonders to convince them.

Taken together, these first impressions provide us with interesting and meaningful observations about who Jesus was and what His values and mission were going to be. John's opening verses tell us clearly "who" Jesus was. This is akin to an enterprise publishing its values, principles, and culture for all to know. The stories that followed inform us how Jesus lived His life as a testament of who He was. Jesus' actions spoke loud and clear. In every respect, Jesus' actions proved He was the Son of God, and like God, there was no shadow of change in Jesus.

A leader will inevitably cast a long shadow over the people they lead. In our cases, though, sometimes our shadow will shift. People will closely observe a leader's actions because actions speak louder than words. First impressions are important, but so is consistency. Being caught in a compromising position "off the record" or making "off the cuff" comments can imperil a leader's credibility.

While opinions vary about right and wrong, moral and immoral behavior, a Christian leader looks to Jesus as the source of their values, principles, and culture. Jesus provides the yardstick by which actions are measured. But even if a leader consistently lives out the values, principles, and culture of a Christian, not everyone will respond favorably to them. Regardless, we are called to imitate as closely as we can the values of Jesus. When we do this, we remain in God's favor. God's favor will then overflow, and we can expect our "first impressions" will benefit all we meet.

REFLECTIONS FOR THE WEEK

1. Read the first impressions of Jesus on two other people: Nicodemus, a Pharisee and leader of the Sanhedrin (John 3:1–21), and the woman of Samaria (John 4:1–42). What do these encounters tell you about Jesus?

2. Consider the type of first impression you might be making to new employees or people first coming into contact with your organization. Are there things you wish you could convey? Are there things you might want to change in the future?

3. Someday you will have a clear "first impression" of Jesus. What person will Jesus see in you?

PRAYER

Jesus, thank You for Your life on earth. You modeled for us a way of living that brings the kingdom of the Father to earth now. You modeled for us a way to live that would be a blessing to us and others if we imitate You. Help me to imitate You. We are called to follow You by the grace of the Father. Help me to follow You more closely. Help me to see You in others that I meet, and help me to be a reflection of You to everyone.

Amen

JULY—WEEK TWO

ESTABLISHING THE VALUES AND CULTURE OF THE ORGANIZATION

The eye is the lamp of the body; so then if your eye is clear, your whole body will be full of light. But if your eye is bad, your whole body will be full of darkness. If then the light that is in you is darkness, how great is the darkness!
~ Matthew 6:22–23 NASB

Therefore everyone who hears these words of Mine and acts on them, may be compared to a wise man who built his house on the rock. And the rain fell, and the floods came, and the winds blew and slammed against that house; and yet it did not fall, for it had been founded on the rock. Everyone who hears these words of Mine and does not act on them, will be like a foolish man who built his house on the sand. The rain fell, and the floods came, and the winds blew and slammed against that house; and it fell—and great was its fall.
~ Matthew 7:24–27 NASB

Then I said, "Look, I have come.
As is written about me in the Scriptures:
I take joy in doing your will, my God,
for your instructions are written on my heart."
I have told all your people about your justice.
I have not been afraid to speak out,
as you, O Lord, well know.
I have not kept the good news of your justice hidden in my heart;
I have talked about your faithfulness and saving power.
I have told everyone in the great assembly
of your unfailing love and faithfulness.
~ Psalm 40:7–10 NLT

Order is better than chaos. Order allows employees within an enterprise to work collaboratively toward achieving common goals. Order is enhanced when an organization develops policies and procedures for accomplishing tasks. But policies and procedures, like all rules, sometimes require context before they can be applied as they were intended. For example, a policy may call for two signatures before a transaction can be initiated. But what if during an extreme situation, say a hurricane evacuation, the workforce is scattered. Nonetheless, an important decision must be made and only one leader can be found. How that leader reacts and makes a decision—without the advice and counsel of a second leader—will be evaluated in hindsight by how closely the decision was aligned with the "values" and "culture" of the business.

Taking the hurricane example a little further, in New Orleans after Katrina, some individuals reached decisions without the counsel of others, and those decisions imperiled businesses because they were wrong—overcharging those in need, bribing officials to gain lucrative contracts, and committing other crimes.

We all know poor decisions happen, even without a hurricane disaster. People are people, and we are fallen, all of us. It is impossible to create an environment where no bad decisions are reached. But it is possible to enhance the probability that good decisions are the ones being made and to reduce the probability of making bad ones. Identifying and adopting principles of commonly held values will shape the culture of the business, provide important context for interpreting policies and procedures in diverse circumstances, and enhance the probability good decisions will be made.

How should a leader approach the task of establishing a set of commonly held values and cultural principles for the organization they lead and implementing them? I believe the following six steps will lead to a consistent application of core values and cultural principles by which the organization chooses to exist.

- Begin at the beginning: Identify and codify the values and cultural principles, preferably in written form.
- Spread the news: Communicate them to all employees.
- Provide training: Instruct all employees how to interpret the values and cultural principles and what they mean to eliminate confusion about semantics.

- Provide context: Demonstrate the values and cultural principles through examples and by practical application to the activities of the organization.
- Warn them: Instruct employees how they will meet challenges to the values and cultural principles in order to withstand challenges and prevail against them.
- Leave a legacy: Ensure the values and cultural principles will be passed on to others who will follow later.

I have learned it is vital for a leader to be involved in interpreting commonly held values—to spend time and energy in "setting the record straight" when it comes to the values and cultural principles applicable to their particular organization. We all came from different backgrounds and experiences. Our personal values and cultural principles were initially learned from childhood and thereafter modified by peers, mentors, teachers, friends, and heroes, and from schools, neighborhoods, churches, and jobs. People enter the workforce with all of the values and cultural differences of the general population and it is important, if an organization wants uniformity of application of the values and culture it believes in, to spend time, money, and energy in educating, training, and disciplining employees about the ones the employer holds dear. Therefore, it is imperative for a leader to identify the core values and cultural principles important to the organization, to communicate them to everyone, to interpret and clarify their meaning, to demonstrate their application at work, to uphold them when challenged, and to provide for their continued existence over time.

IDENTIFY AND CODIFY THE CORE VALUES AND CULTURAL PRINCIPLES

Jesus is our model for core values and moral principles. This idea may give you pause, even extreme pause, because we live in a secular society that defends the rights of its citizens to believe or not believe anything spiritual in nature. You may believe you have no rights to assert Christian principles on others. But you do have the right and the obligation to identify and affirm the principles and values by which your organization will behave and conduct its business. In the aftermath of many public scandals, the Federal government adopted Sarbanes-Oxley, a series of rules to standardize and discipline how public companies conduct business and ethics. Whether public or private, society expects businesses to "follow the rules."

Certainly no one should assert a principle that is against the law; you would be exposing yourself and your organization to liability if you asserted principles that discriminated against people for any reason or harmed people, physically or mentally. But that is not what we are worried about, is it? Can anyone say Christian principles of behavior are outside of the bounds of the law and commonly held principles of fairness and right and wrong in our society? It is possible and even likely that Christians will hold a more narrow view of fairness and right and wrong than non-Christians, but it is not rational to assert Christians would establish any principles outside of the law or what "normal" society would deem acceptable.

But let me clarify: I am not saying you should sit down with a blank piece of paper and a Bible and start making lists. Rather, what you should do is pass each of your organization's values and cultural principles of right and wrong or fair and unfair through the lens of your Christian conscience.

As a leader, you *are* a judge and arbiter of actions and choices made by your employees in the course of their employment. It is already your responsibility.

The most authoritative source for learning and developing a Christian conscience is the Bible—both the Old and the New Testaments. Reading the Bible opens the mind to the guiding influence of the Holy Spirit, imparting discernment and wisdom.

Jesus said, "These things I have spoken to you while I am still with you. But the Helper, the Holy Spirit, whom the Father will send in my name, he will teach you all things and bring to your remembrance all that I have said to you. Peace I leave with you; my peace I give to you. Not as the world gives do I give to you. Let not your hearts be troubled, neither let them be afraid" (John 14:25–27 ESV).

And the Apostle Paul tells us, "All Scripture is breathed out by God and profitable for teaching, for reproof, for correction, and for training in righteousness, that the man of God may be complete, equipped for every good work" (2 Timothy 3:16–17 ESV).

And the Apostle Peter says, "(know) this first of all, that no prophecy of Scripture comes from someone's own interpretation. For no prophecy was ever produced by the will of man, but men spoke from God as they were carried along by the Holy Spirit" (2 Peter 1:20–21 ESV).

And the psalmist says,
> How can a young person stay pure?
> By obeying your word.
> I have tried hard to find you—
> don't let me wander from your commands.
> I have hidden your word in my heart,
> that I might not sin against you.
> I praise you, O Lord;
> teach me your decrees.
> I have recited aloud
> all the regulations you have given us.
> I have rejoiced in your laws
> as much as in riches.
> I will study your commandments
> and reflect on your ways.
> I will delight in your decrees
> and not forget your word.
>
> ~ Psalm 119:9–16 NLT

Jesus taught his followers the core values and moral principles that are pleasing to God. His audience was principally a Jewish audience, familiar with what we now call the Old Testament. Jesus did not take issue with the message of the Old Testament. He did, however, take exception to how some interpreted it and applied it in daily life. In this regard, Jesus was a teacher and interpreter of the Old Testament—he gave people context in which to live the principles and values of God.

SPREAD THE NEWS

Jesus reaffirmed for His disciples and followers that the Scriptures were the true source of His values and principles. When Satan came to tempt Jesus at the beginning of His ministry, Jesus said, "It is written, One does not live by bread alone, but by every word that comes from the mouth of God" (Matthew 4:4 NRSV). Each of the three times Satan confronted Him, Jesus used Scripture to defend Himself.

Jesus also said and taught the disciples, "Do not think that I have come to abolish the law or the prophets; I have come not to abolish but to fulfill" (Matthew 5:17 NRSV). Jesus made it very clear the source of their core values and principles was the Scriptures.

PROVIDE TRAINING

Jesus communicated the core values and principles to His disciples in a number of ways, but initially He accomplished this by attending synagogue and teaching and preaching. "Jesus went throughout Galilee, teaching in their synagogues and proclaiming the good news of the kingdom and curing every disease and every sickness among the people" (Matthew 4:23 NRSV).

PROVIDE CONTEXT

The book of Matthew tells us that as Jesus' fame increased and large crowds began to follow Him, He took His disciples up on a mountain and began to instruct them specifically in how to apply and interpret the Scriptures in a manner consistent with the values and principles God desires (Matthew 5:1). We have come to call this conversation with His disciples the "Sermon on the Mount."

In the Sermon on the Mount (Matthew 5–7), Jesus affirmed the authority of all the Scriptures but chastised the widespread conventional wisdom used to interpret and apply them. A common theme of Jesus' harsh criticism of the religious leaders of Israel was their legalistic ("form over substance") interpretation of Scriptures. Using the practices of the religious leaders as examples of ungodly behavior, Jesus called His followers to adhere to the tenets of Scripture in spirit as well as deed. Because God knows all the thoughts of men, He cannot overlook evil thoughts and evil intent. Jesus called His followers to be aware their thoughts and behaviors had to be perfect and holy because God was perfect and holy.

Readers of the Sermon on the Mount today must find, as did the original hearers of Jesus' instructions, it is impossible for anyone to live a life so perfect. In spite of our incredulity, Jesus says to us and them,

"Whoever then annuls one of the least of these commandments, and teaches others to do the same, shall be called least in the kingdom of heaven; but whoever keeps and teaches them, he shall be called great in the kingdom of heaven. For I say to you that unless your righteousness surpasses that of the scribes and Pharisees, you will not enter the kingdom of heaven" (Matthew 5:19-20 NASB).

Unlike the original hearers, we interpret Jesus' sayings from the perspective of the cross and resurrection of Jesus. To our sorrow, we realize we are incapable of adhering to the righteous requirements of God's laws, but we rejoice because we can trust Jesus in faith to be our righteousness.

WARN THEM

Jesus taught His disciples the practical application of the core values and moral principles of God so they could defend themselves and the gospel. In Matthew chapter ten, Jesus gave detailed instructions to His disciples as they prepared to go on their first missionary assignment—where they were to go and not to go, who was to receive the message, how the disciples were to be compensated, what message they were to speak, and how they were to behave when their testimony was rejected.

LEAVE A LEGACY

Jesus instructed His disciples how they were to carry on in His absence (cf. Matthew 24-25) (as good servants doing the Master's bidding and remaining prepared for His return), how they were to treat each other (forgiving one another's sins and offering mercy since their sins had been forgiven and God had granted them mercy), and how they could expect to be treated by civil and other worldly authorities for the message they would preach and teach (to be persecuted and rejected and face physical peril upon occasion).

The book of Matthew concludes with Jesus giving His followers clear instructions to ensure His message continued on after His departure into heaven. "And Jesus came and said to them, All authority has been given to Me in heaven and on earth. Go therefore and make disciples of all the nations, baptizing them in the name of the Father and the Son and the Holy Spirit, teaching them to observe all that I commanded you; and lo, I am with you always, even to the end of the age" (Matthew 28:18-20 NASB).

As a Christian, you are called to follow Jesus. You are called to follow Jesus at work and at home. You are called to follow Jesus without differentiation among different life circumstances. Following Jesus in your heart requires diligent observance of what He said and strengthening your relationship with Jesus through prayer and meditation on His teaching. Jesus promised you will be given everything you need to follow Him when obedience is your heart's desire.

As a Christian leader, you are called to integrate your organization's core values and cultural principles with those placed in your heart and conscience by Jesus. When there is close congruence of the values and cultural principles you follow at work with those Jesus taught, there is peace. When the congruence is not there, neither will there be peace.

REFLECTIONS FOR THE WEEK

1. Read Matthew chapters 5 through 7. Imagine you are on a hillside in Galilee and you hear Jesus teach these things. Prayerfully reflect upon what these statements mean to you.

2. Speaking through the prophet Isaiah, God said, "Thus says the Lord, your Redeemer, the Holy One of Israel: I am the Lord your God, who teaches you for your own good, who leads you in the way you should go. O that you had paid attention to my commandments! Then your prosperity would have been like a river, and your success like the waves of the sea" (Isaiah 48:17-18 NRSV). Isaiah also warns, "There is no peace," says the Lord, "for the wicked" (Isaiah 48:22 NRSV). How do you approach an understanding of these passages in light of the teachings of Jesus?

PRAYER

Almighty God, forgive me for falling short of the standard of Jesus. I sadly acknowledge that I have often fallen away from actions and thoughts that would be pleasing to You. It is in my helpless condition that I cling to Jesus. Lord Jesus, by Your saving work I can stand. Help me to learn from my failures so that I grow ever more like Jesus. Do not abandon me. Open my mind, I pray, to wisdom and strengthen me for obedience.

Amen

JULY—WEEK THREE

PROTECTING THE REPUTATION OF THE ORGANIZATION

> Finally then, brethren, we request and exhort you in the Lord Jesus, that as you received from us instruction as to how you ought to walk and please God (just as you actually do walk), that you excel still more. For you know what commandments we gave you by the authority of the Lord Jesus. For this is the will of God, your sanctification; that is, that you abstain from sexual immorality; that each of you know how to possess his own vessel in sanctification and honor, not in lustful passion, like the Gentiles who do not know God; and that no man transgress and defraud his brother in the matter because the Lord is the avenger in all these things, just as we also told you before and solemnly warned you. For God has not called us for the purpose of impurity, but in sanctification. So, he who rejects this is not rejecting man but the God who gives His Holy Spirit to you.
>
> ~ 1 Thessalonians 4:1–8 NASB

We are all too familiar with fallen heroes. Every generation has them, and it is likely every succeeding generation will have them. Some of the most memorable human failures occur in sports, politics, business, and religion. Individuals and organizations alike can stumble and make errors in judgment that plummet them into disgrace. Past presidents (the USA and other countries), congressmen, senators, governors, mayors, city council members, school board members, and judges; past football, baseball, and basketball athletes, coaches, athletic directors, and teams (the USA and other countries); past CEOs, CFOs, investment bankers, investment advisors, and even accounting firms; past pastors and priests and churches have all experienced disgrace from mistakes and misdeeds. I am certain as you read the list of categories in the preceding sentence, more than one qualifying name came to your mind.

As a leader, you have a particular charge to keep the reputation of the business above reproach. In my opinion, this means the reputation of the leader must also be kept above reproach.

Like a pebble dropped into water, an organization's or individual's personal failure in moral or ethical behavior never affects just the offending party. I believe a failure in moral or ethical behavior by a leader and/or his organization will have a serious negative effect on at least six different persons or groups.

- Lapses in moral judgment and ethical behavior do not happen in a vacuum. These events will always have a victim who may suffer in a number of ways. A victim may experience great personal indignity, perhaps even suffering physical, emotional, or psychological harm. A victim may also experience a loss of property or other valuables. Recovery for the victim is never easy or assured. Close friends and family of the victims will also be affected emotionally by the offense against the victim.
- The offense will cause disruptions in the internal community surrounding the perpetrator. Within an organization, coworkers will be affected. For an individual, family members may suffer emotionally. Loss of camaraderie and trust, feelings of betrayal, loss, anger, and confusion and a misplaced sense of purpose are all likely responses of the people who have invested belief, time, and trust with the organization or the leader who chose to behave in an unethical or immoral way and is exposed.
- The offense will cause disruptions in the external community surrounding the perpetrator. Those who are served by the organization or individual will experience emotional responses similar to those experienced by members of the internal community who work or live closely with the perpetrator.
- It is likely the mission of the organization served by the perpetrator will suffer immense consequences. Those who support its purpose with revenues will find it difficult to continue doing so. Those who use its services will face concerns of trust and

issues of confidence and may very well not desire to be associated with the organization or individual. The consequences may be so significant the organization ceases to exist.

- The history of the organization served by the perpetrator will be tarnished—its legacy will be consumed with the tragic circumstances of the ethical or moral failure. Those who were part of the history will suffer consequences because events and circumstances of which they were proud are now seen in the context of the present humiliation.

- Finally, it is not only the victims or the innocent associates of the perpetrator who suffer. Often a lapse in ethical behavior or moral judgment will include one or more willing co-conspirators. Those who were willing contributors to the moral or ethical lapse will also suffer damage to themselves. And they, in turn, will ripple on with effects on those who looked to them for honesty, integrity, leadership, trust, hope, a future, and a mission.

The Bible does not shy away from human failure and the effects of such failure on others. Through stories of the best and brightest as well as stories of villains and folks who make bad decisions, we see ourselves more clearly—what we are capable of doing to ourselves and each other.

We also gain insight into the personality of God, who stands holy and who is concerned with any sin and oppression. For illustration, I have selected two stories to show the inter-related consequences of lapses of moral conduct and ethical behavior: the story of Amnon and Tamar; and the "inside" story of the apostasy of the rulers and religious leaders of Judah in the days of the prophet Jeremiah.

AMNON AND TAMAR

Amnon was one of King David's sons, and Tamar was one of his daughters, but each had a different mother. Their tragic story is told in 2 Samuel beginning in chapter 13. The story reveals that Amnon became obsessed with a physical desire for Tamar.

> David's son Absalom had a beautiful sister whose name was Tamar; and David's son Amnon fell in love with her. Amnon

was so tormented that he made himself ill because of his sister Tamar, for she was a virgin and it seemed impossible to Amnon to do anything to her.

~ 2 Samuel 13:1b–2 NRSV

Using a carefully contrived ruse, Amnon found a way to be alone with Tamar. Amnon seized her, and she cried out, "No, my brother, do not force me; for such a thing is not done in Israel; do not do anything so vile! As for me, where could I carry my shame? And as for you, you would be as one of the scoundrels in Israel. Now therefore, I beg you, speak to the king; for he will not withhold me from you." But he would not listen to her; and being stronger than she, he forced her and lay with her (2 Samuel 13:12–14 NRSV).

As if incest and rape was not bad enough, Amnon continued his vile behavior when he cast her away from him. By this action he condemned her to a life of disgrace and ridicule.

> Then Amnon was seized with a very great loathing for her; indeed, his loathing was even greater than the lust he had felt for her. Amnon said to her, "Get out!" But she said to him, "No, my brother; for this wrong in sending me away is greater than the other that you did to me." But he would not listen to her. He called the young man who served him and said, "Put this woman out of my presence, and bolt the door after her." (Now she was wearing a long robe with sleeves; for this is how the virgin daughters of the king were clothed in earlier times.) So his servant put her out, and bolted the door after her. But Tamar put ashes on her head, and tore the long robe that she was wearing; she put her hand on her head, and went away, crying aloud as she went.

~ 2 Samuel 15–19 NRSV

A number of things occurred as a result of this tragic event. First, David learned about the event but did nothing to discipline his son or to heal Tamar. Second, Absalom, Tamar's brother and a rival of Amnon to succeed to the throne of David, used the event to bring about the murder of Amnon with revenge as the stated motive. We do not know what the

JULY—WEEK THREE

people David governed thought of David's lack of discipline, but we do see a rift begin in his family that would not be healed. That rift led to murder and conspiracy.

Because of his act of revenge, Absalom was forced to flee the kingdom. Again, King David did nothing to discipline a child who committed the murder of another son. After a few years, David reluctantly allowed Absalom to return to Jerusalem. The continued estrangement (and perhaps the perception of Absalom that David was weak) emboldened Absalom to seek to overthrow David. David was chased out of Jerusalem, and Absalom slept with his father's harem. In the end, David's troops rallied, and Absalom was killed.

The ripple effect of this family tragedy now affected the general population. Upon hearing of Absalom's death, David mourned so greatly that he was rebuked by Joab, one of his advisors who said,

> "Today you have covered with shame the faces of all your officers who have saved your life today, and the lives of your sons and your daughters, and the lives of your wives and your concubines, for love of those who hate you and for hatred of those who love you. You have made it clear today that commanders and officers are nothing to you; for I perceive that if Absalom were alive and all of us were dead today, then you would be pleased. So go out at once and speak kindly to your servants; for I swear by the Lord, if you do not go, not a man will stay with you this night; and this will be worse for you than any disaster that has come upon you from your youth until now."
>
> ~ 2 Samuel 19:5–7 NRSV

Tamar, Absalom, David, David's harem, David's successor, the people of Israel, and Amnon were all negatively affected by the tragic circumstances set in motion by Amnon. Along the way, those affected by the act of violence against Tamar made their own mistakes and errors that allowed the terrible initial act to continue to create problems. But this does not seem to me to be an unusual circumstance—we are all sinners and prone to error. Nonetheless, the story of Amnon and Tamar illustrates the significant ripples that affect many others when a lapse in moral values occurs with an individual.

AN "INSIDE" LOOK AT JERUSALEM BEFORE THE BABYLONIAN CONQUEST

The books of Ezekiel and Jeremiah provide examples of the negative consequences brought about by the immoral and unethical behavior of the ancient leaders of Judah. The immoral and unethical behavior was most characterized by the apostasy of the leaders of Judah just before the Babylonian conquest. Condemning the leaders and holding them accountable was none other than God Almighty. The negative consequences affected the historical record of the people in exile. The internal community was disrupted at the cost of their homes, their possessions and, for many thousands of them, their very lives. In these books we also see the consequences to co-conspirators (false prophets) and the beginning of a radical change in the "mission" of the Jewish people as God's chosen people. The fall of Jerusalem and the exile of the people to Babylon exhibit the judgment of God on His people who had broken the covenant relationship with Him.

The exile of the Jews and the Babylonian conquest took place in two different waves. The book of Ezekiel is written about the first wave of Israelites who were deported to Babylon while Jerusalem still remained. The captive people were experiencing many emotional trials, and their pain was exacerbated by their own countrymen. The non-exiled residents of Jerusalem were telling the captives two things: on the one hand, they were being told that they were the ones chosen by God to be punished—hence, they had gotten what they deserved; on the other hand, they were being told by false prophets inside Jerusalem that God would quickly restore them back to Judah. Neither of these assertions was true. Upon the scene came Ezekiel, whom God appointed to speak the truth to the captives.

> In the thirtieth year, in the fourth month, on the fifth day of the month, as I was among the exiles by the river Chebar, the heavens were opened, and I saw visions of God.
>
> Ezekiel 1:1 NRSV

> He said to me, Mortal, I am sending you to the people of Israel, to a nation of rebels who have rebelled against me; they and their ancestors have transgressed against me to this very day. The descendants are impudent and stubborn. I am sending you to them, and you shall say to them, "Thus says the Lord God." Whether they hear or refuse to hear (for they are a rebellious house), they shall know that there has been a prophet among them.
>
> Ezekiel 1:3–5 NRSV

Jeremiah was a prophet within Jerusalem who continually pronounced a message of destruction at God's hand for the sins of the people. Jeremiah was in the city when it fell to the Babylonians and his prophecies were proved to be true.

What is done in secret is not a secret to God. The leaders of the people were committing terrible acts of idolatry and apostasy; some were even offering human sacrifices to foreign gods. False prophets were telling the people that God would deliver them from harm, yet God through Jeremiah told them what fate they would suffer if they did not repent of their sin. Later, Jeremiah at God's word told the people that they should surrender to avoid slaughter, but Jeremiah was threatened, ignored, and arrested.

To those people who had already suffered exile, God revealed through Ezekiel (and also Jeremiah) *they* were actually going to form the remnant of Israel God would use to restore His people. God had actually spared them by getting them out of Jerusalem and Judah before the slaughter.

For us modern readers, the slaughter and devastation of Jerusalem is hard to grasp. It is even harder for us to think a God of love would call down upon the people the acts of violence the book of Lamentations records as coming against them. Yet the Old Testament is clear God did cause the destruction of Jerusalem. Jeremiah says,

> *Is it nothing to you, all you who pass by?*
> *Look and see*
> *if there is any sorrow like my sorrow,*
>   *which was brought upon me,*
>   *which the Lord inflicted*
>   *on the day of his fierce anger.*

> *From on high he sent fire;*
> *it went deep into my bones;*
> *he spread a net for my feet;*
> *he turned me back;*
> *he has left me stunned,*
> *faint all day long.*
> *My transgressions were bound into a yoke;*
> *by his hand they were fastened together;*
> *they weigh on my neck,*
> *sapping my strength;*
> *the Lord handed me over*
> *to those whom I cannot withstand.*
>
> ~ Lamentations 1:12–14 NRSV

> *The Lord has become like an enemy;*
> *he has destroyed Israel.*
> *He has destroyed all its palaces,*
> *laid in ruins its strongholds,*
> *and multiplied in daughter Judah*
> *mourning and lamentation.*
>
> ~ Lamentations 2:5 NRSV

The descriptions in Lamentations of the slaughter are hard to read. No one, not even the elderly, infants, children, or women were spared. Before the slaughter, the siege and disease killed many.

God knows our inability to grasp these events. Therefore, God revealed to Ezekiel a vision of the idolatry, the worship of foreign gods and other sins occurring inside the Temple in Jerusalem as evidence for the coming destruction on the city (Ezekiel chapter 8).

> He said to me, "Go in, and see the vile abominations that they are committing here." So I went in and looked; there, portrayed on the wall all around, were all kinds of creeping things, and loathsome animals, and all the idols of the house of Israel. Before them stood seventy of the elders of the house of Israel, with Jaazaniah son of Shaphan standing among them. Each had his censer in his hand, and the fragrant cloud of incense was ascending. Then he said to me, "Mortal, have you seen what the elders of the house of Israel are doing in the dark, each in

his room of images? For they say, 'The Lord does not see us, the Lord has forsaken the land.'" He said also to me, "You will see still greater abominations that they are committing."

~ Ezekiel 8:9-13 NRSV

At the end of these visions, Ezekiel saw the glory of God leave the Temple. This vision was new and astounding. Heretofore, the people of Israel believed God resided physically in the Temple and His presence there would never allow the city to fall. By leaving the Temple, God showed Ezekiel that (1) He could be anywhere, even with the exiles in Babylon, (2) He would carry out His judgment on the city and its people, and (3) He would restore the exiles in captivity back to the land of Israel.

Meanwhile, in Jerusalem, Jeremiah was prophesying about the coming judgment and calling the people to repent.

Run to and fro through the streets of Jerusalem,
look around and take note!
Search its squares and see
if you can find one person
who acts justly
and seeks truth—
so that I may pardon Jerusalem.

~ Jeremiah 5:1 NRSV

Tragically, dishonesty and sin was everywhere. No one was found to be upright.

Then I said, "These are only the poor,
they have no sense;
for they do not know the way of the Lord,
the law of their God.
Let me go to the rich
and speak to them;
surely they know the way of the Lord,
the law of their God."
But they all alike had broken the yoke,
they had burst the bonds.

~ Jeremiah 5:4-5 NRSV

God is dramatically revealed in the book of Jeremiah as a God who cares and grieves for His people who have rejected Him. God does not wish the punishment to occur, but His righteousness calls for it even though His grace and mercy had forestalled it for a long time.

> Shall I not punish them for these things?
> says the Lord,
> and shall I not bring retribution
> on a nation such as this?
> An appalling and horrible thing
> has happened in the land:
> the prophets prophesy falsely,
> and the priests rule as the prophets direct;
> my people love to have it so,
> but what will you do when the end comes?
> ~ Jeremiah 5:29-31 NRSV

But Jeremiah is also called to preach a message of hope that, after judgment, God will restore the remnant to himself.

> The Lord appeared to him (Israel) from far away.
> I have loved you with an everlasting love;
> therefore I have continued my faithfulness to you.
> Again I will build you, and you shall be built,
> O virgin Israel!
> Again you shall adorn yourself with tambourines
> and shall go forth in the dance of the merrymakers.
> Again you shall plant vineyards
> on the mountains of Samaria;
> the planters shall plant
> and shall enjoy the fruit.
> For there shall be a day when watchmen will call
> in the hill country of Ephraim:
> "Arise, and let us go up to Zion,
> to the Lord our God."
> ~ Jeremiah 31:3-6 ESV

The story of the fall of Jerusalem and the Babylonian exile are terrible examples of how lapses in moral and ethical behavior of leaders ultimately infect the entire population with sin. Calamity fell on everyone. The remnant went into exile where they had to learn to understand what had happened in order to hope for a better future.

As a Christian leader, you have resources available to help you avoid falling into moral and ethical sins. The Bible reveals the will of God and imparts wisdom and discernment. The church will edify you with relationships shaped by the very image of Christ. Your prayers will be heard because they will be delivered to heaven by the Holy Spirit. Jesus sits at the right hand of God the Father to intercede on your behalf. Jesus' death on the cross will cover over your sins—past, present, and future if you heed His call to repent and return to His grace.

And God will not leave His children in disobedience, but by and through discipline will bring about salvation and repentance.

Be alert always. Pray that you will discern the hand of God moving in your life when you face situations that could result in moral or ethical failures.

REFLECTIONS FOR THE WEEK

1. Undoubtedly you have experienced the effects of a lapse in moral or ethical behavior from one or more of the six vantage points listed at the beginning of this chapter. Are you still experiencing emotional bondage to that event? Jesus suffered violence at the hands of His people, His very creation. Against all insult and injury, He loved the Father and He loved us to the end. What characteristic of Jesus might offer you solace and hope?

2. Evil lurks everywhere and can find each of us. The Apostle Paul admonished us to be careful about judging the sins of others too quickly. Paul also provided us the source of our ability to withstand temptation.

> So if you think you are standing, watch out that you do not fall. No testing has overtaken you that is not common to everyone. God is faithful, and he will not let you be tested beyond your strength, but with the testing he will also provide the way out so that you may be able to endure it.
>
> ~ 1 Corinthians 10:12–13 NRSV

3. Be alert to a time this week when next your conscience speaks out against an act or thought you have done. Examine carefully how and why you failed to heed the warning of the Spirit.

PRAYER

Father, You judge all motives of men, and You will judge me. You know my fears, my hopes, and my inner secrets. You knew them before I was born. Yet You sent Jesus to be the atoning sacrifice that saved me. Give me continued strength to remain in the path of righteousness. Forgive my mistakes and use them to shape me into the person of God You desire me to be, visible to the world, and an example of the love of Christ.

Amen

JULY—WEEK FOUR

PROTECTING THE REPUTATION OF THE ORGANIZATION

Your decrees are wonderful;
  therefore my soul keeps them.
The unfolding of your words gives light;
  it imparts understanding to the simple.
With open mouth I pant,
  because I long for your commandments.
Turn to me and be gracious to me,
  as is your custom toward those who love your name.
Keep my steps steady according to your promise,
  and never let iniquity have dominion over me.
Redeem me from human oppression,
  that I may keep your precepts.
Make your face shine upon your servant,
  and teach me your statutes.
My eyes shed streams of tears
  because your law is not kept.

~ Psalm 119:129–136 NRSV

Then he went down with them and came to Nazareth, and was obedient to them. His mother treasured all these things in her heart. And Jesus increased in wisdom and in years, and in divine and human favor.

~ Luke 2:51–52 NRSV

(When all the people heard this, and the tax collectors too, they declared God just, having been baptized with the baptism of John, but the Pharisees and the lawyers rejected the purpose of God for themselves, not having been baptized by him.)
"To what then shall I compare the people of this generation, and what are they like? They are like children sitting in the marketplace and calling to one another,
"'We played the flute for you, and you did not dance;

we sang a dirge, and you did not weep.'
"For John the Baptist has come eating no bread and drinking no wine, and you say, 'He has a demon.' The Son of Man has come eating and drinking, and you say, 'Look at him! A glutton and a drunkard, a friend of tax collectors and sinners!' Yet wisdom is justified by all her children."

~ Luke 7:29–35 ESV

Immorality and unethical behavior by a leader of an organization or by other members within its community can have devastating effects on the organization. And lapses in moral or ethical behavior invariably have negative consequences to others beyond the immediate effects on the perpetrator, the victim, and the internal community most closely associated with the sinner. Sadly, the negative effects arising out of lapses in moral and ethical behavior can continue to disrupt harmony and create emotional difficulties for many years after the event occurs or is first detected.

With so much to lose from unethical and immoral behavior, what can be done to enable us to make better choices? And what should be the source of our moral and ethical standards?

Christians believe God has established right and wrong, but not everyone agrees with the Christian ethic. We live in a highly secular society that is increasingly becoming indignant when morals are professed as black or white. The name given to this moral indignation is Moral Relativism. This life model believes what is moral for one person may not be moral for another and in fact can vary across different peoples and cultures. The conclusion drawn from moral relativism is there is no clear definition of what is "right" or "wrong."

In our history, polygamy has been practiced and sanctioned, and then declared illegal. In our history, slavery has been practiced and sanctioned, and then declared illegal. In our history, segregation has been practiced and sanctioned, and then declared illegal.

In our history, abortion has been declared illegal, and then sanctioned and practiced. In our history, the Ten Commandments were once displayed in American schools, but now they are no longer allowed there. The speed limit for automobiles on limited access highways was once 70 miles per hour, then 55 miles per hour, and now is back to 70 or more miles per hour.

Women once were prohibited from voting in general elections, but now they cannot be refused a vote. Once upon a time, Creation was taught in our public schools; now evolution is taught, and Creation is dismissed if mentioned at all.

You get the point.

We seem to know a great deal about deciding what is best or right or wrong—we just seem to change our minds a lot.

If you are a Christian, the sovereign judge and arbiter of right and wrong, good and evil, sin and righteousness, is vested with God. And God chose to enlighten us with His views on right and wrong: God's wisdom and commands are set forth in the Bible.

But if you are not someone who believes in the Judeo-Christian God, then this source of right and wrong is unpersuasive. Around the world, other religions provide guidance to their believers on right and wrong behavior, but if you do not believe in these supernatural and divine sources, what they say is also unpersuasive. Accordingly, if you do not believe in any deity, you look to the human spirit or within yourself to develop moral precepts of right and wrong behavior. But the obvious next question is of what value are these if there is no universal agreement on what is truly right or wrong behavior? C. S. Lewis took on this question in his book, *Mere Christianity*.

Lewis observed that although people will argue a Natural Law (a universal law of right and wrong behavior) does not exist, they do not behave that way in practice. Lewis noted people know when they have been treated poorly by others, and this implies there must be a Natural Law at work acting as the yardstick by which actions are measured.

> Whenever you find a man who says he does not believe in a real Right and Wrong, you will find the same man going back on this a moment later. He may break his promise to you, but

> if you try breaking one to him, he will be complaining "It's not fair" before you can say Jack Robinson. A nation may say treaties don't matter; but then, next minute, they spoil their case by saying that the particular treaty they want to break was an unfair one. But if treaties do not matter, and if there is no such thing as Right and Wrong—in other words, if there is no Law of Nature—what is the difference between a fair treaty and an unfair one? Have they not let the cat out of the bag and shown that, whatever they say, they really know the Law of Nature just like anyone else? It seems, then, we are forced to believe in a real Right and Wrong.
>
> ~ *Mere Christianity*

I think Lewis's logic is correct. Whatever people say to the contrary, each of us acknowledges there is a universal right or wrong, because we all use such a yardstick in measuring other's behaviors toward ourselves. This is so even though we often do not judge ourselves with the same yardstick. So while it may appear there are two "authorities" for establishing right and wrong—Divine authority through revelation (although disagreement exists on "who" God is), and man's own intrinsic ability to create his own morality—we all act as if there is a source of universal right or wrong existing outside of ourselves.

I am not going to argue either the merits of moral relativism or following the tenets of any "god" other than the Judeo-Christian God—there are proponents of these philosophies who can speak for themselves. I will, however, argue that only **God** (YHWH, the great I AM, consisting of one God in three persons—Father, Son, and Holy Spirit) has the authority to establish ethical and moral standards.

There are three reasons why I believe only God has the authority to establish a uniform measure of right and wrong behavior: His character, His promises, and His reliability.

HIS CHARACTER

> Moses said, "Show me your glory, I pray." And he said, "I will make all my goodness pass before you, and will proclaim before you the name, 'The Lord'; and I will be gracious to whom I will

be gracious, and will show mercy on whom I will show mercy. But," he said, "you cannot see my face; for no one shall see me and live." And the Lord continued, "See, there is a place by me where you shall stand on the rock; and while my glory passes by I will put you in a cleft of the rock, and I will cover you with my hand until I have passed by; then I will take away my hand, and you shall see my back; but my face shall not be seen."
~ Exodus 33:18–23 NRSV

The Lord descended in the cloud and stood with him there, and proclaimed the name, "The Lord." The Lord passed before him, and proclaimed,
"The Lord, the Lord,
a God merciful and gracious,
slow to anger,
and abounding in steadfast love and faithfulness,
 keeping steadfast love for the thousandth generation,
forgiving iniquity and transgression and sin,
yet by no means clearing the guilty,
but visiting the iniquity of the parents
upon the children
and the children's children,
to the third and the fourth generation."
~ Exodus 34:5–7 NRSV

God is unique and one of a kind. He alone is holy. Some of His character attributes are omnipotence, omniscience, omnipresence, pre-existent and eternal (without beginning and without end), faithful, merciful, loving, good, immutable, wise, self-sufficient and self-existent, righteous, and just. God is also Creator of everything and therefore both capable of caring for and maintaining His creation. God's personal attributes qualify Him to establish moral and ethical standards of behavior.

HIS PROMISES

As surely as God is faithful, our word to you has not been "Yes and No." For the Son of God, Jesus Christ, whom we proclaimed among you, Silvanus and Timothy and I, was not "Yes and No"; but in him it is always "Yes." For in him every one of God's promises is a "Yes." For this reason it is through him that we say

> the "Amen," to the glory of God. But it is God who establishes us with you in Christ and has anointed us, by putting his seal on us and giving us his Spirit in our hearts as a first installment.
>
> ~ 2 Corinthians 1:18–22 NRSV

God initiated the revelation of Himself to mankind; had He chosen to withhold Himself, we would not have found Him. And God, by revelation, entered into covenant relationship with man and made promises.

God made covenants with Noah, with Abraham, with Moses, with David, and with all creation through the merciful and gracious gift of Jesus Christ. God's promises are revealed throughout Scripture and too exhaustive to list here. However, among them are promises to love us, to save us from sin, to forgive our sins, to grant us everlasting life with him, to bless us, to protect us, to guide us in wisdom, to sustain us, to bear with us in times of trouble, to answer our prayers, to be available when we call, and to treat us with compassion, mercy, and justice.

God's ever directed will toward us is to favor us and bless us. The nature of God's promises qualifies Him to establish moral and ethical standards of behavior for us.

HIS RELIABILITY

> Every generous act of giving, with every perfect gift, is from above, coming down from the Father of lights, with whom there is no variation or shadow due to change. In fulfillment of his own purpose he gave us birth by the word of truth, so that we would become a kind of first fruits of his creatures.
>
> ~ James 1:16–18 NRSV

The Bible reveals God always keeps His promises. No promise of God has ever been broken. In Jesus Christ, God's promises of salvation and restoration were fulfilled. The resurrection of Christ proved all that Jesus preached and proclaimed was true. Our faith and our hope are based upon Jesus and His resurrection from the dead. God, and God alone, is reliable and trustworthy.

MORAL AND ETHICAL DISCERNMENT

We learn what God believes is right and wrong behavior by employing five inter-related methods of inquiry and practice over time. Those methods are: (1) reading Scripture, (2) studying and meditating on its meaning, (3) discussing and seeking the counsel of informed Christian teachers and friends, (4) making prayer with God an important and consistent practice in our daily lives, and, (5) through patiently allowing God to teach us through discipline when our choices are not consistent with His will.

The starting point for understanding who God is and what He requires of us is the Bible. We have listed elsewhere in this book references about the reliability of Scripture to instruct and guide our lives. Some of those passages are found in 2 Peter 1:21, and 2 Timothy 3:15–17. Jesus spoke of the Bible as having divine authority (cf. Matthew 5:18 and John 10:35), and the Old Testament authors point to Scripture as the source of knowledge for knowing God's will and obeying Him.

While our faith and the conviction of the Holy Spirit testify that the Bible is sufficient unto itself, there are books external to the Bible that argue for the historical accuracy of the events recorded in the Bible, that say the Bible compares favorably with other historical records and ancient texts. Two of these are *The Case for Faith: A Journalist Investigates the Toughest Objections to Christianity* by Lee Strobel, and *Faith on Trial: An Attorney Analyzes the Evidence for the Death and Resurrection of Jesus* by Pamela Binnings Ewan.

Some Scripture is unambiguous and clear. This most often occurs when a passage commands an action or prohibits an action, and the interpretation of the precept is straightforward. But such a clear reading of the Bible is not always nor usually the case.

This leads us to some interesting questions that confront all Christians pursuing a study of the Bible: How is it so many people of faith can disagree on what God requires of us? Moreover, how are we to know our interpretation of God's laws of moral and ethical behavior is correct?

When disagreements exist in interpretation, it can stem from one reader taking a passage of Scripture out of context. Consider the passage, "I will do whatever you ask in my name, so that the Father may be glorified in the Son. If in my name you ask me for anything, I will do it" (John 14:13-14 NRSV). This is a true statement, but in my opinion it is not a formula for having God behave like a genie and grant our every wish when we invoke the name of Jesus. Some Christians disagree with me and believe this promise is clear and unambiguous. In my reading, however, I also have read the following story:

> God did extraordinary miracles through Paul, so that when the handkerchiefs or aprons that had touched his skin were brought to the sick, their diseases left them, and the evil spirits came out of them. Then some itinerant Jewish exorcists tried to use the name of the Lord Jesus over those who had evil spirits, saying, "I adjure you by the Jesus whom Paul proclaims." Seven sons of a Jewish high priest named Sceva were doing this. But the evil spirit said to them in reply, "Jesus I know, and Paul I know; but who are you?" Then the man with the evil spirit leaped on them, mastered them all, and so overpowered them that they fled out of the house naked and wounded. When this became known to all residents of Ephesus, both Jews and Greeks, everyone was awestruck; and the name of the Lord Jesus was praised.
>
> ~ Acts 19:11–17 NRSV

I believe there are no contradictions in the Bible; otherwise, who could rely upon any of it? So clearly in these two examples some interpretation is required to fully discern the meaning. Therefore, and without belaboring the point, if a passage contradicts other parts of Scripture, it is a warning something is imperfect with our understanding.

Differences in interpretation have led to schisms in the body of Christ—His Church. Yet there is almost universal agreement on the key tenets of Scripture, summarized by the Apostle Paul in Philippians 2:5-11 below.

> *Let the same mind be in you that was in Christ Jesus,*
> *who, though he was in the form of God,*
> *did not regard equality with God*

> *as something to be exploited,*
> *but emptied himself,*
> *taking the form of a slave,*
> *being born in human likeness.*
> *And being found in human form,*
> *he humbled himself*
> *and became obedient to the point of death—*
> *even death on a cross.*
> *Therefore God also highly exalted him*
> *and gave him the name*
> *that is above every name,*
> *so that at the name of Jesus*
> *every knee should bend,*
> *in heaven and on earth and under the earth,*
> *and every tongue should confess*
> *that Jesus Christ is Lord,*
> *to the glory of God the Father.*

If you are interested in understanding more fully the doctrinal difference of our Christian faith, an excellent source is the book *The Doctrines That Divide: A Fresh Look at the Historic Doctrines That Separate Christians* by Erwin Lutzer.

We need not be overly anxious about misinterpreting Scripture, because God has promised He will teach us His laws. We can be confident the careful reading and meditation on the Bible's overall message and the diligent search for its meaning will be revealed to us.

> So I say to you, Ask, and it will be given you; search, and you will find; knock, and the door will be opened for you. For everyone who asks receives, and everyone who searches finds, and for everyone who knocks, the door will be opened. Is there anyone among you who, if your child asks for a fish, will give a snake instead of a fish? Or if the child asks for an egg, will give a scorpion? If you then, who are evil, know how to give good gifts to your children, how much more will the heavenly Father give the Holy Spirit to those who ask him!
> ~ Luke 11:9–13 NRSV

Still, it is perilous to believe that individually we will always interpret the Scriptures correctly. The Jews of Jesus' day believed they were correctly interpreting Scripture, but Jesus taught them they were not. Therefore, we would be wise to add to our reading and meditating upon Scripture the informed opinions and insights of others.

Jesus established the church to provide a community of believers who could witness to each other, encourage each other, instruct each other, admonish each other, and love each other. The church and pastors and teachers are therefore also sources of illumination of God's moral and ethical standards for situations where clear direction seems uncertain. Many churches provide long and short-term studies on the Bible. One such long-term study that I found very useful is the Disciple Bible Study series. There is much benefit in associating with other Christians for the purpose of challenging each other and encouraging each other to gain new insights into the appropriate interpretation of Scripture.

I believe God indwelt us in the person of the Holy Spirit when we trusted Jesus as our Savior. Therefore, the Holy Spirit also guides us toward making decisions that are pleasing to God. This is always the case when we read Scripture.

> But the Advocate, the Holy Spirit, whom the Father will send in my name, will teach you everything, and remind you of all that I have said to you.
>
> ~ John 14:26 NRSV

The Apostle Paul also said, "But you are not in the flesh; you are in the Spirit, since the Spirit of God dwells in you. Anyone who does not have the Spirit of Christ does not belong to him. But if Christ is in you, though the body is dead because of sin, the Spirit is life because of righteousness" (Romans 8:9–10 NRSV).

And the Holy Spirit also guides us in another valuable way. When we are comforted and instructed by other Christians, we open ourselves to receive the counsel they have come to know through the leading of the Holy Spirit in their lives. Other Christians clearly bring their own views and experiences to play in offering advice and counsel. But it cannot be lost on us that dwelling within all Christians is the Holy Spirit. He will guide counselors and teachers in what to say in certain situations.

Our prayer life is invaluable in leading us into deeper and deeper understanding of God and His purpose and will for our lives, including instructing us in moral and ethical behavior. Consider the following Scriptures:

> "Simon, Simon, listen! Satan has demanded to sift all of you like wheat, but I have prayed for you that your own faith may not fail; and you, when once you have turned back, strengthen your brothers."
> ~ Luke 22:31–32 NRSV

> When he reached the place, he said to them, "Pray that you may not come into the time of trial."
> ~ Luke 22:40 NRSV

> When they had prayed, the place in which they were gathered together was shaken; and they were all filled with the Holy Spirit and spoke the word of God with boldness.
> ~ Acts 4:31 NRSV

> Rejoice always, pray without ceasing, give thanks in all circumstances; for this is the will of God in Christ Jesus for you.
> ~ 1 Thessalonians 5:16–18 NRSV

Finally, we also come to know God's will through trial and error. God has promised to reveal Himself and His will for our lives to us, and to instruct us in living our lives in obedience to Him. Through trial and error, including correction and discipline, God will lead us in the paths we should go.

A Christian therefore can know with confident certainty what actions are pleasing to God, and which ones are not pleasing to God. Given the attributes of God, His promises to us, and His reliability, we would be foolish to ignore His teaching and His will for our lives. In response to those who continue to believe we can determine right and wrong by looking inward to develop a moral and ethical code, consider the attributes of man apart from God: sinful and fallen, conceited, selfish, covetous, gossips and slanderers, foolish, unkind, unloving, arrogant, untrustworthy, unstable, unreliable, angry, profane, bitter, and full of pride.

Our world history reveals the twisting and turning of our treatment of each other and our "evolving" moral principles. Too often our leaders betray us and are no wiser than us. Nonetheless, God has established human authority to rule our lives for our good, and many sound ethical and moral principles are part of our secular culture.

What then can we say about the leader's role in protecting the reputation of the business? Here are four conclusions:

1. Obey civil authorities unless the law is clearly against God's directives.
> For the Lord's sake accept the authority of every human institution, whether of the emperor as supreme, or of governors, as sent by him to punish those who do wrong and to praise those who do right. For it is God's will that by doing right you should silence the ignorance of the foolish. As servants of God, live as free people, yet do not use your freedom as a pretext for evil. Honor everyone. Love the family of believers. Fear God. Honor the emperor.
>
> ~ 1 Peter 2:13–17 NRSV

2. Be prepared to bear the consequences associated with your actions if your conscience, prayerfully considered and laid as a burden on your heart, leads you to civil disobedience to obey a command of God rather than human authority.
> When they had brought them, they had them stand before the council. The high priest questioned them, saying, "We gave you strict orders not to teach in this name, yet here you have filled Jerusalem with your teaching and you are determined to bring this man's blood on us." But Peter and the apostles answered, "We must obey God rather than any human authority. The God of our ancestors raised up Jesus, whom you had killed by hanging him on a tree. God exalted him at his right hand as Leader and Savior that he might give repentance to Israel and forgiveness of sins. And we are witnesses to these

things, and so is the Holy Spirit whom God has given to those who obey him."

~ Acts 5:27–32 NRSV

3. Make it your ambition and your choice to use God's measuring stick in making decisions of a moral or ethical nature. Be alert to provide godly counsel to others. Man's yardstick is nothing compared with God's.

> The gifts he gave were that some would be apostles, some prophets, some evangelists, some pastors and teachers, to equip the saints for the work of ministry, for building up the body of Christ, until all of us come to the unity of the faith and of the knowledge of the Son of God, to maturity, to the measure of the full stature of Christ.
>
> ~ Ephesians 4:11–13 NRSV

4. Make it a practice to constantly remind yourself of three things:

- God loves you, and His love will not be withheld from you.
- Jesus saved you from your sins, all of them—past, present, and future.
- God does not want His children to wallow in guilt and fear.

> Be careful then how you live, not as unwise people but as wise, making the most of the time, because the days are evil. So do not be foolish, but understand what the will of the Lord is. Do not get drunk with wine, for that is debauchery; but be filled with the Spirit, as you sing psalms and hymns and spiritual songs among yourselves, singing and making melody to the Lord in your hearts, giving thanks to God the Father at all times and for everything in the name of our Lord Jesus Christ.
>
> Be subject to one another out of reverence for Christ.
>
> ~ Ephesians 5:15–21 NRSV

REFLECTIONS FOR THE WEEK

1. Jesus was once asked to name the greatest commandment. He replied, "'You shall love the Lord your God with all your heart, and with all your soul, and with all your mind.' This is the greatest and first commandment. And a second is like it: 'You shall love your neighbor as yourself.' On these two commandments hang all the law and the prophets" (Matthew 22:37-40 NRSV). Jesus later gave the people the parable of the Good Samaritan to illustrate who is our "neighbor." (See Luke 10:25-37). Who do you feel is your neighbor? Who is not your neighbor?

2. Can you recall any choices you have made recently that created a struggle in your conscience regarding how God would have wanted you to choose? Prayerfully reconsider those choices now, asking God to continue to illuminate your mind to His desires and to provide you with any additional insights for the future.

PRAYER

Almighty God, Your Scriptures speak of sins that so easily entangle us, sins that have become so much a part of our lives that we scarcely notice them. I ask You to shine a light on my sins that no longer seem to bother me. Let them bother me as much as they bother You. They block out Your truth, and they are damaging me. Thank You for Your patience with me and thank You for Your guiding influence through the Scriptures and godly teachers and counselors who keep me in touch with Your will. In this moment of humility and awareness, hear my call to never let me go, to never leave me when I stray from Your will, and to always bring me safely back into Your grace.

Amen

AUGUST

For the creation waits with eager longing for the revealing of the children of God; for the creation was subjected to futility, not of its own will but by the will of the one who subjected it, in hope that the creation itself will be set free from its bondage to decay and will obtain the freedom of the glory of the children of God. We know that the whole creation has been groaning in labor pains until now; and not only the creation, but we ourselves, who have the first fruits of the Spirit, groan inwardly while we wait for adoption, the redemption of our bodies. For in hope we were saved. Now hope that is seen is not hope. For who hopes for what is seen? But if we hope for what we do not see, we wait for it with patience.
Likewise the Spirit helps us in our weakness; for we do not know how to pray as we ought, but that very Spirit intercedes with sighs too deep for words. And God, who searches the heart, knows what is the mind of the Spirit, because the Spirit intercedes for the saints according to the will of God.

~ Romans 8:19–27 NRSV

What good is it, my brothers and sisters, if you say you have faith but do not have works? Can faith save you? If a brother or sister is naked and lacks daily food, and one of you says to them, "Go in peace; keep warm and eat your fill," and yet you do not supply their bodily needs, what is the good of that? So faith by itself, if it has no works, is dead.

~ James 2:14–17 NRSV

The month of August has always intrigued me because two significant relatives of mine had the name "August." August Adolph Bablitz was my great-grandfather. Great-grandfather August was born in the tiny village of Konitz in West Prussia. He immigrated to the United States when he was a ten–year-old boy, arriving in Chicago on Christmas morning in the year 1886.

It was fascinating to hear him tell his story of coming to America. Initially settling with his father and brother in Chicago, Great-grandfather August eventually moved to Lexington, Kentucky, in 1903 and lived there until he died at the age of 87. He attended law school at the University of Kentucky, played football for the University of Kentucky (letterman 1910-1911), and was also an expert cooper (barrel maker), a trade he learned from his father. He spoke with a distinctive German accent, and when he was 85 years old taught my brother Charlie and me how to stand on our heads by demonstrating the feat. The entire house shook when he tipped over. Grandfather August was larger than life to me, and I was proud of our German heritage. He lived a long life, accomplished many things, and had a tremendous influence on my father and his family.

One of my favorite uncles was named after Great-grandfather August—August Adolph Moore. As a child, I enjoyed visiting all of my aunts, uncles, and cousins on both sides of my family. Uncle August, though, was special to me. Perhaps it was his great sense of humor, or perhaps it was how close he was to my father that attracted me particularly to him. Whatever the reason, I eagerly looked forward to our visits with his family during summer vacations.

When I was grown with a family of my own, Uncle August died. My older brother Charlie, my father Charles, and I went to the funeral in Birmingham, Alabama. My father told us stories about growing up with August, and I am sure the re-telling of those tales helped him cope with some of his grief. When we arrived at the church where the funeral services were being held, I was surprised at the crowd that had turned out for my uncle and his family. It seemed to me the entire church was filled. The service was more of a celebration of my uncle's life than a sad affair. After the service the church held a dinner for the family. Great stories were told, and I continued to be amazed an event I had expected to be filled with overwhelming sorrow contained so much joy.

The funeral service included stories of Uncle August within the context of his everyday life, and the stories continued to be told during the meal afterwards. I reflected that Uncle August was a true believer in Jesus; he was a man who had not died apart from the glory to come.

Do you recall someone in your life who has made a similar impression on you? Someone whose quiet faith and manner of living indicates they are separate, somehow, from the rest of the world?

It was at Uncle August's funeral I became aware of and impressed with positive attributes associated with the fellowship of the church. The image of his funeral has stayed with me ever since. I think it is safe to say his funeral haunted me in some way. It had given me a glimpse of what death means to people filled with the hope of God.

And as we drove home, I realized I stood in contrast to the man my uncle had been.

When Uncle August died and we attended the funeral, I was a "believer," but my life did not demonstrate my beliefs. The author of the book of James described me perfectly: "But be doers of the word, and not merely hearers who deceive themselves. For if any are hearers of the word and not doers, they are like those who look at themselves in a mirror; for they look at themselves and, on going away, immediately forget what they were like" (James 1:22–24 NRSV).

In the months following the funeral, I reflected long and hard about how Uncle August had lived a life of faith. Slowly, I found myself wanting to experience life as he had. I wanted to know the Christ he had known. I wanted to change my direction. As a result, I began to read the Bible, more hoping to find the escape clauses and loop holes than to be confronted with the truth. But God kept illuminating each passage that reflected the difference between my life and His call. God was relentless with me.

When I had finished reading the Bible from cover to cover, I knew my sense of being "in control" of my life had to be abandoned if I was to find what I was looking for. This caused me both anxiety and sadness, and I resisted for longer than I should have. But finally, years later, after causing much sadness and sorrow in others' lives, I cried out to God to save me. I claimed Jesus as my Lord, and I gave what was left of my life to Him. Each day since that day has been a better day. Each adversity leads me closer to Him; each blessing leads me closer to Him; everything leads me closer to Him. "Just a closer walk with thee, grant it, Jesus, is my plea. Daily, walkin' close to thee, let it be, dear Lord, let it be."[3]

God places us in situations that bring us into clear recognition of Him. In one sense, how could it be otherwise? God is everywhere, after all. We grope about, but God sees us and interposes Himself so that we find Him. God is patient with us too. But, sooner or later, we who remain unresponsive to His quiet call can become so "hardened" in the heart that our opportunity to find Jesus is lost. Thus we are admonished to accept Him at the opportune time. Today is the opportune time.

John Wesley, the founder of the Methodist church, used a special word to describe God's grace before we are saved—he called it "prevenient" grace, a grace that goes before us. Attending Uncle August's funeral was prevenient grace for me. God used my time of reflection and soul searching to interpose a vision of God—to present to me the amazing idea that God can be vibrant and real and a commanding presence in a life. That vision ultimately led me to change the course of my life. Someday in the future I expect to tell Uncle August all about it.

As we move through the month of August, I pray God will reveal Himself to you in astonishing ways only you can see. When God touches your heart, your very own heart, in a manner that makes you realize He knows you in the innermost hidden place of "who" you are, it is amazing. If such an event happens to you, do not doubt that God is tugging at your heart. Ultimately, such a moment may take you farther than you currently realize—all the way to heaven's door.

REFLECTIONS FOR AUGUST

1. If you are a parent, reflect on how your children see you in relationship with Jesus Christ. Do they see you reading the Bible, participating in Bible study groups, praying, and actively attending church? Do they know you believe that Jesus is the Son of God and that He has saved your life? What would be your "elevator speech" to your children about what Jesus has meant to you in your life?

---

[3] Lyrics for "Just a Closer Walk with Thee" in public domain, author unknown.

2. One of the significant and distinguishing characteristics of the Judeo-Christian God is that He pursues us, reveals Himself to us, seeks relationship with us, and loves us. Our God is faithful. Reflect on how and where you have seen God's hand at work in your life to bring you closer to Him and to protect, comfort, and bless you. Make it a habit this month to recall those special moments where God has uniquely touched your life. Do those moments provide you with an opportunity to witness to others?

PRAYER

Jesus, thank You for Your loving act of salvation. Thank You for being patient with me and for continuing to interpose Yourself into my life in surprising ways. Open my eyes to see Your presence in everything around me. Use me to offer glimpses of Your life to others. Embolden me to witness how You have changed my life for the better. Let me speak encouraging words that uplift others. Let me be a doer of the Word and not just a hearer of the Word.

Amen

AUGUST—WEEK ONE

RETAINING AND RECRUITING TALENTED EMPLOYEES

> O Lord, you have enticed me,
> and I was enticed;
> you have overpowered me,
> and you have prevailed.
> I have become a laughingstock all day long;
> everyone mocks me.
> For whenever I speak, I must cry out,
> I must shout, "Violence and destruction!"
> For the word of the Lord has become for me
> a reproach and derision all day long.
> If I say, "I will not mention him,
> or speak any more in his name,"
> then within me there is something like a burning fire
> shut up in my bones;
> I am weary with holding it in,
> and I cannot.
>
> ~ Jeremiah 20:7–9 NRSV

The word of the Lord came to me: Mortal, with one blow I am about to take away from you the delight of your eyes; yet you shall not mourn or weep, nor shall your tears run down. Sigh, but not aloud; make no mourning for the dead. Bind on your turban, and put your sandals on your feet; do not cover your upper lip or eat the bread of mourners. So I spoke to the people in the morning, and at evening my wife died. And on the next morning I did as I was commanded.

Then the people said to me, "Will you not tell us what these things mean for us, that you are acting this way?" Then I said to them: The word of the Lord came to me: Say to the house of Israel, Thus says the Lord God: I will profane my sanctuary, the pride of your power, the delight of your eyes, and your heart's desire; and your sons and your daughters whom you left behind shall fall by the sword. And you shall do as I have done; you shall not cover your upper lip or eat the bread of mourners. Your turbans shall be on your heads and your sandals on your feet; you shall not mourn or weep, but you shall pine away in your iniquities and groan to one another. Thus Ezekiel shall be a sign to you; you shall do just as he has done. When this comes, then you shall know that I am the Lord God.

~ Ezekiel 24:15–24 NRSV

An organization expends significant time and resources recruiting and retaining talented employees. Talented in this regard means someone who is able to perform the duties assigned in a capable manner while possessing the ethical and interpersonal skills deemed relevant and critical for the job. A talented employee is therefore one who is reliable, accountable, trustworthy, ethical, diligent, and mindful of their job.

Within an organization, not every employee will be found to be talented, and not every talented employee will stay with the organization. Therefore, two critical activities for any organization are recruiting new employees and nurturing and developing current employees so they remain with the organization.

The Bible reveals God historically interacted directly with many people and chose some to be His special messengers. Usually, we do not know from the stories "why" God chose to recruit certain individuals throughout history to be on His team. Some who had what we might call credentials were Noah, "a righteous man, blameless in his generation; Noah walked with God" (Genesis 6:9b NRSV); Abram, who "believed the Lord; and the Lord reckoned it to him as righteousness" (Genesis 15:6 NRSV); and David, of whom God said to the prophet Samuel, "for the Lord does not see as mortals see; they look on the outward appearance, but the Lord looks on the heart" (1 Samuel 16:7b NRSV).

On the other hand, some of God's chosen people had little to commend them. For example, the prophet Samuel is introduced to us as a young boy too small to have done anything noteworthy when he first hears the call of God (1 Samuel 16:7). Moses, after he is grown, is introduced to us as a murderer who has to flee for his life (Exodus 2:12). And the prophets are also generally introduced without particular recommendation.

The general principle we find at work is God chooses whomever He wants. Once chosen, the people respond to God's call. The response and obedience are two important lessons for us to learn.

Another is God can use even the worst of us to accomplish His tasks.

The Old Testament does not provide much testimony about how the chosen messengers or actors on God's stage *felt* about their unique role. Can you imagine what it meant to actually hear audibly the voice of God? Surely such an event would have radically changed their life. After all, the "mystery" would be revealed—they would know with certainty there is in fact a God. Truth would be known. But how or even if they experienced joy in knowing God is more understood by inference than through direct narrative accounts (the Psalms being the notable exception). Sometimes, the person drawn into relationship with God had to deal with conflicting emotions. God is God, after all, and humans are human. God has a purpose and a plan that employs humans, but His purpose and plan are unilateral.

So it is not surprising to find God often called His followers to say and do things that put them in difficult situations and even in harm's way. In the passages of Scripture that began this chapter, both Jeremiah and Ezekiel were ordered to pronounce to their countrymen the coming disaster of the destruction of Jerusalem and the slaughter of thousands. Such a message was neither popular nor well received.

Jeremiah lamented that the job of being God's spokesman was not what he had originally expected. But Jeremiah also confessed that he could not keep quiet because the Word of God burned within him even though he was in agony over the message he must proclaim and the condemnation and ridicule he must endure from the people. Jeremiah cried out,

> Cursed be the day
> on which I was born!
> The day when my mother bore me,
> let it not be blessed!
> Cursed be the man
> who brought the news to my father, saying,

> *"A child is born to you, a son,"*
> *making him very glad.*
>
> ~ Jeremiah 20:14-15 NRSV

The prophet Ezekiel was made to act as a symbol for the exiles already in Babylon. In the passage at the beginning of this chapter, he is told not to mourn over the death of his wife just as the Israelites are not to mourn over the destruction of Jerusalem. In other passages he is instructed to act out the siege of the city and the people fleeing into the wilderness to escape. God's message exacted a toll on Ezekiel.

As leaders, we sometimes have to ask people to do things they do not want to do. Sometimes we have to announce news that is difficult to hear.

What is the worst thing you ever had to do as a leader?

I have found letting people go and being let go are very difficult things to do. In my career I have fired or laid-off employees, and I have been fired. Sometimes I have fired people for cause, but sometimes the decisions were made because the business had to cut its costs. Once I had to fire my very best friend. On other occasions I have announced the sale of businesses and the closure of business units, costing some employees their jobs, but also exacting a cost to the communities previously counting on the businesses for services they provided to them. On more than one occasion, I have announced my resignation to loyal and dedicated employees (not to mention my family).

Letting people go usually does not involve a life-threatening situation. What if you were a commander of troops or other public service employees and you had to order them to go into battle or dangerous situations? I have not had to experience such a situation, but I can imagine the difficulty a leader would have in reaching such a decision where lives are risked and often lost.

How should a Christian leader approach those moments when they are required to deliver unpleasant and difficult messages to their followers? I believe there are five things a leader must do in such situations: do not procrastinate, pray for your people, lead them until the end, speak the truth in love, and if possible, paint a picture of the future that offers hope and encouragement.

DO NOT PROCRASTINATE

Procrastination is a poor choice when a difficult announcement or decision has to be made. Certainly a leader should not make rash decisions. Rather, it is prudent to (a) avail oneself of prayer, (b) seek the advice and counsel of others, (c) make a careful interpretation of available information, and (d) apply the best personal instincts and training to make informed decisions. But once the time of evaluation is past, move expeditiously to make, communicate, and execute the critical decision.

Consider this passage about Abraham when he was commanded by God to take his son, his only son, Isaac, and sacrifice him to God on a mountain. "So Abraham rose early in the morning, saddled his donkey, and took two of his young men with him, and his son Isaac; he cut the wood for the burnt offering, and set out and went to the place in the distance that God had shown him" (Genesis 22:3 NRSV).

This was not a journey Abraham wanted to make, but he had the unmistakable word of God giving him the instructions. Just like the prophets that would follow him, Abraham believed God and followed His commands quickly.

Procrastination for a Christian leader is akin to doubting God's will and sovereignty. If you find it difficult to do what you know you must, prayerfully consider how God can strengthen you for the task.

PRAY FOR YOUR PEOPLE

A Christian leader is placed over people to act as a shepherd to them. A Christian leader is to be careful about them, concerned about them, and interested in leading them in ways to present them with opportunities to be successful. Because of this responsibility, a Christian leader should pray for employees and communities when situations are changing that will take the leader out of the primary role of shepherd.

Jesus prayed such a prayer for His disciples the night He was arrested (John 17:6-19). Stephen, the first Christian martyr, prayed for his attackers when they were stoning him to death after first speaking to them the truth about Jesus (Acts 7:54–59). Moses, as he was preparing to die, prayed for Joshua to be an effective leader for the Jewish people about to cross the river Jordan (Deuteronomy 31:7–8).

Our prayers do not always have to be "correct" in order to be accepted by God. Sometimes we pray for the wrong things, but God still uses our prayers to guide and instruct us. Consider the situation Joshua faced when the army of Israel was defeated shortly after the miraculous taking of the city of Jericho. (Remember the "walls came a tumbling down"?) God's command had been that the people would take nothing of value from the city of Jericho—all of it was to "be devoted to the Lord for destruction. Only Rahab the prostitute and all who are with her in her house shall live because she hid the messengers we sent. As for you, keep away from the things devoted to destruction, so as not to covet and take any of the devoted things and make the camp of Israel an object for destruction, bringing trouble upon it" (Joshua 6:17–18 NRSV).

Unfortunately, one of the Israelites, Achan, desired some of the plunder and took it and hid it in his tent. Accordingly, when the Israelites next went out to face the people of Ai, "the men of Ai killed about thirty-six of them, chasing them from outside the gate as far as Shebarim and killing them on the slope. The hearts of the people melted and turned to water" (Joshua 7:5 NRSV).

The defeat caused Joshua to be overcome with despair, and he threw himself in the dirt before the ark of the LORD. Joshua prayed to the LORD for understanding. But Joshua did not initially realize the people had sinned. Rather, Joshua found fault with God. Joshua said, "Ah, Lord God! Why have you brought this people across the Jordan at all, to hand us over to the Amorites so as to destroy us? Would that we had been content to settle beyond the Jordan!" (Joshua 7:7 NRSV).

God would have none of Joshua's confusion. Joshua was the leader! "The Lord said to Joshua, 'Stand up! Why have you fallen upon your face? Israel has sinned; they have transgressed my covenant that I imposed on them. They have taken some of the devoted things; they have stolen, they have acted deceitfully, and they have put them among their own belongings. Therefore the Israelites are unable to stand before their enemies; they turn their backs to their enemies, because they have become a thing devoted for destruction themselves. I will be with you no more, unless you destroy the devoted things from among you'" (Joshua 7:10-12 NRSV).

Upon hearing this, Joshua assembled the people of Israel and, by lot, Achan was identified as the person who stole the devoted things. When confronted, Achan confessed his sin. The people stoned Achan and all of his family, and the Lord's anger passed. As the leader of the people, Joshua took it upon himself to pray for the people and for the return of the blessing of God. God answered Joshua's prayer—even though Joshua erred in initially finding fault with God.

Prayer often works that way. Through prayer we invite God into fellowship with us so He can lead and guide us in ways that are pleasing to Him. Pray for the people being lead during difficult times. Do everything in your power to invite God to intervene and to bless the people.

LEAD UNTIL THE END

At some point "ends" come. Until the time of leadership ends, a leader must continue to lead by sound counsel and good example. As Christians, we stand completely in the will of God our Father. Whatever He decrees for us is what will be, and we are promised "that all things work together for good for those who love God, who are called according to his purpose" (Romans 8:28 NRSV).

To abandon the position of leadership because we lose heart or become disgruntled with an apparently foregone outcome is to behave in an ungodly manner. Leaders are given the opportunity to lead in both good times and bad—and sound opportunity exists in both to demonstrate Christian values to others and make a difference in their lives. Remember, Jesus harshly criticized the scribes and leaders of Israel who were not leading the people into righteousness but were rather taking advantage and putting themselves first (cf. Luke 11:37–54).

A wonderful example of a leader "leading until the end" is found in the Apostle Paul's second letter to Timothy. In it, Paul admonishes and encourages

Timothy to continue to persevere in the leadership role Paul had assigned him, even though Paul himself was in prison and would soon be killed.

> I am grateful to God—whom I worship with a clear conscience, as my ancestors did—when I remember you constantly in my prayers night and day. Recalling your tears, I long to see you so that I may be filled with joy. I am reminded of your sincere faith, a faith that lived first in your grandmother Lois and your mother Eunice and now, I am sure, lives in you. For this reason I remind you to rekindle the gift of God that is within you through the laying on of my hands; for God did not give us a spirit of cowardice, but rather a spirit of power and of love and of self-discipline."
>
> ~ 2 Timothy 1:3-7 NRSV

A godly leader leads as long as he is allowed the opportunity to do so.

SPEAK THE TRUTH IN LOVE

We are told we can be angry, but we are also told not to let our anger lead us into sin (Ephesians 4:26). Firing an employee who has broken a rule or who has not performed in a manner satisfactory for the job can lead to situations where the leader experiences anger toward the employee. Anger can lead to harsh words inflicting emotional wounds on the recipient. "A soft answer turns away wrath, but a harsh word stirs up anger" (Proverbs 15:1 NRSV).

But a Christian is admonished to speak the truth in love. We do not help someone by covering over the truth. If a person was not successful because of poor performance, it is wrong not to tell them clearly the causes for their loss of employment. However, the telling should not be demeaning or insulting. "Whoever rebukes a person will afterward find more favor than one who flatters with the tongue" (Proverbs 28:23 NRSV).

The story of Joseph (Genesis 37-45) provides an interesting example of speaking the truth in love. Joseph was one of the sons of Jacob (Israel), a patriarch of the Jewish people. Jacob loved Joseph and the favoritism was irksome to his brothers. At an opportune moment, Joseph's brothers sold him into slavery into Egypt and then reported to their father that Joseph had been killed by a wild animal. After many years and many interesting experiences as a slave in Egypt, Joseph is elevated to second in command only to Pharaoh.

When a famine occurs in the land, Joseph's brothers are forced to go to Egypt to seek food. They are unaware of what has happened to Joseph and are frightened when Joseph reveals himself to them from a position of such great power. They expected harsh retribution from Joseph, but Joseph understood God had been guiding and protecting him even in the midst of his brothers' treachery.

> But Joseph said to them, "Do not be afraid! Am I in the place of God? Even though you intended to do harm to me, God intended it for good, in order to preserve a numerous people, as he is doing today. So have no fear; I myself will provide for you and your little ones." In this way he reassured them, speaking kindly to them.
>
> ~ Genesis 50:19–21 NRSV

A godly leader chooses his words carefully so as not to inflict harm on others. Nonetheless, a leader speaks the truth and leaves the rest to God.

OFFER ENCOURAGEMENT FOR THE FUTURE

The prophets Jeremiah and Ezekiel pronounced difficult news to hear. But God also told them the period of difficulty would not last forever. God Himself promised to bring a remnant of the people back to the land He had promised to Abraham, Isaac, and Israel. As Christians, we stand in a hope for the future non-Christians do not have. Jesus said, "Peace I leave with you; my peace I give to you. I do not give to you as the world gives. Do not let your hearts be troubled, and do not let them be afraid" (John 14:27 NRSV). Accordingly, we can face difficult circumstances and still offer encouragement to those we lead.

The Apostle Paul offered great encouragement to Titus (one of his coworkers) as the time of Paul's ministry was coming to a close.

> For the grace of God has appeared, bringing salvation to all, training us to renounce impiety and worldly passions, and in the present age to live lives that are self-controlled, upright, and godly, while we wait for the blessed hope and the manifestation of the glory of our great God and Savior, Jesus Christ. He it is who gave himself for us that he might redeem us from all iniquity and purify for himself a people of his own who are zealous for good deeds.

Declare these things; exhort and reprove with all authority. Let no one look down on you.

~ Titus 2:11-15 NRSV

Words of encouragement and comfort are always welcome. Offering words of encouragement and comfort in difficult circumstances is a sign of the Holy Spirit living and working in the life of the leader.

A leader will inevitably face times when they must bear difficult news to hear. Such situations provide a unique opportunity for witness to the power of God in the leader's life. Such situations also present a springboard for a better future for those affected if the leader remains confident and at peace with God. In the end, such difficult times can either point participants toward greater wholeness and healing, or further brokenness and bitterness.

REFLECTIONS FOR THE WEEK

1. Were you ever fired from a job? How would you evaluate that event in light of the discussion above?

2. Find a copy of the Gettysburg Address and read it. What godly characteristics of leadership during difficult times do you see in this historical speech? Why has this speech stood the test of time?

PRAYER

Almighty God, the gift of leadership is from You, and it is a blessing. Regardless of my current circumstances, help me to celebrate the call You have placed on me. When I feel weak and anxious, strengthen me in accordance with Your promise that "I can do all things through Christ who strengthens me." When things are going well, remind me that nothing is certain in life except Your unfailing love and grace. Therefore, remind me of past struggles as well as victories so that I grow confident in being a leader even in difficult times. Let me move forward in confidence and lead others to the absolute best of my ability. Be with me this day, I pray.

Amen

AUGUST—WEEK TWO

MANAGING THE BALANCE SHEET AND ANTICIPATING TROUBLE

After saying this Jesus was troubled in spirit, and declared, "Very truly, I tell you, one of you will betray me."
~ John 13:21 NRSV

Who is a God like you, pardoning iniquity
and passing over the transgression
of the remnant of your possession?
He does not retain his anger forever,
because he delights in showing clemency.
He will again have compassion upon us;
he will tread our iniquities under foot.
You will cast all our sins
into the depths of the sea.
You will show faithfulness to Jacob
and unswerving loyalty to Abraham,
as you have sworn to our ancestors
from the days of old.
~ Micah 7:18-20 NRSV

At that time the seer Hanani came to King Asa of Judah, and said to him, "Because you relied on the king of Aram, and did not rely on the Lord your God, the army of the king of Aram has escaped you. Were not the Ethiopians and the Libyans a huge army with exceedingly many chariots and cavalry? Yet because you relied on the Lord, he gave them into your hand. For the eyes of the Lord range throughout the entire earth, to strengthen those whose heart is true to him. You have done foolishly in this; for from now on you will have wars."
~ 2 Chronicles 16:7-9 NRSV

I read a story about leadership many years ago when I was working for Arthur Andersen & Co. It was about vigilance and the importance of a leader to remain watchful and alert for trouble. The story used the analogy that leaders are like old stags of the forest, always on duty and keeping watch for danger while the herd moves and feeds at peace. The story pointed out "watchfulness" is a constant for the leader. The leader must never lose their sense of vigilance. When I read the story, I had not advanced far enough in my career for it to have any direct implication to my then existing role and responsibilities, but the story brought to my attention the truth that somewhere in our firm there were leaders who were watching out for the good of the firm, literally at all hours of the day. Somewhere, there were leaders with the responsibility to ensure safeguards were in place to protect the firm and its employees and clients.

I worked for Arthur Andersen & Co. for ten very enjoyable and educational years, and during my career I met some of those leaders—those watchful "stags" alert for trouble. They were men and women of high ethical ideals and vision. Nonetheless, in 2002 Arthur Andersen & Co. voluntarily gave up its licenses to practice as certified public accountants in the United States after being found guilty of charges related to its audits of Enron. Arthur Andersen & Co. has essentially ceased to exist in any significant capacity even though the Supreme Court subsequently overturned the verdict.

Each of us knows with certainty that trouble is going to come knocking on our door; we just do not know when it will happen. We know trouble is coming because we have seen it come to so many others and to ourselves. We know trouble is coming because our parents and others told us the world is not always fair.

Biblically, we know trouble is coming because trouble is a constant theme in the Bible. Jesus said to the disciples, "I have said this to you, so that in me you may have peace. In the world you face persecution. But take courage; I have conquered the world!" (John 16:33 NRSV).

Trouble arrived in Eden at the beginning of the human race. We know about the fall from grace Adam and Eve suffered and that, as a result of their disobedience, sin (and trouble) entered the world and leaves no one exempt from its deadly effects. Trouble soon found Cain and Abel. Trouble was here to stay.

> The Scriptures say,
> *The Lord looks down from heaven on humankind*
> *to see if there are any who are wise,*
> *who seek after God.*
> *They have all gone astray, they are all alike perverse;*
> *there is no one who does good,*
> *no, not one.*
> ~ Psalm 14:2–3 NRSV

If no one does any good, then it is no wonder trouble finds each of us.

For those of us who believe in God, the idea of "trouble" is itself troubling to consider. Two of the hardest questions a Christian will face are why does God allow suffering (trouble) in the world and why do bad things (trouble) happen to good people? A related question, more about "fairness" than trouble, is why do good things seem to happen to bad (undeserving) people?

These questions can surface for each of us at any time based upon our own personal and unique circumstances, but they are always asked whenever something tragic happens. For me, any of the following things constitute tragic events: the loss of a child, regardless of the circumstances; child abuse; murder; suicide; and prolonged and horrifying illnesses (such as Alzheimer's or cancer) that lead to death.

As Christians, we are taught God is sovereign and *no one* is stronger than God. God alone is omniscient, omnipotent, and omnipresent. In addition to unsurpassed strength, God's attributes include love, mercy, compassion, longsuffering, patience, faithfulness, righteousness, integrity, and truthfulness. Accordingly, we struggle to understand how God, with these attributes, can stand by and allow trouble and suffering to exist.

When we question why God chooses to allow bad things to happen and trouble to come, we are really superimposing our thoughts and feelings onto God. In essence, we are saying if we possessed such attributes, we would choose to intervene and prevent trouble from happening.

Yet God does not always intervene. Sometimes God allows trouble to come, and we struggle to understand why. The novel *The Shack* by William P. Young explores the issues surrounding God's viewpoint about the senseless abduction and murder of an eight-year-old girl. When I read *The Shack*, one of my daughters was then eight years old. The novel affected me in a visceral way, and I wept over the characters and the loss of that child.

It is also a common and fair question for Christians to ask why God allows Satan to continue to work evil in the world. We know from the story of Adam and Eve that there is a great enemy of God and man loose in the world, and this enemy is a source of trouble. The Book of Job tells us more about Satan and the trouble he caused Job (Job 1:9–12). We are told in the Book of Daniel about disobedient angels aligned in the world with evil men who look to pursue evil, particularly against the chosen people of God (Daniel 10:13). The Gospels of Matthew, Mark, and Luke each include stories of Jesus being tempted by Satan. And we hear Jesus speak of God having an enemy in the parable of the wheat and tares—an enemy whose sole purpose was to cause trouble (Matthew 13:24–30).

There is trouble in the world, and it continues unabated, generation after generation. Christians are taught that some trouble is caused by the enemy of God, yet God allows that enemy to exist in the world.

Theologically, because Jesus rose from the dead, we know the power of Satan, demonstrated in this world by our physical death, was overcome. Theologically, we know Jesus' death was offered as atonement for the sins of all men, and God accepted Jesus' sacrifice, imputing to us the righteousness Jesus possessed. This was God's gift we call "grace" (unmerited favor).

Rather than judgment and condemnation, Christ offers us mercy. In the long view, the Bible assures us Satan will one day be completely eliminated, and our world will be restored. In the intervening time, we wait and contend with Satan in this life.

On a basic level, since we were created in the likeness of our Creator and we have feelings and emotions, we know our Creator must also have feelings and emotions. Therefore, God cannot be unaffected emotionally when we experience trouble. The Scriptures reveal to us the depth of emotion God feels toward us, particularly in troubling situations. Consider the following examples of God speaking with emotion.

> The Lord saw that the wickedness of humankind was great in the earth, and that every inclination of the thoughts of their hearts was only evil continually. And the Lord was sorry that he had made humankind on the earth, and it grieved him to his heart. So the Lord said, "I will blot out from the earth the human beings I have created—people together with animals and creeping things and birds of the air, for I am sorry that I have made them." But Noah found favor in the sight of the Lord.
>
> ~ Genesis 6:5–8 NRSV

> *For your Maker is your husband,*
> *the Lord of hosts is his name;*
> *the Holy One of Israel is your Redeemer,*
> *the God of the whole earth he is called.*
> *For the Lord has called you*
> *like a wife forsaken and grieved in spirit,*
> *like the wife of a man's youth when she is cast off,*
> *says your God.*
>
> ~ Isaiah 54:5–6 NRSV

> *Can a woman forget her nursing child,*
> *or show no compassion for the child of her womb?*
> *Even these may forget,*
> *yet I will not forget you.*
> *See, I have inscribed you on the palms of my hands;*
> *your walls are continually before me.*
>
> ~ Isaiah 49:15–16 NRSV

> Jerusalem, Jerusalem, the city that kills the prophets and stones those who are sent to it! How often have I desired to gather your children together as a hen gathers her brood under her wings, and you were not willing!
>
> ~ Luke 13:34 NRSV

The Bible speaks with the very voice of God that God loves us and yearns to have us love Him in return. God grieves when we choose to be disobedient. God is angry when people are oppressed and suffer from injustice. Jesus wept over the death of His friend, Lazarus (John 11:35).

Our unrighteousness and disobedience create a gulf separating us from God, who knows no sin and who alone is holy and righteous. But even against our sins and helplessness, God found a way to reconcile us while remaining true to His holy and righteous character. "For God so loved the world that he gave his only Son, so that everyone who believes in him may not perish but may have eternal life" (John 3:16 NRSV).

So we know with certainty God is love personified. Yet the Old Testament shows us God brought trouble upon the human race in judgment of its evil and sin (for example, the great Flood, the destruction of the Northern Kingdom by the Assyrians, the fall of Jerusalem, and the destruction of the Temple by the Babylonians). The Bible record reveals God brought trouble in judgment of the sin and unrighteous behavior of people. Yet we recoil at the magnitude of the trouble—the death of all living creatures save a remnant kept alive in an ark, the death and destruction of a people at the hands of a ruthless adversary—where even children were butchered. We cannot help but ask, was the verdict too harsh?

Then there is the problem of understanding judgment and hell. The New Testament promises Jesus will come again to judge the living and the dead at the end of time. Those who have a relationship with Christ will be granted everlasting fellowship with God. Those without a relationship with Christ will be judged guilty of sin and condemned to everlasting torment in hell. Since the majority of the world's population is non-Christian, the fate awaiting millions of people is torment and anguish. Jesus often spoke of hell and the separation of God that will be the fate of some people, so we know hell is not just an "idea" subject to some debate of biblical interpretation.

> If any of you put a stumbling block before one of these little ones who believe in me, it would be better for you if a great millstone were hung around your neck and you were thrown into the sea. If your hand causes you to stumble, cut it off; it is better for you to enter life maimed than to have two hands and to go to hell, to the unquenchable fire.
>
> ~ Mark 9:42–44 NRSV

> The poor man died and was carried away by the angels to be with Abraham. The rich man also died and was buried. In Hades, where he was being tormented, he looked up and saw Abraham far away with Lazarus by his side.
>
> ~ Luke 16:22–23 NRSV

> Then he will say to those at his left hand, "You that are accursed, depart from me into the eternal fire prepared for the devil and his angels; for I was hungry and you gave me no food, I was thirsty and you gave me nothing to drink, I was a stranger and you did not welcome me, naked and you did not give me clothing, sick and in prison and you did not visit me."
>
> ~ Matthew 25:41–43 NRSV

At some point, and perhaps even on multiple occasions, each Christian will be forced to evaluate individually how a loving God allows evil and just plain old bad things to continue to exist in the world, and the equally challenging idea of how he could allow some people to be condemned to hell. Whatever the truth of the matter, we will likely not know it or understand it this side of paradise.

But if we must remain ignorant for now, is there anything comforting to learn about trouble? I believe the answer to that question is "yes." I believe at least seven positive things can come from times of trouble and demonstrate that God is an "ever-present help in time of need."

1. God will use trouble to test us, where the word test means an examination or trial that will prove the value or ascertain the nature of something. A test can also mean an event or situation that tries a person's qualities. Using these definitions, trouble will:

> (a) Reveal our character as being either of the world or of the spirit; Therefore, my beloved, just as you have always obeyed me, not only in my presence, but much more now in my absence, work out your own salvation with fear and trembling; for it is God who is at work in you, enabling you both to will and to work for his good pleasure.
>
> Do all things without murmuring and arguing, so that you may be blameless and innocent, children of God without blemish

AUGUST—WEEK TWO

in the midst of a crooked and perverse generation, in which you shine like stars in the world.

~ Philippians 2:12-15 NRSV

Set your minds on things that are above, not on things that are on earth, for you have died, and your life is hidden with Christ in God.

~ Colossians 3:2-3 NRSV

(b) Allow us the opportunity to demonstrate our faith in God; Still, I think it necessary to send to you Epaphroditus—my brother and coworker and fellow soldier, your messenger and minister to my need; for he has been longing for all of you, and has been distressed because you heard that he was ill. He was indeed so ill that he nearly died. **But God had mercy on him, and not only on him but on me also, so that I would not have one sorrow after another.** [bold emphasis mine]

~ Philippians 2:25-27 NRSV

(c) Force us to see idols in our lives that replace God in our lives; I rejoice in the Lord greatly that now at last you have revived your concern for me; indeed, you were concerned for me, but had no opportunity to show it. Not that I am referring to being in need; for I have learned to be content with whatever I have. I know what it is to have little, and I know what it is to have plenty. In any and all **circumstances I have learned the secret of being well-fed and of going hungry, of having plenty and of being in need. I can do all things through him who strengthens me.** [bold emphasis mine]

~ Philippians 4:10-13 NRSV

And, (d) Force us to see strongholds in our life that hold us in bondage. Therefore do not let anyone condemn you in matters of food and drink or of observing festivals, new moons, or sabbaths. These are only a shadow of what is to come, but the substance belongs to Christ. Do not let anyone disqualify you, insisting on self-abasement and worship of angels, dwelling on visions, puffed up without cause by a human way of thinking, and not holding fast to the head, from whom the whole body, nourished and held together by its ligaments and sinews, grows with a growth that is from God.

If with Christ you died to the elemental spirits of the universe, why do you live as if you still belonged to the world? Why do you submit to regulations, "Do not handle, Do not taste, Do not touch"? All these regulations refer to things that perish with use; they are simply human commands and teachings. These have indeed an appearance of wisdom in promoting self-imposed piety, humility, and severe treatment of the body, but they are of no value in checking self-indulgence." [bold emphasis mine]

~ Colossians 2:16-23 NRSV

2. God will use trouble to admonish us and warn us about the consequences of our behavior. The Scriptures say,

Who is wise and understanding among you? Show by your good life that your works are done with gentleness born of wisdom. But if you have bitter envy and selfish ambition in your hearts, do not be boastful and false to the truth. Such wisdom does not come down from above, but is earthly, unspiritual, devilish. **For where there is envy and selfish ambition, there will also be disorder and wickedness of every kind.** [bold emphasis mine]

~ James 3:13-16 NRSV

The Scriptures also say,
Those conflicts and disputes among you, where do they come from? **Do they not come from your cravings that are at war within you?** You want something and do not have it; so you commit murder. And you covet something and cannot obtain it; so you engage in disputes and conflicts. You do not have, because you do not ask." [bold emphasis mine]

~ James 4:1-2 NRSV

3. God will use trouble to strengthen us and make us more useful to Him. Through our troubles, God will equip us for even more difficult circumstances and give us the experience to encourage others who are undergoing similar troubles.

Beloved, I do not consider that I have made it my own; **but this one thing I do: forgetting what lies behind and straining**

forward to what lies ahead, I press on toward the goal for the prize of the heavenly call of God in Christ Jesus. Let those of us then who are mature be of the same mind; and if you think differently about anything, this too God will reveal to you. Only let us hold fast to what we have attained. [bold emphasis mine]

~ Philippians 3:13-16 NRSV

My brothers and sisters, whenever you face trials of any kind, consider it nothing but joy, because you know that the testing of your faith produces endurance; and let endurance have its full effect, so that you may be mature and complete, lacking in nothing. [bold emphasis mine]

~ James 1:2-4 NRSV

If you have raced with foot-runners and they have wearied you, how will you compete with horses?
And if in a safe land you fall down,
how will you fare in the thickets of the Jordan?
For even your kinsfolk and your own family,
even they have dealt treacherously with you;
they are in full cry after you;
do not believe them,
though they speak friendly words to you. [bold emphasis mine]

~ Jeremiah 12:5-6 NRSV

Mordecai told them to reply to Esther, "Do not think that in the king's palace you will escape any more than all the other Jews. For if you keep silence at such a time as this, relief and deliverance will rise for the Jews from another quarter, but you and your father's family will perish. **Who knows? Perhaps you have come to royal dignity for just such a time as this."** [bold emphasis mine]

~ Esther 4:13-14 NRSV

4. God will use trouble in judgment of our actions.

   But if you turn aside and forsake my statutes and my commandments that I have set before you, and go and serve other gods and worship them, then I will pluck you up from the land that I have given you; and this house, which I have consecrated for my name, I will cast out of my sight, and will make it a proverb and a byword among all peoples.

~ 2 Chronicles 7:19–20 NRSV

5. God will use trouble to transform us; we are transformed by confronting trouble with faith.

> Yet whatever gains I had, these I have come to regard as loss because of Christ. More than that, I regard everything as loss because of the surpassing value of knowing Christ Jesus my Lord. **For his sake I have suffered the loss of all things, and I regard them as rubbish, in order that I may gain Christ and be found in him,** not having a righteousness of my own that comes from the law, but one that comes through faith in Christ, the righteousness from God based on faith. I want to know Christ and the power of his resurrection and the sharing of his sufferings by becoming like him in his death, if somehow I may attain the resurrection from the dead. [bold emphasis mine]
>
> ~ Philippians 3:7–11 NRSV

And we can be transformed in response to recognition of the judgment of God.

> The Lord spoke to Manasseh and to his people, but they gave no heed. Therefore the Lord brought against them the commanders of the army of the king of Assyria, who took Manasseh captive in manacles, bound him with fetters, and brought him to Babylon. **While he was in distress he entreated the favor of the Lord his God and humbled himself greatly before the God of his ancestors. He prayed to him, and God received his entreaty**, heard his plea, and restored him again to Jerusalem and to his kingdom. Then Manasseh knew that the Lord indeed was God. [bold emphasis mine]
>
> ~ 2 Chronicles 33:10–13 NRSV

6. God will use trouble to reveal His character to us so we learn to both trust Him and fear (hold in awe and reverence) Him.

> *Then Job answered the Lord:*
> *"I know that you can do all things,*
> *and that no purpose of yours can be thwarted.*

> *'Who is this that hides counsel without knowledge?'*
> *Therefore I have uttered what I did not understand,*
> *things too wonderful for me, which I did not know.*
> *'Hear, and I will speak;*
> *I will question you, and you declare to me.'*
> **I had heard of you by the hearing of the ear,**
> **but now my eye sees you;**
> **therefore I despise myself,**
> **and repent in dust and ashes."** [bold emphasis mine]
> ~ Job 42:1-6 NRSV

7. Ultimately, God will use trouble to bring Himself glory. The word glory can be thought of to mean the ultimate and true reflection of something or someone. When we face troubles due to our own errors, we acknowledge the **righteousness** of God. When God judges us for our decisions that lead us into disobedience and sin, we acknowledge His **holiness**. When God restrains His judgment and when He supplies a comfort to us in our sorrow that "surpasses all understanding," He reveals His **love**, His **compassion**, His **patience**, His **mercy**, and His **grace**. And when we repent and realize our need of a Savior, we come to **Jesus**, God's **ultimate gift and sacrifice for us**. These are attributes of God that express His glory.

In conclusion, we can say with certainty, trouble will come to each of us. We who believe in God know in our hearts God is not apart from trouble and He is with us as we walk through troubling times. God's will is being done on earth in the lives of His children, and He will not forget our times of trouble and sorrow. Through our life experiences, we come to seek God and to know God, and in the trials of life we learn God has an ultimate purpose for us and God alone is worthy to judge rightly. Ultimately, we learn through our own experience and empathy with others to trust God to stand firm in His promise to love us and to be our great Shepherd, who gave His life for the life of the sheep.

REFLECTIONS FOR THE WEEK

1. Spend time this week reflecting on what kind of God would allow trouble to exist in the world. Then spend time reflecting on what kind of God would intervene and not allow free will and the consequences associated with free will. What new insights or new questions come to you as a result?

2. Can you recall now, from a distance, a time of trouble in your life where God chose to not intervene and that was ultimately beneficial for you? What would your life have been like had God chosen to intervene?

3. What trials and troubles in your life have equipped you to be an encourager to someone else undergoing a similar trial?

PRAYER

Father God, sometimes I am afraid because I live in a fallen world where people behave foolishly and even wickedly toward others, disregarding even the civil laws men have enacted, let alone your laws. I am aware of sickness that strikes suddenly and without warning against those who seemed in good health, yet others who have eschewed healthy lifestyles go untouched. I have been physically and emotionally hurt by others, and surely I have reciprocated against others who have wanted to trust me and count on me. Betrayed and betrayer, too often I have sought my own good and not the good of others. I know You can protect us, but I also know that sometimes You will not protect us. Still, I cry out, "Lord, save me! Protect me and those I love!" Lord, please hear me and honor my petition. But, in all events, remember Your promises to never leave me or forsake me. Jesus said that when we are in Your hand, nothing can remove us. Empower me in all trials with Your strength. Let me not fall away because of trials, but let me be encouraged and lifted up in spirit.

Amen

AUGUST—WEEK THREE

MANAGING THE BALANCE SHEET AND ANTICIPATING TROUBLE

O Lord, God of my salvation;
I cry out day and night before you.
Let my prayer come before you;
 incline your ear to my cry!
For my soul is full of troubles,
 and my life draws near to Sheol.
I am counted among those who go down to the pit;
 I am a man who has no strength,
 like one set loose among the dead,
 like the slain that lie in the grave,
 like those whom you remember no more,
 for they are cut off from your hand.
You have put me in the depths of the pit,
 in the regions dark and deep.
Your wrath lies heavy upon me,
 and you overwhelm me with all your waves. Selah
You have caused my companions to shun me;
 you have made me a horror to them.
I am shut in so that I cannot escape;
 my eye grows dim through sorrow.
Every day I call upon you, O Lord;
 I spread out my hands to you.
Do you work wonders for the dead?
Do the departed rise up to praise you? Selah
Is your steadfast love declared in the grave,
 or your faithfulness in Abaddon?
Are your wonders known in the darkness,
 or your righteousness in the land of forgetfulness?
But I, O Lord, cry to you;
 in the morning my prayer comes before you.
O Lord, why do you cast my soul away?
Why do you hide your face from me?

> *Afflicted and close to death from my youth up,*
> *I suffer your terrors; I am helpless.*
> *Your wrath has swept over me;*
> *your dreadful assaults destroy me.*
> *They surround me like a flood all day long;*
> *they close in on me together.*
> *You have caused my beloved and my friend to shun me;*
> *my companions have become darkness.*
> ~ Psalm 88 ESV

> *But now hear, O Jacob my servant,*
> *Israel whom I have chosen!*
> *Thus says the Lord who made you,*
> *who formed you from the womb and will help you:*
> *Fear not, O Jacob my servant,*
> *Jeshurun whom I have chosen.*
> *For I will pour water on the thirsty land,*
> *and streams on the dry ground;*
> *I will pour my Spirit upon your offspring,*
> *and my blessing on your descendants.*
> *They shall spring up among the grass*
> *like willows by flowing streams.*
> *This one will say, "I am the Lord's,"*
> *another will call on the name of Jacob,*
> *and another will write on his hand, "The Lord's,"*
> *and name himself by the name of Israel.*
> ~ Isaiah 44:1–5 ESV

> But seek first the kingdom of God and his righteousness, and all these things will be added to you.
> Therefore do not be anxious about tomorrow, for tomorrow will be anxious for itself. Sufficient for the day is its own trouble.
> ~ Matthew 6:33–34 ESV

One remarkable thing about the Bible is that it does not paint our human condition and the stuff of our lives through rose-colored glasses. We are creatures of the earth. There is the capacity for goodness in us because we were created in the image of God. But when sin entered the world, a curse was placed upon the earth and its inhabitants, mankind included.

> And to Adam he said,
> *"Because you have listened to the voice of your wife*
> *and have eaten of the tree*
> *of which I commanded you,*
> *'You shall not eat of it,'*
> *cursed is the ground because of you;*
> *in pain you shall eat of it all the days of your life;*
> *thorns and thistles it shall bring forth for you;*
> *and you shall eat the plants of the field.*
> *By the sweat of your face*
> *you shall eat bread,*
> *till you return to the ground,*
> *for out of it you were taken;*
> *for you are dust,*
> *and to dust you shall return."*
> ~ Genesis 3:17–19 ESV

The Bible portrays us in all our unflattering details. Psalm 88 quoted above reveals the heart of a person in deep emotional pain who prays to God for relief but is not expecting relief to come. The psalmist is clearly in a place of despair and agony. There are no words of hope expressed. The psalmist has no peace night or day and no comfort from any corner—friends and God alike seem to have spurned him. Psalm 88 is distinctively different from other psalms where feelings of sadness, loss, oppression, and despair are expressed, because the author of Psalm 88 cannot or simply chooses not to express hope in either God or his circumstances. The closing line is particularly haunting: "my companions have become darkness."

My father suffered from clinical depression for most of his adult life. When he was in his blackest moments, there was no consolation for him. My father could have penned Psalm 88 in those times of deep depression.

Last week we concluded that trouble is certainly going to come to each of us sooner or later. One of the effects of trouble in our lives is the emotional response we call stress. Stress can damage our bodies and may lead to sickness and mental anguish so severe that professional help from doctors and counselors is required.

I attended a lecture by H. Martin Blacker, a medical doctor and Neurosurgeon. Dr. Blacker is now retired, but during his career he served as the former Chief, Division of Neurosurgery University of Kentucky Medical Center and Director, Baylor Pain Clinic, Department of Neurosurgery (retired) Baylor College of Medicine. Dr. Blacker discussed in laymen's terms the effects of unchecked stress in our bodies. He began his lecture by explaining what happens when a person experiences stress. First, the brain triggers the output of adrenal cortical trophic hormone (ACTH). ACTH stimulates the outer adrenal gland to secrete a cortisone-like hormone into the bloodstream. The brain simultaneously sends impulses to the inner adrenal gland, which secretes adrenalin, resulting in increased heart rate, increased blood pressure, and the constriction of blood vessels. These involuntary responses to stress are life-saving events when we are confronted with a physical danger, because they give rise to the "fight or flight" response. In response to these chemicals and physical changes, we can run from a predator, dodge an oncoming bus, or defend ourselves from attack. But Dr. Blacker pointed out that these same physical occurrences also happen to us when we are under emotional stress. Prolonged emotional stress can result in hypertension (high blood pressure), gastrointestinal ulceration, adrenal gland enlargement, and thymus gland atrophy resulting in immune system compromise. Emotional stress can exact a terrible toll on our bodies.

Dr. Blacker identified three causes of stress in our lives: environmental, somatogenic, and psychogenic. Environmental causes are the things in our lives that "bug" us, like being late, traffic, long lines, work, etc. Somatogenic causes are the things we do to ourselves to bring on stress, such as obesity and inactivity. Psychogenic stress is created whenever we make things worse than they actually are by enlisting our brains and emotions to "blow out of proportion" a particular situation or circumstance.

Given the serious health issues associated with stress in our lives, Dr. Blacker suggested it would be wise to learn to do things to reduce

AUGUST—WEEK THREE

and shorten the occurrences of stress. Among those suggestions were techniques to:

- Avoid stress by identifying those environmental causes and planning avoidance techniques. For example, if being late is a stressor, plan on leaving early.
- Abort stress through autogenic training (a technique that produces a set of physiologic responses that are the opposite of those exhibited during stress).
- Embark upon a regimen of aerobic fitness that has the benefit of minimizing the physical effect of stress and dissipating them.

As leaders, we must attend to the health of our bodies and minds. Each airline flight includes the admonishment before take-off that in the event the cabin pressure should be compromised, you should put the air bag on your own face first before assisting another with their air bag. Leaders need to take care of themselves first—not because of selfish motives, but because they cannot lead effectively if they are debilitated. Leaders need to periodically take stock of their physical and emotional health.

It is easy for a leader to schedule a periodic physical exam, and most leaders do this either because their employers require it or because they know it is important. It can be much more difficult to evaluate emotional health. When emotional health is under attack, we might be prodded by ourselves or by friends and loved ones to seek counseling (a check-up from the neck-up), but usually our emotional health must already be deteriorating pretty quickly for these observations or assessments to be made.

No one wants to wait until depression and despair are at the door to begin to work on restoring emotional health. Being cognizant of changes in emotional attitudes of peace and confidence within ourselves can be signs we are suffering some emotional let-down. Our Creator has given us an internal warning mechanism we can use to gauge our emotional health and also gauge our relationship with Him. That mechanism is the absence or the presence of the "fruit" of the spirit manifested in our lives. Becoming aware of the absence of the fruit of the spirit in my life serves as a reliable predictor that something is not well with my emotional health.

Since the year 2000, I have kept a series of journals containing a record of many events in my life. The journals are not diaries per se because they are not daily collections. But they are a record of many events—the significant and the mundane, the joyful and the anxious. My memory is faulty. Roger Hall, a friend of mine who holds a PhD Psychology, once told me our brains remember those things that make us sick or afraid and ecstatic experiences, but we quickly forget other events.

Although I remember most of the significant events in my life, the details of them do seem to diminish with time. The journals allow me the opportunity, now from the vantage point of time and distance, to refresh my memory in great detail about whatever was going on in my life at the time. But more important than just being an accurate historical record of my life, the journals provide an accurate account of how God historically moved in my life and responded to my prayers, petitions, and desires.

Over time, this written record of my thoughts and conversations with God has bolstered me when new trials and uncertainties arise. Recently I revisited a number of journals from five years or more past, and I gained an important new insight: during times of trial and anxiety, one or more of the fruits of the spirit were also missing in my life. I was able to draw this conclusion by reflecting on the choices of words I used and the types of prayers and petitions I made. I also noticed as circumstances came to their subsequent conclusion (whether my hoped for outcomes were achieved or denied), my language regained the confidence of one who was found under God's care and His loving hand. My choice of words and confidence again reflected the fruit of the spirit. The presence or lack of the fruit of the spirit in my life was a perfect barometer of my emotional health.

What do I mean by the fruit of the spirit? The fruit of the spirit and the benefits of living a spirit-filled life are found in a number of places in Scripture.

> To set the mind on the flesh is death, but to set the mind on the Spirit is life and peace. For this reason the mind that is set on the flesh is hostile to God; it does not submit to God's law—indeed it cannot, and those who are in the flesh cannot please God.
> ~ Romans 8:6–8 NRSV

> By contrast, the fruit of the Spirit is love, joy, peace, patience, kindness, generosity, faithfulness, gentleness, and self-control.
> ~ Galatians 5:22–23a NRSV

> You were taught to put away your former way of life, your old self, corrupt and deluded by its lusts, and to be renewed in the spirit of your minds, and to clothe yourselves with the new self, created according to the likeness of God in true righteousness and holiness.
> ~ Ephesians 4:20–24 NRSV

> As God's chosen ones, holy and beloved, clothe yourselves with compassion, kindness, humility, meekness, and patience. Bear with one another and, if anyone has a complaint against another, forgive each other; just as the Lord has forgiven you, so you also must forgive. Above all, clothe yourselves with love, which binds everything together in perfect harmony. And let the peace of Christ rule in your hearts, to which indeed you were called in the one body.
> ~ Colossians 3:12–15a NRSV

> Train yourself in godliness, for, while physical training is of some value, godliness is valuable in every way, holding promise for both the present life and the life to come.
> ~1 Timothy 4:7b–8 NRSV

I have discovered in my own life joy, peace, and self-control are most often the fruits missing during times of emotional stress. Anxious thoughts replace joy and peace. I seem to be more on edge. Sometimes I have difficulty sleeping. Things get to me in ways they do not when I am emotionally sound. These "dashboard" signals are clear indicators my spirit-filled life needs to be adjusted.

So what do I do with this insight? How do I make an adjustment to get me back on a path to emotional health and stability? What works best for me is to read through my journals.

It is clear my emotional health is good whenever I accentuate words and prayers extolling the faithfulness of God and whenever I ask God to grant me increasing measures of faith and patience. My journals also reveal God answers those prayers, even when other prayers go unanswered or the answer is "no."

My journals reveal that when focusing my thoughts on God's character and His past acts of love, mercy, kindness, compassion, power, and faithfulness rather than on His performance (i.e. His willingness to grant my current petition), my emotional health improves. This change of focus de-sensitizes my problems and anxieties, and I find myself willing and able to release the present troubling situations to God.

Focusing our attention on God's faithfulness and character can stop the decline of emotional health. Until an ultimate resolution is received, we may still emotionally rest below where we hope to be for some period of time. But we will not continue to fall. In contrast to the hopelessness of Psalm 88, the author of Psalm 42 expressed this thought:

> *Why are you cast down, O my soul,*
> *and why are you disquieted within me?*
> *Hope in God; for I shall again praise him,*
> *my help and my God.*
>
> ~ Psalm 42:11 NRSV

The Bible record is very clear: God responds to our acts of faith. Are you concerned you lack the right amount of faith?

I believe that in times of trial and uncertainty, where faith is needed in increasing measure, it is possible to "fake it until we make it." The Bible calls us to rejoice in all things, even when we face adversity. That is a tough command. If rejoicing in times of trouble is more than you are capable of, it is still possible to acknowledge in prayer God will be true to His character in dealing with our needs and He will "hide us under the cover of his wings" (Psalm 17:8). Such assertions are acts of faith, even though we struggle with not knowing when, if, or how God will respond to our needs.

> Jesus asked the [boy's] father, "How long has this been happening to him?" And he said, "From childhood. It has often cast him into the fire and into the water, to destroy him; but if you are able to do anything, have pity on us and help us." Jesus said to him, "If you are able!—All things can be done for the one

who believes." Immediately the father of the child cried out, "I believe; help my unbelief."

~ Mark 9:21-24 NRSV

God will answer the prayer of the child of God in accordance with His own purposes. This means we will not always get the answer we think we want, or an answer may not be as quick in coming as we would like. But we will never lose God as long as we keep Him in our vision. And God is sufficient for us in all things—even in the times of despair and hurt that cannot be explained and linger too long.

Two other comments are in order. First, I believe Psalm 88 demonstrates the depth of emotional despair experienced when someone does not trust God any longer with the circumstances in their life. Sometimes a believer will not or cannot turn to God in trust alone. That is what I hear in Psalm 88. And if a believer who cannot or will not turn to God in trust alone cries out with the pain of Psalm 88, what agony must a non-believer suffer in dark days?

Second, while I firmly believe turning to God in acknowledgement of His character is a step toward healing and wholeness, sometimes depression and emotional stress are too difficult for an individual to conquer without professional help. Therefore, it is important to remember God called people to their various occupations, and some people were called to understand and help people deal with emotional trauma and events of the mind.

I saw the depression my father suffered. He needed professional help. In my life there was a time when I needed professional help too. If the despair is too great, or the hole too deep for you or someone you know to extricate with upward gaze and prayer, I pray God will send people into your life to lead you to the help you need. We are called to form ourselves into unity as the "body of Christ." We are not called to be islands of Christ. Allow a spirit-filled member of the body of Christ to minister to you or someone you know who is in need. Such acts are godly and not indicative of a weak faith.

REFLECTIONS FOR THE WEEK

1. Consider each of the fruits of the spirit individually: love, joy, peace, patience, kindness, goodness, gentleness, faithfulness, and

self-control. Which fruit do you consistently see in your life? Which fruit would you like to have in greater abundance?

2. The fruit of the spirit is an outgrowth of the working of the Holy Spirit of God in our lives. The source is God the Holy Spirit. In your prayer life this week, ask the Holy Spirit to reveal to you why some aspects of His life in you are not manifesting themselves through the fruit of the spirit in your emotional life.

3. John Wesley wrote a "covenant prayer" that acknowledged the sovereign right of God to direct his life. It is an interesting contrast to Psalm 88. Here is that prayer:

> I am no longer my own, but thine. Put me to what thou wilt, rank me with whom thou wilt; put me to doing, put me to suffering. Let me be employed by thee or laid aside for thee, exalted for thee or brought low by thee. Let me be full, let me be empty. Let me have all things, let me have nothing. I freely and heartily yield all things to thy pleasure and disposal. And now, O glorious and blessed God, Father, Son and Holy Spirit, thou art mine, and I am thine. So be it. And the covenant which I have made on earth, let it be ratified in heaven. Amen

4. What does Wesley's prayer say about someone who is filled with the fruit of the spirit? How does this compare or contrast with Psalm 88?

PRAYER

Almighty God, in my weakness you are strong. You know what I can handle. You know what I will need to handle in order to learn to love You and trust You. Abide in me, as You have promised. Do not allow me to face circumstances beyond my capacity. Do not force me to go it alone. Always and forever guide me and protect me and send to me the Counselor and other counselors who will minister to me in time of need.

Amen

AUGUST—WEEK FOUR

HARVESTING AND PRUNING THE ORGANIZATION

Now I saw a new heaven and a new earth, for the first heaven and the first earth had passed away. Also there was no more sea. Then I, John, saw the holy city, New Jerusalem, coming down out of heaven from God, prepared as a bride adorned for her husband. And I heard a loud voice from heaven saying, "Behold, the tabernacle of God is with men, and He will dwell with them, and they shall be His people. God Himself will be with them and be their God. And God will wipe away every tear from their eyes; there shall be no more death, nor sorrow, nor crying. There shall be no more pain, for the former things have passed away." Then He who sat on the throne said, "Behold, I make all things new." And He said to me, "Write, for these words are true and faithful."

And He said to me, "It is done! I am the Alpha and the Omega, the Beginning and the End. I will give of the fountain of the water of life freely to him who thirsts. He who overcomes shall inherit all things, and I will be his God and he shall be My son. But the cowardly, unbelieving, abominable, murderers, sexually immoral, sorcerers, idolaters, and all liars shall have their part in the lake which burns with fire and brimstone, which is the second death."

~ Revelation 21:1–8 NKJV

Jesus answered and said to them, "The sons of this age marry and are given in marriage. But those who are counted worthy to attain that age, and the resurrection from the dead, neither marry nor are given in marriage; nor can they die anymore, for they are equal to the angels and are sons of God, being sons of the resurrection. But even Moses showed in the burning bush passage that the dead are raised, when he called the Lord 'the God of Abraham, the God of Isaac, and the God of Jacob.' For He is not the God of the dead but of the living, for all live to Him."

~ Luke 20:34–38 NKJV

> Although I heard, I did not understand. Then I said, "My lord, what shall be the end of these things?"
> And he said, "Go your way, Daniel, for the words are closed up and sealed till the time of the end. Many shall be purified, made white, and refined, but the wicked shall do wickedly; and none of the wicked shall understand, but the wise shall understand.
>
> ~ Daniel 12:8–10 NKJV

Businesses and organizations are dynamic entities. In business school and in practice we often think of businesses and organizations as having different life cycles. For example, we might say one enterprise is in the start-up phase and another is in the growth phase. Such names provide us with descriptors of the different challenges and opportunities facing enterprises in various places along their "life cycle."

Businesses and organizations, just as people, undergo dramatically different challenges and opportunities throughout their respective life cycles. As people and businesses move within and across various life cycles, there is often a need to make adjustments—to keep some ideas or things and change others. Using the metaphor of a gardener tending a garden, we can say people and organizations face decisions to prune away unproductive or unfruitful activities in order to clear the way for more beneficial activities.

There are many reasons for a leader to consider pruning a business or an organization. In my career, I have pruned businesses because changing circumstances made me question our ability to meet our goals. On other occasions I pruned the business because we had to cut costs or we needed different skills than afforded by our existing employees. Sometimes we pruned one area in order to pursue opportunities we believed had more promise in another direction.

I have also sold (harvested) businesses where such course of action seemed prudent. Harvesting a business or organization, unlike pruning, usually results in making an end of an enterprise for the existing ownership or senior management and putting the enterprise into someone else's hands. Harvesting can occur for many reasons. Some common reasons for making a decision to harvest an enterprise are the death of an owner, retirement of an owner, simply responding to an offer too good to pass up, or merely recognizing the business has run its course.

The human life cycle is usually a long one, affording many opportunities for pruning away activities and behaviors no longer desired to pursue others deemed more beneficial. Making decisions to "prune" aspects of the human life are often self-directed. For example, consider the activities of weight loss or exercise. Such activities are often associated with a personal desire to change behaviors no longer considered worthwhile and perhaps even harmful. Decisions to change careers or to seek additional education are other examples of self-directed pruning activities made with a view toward bettering individual circumstances and achievements.

God also plays a part in pruning lives. Jesus said,
> I am the true vine, and My Father is the vinedresser. Every branch in Me that does not bear fruit He takes away; and every branch that bears fruit He prunes, that it may bear more fruit.
> ~ John 15:1–2 NKJV

The results of self-directed pruning efforts, like everything in life, are uncertain. Self-directed pruning efforts may lead to greater happiness, satisfaction, and productivity, but a satisfactory result is not guaranteed. On the other hand, when God is pruning a life, the result will always be for the good of the person as the following Scriptures, speaking about God's goodness, attest.

> Every good gift and every perfect gift is from above, and comes down from the Father of lights, with whom there is no variation or shadow of turning.
> ~ James 1:17 NKJV

> O God, You have taught me from my youth;
> And to this day I declare Your wondrous works.
> Now also when I am old and grayheaded,
> O God, do not forsake me,
> Until I declare Your strength to this generation,
> Your power to everyone who is to come.
> ~ Psalm 71:17–18 NKJV

> *Nevertheless I am continually with You;*
> *You hold me by my right hand.*
> *You will guide me with Your counsel,*
> *And afterward receive me to glory.*
> *Whom have I in heaven but You?*
> *And there is none upon earth that I desire besides You.*
> ~ Psalm 73:23–25 NKJV

My life has seen a great deal of pruning. Some things that once seemed important to me no longer seem important. Some activities I pursued no longer tug at my heart. Over the last twenty years I have seen evidence of God's pruning work in my life. Here is my litmus test of whether or not God is at work in changing me: When a change in my life brings about more peace, more joy, more wholeness, and greater awareness of God, I attribute the pruning to God.

Rebellion can hinder God's pruning work. Exercising free will and challenging the changes God is calling an individual to make may for a while thwart God's purposes. But going against the will of God is not a wise personal decision. Consider the story of Jonah and the great fish. Jonah was a prophet of God. God called Jonah to go and preach a message of repentance to Nineveh, one of Israel's great enemies. Jonah rebelled. Rather than go to Nineveh, Jonah took off in the opposite direction because he did not want Nineveh to repent and be saved. Enter the great fish (literally). After three days in the belly of the fish, Jonah was vomited on the shore and made his way from there to Nineveh. The people of Nineveh happened to worship a fish god. Perhaps Jonah's fish experience made his message all the more impressive, because we are told the people repented and God withheld His judgment (Jonah 3:6–10). God seems to turn up the pressure on those who know Him but who choose to willfully disobey.

At some point, all pruning activities will cease. Someday we will all die. What happens after death is a great mystery that must be approached in faith. Perhaps you know what different cultures and religions believe occurs after death. I am not an expert. But when I have philosophically considered how a person with no belief of life after death approaches life, I find it almost impossible to contemplate. A number of years ago, a friend of mine with no belief in God or heaven experienced the terrible tragedy of the death of his daughter. Watching him proceed through his grief, I was struck by the hopelessness he felt and the inability to make sense of the tragedy. She was gone, and that was that. Recently a Christian couple at our church lost their daughter in a terrible accident. Their loss was also immense, but they were not without hope. They are certain they will see their little girl again. The contrast is stark—grief without hope against grief with the hope of heaven and a God who will make all things right.

What about you? Do you believe in heaven? According to the Scriptures quoted above, heaven is real, and some people are going to go there some day. Those who are not going there are going somewhere else, and that somewhere else will not be pleasant.

The Bible teaches the only necessary and sufficient decision for going to heaven is to believe Jesus is the Divine Son of God who gave His life as an atoning sacrifice for all men and that whoever believes in Him will not perish but have everlasting life (John 3:16).

In His closing comments to His disciples on the night of His arrest, Jesus said,

> Let not your heart be troubled; you believe in God, believe also in Me. In My Father's house are many mansions; if it were not so, I would have told you. I go to prepare a place for you. And if I go and prepare a place for you, I will come again and receive you to Myself; that where I am, there you may be also. And where I go you know, and the way you know.
> Thomas said to Him, "Lord, we do not know where You are going, and how can we know the way?"
> Jesus said to him, "I am the way, the truth, and the life. No one comes to the Father except through Me."
> ~ John 14:1–6 NKJV

I have known people who want to believe in heaven but who struggle with believing the literal exclusivity of Jesus as the way there. Many people want to be self-justified in living a life worthy of going to heaven. Of course, such reasoning never answers the question "how good is good enough?" I think such questions lead to anxiety rather than peace. Leaving salvation up to Jesus creates peace for the believer. But what is it about Jesus that is a stumbling block to some people? What makes some people attracted to Jesus and some not attracted to Him? The simple answer is God's awakening call in the life of a sinner. How this happens is the source of some theological disagreement among Christians.

Some Christians believe God chooses to awaken those He calls; God chooses some and does not choose others. God is sovereign and has the right and power to do as He pleases. This view is known as the doctrine of predestination. Other Christians believe God calls out to everyone, but not everyone will listen. Those with this opinion are said to follow the doctrine of arminianism. The primary sources of Scripture for these differing views are found in Romans 9 and Ephesians 1:11 for predestination; and recorded in Matthew 11:28-30 and 1 John 2:2 for arminianism.

The debate over these divergent Christian theologies has existed for centuries and continues to be unresolved. However, among Christian theologians there is almost universal agreement the sole determinative factor for salvation is Jesus and having faith in Him alone.

For this reason, Christians are urged to present Jesus to the world. The Gospel of Matthew ends with the "great commission" to followers of Jesus.

> And Jesus came and spoke to them, saying, "All authority has been given to Me in heaven and on earth. Go therefore and make disciples of all the nations, baptizing them in the name of the Father and of the Son and of the Holy Spirit, teaching them to observe all things that I have commanded you; and lo, I am with you always, even to the end of the age."
>
> ~ Matthew 28:18-20 NKJV

The Apostle Paul reiterates the necessity of proclaiming Jesus when he says,

> How then shall they call on Him in whom they have not believed? And how shall they believe in Him of whom they have not heard? And how shall they hear without a preacher? And how shall they preach unless they are sent? As it is written:

> "How beautiful are the feet of those who preach the gospel of peace,
> Who bring glad tidings of good things!"
> So then faith comes by hearing, and hearing by the word of God
> ~ Romans 10:14–15, 17 NKJV

Jesus told His disciples he was going to prepare a place for them and He was coming back to get them so that where He was, they would also be. Jesus was speaking about heaven. Since Jesus promised that those who believe in Him are going to heaven, what do you think heaven will be like?

The quotes from the book of Revelation at the start of this chapter provide some inkling. The book of Revelation also describes the throne of God and the glorious vision of angels and saints worshiping God and Jesus (Revelation chapter four). The psalmist says,

> *You make known to me the path of life;*
> *in your presence there is fullness of joy;*
> *at your right hand are pleasures forevermore.*
> ~ Psalm 16:11 ESV

Heaven will be unlike anything we have ever known. But these Scriptures reveal it will be wonderful and full of joy.

However, something will be missing in heaven: Sin will not be there. Since sin is the cause of death and suffering here on earth, there will be no death and suffering in heaven.

> Then the angel showed me the river of the water of life, bright as crystal, flowing from the throne of God and of the Lamb through the middle of the street of the city; also, on either side of the river, the tree of life with its twelve kinds of fruit, yielding its fruit each month. The leaves of the tree were for the healing of the nations. No longer will there be anything accursed, but the throne of God and of the Lamb will be in it, and his servants will worship him. They will see his face, and his name will be on their foreheads. And night will be no more. They will need no light of lamp or sun, for the Lord God will be their light, and they will reign forever and ever.
> ~ Revelation 22:1–5 ESV

So I know I will no longer sin when I get to heaven because sin does not exist in heaven. But I sin now, and I sometimes wonder what will turn off my propensity to sin when I die? Sometimes I find the thought I will no longer sin harder to believe than anything else. I remember before Adam sinned, he and Eve lived in Eden—a paradise I believe had to resemble heaven. That paradise was not enough to prevent Adam and Eve from sinning. What gives us confidence we will fare better than they?

I think there are three important differences giving us confidence that we will be without sin in heaven. First, there will no longer be an enemy seeking to entice us to sin. Satan will no longer be a threat to us in heaven.

Second, we will remember all of our trials and troubles on earth and know how God responded to each of them for our good. Unlike Adam and Eve, who were enticed to believe God might withhold something from them worth having, we will know with certainty that God never let us down, never lied to us, never failed us, and never withheld anything of value from us. The most important evidence of this is God did not withhold Jesus from us.

And finally, Jesus, the Savior of our souls, the "lamb of God who takes away the sin of the world" (John 1:29b ESV) will be with us in heaven. Looking upon the person who died in my place will give me pause about wanting to do, think, or say anything that would not bring Him honor and glory.

REFLECTIONS FOR THE WEEK

1. Jesus, when He began to preach, said that the kingdom of God was near and that people should repent and receive that good news (cf. Mark 1:15 and Matthew 4:17). In the midst of a fallen world, do the words of Jesus offer you any hope of experiencing heaven in this world, not in the future but now?

2. The fact Christians continue to commit sins after coming to Christ is a stumbling block for many Christians and non-Christians alike. Becoming a Christian is a life-changing event. Jesus discussed being "born again" with Nicodemus in John 3:1–21. Being "born again" begins the journey of the Christian to lead

a life in accordance with the will of God. But being born again does not cure our propensity to sin. The Apostle Paul gives a great discussion of this in Romans chapter seven:

> So I find it to be a law that when I want to do right, evil lies close at hand. For I delight in the law of God, in my inner being, but I see in my members another law waging war against the law of my mind and making me captive to the law of sin that dwells in my members. Wretched man that I am! Who will deliver me from this body of death? Thanks be to God through Jesus Christ our Lord! (Romans 7:21–25a).

3. Reflect on Paul's discussion of the war he continued to wage against sin in his life and how it relates to your life.

PRAYER

Lord Jesus, I have one prayer to offer this week—to thank You for saving me. Thank You for taking my sins on Yourself and cleansing me from all sin and unrighteousness! And now, Lord, help me identify continued instances of sin in my life and encourage and empower me to deal with them. Set me firmly on the path to heaven. Guard and protect my thoughts and my actions until I am fully Yours.

Amen

SEPTEMBER

THE END OF THE THIRD QUARTER

For you formed my inward parts;
you knitted me together in my mother's womb.
I praise you, for I am fearfully and wonderfully made.
Wonderful are your works;
my soul knows it very well.
My frame was not hidden from you,
when I was being made in secret,
intricately woven in the depths of the earth.
Your eyes saw my unformed substance;
in your book were written, every one of them,
the days that were formed for me,
when as yet there was none of them.
How precious to me are your thoughts, O God!
How vast is the sum of them!
If I would count them, they are more than the sand.
I awake, and I am still with you.

~ Psalm 139:13–18 ESV

As he passed by, he saw a man blind from birth. And his disciples asked him, "Rabbi, who sinned, this man or his parents, that he was born blind?" Jesus answered, "It was not that this man sinned, or his parents, but that the works of God might be displayed in him. We must work the works of him who sent me while it is day; night is coming, when no one can work. As long as I am in the world, I am the light of the world." Having said these things, he spit on the ground and made mud with the saliva. Then he anointed the man's eyes with the mud and said to him, "Go, wash in the pool of Siloam" (which means Sent). So he went and washed and came back seeing.

~ John 9:1–7 ESV

Our lives have ups and downs. The author of Ecclesiastes proved his wisdom when he wrote the words "For everything there is a season, and a time for every matter under heaven" (Ecclesiastes 3:1 ESV). Ecclesiastes reminds us things will not always go as we want or hope, that what is happening to us now will not likely continue unchanged for long. Good times and bad times do not last forever.

Tough times can make us both stronger and wiser. The vicissitudes of life provide great opportunity for gaining wisdom. Wisdom gained from hard times is often more apparent through hindsight. That has been the case in my life.

On September 9, 2004, my wife and I lived through a difficult and uncertain time associated with the birth of our third daughter. I cannot remember a more trying time in my life. As those events unfolded, I was too hard pressed to do anything other than persevere. With hindsight, I see clearly God's blessings and love were at work within those dark days.

In December 2003 my wife and I had celebrated our wedding anniversary. We were proud parents of two beautiful daughters and had much to celebrate. Shortly thereafter, we learned we were going to have a third child. We received this news with great joy even though we were both already older than are most new parents.

In the late spring of 2004, a routine ultrasound revealed something was wrong with our baby. The ultrasound was incapable of providing an accurate diagnosis other than something abnormal had occurred. The physicians suggested we consider an amniocentesis test to screen for birth defects. After careful consideration and prayer, we elected not to have an amniocentesis test. We agreed the additional information such a test disclosed would not have any bearing on our desire to have the baby and bring it to term.

The physicians believed whatever medical treatment the baby would need could be better accomplished with a full term baby out of the womb. The course of action decided upon was to continue to watch the baby with ultrasounds and check-ups. If the baby's symptoms worsened, then she would be delivered prematurely. If we were able to get to full term, labor would be induced immediately.

In the early morning of September 9, 2004, the baby was at full term, and we entered the hospital. The drug pitocin was administered to induce labor. We waited, and waited, and waited some more. All day long and into the evening, we waited. My wife did not dilate, nor did labor induce. In the early evening the doctor informed us the baby needed to be delivered by caesarian section because the pitocin was not working. We were greatly disappointed and scared, but we agreed.

The caesarian section went well, and our little girl was born, but things worsened quickly. The baby was diagnosed with blood problems immediately—her platelet count was extremely low. Had she been delivered through the birth canal, she would have suffered hemorrhaging and brain damage, likely not surviving. Worse, the baby's blood cells contained cancer cells consistent with leukemia. Physically she displayed certain characteristics of children with Down syndrome, but not all of them. Although most of the nurses and physicians believed our baby had Down syndrome, it would be a week before the DNA test would confirm that opinion. On the night of our baby's birth, we were filled with anxiety and sorrow. Our daughter was alive, but she was a very sick baby and possibly had a serious chromosomal disorder.

My wife had been given an epidural anesthetic during delivery. The epidural was also to provide anesthesia for her post-operative recovery. During the night her epidural became undone, and the anesthesia stopped working. Even though my wife complained of pain all night, the problem went undetected until it was too late to correct. For about 12 hours, my wife experienced the physical pain of post surgery recovery without any anesthesia. Harrowed by the prospects of a sick baby, tired from the operation and pain, she too was in difficult straits.

Our little girl needed a name. We had not yet decided upon a name when we entered the hospital, although a number of names had been considered. In the midst of the fear and anxiety, my wife found Psalm 108:1–2.

My heart is steadfast, O God!
I will sing and make melody with all my being!
Awake, O harp and lyre!
I will awake the dawn! (ESV)

We named our little girl Melody Dawn.

The following day, about six in the morning, exhausted physically and mentally, I left the hospital to go home to be with our two other little girls. As I sat in the car, I found the stillness of being alone a welcome relief. No "brave front" was needed in the car. My solitude allowed the opportunity for every question and concern to come into my mind without a need for a solution. On the way home I made a detour and stopped in the parking lot of our church. I parked the car and cried out to God to reverse the course of these events. He could make our daughter well, and he could make her normal. I went over all of the things on my heart with God. I cried and wept for my little girl, imagining what was in store for her if she did have Down syndrome and confronting my fears of her not surviving the problems with her blood. My prayer was the same as those cried out by others suffering pain and anxiety. "Lord, if you are willing, you can heal her. Nothing is impossible for you." I prayed earnestly and hard. Then I went home.

Over the next few hours and then days, we were encouraged by visits from our pastors and friends, but the anxiety and grief never fully abated. Just as a hiker lost in the woods can draw some comfort knowing a search party is looking for him, that hiker is still lost in the woods. The time of grief and anxiety is truly a uniquely experienced event that only the suffering can know.

Melody Dawn stayed in intensive care for almost three weeks. She had numerous blood transfusions. Eventually her platelets improved. A hurricane came and went near us, but we could not (would not) evacuate with Melody in the hospital. My wife and I would take turns in intensive care holding her against our bare skin. My wife nursed her. Slowly, Melody grew stronger. We were eventually released under the observation and care of specialists at Children's Hospital New Orleans. There we learned that in Down syndrome children, sometimes leukemia present at birth will spontaneously become cured. No one knows why. They call such cases Myeloproliferative Disorder. Melody's leukemia cells disappeared over a few months, although she remains much more likely than the normal population for the onslaught of leukemia in the future.

It is now ten years later. Melody truly brightens the day of everyone she meets. She keeps us in laughter more than she ever frustrates us. She is without guile. She is loving and friendly. She "spins" in circles, really fast and for a really long time. We don't know why, but she does. She loves to sing and to dance—she really does make melody to awaken the dawn!

She is more than we could have hoped for, and we are continually and uniquely blessed by her. Melody has received more unsolicited conversations with strangers who just want to shake her little hand and say "hello" than any of our other beautiful children taken together. There is something blessed about Melody that others can sense.

I often remember my prayer of that early morning of September 10, because my God answered it for my good. We are not making the most of a bad situation. We are living our life in joy because God gave us Melody Dawn just as she was meant to be. The difficulties of those few weeks in September 2004 were real. The anxious moments were real. But God was with us every step of the way. We are convinced God held back the effects of pitocin to save Melody at birth. We are also convinced God's hand removed the leukemia cells in her blood. We thank God for Melody Dawn just the way she is.

Business will mirror life because it is a human endeavor. Humans are the agents of business. Our positive and negative attributes are reflected in the work we do. In business as in life, sometimes things worked for and hoped for are not realized. In business as in life, sometimes blessings come in surprising and unmerited ways. Whether for good or for ill, in business and in life, people will surprise us, and we will surprise others. While there is a time for every purpose under heaven, God is above time. God is in the present and will be in every moment of the future. The possibility for good exists wherever God is found.

REFLECTIONS FOR SEPTEMBER

1. Most people want to believe that some good can be found even in bad circumstances. Franklin Roosevelt said, "When you come to the end of your rope, tie a knot and hang on" to remind us to persevere. Biblically, there are also proverbs and sayings that convey these same thoughts:

When the tempest passes, the wicked is no more, but the righteous is established forever (Proverbs 10:25 ESV).

The righteous is delivered from trouble, and the wicked walks into it instead (Proverbs 11:8 ESV).

For his anger is but for a moment, and his favor is for a lifetime. Weeping may tarry for the night, but joy comes with the morning (Psalm 30:5 ESV).

God is our refuge and strength, a very present help in trouble. Therefore we will not fear though the earth gives way, though the mountains be moved into the heart of the sea (Psalm 46:1–2 ESV).

Even though I walk through the valley of the shadow of death, I will fear no evil, for you are with me; your rod and your staff, they comfort me (Psalm 23:4 ESV).

This week, recall adverse circumstances that you have experienced. Can you with hindsight recognize that good was present in the midst of them? Were there hard times where no good is visible to you?

2. What about adverse circumstances at work? Can you now recognize that good was present in the midst of them? Are there some still where no good is visible to you?

PRAYER

Father, how it must wound Your heart to hear the plaintive cries of Your people as they suffer and experience fear. I thank You for being with us and working all things for the good of those who love You and seek to do Your will. In my humanness, I ask to be delivered from such circumstances. In my faith, I ask for strength to endure trials patiently. Let me always in every way cling to You, O God. You are always and forever my only hope in times of difficulty and trouble.

Amen

SEPTEMBER—WEEK ONE
INCREASING SALES AND REVENUES

One day he got into a boat with his disciples, and he said to them, "Let us go across to the other side of the lake." So they set out, and as they sailed he fell asleep. And a windstorm came down on the lake, and they were filling with water and were in danger. And they went and woke him, saying, "Master, Master, we are perishing!" And he awoke and rebuked the wind and the raging waves, and they ceased, and there was a calm. He said to them, "Where is your faith?" And they were afraid, and they marveled, saying to one another, "Who then is this, that he commands even winds and water, and they obey him?"

~ Luke 8:22–25 ESV

They came to the other side of the sea, to the country of the Gerasenes. And when Jesus had stepped out of the boat, immediately there met him out of the tombs a man with an unclean spirit. He lived among the tombs. And no one could bind him anymore, not even with a chain, for he had often been bound with shackles and chains, but he wrenched the chains apart, and he broke the shackles in pieces. No one had the strength to subdue him.

~ Mark 5:1–4 ESV

When he saw Jesus, he cried out and fell down before him and said with a loud voice, "What have you to do with me, Jesus, Son of the Most High God? I beg you, do not torment me." For he had commanded the unclean spirit to come out of the man.

~ Luke 8:28–29a ESV

Jesus then asked him, "What is your name?" And he said, "Legion," for many demons had entered him. And they begged him not to command them to depart into the abyss. Now a large herd of pigs was feeding there on the hillside, and they begged him to let them enter these. So he gave them permission. Then the demons came out of the man and entered the pigs, and the herd rushed down the steep bank into the lake and drowned.

~ Luke 8:30–33 ESV

> When the herdsmen saw what had happened, they fled and told it in the city and in the country. Then people went out to see what had happened, and they came to Jesus and found the man from whom the demons had gone, sitting at the feet of Jesus, clothed and in his right mind, and they were afraid. And those who had seen it told them how the demon-possessed man had been healed. Then all the people of the surrounding country of the Gerasenes asked him to depart from them, for they were seized with great fear. So he got into the boat and returned. The man from whom the demons had gone begged that he might be with him, but Jesus sent him away, saying, "Return to your home, and declare how much God has done for you." And he went away, proclaiming throughout the whole city how much Jesus had done for him.
>
> ~ Luke 8:34–39 ESV

How much is enough when it comes to setting sales and revenue targets? If you have a specific amount in mind, is it fixed, or is it subject to adjustment in the future? How would you approach solving the question "how much is enough" for your organization?

I can think of only one instance where the idea of increasing revenues would not be an important objective of an enterprise, although there may be others. That exception would be a foundation or other enterprise organized solely for the purpose of going out of existence in the future—such as a charitable foundation established to give away or otherwise completely exhaust a fixed amount of money. Otherwise, I believe every type of enterprise would like to grow sales and revenues in order to provide for "rainy day" reserves, to make a profit, to do more of what the mission is, or to achieve the mission and vision faster. Growing the revenue stream is the primary and most effective way any organization can assure itself it will continue in existence.

It is not, of course, all about the money. Unlike businesses created for the purpose of making a profit, many organizations are comprised of people with common beliefs and shared purposes who unite to advance a common cause or ideal. Religious and charitable organizations, social and political action organizations, and foundations or other organizations established around a "cause" are examples of these types of not-for-profit organizations. Such organizations can spontaneously grow in membership based on word-of-mouth testimonies and personal attraction to the ideals and causes they promote. If a belief or cause is strong enough to ignite grass roots support, the belief or cause can spread irrespective of revenues. Revenues can be beneficial to not-for-profit entities, however. More money provides more opportunity to reach more people, enhancing the odds of achieving the organization's mission. Coupling grass roots growth with revenue growth can lead to exponential progress in achieving such an organization's mission and vision.

All organizations and causes, for profit and not-for-profit alike, have to start somewhere—they all have a beginning. Therefore, the first step in increasing sales and revenues is to have sales and revenues to begin with. And the first step in developing a "grass roots" following is to have a following to begin with.

The Gospels reveal Jesus had no difficulty in attracting crowds (cf. Matthew 4:24–25, 8:18, 9:36; Mark 6:31–44; and Luke 6:17, 8:19, and 9:37). Jesus also attracted a number of followers who listened to Him teach as a rabbi. From among that group of followers, Jesus chose twelve to be His intimate disciples—eleven of whom would carry on His mission after He ascended into heaven.

The story of the voyage across the stormy sea to the land of the Gerasenes illustrates Jesus using events and circumstances to teach the disciples valuable lessons about their future work, their own frailties, and the difficulties they would face in the world.

Because the Gospels of Matthew, Mark, and Luke each include this story, we can infer that Jesus thought the trip was important, as did the authors. What can we learn from the story? How can we apply the lessons of the story in our lives and businesses? Here are some of my observations.

1. "So they set out, and as they sailed he fell asleep." Jesus fell asleep because He was tired. This sentence tells us Jesus was human. At the end of His ministry, Jesus as a man was crucified and killed. Some theories

arose in the years after Jesus' death questioning whether He was truly a man. The apostles were adamant and clear Jesus was both fully human and fully divine. Jesus referred to Himself as both the Son of God and the Son of man.

The Gospel stories provide many other examples of Jesus' humanity in addition to the verse above. The Apostle Paul tells us in Romans 5:12–19 sin entered the world through one man (Adam) and sin was expiated by one man (Jesus Christ). Paul spoke of the surpassing importance of the cross and the crucifixion in 1 Corinthians 1:18–30, and in 1 Corinthians 15 explained the importance to Christians of the truth of the bodily resurrection of Jesus. Both the disciples John and Peter refuted arguments Jesus was not a man. (cf. 1 John 1:3 and 4:1–3 and 2 Peter 1:16–18 and 2:1. The humanity of Christ makes His sacrificial offering something of inestimable value. Jesus suffered and died to save us. His suffering and death were real.

2. "And a windstorm came down on the lake, and they were filling with water and were in danger. And they went and woke him, saying, 'Master, Master, we are perishing!' And he awoke and rebuked the wind and the raging waves, and they ceased, and there was a calm." Jesus was also fully Deity. Jesus had complete control over the physical world. When we realize Jesus had such great power, we learn Jesus was not a victim of His opposition. Rather, Jesus was a king in charge of His mission—a mission He successfully completed. Jesus' disciples needed to learn, believe, and remember Jesus was truly King of Kings and Lord of Lords. We can draw comfort from His willing sacrifice for our behalf; we can have assurance His awesome power is available to us through the Holy Spirit.

3. "He said to them, 'Where is your faith?' And they were afraid, and they marveled, saying to one another, 'Who then is this, that he commands even winds and water, and they obey him?'" This passage reveals three important points.

First, Jesus' power alarms the disciples even more than the threat of the storm. These men have been His closest companions and have been with Him for some time, yet they cannot comprehend how Jesus was able to accomplish the calming of the storm. Their struggle to understand the person of Jesus (fully human Son of man and fully divine Son of God) would continue for His entire mission on earth. On the night of His betrayal, Jesus asked Philip, "Have I been with you so long, and you still do not know me, Philip? Whoever has seen me has seen the Father. How can you say, 'Show us the Father'"? (John 14:9 ESV). Because the disciples struggled with understanding the person of Jesus, it is likely that even His followers today will struggle with understanding Him as fully human and fully divine.

Second, in calming the storm Jesus revealed He had the power to protect His disciples and even strangers from physical and spiritual dangers. One might surmise, therefore, Jesus would use His power in a preventative or pre-emptive way to ward off danger. But Jesus did not do that. Jesus allowed physical and spiritual dangers to come against His followers then, and they still come against His followers today.

Third, Jesus expected His followers to have faith in Him, particularly in extremely difficult situations. Just as God the Father used trials to perfect faith, Jesus used trials to perfect the faith of His followers. Often, as in this story, the disciples struggled with their faith. For example, Matthew 14:22–33 contains another account of Jesus and the disciples on a stormy sea. The story is the one where Jesus walks on the stormy waters to His disciples, who are alone and struggling in their boat. Even though this story chronologically occurs after Jesus had already calmed a stormy sea once before, the disciples still react in surprise and fear at Jesus' display of power. If the disciples struggled with their faith, we too will struggle with our faith from time to time.

4. "When he saw Jesus, he cried out and fell down before him and said with a loud voice, 'What have you to do with me, Jesus, Son of the Most High God? I beg you, do not torment me.'" Although the disciples struggled to understand the person of Jesus, the spiritual world had no problem recognizing Jesus as the Son of God. The enemy was not unaware, but the evil spirits in the man had no power over Jesus. It is as important for us to remember as it was important for the disciples to see that Jesus

is stronger than the enemy. Therefore, whatever trials and dangers may come against us, we can be confident nothing happens apart from the sovereign will of God. Our hope and confidence is in the Lord regardless the outcome we experience personally. In this we mimic the faith of Shadrach, Meshach, and Abednego who, in the trial of the fiery furnace, told king Nebuchadnezzar, "O Nebuchadnezzar, we have no need to answer you in this matter. If this be so, our God whom we serve is able to deliver us from the burning fiery furnace, and he will deliver us out of your hand, O king. But if not, be it known to you, O king, that we will not serve your gods or worship the golden image that you have set up" (Daniel 3:16–18 ESV).

5. "And those who had seen it told them how the demon-possessed man had been healed. Then all the people of the surrounding country of the Gerasenes asked him to depart from them, for they were seized with great fear." We learn from this passage that Jesus will not be accepted everywhere. In fact, as the Gospels reveal, He will be rejected by most people. But just as the Father does, Jesus respects free will and the wishes of some to not heed His call. In imitation of Christ, a Christian should be willing to discuss their faith with another. Joy, alone, should be the stimulus to share gratefully what God has done in the Christian's life. But like Jesus, we should respect the opinions of others.

In addition to these observations, I believe three other significant observations can be made about the story of the demon-possessed man across the stormy sea in the land of the Gerasenes.

The first is that Jesus' mission of salvation is of all-surpassing importance to us because the enemy is great who fights against our souls; the story reveals the horror awaiting mankind without a Savior. The legion of demons are malevolent, entirely evil, and seeking the destruction of the man. The severity of the demon possession is presented in clear and graphic detail, as discussed by both John MacArthur (*The MacArthur Study Bible*) and Joh. Ylvisaker (*The Gospels: a Synoptic Presentation of the Text in Matthew, Mark, Luke, and John with Explanatory Notes*). The demons wanted only to torture and inflict pain on the man, and when cast out, the demons could not restrain themselves from destroying a herd of pigs that, according to Mark (Mark 5:13), numbered about two thousand. The extent of the evil in possession of the demoniac could not have been lost on the disciples. The message to the disciples was very clear: Even though they would face great opposition from sinful men and evil spirits, the world and its people need saving. The mission is so urgent to Jesus and the Father, the risks so great, that Jesus "who, though he was in the form of God, did not count equality with God a thing to be grasped, but emptied himself, by taking the form of a servant, being born in the likeness of men. And being found in human form, he humbled himself by becoming obedient to the point of death, even death on a cross" (Philippians 2:6–8 ESV).

The second observation concerns how Jesus might have answered the question, "how much is enough?" with respect to His mission on earth. We know Jesus did not care about money. He was an itinerant preacher. But because He is the founder of the Christian church, it is possible to consider the work of Jesus in the business contexts of "missions" and "visions." You will recall missions answer the question, "what do we do?" Visions are related to missions and answer the question, "what do we want to be?" Jesus came to ignite a grass roots effort to change the world. Simply stated, Jesus' mission was to offer Himself as an atoning sacrifice for the sins of the world. His vision was to usher in God's kingdom on earth and restore mankind to right relationship with God by canceling sin and the death that sin demands.

Therefore, rather than thinking about the question "how much is enough" in terms of money, think about "how much is enough" in relation to Jesus' mission of salvation. How many followers did Jesus want? The answer to the question in my opinion is at least "one more." **Jesus made the decision to cross the lake that night to save *one* person.** He did not preach a message to the people on the other side, and He got in the boat and returned home when the townspeople asked Him to leave. Jesus cared enough about *one* person to get in a boat exhausted (for He fell asleep) and sail through a storm just to meet one man in need of a Savior.

Because of the importance to Jesus of the **one** person waiting on the other side of the lake, (**someone** just like us in desperate need of a Savior), Jesus tells His disciples to get in the boat and go to the other side of the lake. The stories of the one lost sheep and the one lost coin (Luke 15:1–10) reinforce the idea that Jesus considers the salvation of one person to be of great importance. Certainly Jesus used the trip and the stormy sea to give the disciples the opportunity to grow in the knowledge of His person and their faith. We are given no other reason for Jesus making the journey than the encounter with the demoniac and the testing of the disciples through the storm and the spiritual encounter. But it seems clear to me that Jesus used the trip to reinforce for His disciples that every soul was important to the Father and to the Son.

And in light of the surpassing importance of the work of Jesus and His mission on earth, the final and most important point to me of the trip across the lake is Jesus used the exercise to provide us with foundational training also. **We are also in the boat with the disciples**. We are now part of the educated and committed followers of Christ who can continue the grass roots effort to bring others to Christ. Jesus wants you to know exactly who He is and what His purpose was in coming to earth. Jesus wants you to know He cares about the one. Jesus needs workers who also care about the one. Jesus needs workers who are willing to risk their pride, their time, their wealth, their energy, and their commitment to gain "market share" for His kingdom.

For those who do so, for those who follow Him, Jesus promises an unsurpassed benefit to His followers—"even eternal life."

REFLECTIONS FOR THE WEEK

1. The magnitude and importance of Jesus' redemptive work for mankind can sometimes be lost to the **one**. This week, reflect on what Jesus' redemptive work means to you, personally, apart from the Christian community at large. Consider afresh that Jesus died for **your** sins, so that **you** could be reconciled to God.

2. Some people are timid in discussing their faith and relationship with Jesus with others. Some people feel they lack theological training or will not have an answer to difficult questions. Reflect on how you feel about being a witness for Christ in your life, your actions, your faith, and your work. Remember that Jesus also came looking for you.

PRAYER

Jesus, Son of the Most High God, I pray that Your redemptive work on earth will continue until the last "one" is called to Your salvation. Lord, empower me to be an example that leads others to You. Remove any doubts I may feel of inadequacy to the challenge of presenting You to a fallen world. Embolden me to speak Your truth in love when opportunity arises. Let me be willing to spend a night on a stormy sea to deliver some "one" from sin and death.

Amen

SEPTEMBER—WEEK TWO

DETERMINING PRIORITIES, SETTING GOALS, AND COMMUNICATING THEM TO OTHERS

After the death of Moses the servant of the Lord, the Lord said to Joshua the son of Nun, Moses's assistant, "Moses my servant is dead. Now therefore arise, go over this Jordan, you and all this people, into the land that I am giving to them, to the people of Israel. Every place that the sole of your foot will tread upon I have given to you, just as I promised to Moses. From the wilderness and this Lebanon as far as the great river, the river Euphrates, all the land of the Hittites to the Great Sea toward the going down of the sun shall be your territory. No man shall be able to stand before you all the days of your life. Just as I was with Moses, so I will be with you. I will not leave you or forsake you. Be strong and courageous, for you shall cause this people to inherit the land that I swore to their fathers to give them. Only be strong and very courageous, being careful to do according to all the law that Moses my servant commanded you. Do not turn from it to the right hand or to the left, that you may have good success wherever you go. This Book of the Law shall not depart from your mouth, but you shall meditate on it day and night, so that you may be careful to do according to all that is written in it. For then you will make your way prosperous, and then you will have good success. Have I not commanded you? Be strong and courageous. Do not be frightened, and do not be dismayed, for the Lord your God is with you wherever you go."

~ Joshua 1:1–9 ESV

A long time afterward, when the Lord had given rest to Israel from all their surrounding enemies, and Joshua was old and well advanced in years, Joshua summoned all Israel, its elders and heads, its judges and officers, and said to them, "I am now old and well advanced in years. And you have seen all that the Lord your God has done to all these nations for your sake, for it is the Lord your God who has fought for you. Behold, I have allotted to you as an inheritance for your tribes those nations that remain, along with

all the nations that I have already cut off, from the Jordan to the
Great Sea in the west. The Lord your God will push them back
before you and drive them out of your sight. And you shall possess
their land, just as the Lord your God promised you. Therefore, be
very strong to keep and to do all that is written in the Book of the
Law of Moses, turning aside from it neither to the right hand nor
to the left, that you may not mix with these nations remaining
among you or make mention of the names of their gods or swear
by them or serve them or bow down to them, but you shall cling to
the Lord your God just as you have done to this day. For the Lord
has driven out before you great and strong nations. And as for you,
no man has been able to stand before you to this day.

~ Joshua 23:1–9 ESV

The book of Joshua chronicles the culmination of God's covenant with Abraham. God told Abraham,

> Know for certain that your offspring will be sojourners in a
> land that is not theirs and will be servants there, and they will
> be afflicted for four hundred years. But I will bring judgment
> on the nation that they serve, and afterward they shall come
> out with great possessions. As for you, you shall go to your
> fathers in peace; you shall be buried in a good old age. And
> they shall come back here in the fourth generation, for the
> iniquity of the Amorites is not yet complete.
>
> ~ Genesis 15:13–16 ESV

On that day the Lord made a covenant with Abram, saying, "To your offspring I give this land, from the river of Egypt to the great river, the river Euphrates."

~ Genesis 15:18 ESV

The fulfillment of the covenant spanned over 400 years. During that time, just as God had foretold, the Israelites went from being guests of Pharaoh, during the time Joseph served as Pharaoh's executive, to slaves of Pharaoh.

The fulfillment of the covenant was God's work. Only God was able to protect the Israelites from their enemies and deliver to them freedom and then a land of their own. But more important than freedom, God gave the Israelites access to Himself—the One True God. God gave them the Ten Commandments and the other aspects of the Law that brought order and justice to their people. From one man (Abraham) God brought forth a people. From a people, God brought forth a nation. From a nation, God brought forth a Savior of the world.

Every step of the way, God chose the leaders who would work as His agents in fulfilling the covenant. Moses was called by God to bring the people out of bondage in Egypt and to lead them to the Promised Land. But the Israelites refused to take possession of the Promised Land when they first approached it, and so they were forced to sojourn for 40 years in the desert until that entire adult generation had died. In the passages of Scripture above, Moses has died. And now, with Moses dead, God appoints Joshua to lead the people in Moses's place.

God established the mission for Joshua (lead the people), the vision (take the land), and the values Joshua had to keep in exercising his duties as leader (follow the Law of God and be strong and courageous). Choosing the right priorities for the mission and vision became one of Joshua's most important roles as a leader. Joshua's first priority was to rely upon God in all that he did.

Joshua was well acquainted with God and the covenant. Joshua had been the "aide" of Moses and was with Moses on many occasions when God and Moses would meet and speak. For example, Joshua was on the mountain with Moses when God gave him the Ten Commandments (Exodus 24:13). Joshua stayed with Moses in the Tent of Meeting when God visited Moses (Exodus 33:11). Joshua was with the spies who initially scouted the Promised Land, although the people were afraid to take possession of it at that time and so were punished by God by being forced to remain in the wilderness for forty years (Numbers 14:6). And Joshua was with Moses when God foretold that the people would rebel and turn away from Him once they entered the Promised Land (Deuteronomy 31:14-18).

As he accepted his commission from God, Joshua had firsthand knowledge of the holiness of God that demanded obedience and reverence (fear) from the people. But Joshua had also seen God was patient, trustworthy, and committed to fulfilling the covenant He had made to Abraham. The knowledge of God was truly the beginning of wisdom for Joshua.

The book of Joshua illustrates excellent principles of leadership in executing priorities. Joshua completed the following steps in fulfilling his role as God's agent to lead the people into the Promised Land.

1. Joshua first **restated the vision—the people were going to cross the Jordan and take the land (Joshua 1:10-11).**

2. Remembering the past failures of the people to enter the land, Joshua **tested** the people by sending spies into the land just as Moses had done. When the spies returned this time, however, the people were ready to enter the land, confident that the LORD was with them (Joshua 2).

3. Joshua made a **first step**—a beginning. He got the people organized and moving (Joshua 3).

4. Joshua **commemorated success in a communal way.** Joshua erected a stone monument using stones taken from the Jordan River bed that God had dried up to allow the people to cross over into the Promised Land (Joshua 4).

5. Joshua called the people to **affirm the commandments (values)** of the LORD. Joshua had the men circumcised as a sign of the covenant with God that was being fulfilled. Joshua kept the people firmly grounded in their hope of victory—God, and God alone (Joshua 5).

6. **Joshua modeled the values (obedience, trust, and faithfulness) for the people**. God had told Joshua that every place he set his foot would be his. Joshua led the people to Jericho. When God sent an angel to explain the battle strategy to Joshua, Joshua listened and obeyed fully (Joshua 6).

7. **Joshua held the people accountable for their actions**. When an Israelite chose to take possessions as spoils of war from Jericho against the will of God, God withdrew His protection from the people. Joshua suffered a momentary loss of faith in God (Joshua 7:6-9), but when God pointed out the sinner, Joshua was resolute before the people in carrying out God's justice (Joshua 7:24-26). In doing this, Joshua continued to model the values of God before the people. Moreover, the people learned that a single sinner in their midst would bring serious consequences.

8. Joshua **completed the work** assigned to him. He then **"restated" and summarized** all that God and the people had accomplished—the mission,

the vision, and the values in order to leave a legacy for those that would come after him (Joshua 23).

The book of Joshua is a book of success for the Israelites and the Jewish people. God's covenant made to Abraham over 400 years earlier was fulfilled. But we know the success did not last. The rest of the history of the Israelites contained in the Old Testament reveals that after Joshua's generation passed away, the people forgot their unique relationship with God.

> When Joshua dismissed the people, the people of Israel went each to his inheritance to take possession of the land. And the people served the Lord all the days of Joshua, and all the days of the elders who outlived Joshua, who had seen all the great work that the Lord had done for Israel.
>
> ~ Judges 2:6–7 ESV

> And all that generation also were gathered to their fathers. And there arose another generation after them who did not know the Lord or the work that he had done for Israel. And the people of Israel did what was evil in the sight of the Lord and served the Baals. And they abandoned the Lord, the God of their fathers, who had brought them out of the land of Egypt. They went after other gods, from among the gods of the peoples who were around them, and bowed down to them. And they provoked the Lord to anger.
>
> ~ Judges 2:10–12 ESV

As a leader, how would you feel if you knew some project you were working on would last only a short while before it was destroyed or forgotten by those who came after you? Has such a question ever entered your mind? It has entered my mind. When I worked for Arthur Andersen & Co. as an auditor, I greatly enjoyed my work and believed we were doing work of value. But I often wondered what the real point of the work was. Who would care years down the road about the work we were doing? For that matter, the firm's policy was to destroy audit workpapers after some legal and statutory number of years had elapsed. So I was sadly and completely aware that not even the physical evidence of the work I had done would last long.

I have now been employed by five other enterprises since Arthur Andersen & Co., and I still wonder if those who followed after me in my footsteps cared one hoot about the work I did. Perhaps this same reasoning was what the author of Ecclesiastes had in mind when he said,

> "Meaningless! Meaningless!"
> says the Teacher.
> "Utterly meaningless!
> Everything is meaningless."
>
> ~ Ecclesiastes 1:2 NIV

Yet, Joshua knew before he embarked on his mission to lead the people into the Promised Land that they would fall away. In Exodus 31:16, God told Joshua and Moses the people would fall away after they had entered the Promised Land. Even with knowledge of the ultimate betrayal of the people, Joshua followed through and carried out his mission. How is it that Joshua persevered?

The answer, in my opinion, is Joshua knew God intimately. At the end of his mission, Joshua said this to the people,

> Now therefore revere the Lord, and serve him in sincerity and in faithfulness; put away the gods that your ancestors served beyond the River and in Egypt, and serve the Lord. Now if you are unwilling to serve the Lord, choose this day whom you will serve, whether the gods your ancestors served in the region beyond the River or the gods of the Amorites in whose land you are living; but as for me and my household, we will serve the Lord.
>
> ~ Joshua 24:14–15 NRSV

Joshua did his job because God called him to do it. In the years in the desert serving as Moses's aide, Joshua had come to know the LORD. Joshua knew God was holy and trustworthy; the ultimate outcome of his assignment was not anything he had to worry about. The future was in God's good hands. Joshua was pleased to have played a part in God's plan and to have come to know God.

The Apostle Paul shared a similar sentiment in one of his last letters to Timothy, a devoted follower of Paul. Near the end of his life, Paul gave the following summary:

> As for me, I am already being poured out as a libation, and the time of my departure has come. I have fought the good fight, I have finished the race, I have kept the faith. From now on there

is reserved for me the crown of righteousness, which the Lord, the righteous judge, will give me on that day, and not only to me but also to all who have longed for his appearing.

~ 2 Timothy 4:6–8 NRSV

Centuries of Jewish history and a personal experience with Jesus meant Paul had come to know more than Joshua. Paul knew what Joshua must have hoped—in spite of the failures of the Israelites, God remained faithful and had brought forth Jesus Christ as Savior of the world. But even Paul did not see the end of the story—the ultimate return of Jesus to the world to bring justice and to establish His church. Neither have we yet seen the ultimate conclusion. We still walk in a fallen world where sin and evil reside and death still claims everyone.

How then do we claim peace and satisfaction for our jobs, whatever they are, when they are completed and "well done?" The answer: In the same way as Joshua and Paul. We find our satisfaction in God alone. Paul said,

> So, whether you eat or drink, or whatever you do, do everything for the glory of God. Give no offense to Jews or to Greeks or to the church of God, just as I try to please everyone in everything I do, not seeking my own advantage, but that of many, so that they may be saved.
>
> 1 Corinthians 10:31–33 NRSV

Paul also said,
> And let the peace of Christ rule in your hearts, to which indeed you were called in the one body. And be thankful. Let the word of Christ dwell in you richly; teach and admonish one another in all wisdom; and with gratitude in your hearts sing psalms, hymns, and spiritual songs to God. And whatever you do, in word or deed, do everything in the name of the Lord Jesus, giving thanks to God the Father through him.
>
> ~ Colossians 3:15–17 NRSV

Since we find our joy, our purpose, our fulfillment in Christ, shouldn't we make it our priority to grow in the knowledge of God and Jesus Christ? Consider what we also see from the passages of Scripture above and the book of Joshua. God is involved in the world, and His involvement is active and purposeful. God has a plan, and He is working his plan. God is holy and righteous, and the actions of men have consequences before Him. Even a little sin can be deadly, and a lost opportunity can lead to great regret.

I urge you to continue to study the Word of God, to fellowship with believers in a church of your choice, to pray, and seek to God's will for your life. As Joshua and Paul before you, make your first and true priority understanding God and being in fellowship with Him. All else will fail and fade away, but God will be forever. In Christ, we too will be forever with God.

REFLECTIONS FOR THE WEEK

1. This week, select a common task that you perform in your role in your organization and work "as for the Lord." Decide what differences in method and approach might be called for. Consider whether your level of job satisfaction changes as a result.

2. This week, record on your calendar the time you actually spend in getting to know God. If getting to know God were your first priority, how do you allocate your time to it?

PRAYER

Almighty God, I sometimes find it difficult to grasp Your involvement in the world in any physical way. It is easier for me to be philosophical about Your love, Your care, and Your plan. Sometimes I even find it repugnant to think that You influence people directly, moving resources and opportunities around Your world as You see fit for Your plan. Illuminate my mind through Your Scriptures and the guiding influence of Your Holy Spirit. Forgive my inability to grasp the true scope of Your plans, and forgive my ignorance to not even seek to understand Your purpose in my life. I humbly ask now, in this time of reflection and meditation, that You create in me a spark to know Your Word, to see a glimpse of Your majesty, and to submit my will to Yours. Guide me and protect me, Lord.

Amen

SEPTEMBER—WEEK THREE

RECOGNIZING WHEN CHANGE IS NECESSARY

Now the serpent was more crafty than any other wild animal that the Lord God had made. He said to the woman, "Did God say, 'You shall not eat from any tree in the garden'?" The woman said to the serpent, "We may eat of the fruit of the trees in the garden; but God said, 'You shall not eat of the fruit of the tree that is in the middle of the garden, nor shall you touch it, or you shall die.'" But the serpent said to the woman, "You will not die; for God knows that when you eat of it your eyes will be opened, and you will be like God, knowing good and evil." So when the woman saw that the tree was good for food, and that it was a delight to the eyes, and that the tree was to be desired to make one wise, she took of its fruit and ate; and she also gave some to her husband, who was with her, and he ate. Then the eyes of both were opened, and they knew that they were naked; and they sewed fig leaves together and made loincloths for themselves.

~ Genesis 3:1–7 NRSV

In the course of time Cain brought to the Lord an offering of the fruit of the ground, and Abel for his part brought of the firstlings of his flock, their fat portions. And the Lord had regard for Abel and his offering, but for Cain and his offering he had no regard. So Cain was very angry, and his countenance fell. The Lord said to Cain, "Why are you angry, and why has your countenance fallen? If you do well, will you not be accepted? And if you do not do well, sin is lurking at the door; its desire is for you, but you must master it."
Cain said to his brother Abel, "Let us go out to the field." And when they were in the field, Cain rose up against his brother Abel, and killed him. Then the Lord said to Cain, "Where is your brother Abel?" He said, "I do not know; am I my brother's keeper?" And the Lord said, "What have you done? Listen; your brother's blood is crying out to me from the ground! And now you are cursed from the ground, which has opened its mouth to

receive your brother's blood from your hand. When you till the ground, it will no longer yield to you its strength; you will be a fugitive and a wanderer on the earth." Cain said to the Lord, "My punishment is greater than I can bear! Today you have driven me away from the soil, and I shall be hidden from your face; I shall be a fugitive and a wanderer on the earth, and anyone who meets me may kill me." Then the Lord said to him, "Not so! Whoever kills Cain will suffer a sevenfold vengeance." And the Lord put a mark on Cain, so that no one who came upon him would kill him. Then Cain went away from the presence of the Lord, and settled in the land of Nod, east of Eden.

~ Genesis 4:3–16 NRSV

Then the Jews began to complain about [Jesus] because he said, "I am the bread that came down from heaven." They were saying, "Is not this Jesus, the son of Joseph, whose father and mother we know? How can he now say, 'I have come down from heaven'?" Jesus answered them, "Do not complain among yourselves. No one can come to me unless drawn by the Father who sent me; and I will raise that person up on the last day. It is written in the prophets, 'And they shall all be taught by God.' Everyone who has heard and learned from the Father comes to me."

~ John 6:41–45 NRSV

John P. Kotter, a professor at Harvard Business School, has spent a large part of his career studying how businesses implement organizational change. In his article, "Leading Change: Why Transformation Efforts Fail" (Harvard Business Review, Mar/Apr 1995), Mr. Kotter states, "These efforts have gone under many banners: total quality management, reengineering, right sizing, restructuring, cultural change, and turnaround. But, in almost every case, the basic goal has been the same: to make fundamental changes in how business is conducted in order to help cope with a new, more challenging market environment." In the balance of the article, Mr. Kotter identifies eight errors that commonly occur whenever a transformation effort fails. Those are the following: not establishing a great enough sense of urgency; not creating a powerful enough guiding coalition; lacking a vision; undercommunicating the vision by a factor of ten; not removing obstacles to the new vision; not systematically planning for and creating short-term wins; declaring victory too soon; and not anchoring changes in the corporation's culture. Mr. Kotter's article illustrates change management is "big business."

Why is change management such big business? Change management is big business because the stakes associated with its success or failure are extremely high. Leadership decides to embark upon a fundamental change in how business is conducted in response to a perceived crisis. The crisis is what prods the action. Yet, even when the leadership and employees are aware of the serious consequences the organization will suffer if an effort to adopt change fails, Mr. Kotter's work found more failures than successes. Why? Mr. Kotter points to the answer by implication through his eight common errors—people are the instruments of change, and people are change-resistant.

This conclusion is also drawn by Mark J. Dawson and Mark L. Jones in an article entitled "Human Change Management: Herding Cats" (published on the PwC website pwc.com). In their article, Messrs Dawson and Jones note about "75% of organizational change programs fail, largely because employees feel left out of the process and end up lacking the motivation, skills, and knowledge to adopt new systems and procedures." Messrs Dawson and Jones go on to say that "organizations don't adapt to change; their people do."

Prosci Research, an independent research company specializing in the areas of change management, developed a model to achieve successful change management for all types of organizations called the ADKAR Model. The ADKAR Model focuses on the people side of change with the intention of eliminating many of the negative side effects associated whenever change is introduced within an organization. ADKAR is an acrostic for five inter-related components of successful change management:

- Awareness: Simply stated, an organization must be made aware of the need for change—the fundamental reasons why the change is required. For Mr. Kotter, this awareness takes the form of instilling a sense of urgency for the change process.

- Desire: Leadership must translate awareness into desire. The need for change must answer the personal question, "what's in it for me?"
- Knowledge: A method must be selected and employed to accomplish the steps necessary to effect change.
- Ability: Ability translates into training employees to do work in a different way as a result of the change.
- Reinforcement: During a change process, as Mr. Kotter noted, early successes are key. Even if only on a small scale, it is important to identify and celebrate wins early. This reinforces the new behaviors and processes.

My purpose in calling your attention to these authors and ideas on implementing change was not to recommend their methods or ideas, although I find their work compelling. But since "change management" is such a big business, there are many consultants, ideas, practices, and theories that speak to the problems associated with winning when it comes to effecting change in an organization. If you are about to embark upon a change effort in your organization, you would do well to research different points of view to select your model for success. Rather, it was my intention to point out that people are fundamentally opposed to being told they have to change anything. In the end, successful change within an organization requires convincing many people that the change will be beneficial to them even more than convincing them the change will benefit the organization.

If people are resistant to being told they have to change or should change something about themselves, they have little difficulty in initiating for themselves a change they deem to be desirable. We can see these human characteristics at work from the beginning of time in the passages above from the book of Genesis. Here we see three aspects of how change is willfully accepted or rejected in people. Those aspects are (1) moving in a new direction as a result of a change in thinking or attitude, (2) refusing to acknowledge a change is necessary in spite of evidence that without change certain behaviors will be destructive, and (3) the positive aspects of accepting the need to change in spite of difficulty.

MOVING IN A NEW DIRECTION

In Genesis 3:1-7, Eve is contemplating a number of new ideas. Simply stated, Eve is changing her mind about certain things she knew about God and what she had been told. The author of the book of James records the process of sin taking control of a person's life: "No one, when tempted, should say, 'I am being tempted by God'; for God cannot be tempted by evil and he himself tempts no one. But one is tempted by one's own desire, being lured and enticed by it; then, when that desire has conceived, it gives birth to sin, and that sin, when it is fully grown, gives birth to death" (James 1:13-15 NRSV). Eve allowed the thought to cross her mind that God was withholding something good from her. She allowed herself to think she could disobey God without consequences. Then, she decided to act upon her new ideas. Worse, Eve decided to share her new way of thinking with Adam.

The human race learned a valuable lesson as a result: Not all change is good.

The human race also learned there are consequences associated with change. The first recorded change in history ended very badly. Perhaps as a result, Adam and Eve became change resistant—and so did we. In the words of Mark Twain, "The cat that sat on the hot stove lid will not sit upon a hot stove lid again. But he won't sit upon a cold stove lid, either."

What must life have been like for Adam and Eve after God put them out of the Garden of Eden? The Bible does not record any specific stories of their lives or their relationship with God, but we can discern God stayed in touch with them because Eve gave praise to God upon the birth of her son Cain (Genesis 4:1). And Adam and Eve must have spoken to their sons about God because both Cain and Abel had awareness of God when they took offerings to Him.

But somewhere in the family upbringing of Cain, a time must have come when feelings or emotions of discontent were established, and sin was provided a foothold to lay waiting for its opportunity. In Cain's life, somewhere and somehow, a sense of discontent with God over the toils of life occurred. Perhaps Cain felt obligated to bring his offering, but Abel brought an offering out of love and respect. Where would Cain have gained some understanding that it was possible to question God unless it came from his family? Where would Cain have developed a belief of God's unfairness if not from his family?

STUBBORN REFUSAL TO ACKNOWLEDGE THE NEED TO CHANGE

The second aspect of change is now demonstrated. God, knowing Cain's heart, gives Cain some good advice. In love, God says, "Why are you distressed, and why is your face fallen? Surely, if you do right, there is uplift. But if you do not do right sin couches at the door; its urge is toward you, yet you can be its master" (from the Hebrew Holy Scriptures Tanakh, Genesis 4.6–7).

Cain (like almost all of us) did not like to be told what he should do. Cain did not change. Instead, Cain went from bad to worse and committed the first murder. Suddenly, God's pronouncement on Eve that "I will greatly increase your pains in childbearing" (Genesis 3:16) took on an entirely different meaning. Not only did Eve experience physical pain in child delivery, she further experienced the pain of the death of a son.

God confronted Cain about Abel. Rather than repenting of his crime and pleading with God for forgiveness, Cain fell even further away from God. In spite of Cain's stubborn, sinful obstinacy, God did not require Cain's death. God actually left open the door for Cain to seek forgiveness and restoration of fellowship with God. Notice in God's judgment He invoked a curse on the ground, taking away Cain's livelihood and declaring that Cain would be a restless wanderer. But God did not say Cain was cut off from God.

How did Cain respond to God's judgment? First, he cried the punishment was "more than I can bear." No sorrow. No remorse. And it seems clear Cain did not want a relationship with God. Cain said, "Today you have driven me away from the soil, and I shall be hidden from your face;

I shall be a fugitive and a wanderer on the earth, and anyone who meets me may kill me" (Genesis 4:14 NRSV).

Cain's assertion was silly and further belied the glory of God. Cain could not be hidden from God—God would always know where Cain was just as He knew about Cain's crime and the sins of Adam and Eve when they were hiding in the Garden. In paraphrasing God's judgment, Cain revealed his attitude toward God. Cain did not attribute forgiveness, compassion, or love as characteristics of God.

Cain never turned back to God. And, as recorded in Genesis 4 and 5, Cain's progeny continued along a path of increased separation from God. Ultimately, Cain's side of the family tree was destroyed in the Flood.

ACCEPTANCE THAT CHANGE WILL BE BENEFICIAL

The third illustration of change is revealed in the story of Seth and his progeny. After the death of Abel, the Bible records Eve conceived and had another son whom she named Seth. The story of human civilization takes a divisive turn with the birth of Seth. As opposed to Cain and his offspring, Seth remained close to God. Perhaps Adam and Eve had finally gained wisdom and insight into God and the relationship between God and men in the years since leaving the Garden and in the death of Abel. Perhaps they had recoiled at the sin growing rampantly in the family of Cain. However it occurred, Seth's family line began to actively seek after the Lord. The key difference in the lives of Cain and Seth is found in Genesis 4:26 NRSV. "To Seth also a son was born, and he named him Enosh. At that time people began to invoke the name of the Lord."

What was the result of Seth seeking to learn about God and seeking His favor? Seth's family produced Enoch, a man considered righteous and who walked with God for 300 years before God took him (Genesis 5:24). Enoch produced Noah, and out of Noah was born all the generations of man after the Flood. Cain's generation was obliterated.

Sin came into the world when Eve changed her mind. Because Cain would not change his mind, sin overtook the earth and God brought a flood to cleanse the earth of the wickedness running rampant upon it. Because Seth changed his mind about "who" God was, his generation began to call upon the name of the LORD. As a result, some lives were deemed faithful and righteous by God.

Isaiah speaks with the voice of God about our reluctance to change from our sins:

> *O that you had paid attention to my commandments!*
> *Then your prosperity would have been like a river,*
> *and your success like the waves of the sea;*
> *your offspring would have been like the sand,*
> *and your descendants like its grains;*
> *their name would never be cut off*
> *or destroyed from before me.*
> *"There is no peace," says the Lord, "for the wicked."*
> ~ Isaiah 48:18-19, 22 NRSV

Since God never changes, these words from Isaiah are as applicable to us as they were to Cain and as they were to the Israelites living in their sins. God cries out to those who will hear—but we do not listen.

As a leader, you will likely face a crisis that will prompt you to begin the arduous process of leading your organization through a time of change. Your people will resist adopting new behaviors unless you can prevail upon them that the change will be good for them. This will frustrate you. But as a leader, you must overcome the human tendency to resist change when change is necessary.

When something (the Scriptures, a sermon, a Christian friend) implores and urges you to observe some aspect of your life that needs to be changed, remember your human nature. Remember Eve, Cain, and Seth. Remember to call upon the name of the LORD to give you courage, character, resolve, and a willingness to change.

REFLECTIONS FOR THE WEEK

1. Is there something going on in your life, right now, that seems to be urging you to consider a different path? If so, consider that God is attempting to get your attention and to encourage you to change direction.

2. Read Matthew 5, 6, and 7 (the Sermon on the Mount). What sayings of Jesus conflict with your attitudes or behaviors?

3. Read Revelation 2:1–7 where Jesus urges the church in Ephesus to change and regain its love and zeal for Him. God cares about our actions, but He also cares about our relationship with Him. In fact, our relationship with Him is of first importance. Is there anything you need to change to bring Christ more fully into the center of your life?

PRAYER

Dear God, thank You for Your patience in dealing with me. Thank You for caring about me and urging me to change my ways when they are harming me, harming others, or blocking my relationship with You. Jesus often said, "Let him who has ears, hear." Grant that I may have the eyes to see and the ears to hear so that I might understand with my heart and turn to You and be healed.

Amen

SEPTEMBER—WEEK FOUR

ACCUMULATING SUFFICIENT RESOURCES TO ACHIEVE THE GOALS AND OBJECTIVES OF THE ORGANIZATION

> *The Lord is my shepherd, I shall not want.*
> *He makes me lie down in green pastures;*
> *he leads me beside still waters;*
> *he restores my soul.*
> *He leads me in right paths*
> *for his name's sake.*
> *Even though I walk through the darkest valley*
> *I fear no evil;*
> *for you are with me;*
> *your rod and your staff—*
> *they comfort me.*
> *You prepare a table before me*
> *in the presence of my enemies;*
> *you anoint my head with oil;*
> *my cup overflows.*
> *Surely goodness and mercy shall follow me*
> *all the days of my life,*
> *and I shall dwell in the house of the Lord*
> *my whole life long.*
>
> ~ Psalm 23 NRSV

Therefore I tell you, do not worry about your life, what you will eat or what you will drink, or about your body, what you will wear. Is not life more than food, and the body more than clothing? Look at the birds of the air; they neither sow nor reap nor gather into barns, and yet your heavenly Father feeds them. Are you not of more value than they? And can any of you by worrying add a single hour to your span of life?

~ Matthew 6:25–27 NRSV

An enterprise needs resources to propel it toward fulfillment of its goals and objectives. Without sufficient resources, made available at the right time and in the right place, the mission of the enterprise will be in danger. Ensuring sufficient resources are available to the enterprise is thus one of the most important jobs of a leader.

And while it is true all enterprises need resources in order to achieve goals and objectives, individuals need resources too. Abraham Maslow (1908-1970), a professor of psychology at Brandeis University and Brooklyn College, became interested in studying the needs of humans and how different needs were pursued. The results of his work were published in 1943.

Maslow's work led him to conclude there are certain needs common to all people. He also concluded people pursue needs in a certain order, seeking basic needs for survival first before seeking other needs that are important for happiness and well-being.

Maslow grouped human needs in order of priority as **physiological** needs (breathing, food, water, sex, sleep, homeostasis, excretion), **safety** (security of body, employment, resources, morality, the family, health, property), **love and belonging** (friendship, family, sexual intimacy), **esteem** (self-esteem, confidence, achievement, respect of others, respect by others), and **self-actualization** (morality, creativity, spontaneity, problem solving, lack of prejudice, acceptance of facts).

Maslow's list of human needs is typically illustrated as a pyramid with needs associated with the minimum requirements for living resting at the bottom and needs associated with "betterment" of the individual at the top—hence his list is called a "hierarchy" of needs.

The Bible in many cases provides corroboration of much of Maslow's work—for example, God created the world and everything in it, including the food we eat, and instructed man to work it and subdue it (satisfying the physiological needs). God instituted marriage and intimacy and instructed man to "be fruitful and multiply" (satisfying the needs for love and belonging). God gave man moral laws and directives designed to create order and security (satisfying the need for safety). God gave man an intellect and the desire to achieve and learn so that he could fulfill the purpose for which he was created (satisfying the needs of esteem and self-actualization). Jesus directed his disciples and all Christians to love each other, care for each other's needs, uplift each other and instruct each other, and Jesus gave us the example of serving and sacrificing ourselves for the good of others (satisfying the needs of love and belonging, esteem, and self-actualization).

As Christians, therefore, we can see Maslow's work has some credibility. Jesus knew our basic needs for food, shelter, and clothing were vitally important, and He spoke about them in His Sermon on the Mount (Matthew 6:31–34). But paradoxically, Jesus urged His listeners to not "worry" over such things. Jesus preached that God the Father knows of our needs, including the basic necessities of life, and God will provide them to His people. Therefore, Jesus urged His listeners to "strive first for the kingdom of God and his righteousness, and all these things will be given to you as well" (Matthew 6:33 NRSV).

The implication for Christians is God will work out the details in providing for our basic human needs when we focus on Him, seek to obey Him, and do His will in this world, including the work He has called us to do. And with this conclusion, we begin to shift away from following Maslow's theory.

Maslow puts the need for self-actualization at the top of his hierarchy and concludes we only focus on those *higher* needs when the other *lower* needs have been met. (The self-actualization needs for Maslow included morality, although he did not include any discussion of God and the worship of God in his list of human needs.) To Maslow, if you are hungry or thirsty you will, in fact, not concentrate on anything else until the basic need is met.

But Jesus said we must subdue the human desire to satisfy the need for food, shelter, and clothing and focus instead on knowing God. Jesus implied the same message elsewhere in Scripture when He instructed Martha to consider how Mary (her sister) had made a wiser choice in listening to the words of Jesus than Martha had in being busy preparing a meal to serve to him and becoming impatient with Mary for not offering help (Luke 10:38–42).

Overcoming the urge to satisfy basic human needs is not something easily accomplished—it requires supernatural help from God. The good news is God is willing to provide us with supernatural help if we want to "seek first his kingdom." God provides supernatural help to us when we exercise spiritual disciplines, particularly the spiritual disciplines of faith, hope, and love. And when we practice the spiritual disciplines of faith, hope, and love, we gain access to the most important resource we need to equip us as leaders, regardless the nature of our work. We gain God's blessings in abundance in all we do when we pursue faith, hope, and love.

The Apostle Paul spoke of the spiritual disciplines everyone should strive for in his letter to the Corinthian church when he said, "And now faith, hope, and love abide, these three; and the greatest of these is love" (1 Corinthians 13:13 NRSV). Here is how these spiritual disciplines help us receive the blessings of God.

1. **Faith**: Faith is the first spiritual discipline believers obtain. Faith is important because faith is the basis of our salvation. This is clearly evident in the New Testament. But even in the Old Testament, faith (believing that what God promised or said was absolutely true in spite of evidence to the contrary) was blessed by God. Jesus healed people based upon their faith that they would be healed. Jesus criticized His disciples for times when their faith was insufficient, and He urged His disciples to have faith (trust) in Him as they would trust in the Father.

> And he (Abraham) believed the Lord; and the Lord reckoned it to him as righteousness.
>
> ~ Genesis 15:6 NRSV

> You keep him in perfect peace whose mind is stayed on you, because he trusts in you.
>
> ~ Isaiah 26:3 ESV

> Do not let your hearts be troubled. Believe in God, believe also in me.
>
> ~ John 14:1 NRSV

> For by grace you have been saved through faith, and this is not your own doing; it is the gift of God.
>
> ~ Ephesians 2:8 NRSV

But now, apart from law, the righteousness of God has been disclosed, and is attested by the law and the prophets, the righteousness of God through faith in Jesus Christ for all who believe.

~ Romans 3:21–22 NRSV

Therefore, since we are justified by faith, we have peace with God through our Lord Jesus Christ, through whom we have obtained access to this grace in which we stand; and we boast in our hope of sharing the glory of God.

~ Romans 5:1–2 NRSV

Then he touched their eyes and said, "According to your faith let it be done to you." And their eyes were opened.

~ Matthew 9:29–30a NRSV

Then Jesus answered her, "Woman, great is your faith! Let it be done for you as you wish." And her daughter was healed instantly.

~ Matthew 15:28 NRSV

There is no doubt faith in increasing measure is a valuable resource for the Christian leader. What is the source of faith? The source of faith is hearing the Word of God. "So faith comes from what is heard, and what is heard comes through the word of Christ" (Romans 10:17 NRSV). Faith is increased when you read and meditate on the Word of God and hear it preached.

2. **Hope**: Hope is the evidence of our faith and the bedrock of our ability to do what God asks us to do. Because of hope we are able to face uncertainty and trials, and to persevere and endure in our faith throughout our lifetime. Hope allows a Christian to stand in the face of uncertainty, trusting God to keep His promises. The Holy Spirit is the source of hope in our lives. Hope springs to life when God the Holy Spirit testifies with our inner self, our "spirit," that we have been saved and our future is certain.

We boast in our hope of sharing the glory of God. And not only that, but we also boast in our sufferings, knowing that suffering produces endurance, and endurance produces character, and character produces hope, and hope does not disappoint us, because God's love has been poured into our hearts through the Holy Spirit that has been given to us.

~ Romans 5:2b–5 NRSV

May the God of hope fill you with all joy and peace in believing, so that you may abound in hope by the power of the Holy Spirit.

~ Romans 15:13 NRSV

In the same way, when God desired to show even more clearly to the heirs of the promise the unchangeable character of his purpose, he guaranteed it by an oath, so that through two unchangeable things, in which it is impossible that God would prove false, we who have taken refuge might be strongly encouraged to seize the hope set before us. We have this hope, a sure and steadfast anchor of the soul.

Hebrews 6:17–19a NRSV

A Christian leader possessing hope in increasing measure will be able to meet conflict and danger head-on with resolute courage. Resolute courage is a character trait of great significance to any leader. But our resolute courage is not of ourselves. We stand not on the substance of our work, our prowess, our opinion of right or wrong, the nobility of our cause, or the odds against us. Rather, we stand in hope on God's strength and His promises.

The Apostle Paul wrote,

> What then are we to say about these things? If God is for us, who is against us? He who did not withhold his own Son, but gave him up for all of us, will he not with him also give us everything else? Who will bring any charge against God's elect? It is God who justifies. Who is to condemn? It is Christ Jesus, who died, yes, who was raised, who is at the right hand of God, who indeed intercedes for us. Who will separate us from the love of Christ? Will hardship, or distress, or persecution, or famine, or nakedness, or peril, or sword? As it is written,
> "For your sake we are being killed all day long;
> we are accounted as sheep to be slaughtered."
> No, in all these things we are more than conquerors through him who loved us. For I am convinced that neither death, nor life, nor angels, nor rulers, nor things present, nor things to come, nor powers, nor height, nor depth, nor anything else in

all creation, will be able to separate us from the love of God in Christ Jesus our Lord.
> ~ Romans 8:31-39 NRSV

The Apostle Paul possessed hope in increasing measure and used it as an invaluable resource in completing his work.

3. **Love**: Love proves our lives have been transformed into the image of Christ and that we have fellowship with Him. And if we have fellowship with Christ, we have fellowship with God the Father. Love presents opportunities where there were none before.

Jesus said,
> "If you love me, you will keep my commandments."
> ~ John 14:15 NRSV

> "Those who love me will keep my word, and my Father will love them, and we will come to them and make our home with them. Whoever does not love me does not keep my words; and the word that you hear is not mine, but is from the Father who sent me."
> ~ John 14:23-24 NRSV

> "This is my commandment, that you love one another as I have loved you."
> ~ John 15:12 NRSV

From the Apostle Paul:
> Love is patient; love is kind; love is not envious or boastful or arrogant or rude. It does not insist on its own way; it is not irritable or resentful; it does not rejoice in wrongdoing, but rejoices in the truth. It bears all things, believes all things, hopes all things, endures all things. Love never ends.
> ~ 1 Corinthians 13:4-8a NRSV

Who would not desire a personal resource that always protects, always trusts, always hopes, always perseveres and never fails?

How does a leader gain increasing measures of Christian love—the type of love of which Paul wrote in the passage of Scripture above? Here again, the answer is found in Scripture.

The Bible tells us our capacity for Christian love occurs because of God. "We love because he first loved us" (1 John 4:19 NRSV). Our awareness of the depth of the Father's love for us sparks a desire to love in return.

Then, as the Holy Spirit molds us and shapes us, we grow in Christian love as we grow in the likeness of Christ. "Beloved, let us love one another, because love is from God; everyone who loves is born of God and knows God" (1 John 4:7 NRSV).

Further, Jesus was the personification of love and our great example. If there is one admonition I would give everyone, it is this: pursue Christ as an objective. Seek Him, pursue Him, discover Him, desire Him, and love Him.

Read the passage of Scripture above substituting the name Jesus in place of love wherever it occurs in 1 Corinthians 13:4–8. When love as a valuable resource is viewed in this way, we realize Jesus always protects, always trusts, always hopes, always perseveres, and never fails. We love because Christ first loved us.

Through **faith** in Christ and **hope** in the promises of God, we will grow more and more into the likeness of Christ. Whatever you undertake to complete as a leader in your business or your family—whether a problem, a goal, an opportunity, an objective, a mission, or a task—whatever it is you seek to accomplish, it will be easier to accomplish when you have **Christ's love** living in you. The ability to gain increasing measures of faith and hope is enabled only through awareness of the surpassing greatness of Christ's love for His people.

With faith, hope, and love, we can truly say with Paul, "I can do all things through him who strengthens me" (Philippians 4:13 NRSV).

REFLECTIONS FOR THE WEEK

1. A common business quotation is "Hope is not much of a strategy." What is it about Christian hope that would make for a good strategy?

2. The Greek language used in the New Testament had four different words for love that allowed for a distinction between sexual love (eros), family love as between a father and a child or between family members in general (storge), brotherly love as in friendship and affection (philia), and godly love—a love that never changes and is self-giving (agape). The Apostle Paul provided a comprehensive definition of Christian love in 1 Corinthians 13:8. Which of those attributes do you find the most difficult to display in your interactions with others?

PRAYER

Holy Spirit, impress upon my spirit the love of Christ that allows me to love. Convince me of the faithfulness of Christ that gives me hope in all circumstances. Use the events in my life to strengthen my faith that God is trustworthy and will meet all of my needs, even in what looks like hopeless situations. Finally, quicken in my mind opportunities for witnessing to others the basis of my faith, my hope, and my love so that the kingdom of God is advanced upon the earth.

Amen

SEPTEMBER—WEEK FIVE

THE END OF THE THIRD QUARTER

ACCUMULATING SUFFICIENT RESOURCES TO ACHIEVE THE GOALS AND OBJECTIVES OF THE ORGANIZATION

> For the kingdom of heaven is like a landowner who went out early in the morning to hire laborers for his vineyard. After agreeing with the laborers for the usual daily wage, he sent them into his vineyard. When he went out about nine o'clock, he saw others standing idle in the marketplace; and he said to them, "You also go into the vineyard, and I will pay you whatever is right." So they went. When he went out again about noon and about three o'clock, he did the same. And about five o'clock he went out and found others standing around; and he said to them, "Why are you standing here idle all day?" They said to him, "Because no one has hired us." He said to them, "You also go into the vineyard." When evening came, the owner of the vineyard said to his manager, "Call the laborers and give them their pay, beginning with the last and then going to the first." When those hired about five o'clock came, each of them received the usual daily wage. Now when the first came, they thought they would receive more; but each of them also received the usual daily wage. And when they received it, they grumbled against the landowner, saying, "These last worked only one hour, and you have made them equal to us who have borne the burden of the day and the scorching heat." But he replied to one of them, "Friend, I am doing you no wrong; did you not agree with me for the usual daily wage? Take what belongs to you and go; I choose to give to this last the same as I give to you. Am I not allowed to do what I choose with what belongs to me? Or are you envious because I am generous?"
>
> ~ Matthew 20:1–15 NRSV

SEPTEMBER—WEEK FIVE

> For who sees anything different in you? What do you have that you did not receive? And if you received it, why do you boast as if it were not a gift?
> ~ 1 Corinthians 4:7 NRSV

When my son was three years old, we enrolled him in our church's preschool program. He would go to preschool for a half-day, three days a week. I do not remember anything he learned in preschool except for a daily prayer he taught us to say before meals. Courtesy of my three-year-old son, here is that prayer:

"Lord, we thank you for our food,
for rest and home, and all things good.
For wind, and rain, and sun above.
But most of all, for those we love.
Amen."

I did not understand then, but I do now, the importance of learning how to say "thank you" to God. And I am grateful for the wisdom possessed by someone in our old church to instruct my son, and me, in the importance of gratitude.

I believe there are three great spiritual resources every leader should strive for: faith, hope, and love. Faith, hope, and love provide the foundation upon which God will mold and shape your life. They will enable you to accomplish things you did not imagine, and to become more than you envisioned.

But there is also another spiritual resource every leader should aspire to accumulate in their heart that is closely associated with faith, hope, and love. That resource is **gratitude.** I am not speaking about the common, everyday, earthly politeness that shares the name gratitude. Too often, being grateful and expressing gratitude is little more than a platitude. What I am speaking about is godly gratitude.

What is godly gratitude in comparison with any other type of gratitude? Merriam-Webster's dictionary defines gratitude as the state of being thankful. Godly gratitude and worldly gratitude share that fundamental definition.

But godly gratitude is fundamentally different in quality because the object toward which the gratitude is being offered is God.

Godly gratitude is grounded in a humble spirit and enlightened by godly wisdom. Godly gratitude enhances a person's quality of life and provides a resource to meet and handle all new situations—even the most difficult ones.

Gratitude, standing alone, is a character trait we recognize and admire in others. Godly gratitude, on the other hand, does not stand alone, but works with faith, hope, and love to transform a Christian's life.

Godly gratitude interacts with, sustains, and propels faith, hope, and love. Faith combined with gratitude yields courage; hope combined with gratitude yields confidence. And love, when combined with gratitude, grows into the quality of love described by the Apostle Paul in his famous discourse on love found in 1 Corinthians 13.

Godly gratitude is grounded in humility. We know from Scripture that God approves of a humble spirit.

> And all of you must clothe yourselves with humility in your dealings with one another, for "God opposes the proud, but gives grace to the humble."
>
> ~ 1 Peter 5:5b NRSV

> *Good and upright is the Lord;*
> *therefore he instructs sinners in the way.*
> *He leads the humble in what is right,*
> *and teaches the humble his way.*
>
> ~ Psalm 25:8–9 NRSV

> But you are not to be called rabbi, for you have one teacher, and you are all students. And call no one your father on earth, for you have one Father—the one in heaven. Nor are you to be called instructors, for you have one instructor, the Messiah. The greatest among you will be your servant. All who exalt themselves will be humbled, and all who humble themselves will be exalted.
>
> ~ Matthew 23:8–12 NRSV

The Apostle Paul was keenly aware of God's approval of humility. The passage above from 1 Corinthians 4:7 clearly illustrates godly humility—the foundation for godly gratitude. "What do you have that you did not receive?"

Paul was pointing out to the Corinthians they should not quarrel over which messenger of the gospel (in this case Paul or Apollos) had more authority or better credentials. The only thing of importance was the message of salvation itself. And that message came from Jesus and was made perfect only in Jesus. There was no basis for anyone to claim anything about it. Paul was saying, "be glad you received the message, just as everyone else who received the message should be glad."

As Christians we focus on humility and gratitude, for without Christ there would be no salvation. Christ is the beginning of everything true for a Christian. All of our faith, our hope, and our love flow from Him. Personal awareness that God supplies everything we need, combined with a posture of humility, allows our gratitude to flow upwards to God, and it is pleasing to Him.

While godly gratitude has as its genesis humility of character, it is **godly wisdom** that shapes humility and creates the framework in which a Christian learns to appreciate all God has done and to eagerly anticipate what else He is doing. Godly wisdom provides the prism through which our lives and the substance of our experiences can be truthfully and fully observed.

> But the wisdom from above is first pure, then peaceable, gentle, willing to yield, full of mercy and good fruits, without a trace of partiality or hypocrisy.
>
> ~ James 3:17 NRSV

> And let the peace of Christ rule in your hearts, to which indeed you were called in the one body. And be thankful. Let the word of Christ dwell in you richly; teach and admonish one another in all wisdom; and with gratitude in your hearts sing psalms, hymns, and spiritual songs to God. And whatever you do, in word or deed, do everything in the name of the Lord Jesus, giving thanks to God the Father through him.
>
> ~ Colossians 3:15-17 NRSV

> *I, wisdom, live with prudence,*
> *and I attain knowledge and discretion.*
> *The fear of the Lord is hatred of evil.*
> *Pride and arrogance and the way of evil*
> *and perverted speech I hate.*
> *I have good advice and sound wisdom;*
> *I have insight, I have strength.*
> *By me kings reign,*
> *and rulers decree what is just;*
> *by me rulers rule,*
> *and nobles, all who govern rightly.*
> *I love those who love me,*
> *and those who seek me diligently find me.*
> ~ Proverbs 8:12–17 NRSV

Godly gratitude is grounded in humility and informed by wisdom. God approves of godly gratitude and blesses it. Conversely, God condemns ingratitude in harsh and unambiguous language. Scripturally, the conversation about gratitude is not associated with earthly politeness and graciousness but is all about godly gratitude.

Matthew 20:1–15, quoted at the start of this chapter, is one example of God's displeasure in ingratitude. Buried in the grumbling of the laborers who went to work early was their sense of unfairness. They were not grateful for the work at the agreed upon wage. They were not humble in heart. Their pride prevented them from rejoicing in the fortune of other laborers who needed work and wages too. Their pride prevented them from recognizing and honoring a man who had a generous spirit and belittled his right to do with his own property whatever he desired to do.

Here are other examples of God's displeasure on those without godly gratitude in their hearts.

> A son honors his father, and servants their master. If then I am a father, where is the honor due me? And if I am a master, where is the respect due me? says the Lord of hosts to you, O priests, who despise my name. You say, "How have we despised your name?" By offering polluted food on my altar. And you say, "How have we polluted it?" By thinking that the Lord's table may

be despised. When you offer blind animals in sacrifice, is that not wrong? And when you offer those that are lame or sick, is that not wrong? Try presenting that to your governor; will he be pleased with you or show you favor? says the Lord of hosts.

~ Malachi 1:6-8 NRSV

Now when the Pharisee who had invited him saw it, he said to himself, "If this man were a prophet, he would have known who and what kind of woman this is who is touching him—that she is a sinner." Jesus spoke up and said to him, "Simon, I have something to say to you." "Teacher," he replied, "speak." "A certain creditor had two debtors; one owed five hundred denarii, and the other fifty. When they could not pay, he canceled the debts for both of them. Now which of them will love him more?" Simon answered, "I suppose the one for whom he canceled the greater debt." And Jesus said to him, "You have judged rightly." Then turning toward the woman, he said to Simon, "Do you see this woman? I entered your house; you gave me no water for my feet, but she has bathed my feet with her tears and dried them with her hair. You gave me no kiss, but from the time I came in she has not stopped kissing my feet. You did not anoint my head with oil, but she has anointed my feet with ointment. Therefore, I tell you, her sins, which were many, have been forgiven; hence she has shown great love. But the one to whom little is forgiven, loves little."

~ Luke 7:39-47 NRSV

When he saw them, he said to them, "Go and show yourselves to the priests." And as they went, they were made clean. Then one of them, when he saw that he was healed, turned back, praising God with a loud voice. He prostrated himself at Jesus' feet and thanked him. And he was a Samaritan. Then Jesus asked, "Were not ten made clean? But the other nine, where are they? Was none of them found to return and give praise to God except this foreigner?"

~ Luke 17:14-18 NRSV

Why is godly gratitude so important to God? I believe godly gratitude demonstrates to God our faith in Him (we believe Him), our hope in

Him (we trust Him), and our love for Him (He is our all, in all). Godly gratitude displaces pride and hinders our propping up idols that would supplant God's sovereign role in our lives. Godly gratitude gives God all the glory—for everything.

J. Ellsworth Kalas, former president of Asbury Theological Seminary, wrote a book entitled, *I Bought a House on Gratitude Street: and Other Insights on the Good Life*. Kalas writes, "I have learned never to leave gratitude to chance. My place on Gratitude Street depends on consistent awareness. So each morning, within the first half-hour of the day, I list the three or four matters from the previous day for which I am most grateful." Kalas goes on to say, "Gratitude is love with a memory." Kalas is someone who has become familiar with the benefits of living a life of gratitude, particularly toward God.

The advice of Kalas to make a practice and a habit of remembering events and things for which he is grateful is good advice. Since Christians are called (Philippians 4:4-7) to be anxious about nothing, and to be thankful about everything, maintaining a memory of God's blessings and promises and His prior acts in our lives allows us to live grateful, peaceful, joyful, and abundant lives.

A very good friend of mine developed a list of bedrock promises of God that comfort him in difficult times. I think he is right to always know and have accessible in memory God's promises and blessings that are real and true for each person. Here are some of the items on my list:

1. **We have been adopted as heirs of God, and nothing can rob us of that heritage.**

> For in Christ Jesus you are all children of God through faith. As many of you as were baptized into Christ have clothed yourselves with Christ.
> ~ Galatians 3:26-27 NRSV

> For you did not receive a spirit of slavery to fall back into fear, but you have received a spirit of adoption. When we cry, "Abba! Father!" it is that very Spirit bearing witness with our spirit that we are children of God, and if children, then heirs, heirs

of God and joint heirs with Christ—if, in fact, we suffer with him so that we may also be glorified with him.

~ Romans 8:15–17 NRSV

2. **God is with us in all trials and will uphold us through His power and strength. Christ will never leave us or forsake us.**

He has said, "I will never leave you or forsake you." So we can say with confidence,
"The Lord is my helper;
 I will not be afraid.
What can anyone do to me?"

~ Hebrews 13:5a, 6 NRSV

I am the good shepherd. I know my own and my own know me, just as the Father knows me and I know the Father. And I lay down my life for the sheep

~ John 10:14–15 NRSV

3. **God hears our prayers and answers them.**

Beloved, if our hearts do not condemn us, we have boldness before God; and we receive from him whatever we ask, because we obey his commandments and do what pleases him.

~ 1 John 3:21–22 NRSV

Is there anyone among you who, if your child asks for bread, will give a stone? Or if the child asks for a fish, will give a snake? If you then, who are evil, know how to give good gifts to your children, how much more will your Father in heaven give good things to those who ask him!

~ Matthew 7:9–11 NRSV

4. **The Holy Spirit has been given to us. The Holy Spirit, living within us, provides immense benefits to us in our everyday lives.**

Likewise the Spirit helps us in our weakness; for we do not know how to pray as we ought, but that very Spirit intercedes with sighs too deep for words. And God, who searches the heart, knows what is the mind of the Spirit, because the Spirit intercedes for the saints according to the will of God.

~ Romans 8:26–27 NRSV

> For this reason I bow my knees before the Father, from whom every family in heaven and on earth takes its name. I pray that, according to the riches of his glory, he may grant that you may be strengthened in your inner being with power through his Spirit, and that Christ may dwell in your hearts through faith, as you are being rooted and grounded in love. I pray that you may have the power to comprehend, with all the saints, what is the breadth and length and height and depth, and to know the love of Christ that surpasses knowledge, so that you may be filled with all the fullness of God.
> ~ Ephesians 3:14–19 NRSV

> But the Advocate, the Holy Spirit, whom the Father will send in my name, will teach you everything, and remind you of all that I have said to you.
> ~ John 14:26 NRSV

> But when he, the Spirit of truth, comes, he will guide you into all truth.
> ~ John 16:13

> Live by the Spirit, I say, and do not gratify the desires of the flesh. For what the flesh desires is opposed to the Spirit, and what the Spirit desires is opposed to the flesh; for these are opposed to each other, to prevent you from doing what you want. But if you are led by the Spirit, you are not subject to the law. Now the works of the flesh are obvious: fornication, impurity, licentiousness, idolatry, sorcery, enmities, strife, jealousy, anger, quarrels, dissensions, factions, envy, drunkenness, carousing, and things like these. I am warning you, as I warned you before: those who do such things will not inherit the kingdom of God. By contrast, the fruit of the Spirit is love, joy, peace, patience, kindness, generosity, faithfulness, gentleness, and self-control. There is no law against such things.
> ~ Galatians 5:16–23 NRSV

5. **We have been granted everlasting life.**

> But our citizenship is in heaven, and from it we await a Savior, the Lord Jesus Christ, who will transform our lowly body to

be like his glorious body, by the power that enables him even to subject all things to himself.

~ Philippians 3:20–21 ESV

And which now has been manifested through the appearing of our Savior Christ Jesus, who abolished death and brought life and immortality to light through the gospel.

~ 2 Timothy 1:10 ESV

For God so loved the world, that he gave his only Son, that whoever believes in him should not perish but have eternal life.

~ John 3:16 ESV

6. **God's strength is available to us.**

Finally, be strong in the Lord and in the strength of his might. Put on the whole armor of God, that you may be able to stand against the schemes of the devil."

~ Ephesians 6:10–11 ESV

At my first defense no one came to stand by me, but all deserted me. May it not be charged against them! But the Lord stood by me and strengthened me, so that through me the message might be fully proclaimed and all the Gentiles might hear it. So I was rescued from the lion's mouth. The Lord will rescue me from every evil deed and bring me safely into his heavenly kingdom. To him be the glory forever and ever. Amen.

~ 2 Timothy 4:16–18 ESV

7. **God's blessings are renewed every day.**

But this I call to mind,
 and therefore I have hope:
The steadfast love of the Lord never ceases;
 his mercies never come to an end;
 they are new every morning;
 great is your faithfulness.

~ Lamentations 3:21–23 ESV

For I know the plans I have for you, declares the Lord, plans for welfare and not for evil, to give you a future and a hope.

~ Jeremiah 29:11 ESV

8. **The Bible instructs us in wisdom and knowledge of God.**

> For the word of God is living and active, sharper than any two-edged sword, piercing to the division of soul and of spirit, of joints and of marrow, and discerning the thoughts and intentions of the heart. And no creature is hidden from his sight, but all are naked and exposed to the eyes of him to whom we must give account.
>
> ~ Hebrews 4:12–13 ESV

> But as for you, continue in what you have learned and have firmly believed, knowing from whom you learned it and how from childhood you have been acquainted with the sacred writings, which are able to make you wise for salvation through faith in Christ Jesus. All Scripture is breathed out by God and profitable for teaching, for reproof, for correction, and for training in righteousness, that the man of God may be complete, equipped for every good work.
>
> ~ 2 Timothy 3:14–17 ESV

When I remember the great promises of God available to me through Jesus Christ, I am exceedingly grateful. When I consider the sacrifice of Christ to save me from all my sins, I am overwhelmed with gratitude. Because God has comforted me in times of sorrow, or fear, or trial, or uncertainty, I rejoice and give thanks for His compassion, His love, and His great mercy. When I remember God has never disappointed me in anything, I thank Him for His faithfulness.

As I study the Scriptures, I gain wisdom into the character of God and the unsurpassed glory of Jesus; I gain confidence in living the life He has called me to live.

In recognition of all of this, I am becoming more and more willing to trust Him in any and all circumstances, even when the purpose for those circumstances is unclear, uncertain, and difficult. As my understanding of Him increases, godly gratitude also grows in me, and it provides fuel to increase my faith, my hope, and my love.

Godly gratitude requires my awareness of humility and reliance on God. In gratitude I can say, "God is able and willing to provide all my needs."

REFLECTIONS FOR THE WEEK

1. What promises of God would you include on your list of God's promises that are bedrock promises to you, able to strengthen you in times of uncertainty, disappointment, and difficulty?

2. How do you respond to Paul's question to the Corinthians, "What do you have that you did not receive?"

3. If all that you have is a gift, how does that thought free up your use of time, resources, and gifts?

PRAYER

Almighty God, Father, Son, and Holy Spirit, I humbly approach you in gratitude for all the gifts You have given me. I acknowledge again Your great glory, Your wisdom, Your mercy, Your strength, Your willingness to instruct me, Your sacrifice to save me, Your call upon my life, and Your plans for me. I remember the great things You have done. I look forward with great anticipation to Your blessings that are renewed each day. Through Your Holy Spirit I ask that these great acts of Your love be never far from my memory so that I am never ungrateful. Through humble and holy gratitude, increase my faith, my hope, and my love.

Amen

OCTOBER
THE BEGINNING OF THE FOURTH QUARTER

In the morning sow your seed,
And in the evening do not withhold your hand;
For you do not know which will prosper,
Either this or that,
Or whether both alike will be good.
Truly the light is sweet,
And it is pleasant for the eyes to behold the sun;
But if a man lives many years
And rejoices in them all,
Yet let him remember the days of darkness,
For they will be many.
All that is coming is vanity.
Seek God in Early Life
Rejoice, O young man, in your youth,
And let your heart cheer you in the days of your youth;
Walk in the ways of your heart,
And in the sight of your eyes;
But know that for all these
God will bring you into judgment.
Therefore remove sorrow from your heart,
And put away evil from your flesh,
For childhood and youth are vanity.
~ Ecclesiastes 11:6–10 NKJV

Do you have a favorite month? Our calendar is so judiciously separated into holidays, birthdays, school days, holy days, and sports seasons (I just added that since I like college basketball and professional football) that it can be difficult to focus on one particular favorite month. But since I was a young man in my twenties, I have eagerly looked forward each year to the arrival of October. There are probably many reasons for this, some I may even be unaware of, but the principal reasons for my delight in the month of October have to do with color, reflection, and renewal.

It is true our sky is blue; but not all blues are equal. For me, an October sky is unsurpassed in its beauty, and its "blueness" is different from any other month. I perceive the October sky as a mirrored, almost silver-hued blue. I attribute the color to the effects of the bright sunlight now lower in the horizon that refracts either off my retinas or the moisture in the air, or both, into shimmers of white that polish and change the blue, giving it a sharper edge and deeper clarity. The hints of coolness on the air accentuate the coldness of blue. There is no mistaking an October sky for winter, summer, or spring. The October sky, coupled with a walk in the beautiful autumn foliage, is pure joy for me.

With such a magnificent sky, and with the changing of the season, October provides ample opportunity for reflection. In business, the year is rapidly drawing to a close. Plans for the New Year will begin to be developed based upon results through the third quarter. Because of the rapidly approaching holiday season, acquisitions, divestitures, financing, and fund-raising activities take on a sense of urgency in October—a deal not done by Thanksgiving may not get done until January.

Given all of this, October is naturally a time for leaders to reflect on the year that is slipping past and to set sights for what is going to come. Contemplative moments are not morbid in October. If things are not well, they can still improve. If things are well, they can be celebrated and reinforced. October does not easily tolerate spilled milk dispositions.

This brings me to renewal. Honest self-assessments in October have great opportunity to lead to renewal of purpose. If all is not lost—then work must be rejoined to bring victory. If results are not to be as hoped for, something still can be achieved if hope is renewed and effort applied. Standing between the vitality of summer and the bleakness of winter is October, a time to renew commitments, effect change, and establish a better future.

Spiritually, I find myself to now possess an "October soul," and I like that. What do I mean by an October soul? Age has something to do with it—at the time of writing, I am fifty-seven—and there are fewer days in front of me than behind me. This is not a morbid thought. I retain my health, my zest for life, my pursuit of knowledge, my striving to become what God wants me to be, and my desire to be a better husband, father, friend, and leader. In many respects I am at my peak performance—I have experienced much and gained much wisdom. I have done good things and bad things, smart things and foolish things. In honest reflection I find both wonder and blessing because God has used these things to make my soul prosper. I am very grateful.

In my October soul, I know who I am; my identity causes me no anxiety. I know how I will respond to crises, to trouble, to testing, to hurt, to disappointment, to unfairness, to prosperity, and to need. I know how to laugh and how to make—and take—a joke. I know what kind of husband I am. I know what kind of father I am. Over the last dozen years, I have come to know Jesus, my God and king. I am at peace with me.

Because of Jesus, I know what to do when I fall short of being who God wants me to be. In my October soul, I allow past regrets to wash over me, but I do not wallow in them. I remember with remorse, but not with continuing indictment, my mistakes and those times when I was much less than I should have been. To paraphrase the words of an old bluegrass song, "I have done my *time*."[4] And through God, I have moved on to restoration and healing. I pray for those I have hurt, trusting God to make all things right. In my October soul, good memories comfort me, and hurtful memories merely mark the road I have traveled.

And in my October soul, I look forward to enjoying a harvest. I look forward to helping my family make their own journey through life so that they too, somewhere in the future, arrive safely in their October souls.

Randy Pausch, a professor at Carnegie Mellon University, contracted pancreatic cancer in 2007 and passed away in 2008. His final lecture is available to view on YouTube. It is a remarkable lecture, and Randy must have been a remarkable man. Shortly before he died, he was interviewed by Diane Sawyer. In that interview, Randy spoke candidly about his terminal illness, and he said something that I found very uplifting. Randy said that inevitably with his passing, his wife and children would

---

[4] "Doin' My Time" by Jimmie Skinner.

find themselves being thrown over a cliff, and he would not be there to catch them. Since that was the case, he had decided he would spend his remaining time preparing nets that would catch them when he could not.

In my October soul, I also want to prepare nets to protect my wife and children if they fall and I am not there to catch them. My nets will be sown using strong fabric and fiber, and my nets will be filled with the cushioning power of faith, hope, love, and goodness even in the midst of evil. My nets will offer healing, forgiveness, redemption, and an everlasting future because my God has promised those blessings to me, and He will give them abundantly to my family.

It's October—a rare and beautiful month. I pray *this* October will hold rich blessings for you.

REFLECTIONS FOR OCTOBER

1. Of what fabric would you sew nets for those you care about?

2. Are there any regrets and recriminations in your life that still exert a negative influence on your peace and joy? In your circumstance, what kind of a God would meet your needs to bring you hope and healing?

3. The author of Ecclesiastes questions to what purpose is anything in life since even those things that we avidly pursue do not last, and we perish and are quickly forgotten. But the author of Ecclesiastes does not question the existence of God. To him, God is real. His conclusion is,

Let us hear the conclusion of the whole matter:
Fear God and keep His commandments,
For this is man's all.
For God will bring every work into judgment,
Including every secret thing,
Whether good or evil.

Ecclesiastes 12:13–14 NKJV

Spend some time this month reflecting on God's call on your life.

PRAYER

Gracious and wonderful Father, thank You for giving us the seasons to mark our time. Thank You for providing me with certain seasons in my life where I can pause and reflect on myself, renew my spirits, and re-commit myself to those ventures and relationships that mean much to me. The Bible says, "There is no peace apart from God." Draw me ever closer to You. Be near, O God, be near, and let my spirits soar into the freedom that Christ has given me.

Amen

OCTOBER—WEEK ONE

HOLDING YOURSELF AND OTHERS ACCOUNTABLE TO KEEP PROMISES AND COMMITMENTS

And Jephthah made a vow to the Lord, and said, "If You will indeed deliver the people of Ammon into my hands, then it will be that whatever comes out of the doors of my house to meet me, when I return in peace from the people of Ammon, shall surely be the Lord's, and I will offer it up as a burnt offering."

So Jephthah advanced toward the people of Ammon to fight against them, and the Lord delivered them into his hands.

~ Judges 11:30–32 NKJV

When Jephthah came to his house at Mizpah, there was his daughter, coming out to meet him with timbrels and dancing; and she was his only child. Besides her he had neither son nor daughter. And it came to pass, when he saw her, that he tore his clothes, and said, "Alas, my daughter! You have brought me very low! You are among those who trouble me! For I have given my word to the Lord, and I cannot go back on it."

So she said to him, "My father, if you have given your word to the Lord, do to me according to what has gone out of your mouth, because the Lord has avenged you of your enemies, the people of Ammon."

~ Judges 11:34–36 NKJV

Walk prudently when you go to the house of God; and draw near to hear rather than to give the sacrifice of fools, for they do not know that they do evil.
Do not be rash with your mouth,
And let not your heart utter anything hastily before God.
For God is in heaven, and you on earth;
Therefore let your words be few.
For a dream comes through much activity,
And a fool's voice is known by his many words.
When you make a vow to God, do not delay to pay it;

For He has no pleasure in fools.
Pay what you have vowed—
Better not to vow than to vow and not pay.
Do not let your mouth cause your flesh to sin, nor say before the messenger of God that it was an error. Why should God be angry at your excuse and destroy the work of your hands? For in the multitude of dreams and many words there is also vanity. But fear God.

~ Ecclesiastes 5:1–7 NKJV

There were also two others, criminals, led with Him to be put to death. And when they had come to the place called Calvary, there they crucified Him, and the criminals, one on the right hand and the other on the left. Then Jesus said, "Father, forgive them, for they do not know what they do."

~ Luke 23:32–34a NKJV

Then one of the criminals who were hanged blasphemed Him, saying, "If You are the Christ, save Yourself and us."
But the other, answering, rebuked him, saying, "Do you not even fear God, seeing you are under the same condemnation? And we indeed justly, for we receive the due reward of our deeds; but this Man has done nothing wrong." Then he said to Jesus, "Lord, remember me when You come into Your kingdom."
And Jesus said to him, "Assuredly, I say to you, today you will be with Me in Paradise."

~ Luke 23:39–43 NKJV

Do you, like me, find some passages in the Bible emotionally challenging to read and harder still to understand because of the descriptions of extreme human suffering they contain? For example, the story of the great Flood that destroyed the world (Genesis 6:9–8:22), the stoning of Achan's family rather than just Achan (Joshua 7:22–26), Joshua's complete and total destruction of Jericho (all of its men, women, and children and livestock) when the Israelites entered the Promised Land (Joshua 6:21), and the descriptions of the horrors in Jerusalem during the siege by the Babylonians (Lamentations 2:19–22), reveal the horror of violence on the global, national, and personal level.

The magnitude of the human suffering brought about by the Flood, and the destruction of Jericho and Jerusalem are clearly placed in the context of God's sovereign and righteous judgment for the sins of the people being judged. The depth of the destruction startles us, but as we consider the stories, we become undeniably aware of the majesty of God and His judgments against sin. We learn God is active in the world—"God is not dead, nor doth He sleep" ("Christmas Bells" by Henry Wadsworth Longfellow). Mankind's acts of rebellion and obedience are equally available to God to use to accomplish His divine purpose in the world, as are those moments when humans trust and obey God's commands.

Standing among the truly difficult passages of Scripture to read is the story of Jephthah's vow, because it is markedly different from the stories of human suffering noted above that were precipitated by sin and carried out by God's judgment. Jephthah's story is self-inflicted and needless (because God's favor already rested on Jephthah when He uttered it), it caused harm to befall an innocent child, it was careless and horrific in its result, and the vow itself was ungodly, even when the purpose for it and the foolish obedience to it was, at least in part, aimed at somehow honoring God.

Particularly disconcerting is that the author of the book of Judges provides no editorial comment on how we should interpret the story of Jephthah's vow. The story stands as it is presented, leaving the reader to struggle with its message. It is also disturbing because it gets clearly to the conflict and consequences associated with a particular type of human sin—broken promises.

Commentators disagree and have struggled with what really happened to Jephthah's daughter for thousands of years. Rabbi Moshe Reiss, in an article entitled "Jephthah's Daughter" discusses how Jephthah's vow and his daughter's fate have been interpreted over the years—both by Jewish and Christian theologians. According to Rabbi Reiss, almost all early commentators (Jewish and Christian) believed Jephthah carried out his vow and physically sacrificed his daughter on an altar. However, later commentators believed Jephthah did not kill his daughter, but rather committed her to a life of celibacy and isolation in devotion to God. In support of the latter assertion, such commentators note that the writer of the book of Judges does not condemn Jephthah's actions even though they are clearly in violation of the Hebrew Law (Leviticus 18:21, 20:2–5, and Deuteronomy 12:31, 18:10), implying therefore that the daughter was not killed. In this reasoning, the vow, while foolish, was not illegal and therefore was fulfilled in righteousness by Jephthah even though it caused grief to both he and his daughter.

Against this reasoning is the brutal time period described in the book of Judges and its closing sentence: "In those days there was no king in Israel; everyone did what was right in his own eyes" (Judges 21:25 NKJV). So we are left with ambiguity—and plenty of it. The absolute truth of what happened is not known. What is written is all the information we have.

In spite of its ambiguity, the story does provide instruction on the importance of taking promises seriously. The author of Ecclesiastes in the passage of Scripture above concluded the same thing. In the book of Numbers, Moses provides regulations governing making and keeping vows (Numbers 30:1–16).

God's viewpoint about this particular vow and what might have been the outcome had Jephthah chosen to break his vow is not revealed in the story. Jephthah did not ask God what he should do; rather he chose to keep his foolish and ill-advised vow and the results, whether by her death or seclusion, were terrible for the daughter and Jephthah. Worse still, no honor was brought to God. The story presents a true "lose-lose" situation.

I can't help but wonder what would have been the result if Jephthah had broken his ill-advised vow. Fortunately, another story in the Bible illustrates the implications of breaking a vow to God, but in that story the ending is restoration from sin. The story concerns Peter and his re-commissioning as an apostle and leader of the early Christian church by Jesus—the person to whom Peter had made and then broken a vow. The story is found in John 13:37 and John 18:15–27. Here are some highlights:

On the night of his arrest, Jesus gathered with His disciples for their last supper together. During the evening, Jesus became distressed and told them one of them was going to betray him, and the rest would all fall away. Peter says, "I will lay down my life for Your sake" (John 13:37b NKJV). Jesus replies that Peter will, in fact, deny he knows Jesus three times before morning. After Jesus predicts his betrayal, Peter insisted, "If I have to die with You, I will not deny You!" (Mark 14:31 NKJV). We all are familiar with the story and know that Peter did, indeed, deny Jesus three times that night.

In assessing the magnitude of the betrayal, it is important to recall some facts about Peter and his relationship with Jesus. Peter was a member of Jesus' inner circle (along with John and James) and was with him on certain key occasions. Peter was there when Jesus brought Jairus' daughter back to life (Luke 8:51–56). Peter was there when Jesus was transfigured into glory on the mount of transfiguration (Luke 9:28–36). Peter stepped out of the boat and walked (briefly) on the water (Matthew 14:28–33). And it was Peter who acknowledged before the other disciples that Jesus was "The Christ of God" (Luke 9:20). Jesus took Peter (along with John and James) to be close to Him and to pray with Him during the hours in Gethsemane before His arrest. And Luke records Jesus lifted a special prayer for Peter in advance of his betrayal. "And the Lord said, 'Simon, Simon! Indeed, Satan has asked for you, that he may sift you as wheat. But I have prayed for you, that your faith should not fail; and when you have returned to Me, strengthen your brethren'" (Luke 22:31–32 NKJV).

Peter knew with certainty Jesus was the Messiah, the Son of God. And yet, he betrayed him and broke his vow of allegiance and protection.

Making and breaking vows to God are not isolated instances. People make and break vows to God all the time. A common example of a broken vow to God is divorce. Jesus preached we should not divorce except on the grounds of infidelity (Matthew 5:31–32), yet divorce happens. Or consider situations where a sin, such as sexual promiscuity or drug dependency, is habitual and holds great power over the person. Such a person may become deeply grieved such that they cry out a promise to not "do it again," only to fail. And there are examples of people in deep distress who pray "if only" God will deliver them, then they, in turn, will "do something" for God—yet they find they cannot, or will not, do whatever "that something" is for God, and a vow is broken.

In the passage from Luke 23:39-43 above, Jesus forgave a criminal on the cross, so we know with certainty those who truly repent of their sins and who call Jesus Lord will also have their sins forgiven. We also know Jesus' act of salvation was once for all—it covered all of our sins before we came to Christ, and all of our sins that have or will occur afterward too. Peter had confessed Christ as Lord, and Jesus had pronounced him "clean" (John 13:10). Forgiveness of broken vows is accomplished just the same as forgiveness of any other sin is accomplished—not by anything we do, but solely by Jesus' act of salvation.

But, you may ask, what about the consequences associated with breaking a vow? How are they resolved? The answer to this question is ambiguous. It is very likely a broken vow will have earthly consequences notwithstanding Jesus' forgiveness of the sinner. Divorce has ramifications—emotional and monetary, and those consequences have to be dealt with. But, as in Peter's case, breaking a vow does not necessarily mean you are no longer empowered to serve in the capacity God has called you. Jesus went to extraordinary lengths to restore Peter to his role as apostle (John 21:15-19). And Jesus restored Peter fully—he was not left in a lesser role.

I believe Peter, in the process of his full restoration to service, displayed certain key characteristics. First, he was truly repentant of his sin. Luke records, "And the Lord turned and looked at Peter. Then Peter remembered the word of the Lord, how He had said to him, 'Before the rooster crows, you will deny Me three times.' So Peter went out and wept bitterly" (Luke 22:61-62 NKJV). Peter's sin brought him face to face with his pride, his self-righteousness, and his courage based only on the thin air of "himself." Peter learned that "apart from Jesus, he could do nothing." But, from his newfound humility, Peter would and could be useful to Jesus again.

Second, Peter acknowledged his sin in front of others. Confession to Jesus is vitally important—but confession to friends who have been wronged or who have been disappointed because of our actions can bring healing to everyone. On the beach, Peter confessed his love for Jesus three times in front of his friends. The dialogue with Jesus was painful to Peter, but he answered Jesus each time.

Third, Peter chose to love Jesus and left it up to Jesus to decide his fate. Had Jesus not fully restored Peter to the office of apostle, I believe Peter would have gladly accepted whatever role Jesus gave him. But Peter, from his new self-awareness that he was nothing without Christ, had meditated on all the things Jesus had said, particularly on the night of his betrayal, and Jesus' words rang out with hope of forgiveness and restoration. After he had predicted Peter's denial, Jesus said these things:

> Let not your heart be troubled; you believe in God, believe also in Me.
>
> ~ John 14:1 NKJV

> Most assuredly, I say to you, he who believes in Me, the works that I do he will do also; and greater works than these he will do, because I go to My Father. And whatever you ask in My name, that I will do, that the Father may be glorified in the Son. If you ask anything in My name, I will do it."
>
> ~ John 14:12–14 NKJV

> You are already clean because of the word which I have spoken to you. You did not choose Me, but I chose you and appointed you that you should go and bear fruit, and that your fruit should remain, that whatever you ask the Father in My name He may give you.
>
> ~ John 15:3,16 NKJV

Christ's words spoke of forgiveness, but also of usefulness.

There was one other thing I believe Peter did in order to be made fully useful to Jesus again. Peter understood the past could haunt the future, but it did not have to irrevocably affect the future. In order to put the past in the past, Peter had to forgive himself.

We hear this same advice from the Apostle Paul, who said, "Brethren, I do not count myself to have apprehended; **but one thing I do, forgetting those things which are behind and reaching forward to those things which are ahead**" (Philippians 3:13 NKJV bold emphasis mine).

If Christ was willing to put the matter behind Him, Peter also had to do the same. And with a humble and forgiven heart, Peter could hope to be restored to service—to be used again by Christ in the office he held before his act of betrayal.

In the meeting between Jesus and Peter on the beach (John 21:15–19), Jesus informed Peter of how difficult his life as an apostle would be. In fact, Peter is told that he would be killed somewhere in the future for his work in evangelizing the world—in essence once again being accused, at his great peril, of knowing and loving Christ. Jesus made it very clear Peter was not to worry about anything except looking after Jesus' sheep and following Him. Peter accepted the assignment and chose to follow Jesus. This time, with Christ as his rock and sure foundation, Peter was successful.

Only God can determine what consequences we will face in our failures and broken vows. And only God can heal us. It is possible that God will not restore us to where we were before our sin. It is possible God will take from us something our own actions had already made forfeit. But it is also possible God will restore us fully in addition to forgiving our sins. In our contrition we must not lose sight of God's sovereignty. By faith we know our sins are forgiven; we can also ask to have the consequences of sin changed. We must not, however, think God has not heard us if His answer is "no." In our faith, with a forgiven heart, we must lift up our wants and accept what God requires. In the long run, humility, confession, and grace will bring us to restoration.

Who knows what would have happened if Jephthah had repented of his foolish vow? Perhaps God would have taken from him his role as judge—but his daughter would have been restored. Jephthah did not posses humility, and as a result he withdrew from the healing that would have come from confession and grace.

Choose to allow God to show you grace in your times of brokenness. Seek Him with a humble and penitent heart. Ask for what you desire. Gladly accept His judgment. And as a leader, when someone breaks a vow to you, ask God for the courage and the wisdom to treat them in a godly fashion. If possible (it is not always possible), restore them as Peter to continued relationship and service.

REFLECTIONS FOR THE WEEK

1. Judges 11:27 says God's Spirit came upon Jephthah. This anointing from God occurred **before** Jephthah's vow. What might have been the reasons that Jephthah made his foolish vow even though God had already blessed him unilaterally?

2. In what way does trust play a part in both forgiveness of sins and restoration to work?

3. If Christ is willing to forgive, what hinders us in forgiving others and ourselves?

PRAYER

Fairest Lord Jesus, Son of God and Son of man, hear my prayers of contrition over broken promises. Thank You for removing my trespasses. Through Your Holy Spirit in me, help me to lay aside my pain and guilt, and look forward to freedom of spirit and useful occupation in the kingdom. Let me use my freedom to loosen the bonds of guilt that hold my brothers. All things are possible for You, and in Your love I find hope of renewal and usefulness.

Amen

OCTOBER—WEEK TWO

RETAINING AND RECRUITING TALENTED EMPLOYEES

> From that time many of His disciples went back and walked with Him no more. Then Jesus said to the twelve, "Do you also want to go away?"
>
> But Simon Peter answered Him, "Lord, to whom shall we go? You have the words of eternal life. Also we have come to believe and know that You are the Christ, the Son of the living God."
>
> Jesus answered them, "Did I not choose you, the twelve, and one of you is a devil?" He spoke of Judas Iscariot, the son of Simon, for it was he who would betray Him, being one of the twelve.
>
> ~ John 6:66–71 NKJV

And Stephen, full of faith and power, did great wonders and signs among the people. Then there arose some from what is called the Synagogue of the Freedmen (Cyrenians, Alexandrians, and those from Cilicia and Asia), disputing with Stephen. And they were not able to resist the wisdom and the Spirit by which he spoke.

~ Acts 6:8–10 NKJV

And they stoned Stephen as he was calling on God and saying, "Lord Jesus, receive my spirit." Then he knelt down and cried out with a loud voice, "Lord, do not charge them with this sin." And when he had said this, he fell asleep.

Now Saul was consenting to his death.

At that time a great persecution arose against the church which was at Jerusalem; and they were all scattered throughout the regions of Judea and Samaria, except the apostles. And devout men carried Stephen to his burial, and made great lamentation over him.

As for Saul, he made havoc of the church, entering every house, and dragging off men and women, committing them to prison.

~ Acts 7:59–8:3 NKJV

> Now there was a certain disciple at Damascus named Ananias; and to him the Lord said in a vision, "Ananias."
> And he said, "Here I am, Lord."
> So the Lord said to him, "Arise and go to the street called Straight, and inquire at the house of Judas for one called Saul of Tarsus, for behold, he is praying. And in a vision he has seen a man named Ananias coming in and putting his hand on him, so that he might receive his sight."
> Then Ananias answered, "Lord, I have heard from many about this man, how much harm he has done to Your saints in Jerusalem. And here he has authority from the chief priests to bind all who call on Your name."
> But the Lord said to him, "Go, for he is a chosen vessel of Mine to bear My name before Gentiles, kings, and the children of Israel. For I will show him how many things he must suffer for My name's sake."
>
> ~ Acts 9:10–16 NKJV

Imagine an urgent new project has just been identified in your organization. The project is multi-disciplinary and cannot be accomplished by a single individual—even you cannot complete the project without help. The rewards associated with the successful completion of the project are great, but the damages associated with an unsuccessful completion are catastrophic. The project must be undertaken; it cannot be ignored. How do you choose who will work on the project? What criteria do you use to screen possible members of your team?

In the space provided below, list as many attributes as you can think of to help you evaluate and select a team from among alternative candidates.

My list included the following: demonstrated expertise in skills and knowledge or relevant experience in previous pressure-filled situations, desire (self-motivation) on the part of the employee, a balance of risk and risk-averse behaviors, dependability, forthrightness, an ability to persuasively defend their work, problem solving and insight, intuition, intelligence, courage, ethics, a history of delivering quality work, practical wisdom, availability, accountability, confidence but not arrogance, a team player unafraid of assuming a leadership role, assertive, and trustworthy.

In such a hypothetical situation, a wide variation in answers is possible. I am sure your list had many similarities and probably had other characteristics I overlooked. But I believe the exercise demonstrated the importance of a leader being aware of the attributes and capabilities of their employees in order to fairly evaluate their effectiveness in the jobs for which they were hired. One of the key roles of a leader is to ensure the mission and the related goals and objectives of the organization are achieved. Since the mission and the related goals and objectives of an organization are usually predominantly achieved through its employees, a leader must be able to answer the questions: Are the organization's employees successfully discharging their duties, and is the organization realizing full benefit from their employment?

Perhaps you have heard the old adage, "Winning isn't everything—it's the only thing." As a Christian leader, winning is important, but it is never as important as living life in a godly and ethical manner. Winning is a goal to be achieved, but it is to be achieved in the right way. To win in an unethical manner would be to mock our God who cares about right and wrong and not about temporal victories in a world that is fading away. Therefore, I believe employee evaluations must include two perspectives: were the goals and objectives met, and were the methods employed in working toward the goals and objectives ethical and consistent with the core values espoused by the organization?

With these questions in mind, a matrix can be prepared, allowing an employer to rate the performance and values of each employee and assigning them into one of four quadrants: low values and low productivity

(Quadrant 1), high values and low productivity (Quadrant 2), high productivity and low values (Quadrant 3), and high productivity and high values (Quadrant 4). The matrix would look like the following chart.

High Values Low Productivity	High Values High Productivity
Low Values Low Productivity	Low Values High Productivity

Values (y-axis) / Productivity (x-axis)

The evaluation process requires assigning numerical values to both the subjective human characteristics associated with the values of the organization and the more objective measures of productivity so that the employee's total evaluation can be plotted within one of the four quadrants. The attributes and personal characteristics I listed above can easily be categorized into attributes of human character or values and attributes of productivity. Here is how my list breaks down into those two categories:

Human Character and Values	Productivity
Dependability	Relevant skills and knowledge
Forthrightness	Prior experience
Intuition	Desire (self-motivation)
Courage	Balance of risk and risk-averse traits
Ethics	Ability to persuade others
Accountability	Problem solving ability and insight

OCTOBER—WEEK TWO

Confidence	Intelligence
Team player with leadership capabilities	Quality work
Assertiveness	Practical wisdom
Trustworthiness	Availability

Having established a list of desired attributes, I am able to evaluate how strong (or even if) a candidate possesses each attribute and rank employees in comparison with one another in the matrix by plotting their productivity measures on the x axis and their character values on the y axis.

In the passages of Scripture above, three important people in the Bible are mentioned: Judas, Stephen, and Paul. *Where would they fit on our matrix?*

Here is how I would position each of them in the four quadrant matrix with the viewpoint and assumption that God is the employer of each of them.

Judas was selected by Jesus to be one of the twelve disciples. Judas had a role to play in the story of Jesus. Jesus did not prematurely judge Judas. Jesus had fellowship with Judas and gave him every opportunity to be blessed just like the other disciples. Judas must have gone on the missionary trips just as the other disciples did, and Judas is not reported to have returned empty-handed. Until the end, Jesus continued to love Judas, even washing the feet of Judas on the night of his betrayal. But Jesus let Judas make his own decisions. And somewhere in their relationship, Judas decided to betray Jesus.

The manner in which Jesus acted and treated Judas is not different from how God treated the Jewish people in the Old Testament. God, through the words and deeds of the prophets, instructed, chastised, admonished, loved, blessed, forgave, entreated, longed for, and gave freedom to the Jewish people in both the Northern and Southern kingdoms before ultimately judging them with the conquests by the Assyrians and the Babylonians. In the years leading up to conquest, there were times under "good" kings when the nations of Israel and Judah prospered. There were times when there was great productivity and religious conviction. But there were also times under "bad" kings when religious conviction was forfeit. Sometimes this forfeiture of religious conviction led to times of trouble and poor productivity, but not always. Sometimes prosperity existed without religious conviction.

The ancient Jewish people of Israel and Judah, prior to their destruction at the hands of the Assyrians and Babylonians, would be characterized as low values, high productivity or low values, low productivity depending on how God was working at the time in their national history to bring them to their senses. Periods of high values and high productivity never lasted very long—the tendency was always one of moving toward low values and a corresponding low productivity.

Judas, before he determined to void the principles that Jesus taught, would be characterized as low values and high productivity. As one of the disciples, Judas likely achieved much, but he had not comprehended or internalized the values of Jesus. Whatever gains Judas had were achieved in his own way. Therefore, Judas enjoyed success (high productivity), but the success was not achieved with high values. Had Jesus not been God, Judas would have destroyed the "business." If Judas worked for us, we might experience gains in productivity, but they would come at great risk to the enterprise.

Stephen was the first Christian to be killed for his profession of belief in Jesus as the Son of God. Stephen was a "high values" man. He is described in Acts 6:5 as "a man full of faith and of the Holy Spirit." When a dispute arose that threatened to take the attention of the apostles away from preaching and evangelism, Stephen, along with six other men, was chosen to administer the distribution of food in Jerusalem among the Christian widows of Greek and Hebrew nationality. Their work was highly productive, and many people in Jerusalem believed in Christ (Acts 6:7).

Stephen also captured the attention of others in Jerusalem through his work (he did great wonders and miraculous signs among the people) and in his testimony that were both fully consistent with his values as a follower of Christ. People of courage and conviction are always noticed by those around them. Stephen was a high values, high productivity servant of God during his life, and his story of faith, love, courage, devotion, compassion, and obedience continues to inspire us today.

The story of the Apostle Paul is historically set out in the book of Acts. Paul's influence on the Christian church is significant—of the twenty-seven books comprising the New Testament, he authored or inspired others to write using his name, thirteen of them. The importance of Paul in the establishment of the church among the Gentiles (non-Jewish) and the development of Christian theology cannot be overestimated.

But when we first meet Paul (then called Saul) he is an enemy of the Christian church and an enemy of Christ. Saul could therefore be characterized as high values and low productivity when assessed from Christ's perspective. Saul had high values because he was highly educated in the Hebrew Scriptures, was fully devoted to those Scriptures, and was fully dedicated to serving God. I think of Saul as someone like Nicodemus—devoted to God but unconvinced of who Jesus truly was. But unlike Nicodemus, Saul chose to persecute the early church—he initially concluded Jesus and profession of faith in Him was blasphemy. Therefore, he was low productivity because he was misguided with respect to Jesus. Here is how Paul described himself before his conversion to Christ:

> If anyone else thinks he has reason for confidence in the flesh, I have more: circumcised on the eighth day, of the people of Israel, of the tribe of Benjamin, a Hebrew of Hebrews; as to the law, a Pharisee; as to zeal, a persecutor of the church; as to righteousness under the law, blameless.
>
> ~ Philippians 3:4b–6 ESV

As told in the Scriptures that began this chapter, on the road to Damascus, with evil intent against the Christians in his heart, Saul met Jesus. After three days of fasting, praying, and blindness, Jesus sent Ananais, who healed Paul and baptized him in the name of Jesus. And for the rest of his life, Paul became more and more useful and productive for Christ. In his service to Jesus, Paul established both churches and leaders to advance the gospel of Jesus. Paul became a "top box" high values, high productivity servant of God.

I have not presented an example from Scripture of someone who would be ranked within the first quadrant—low values and low productivity. Such a person in a work environment would be considered questionable or "probationary." Quadrant 1 should not long be the home of employees—they must either move up in productivity or values or both or risk losing their jobs. During the evaluation period, it is important to gain insight and knowledge into their comprehension and acceptance of the organization's core values and their skills in successfully performing their work.

Employees who fall in Quadrant 2 (high values, low productivity) are something of a quandary in an organization. Their comprehension and expression of core values is highly beneficial, but their lack of productivity imperils their overall success. Given their adoption of core values, the challenge of leadership is to find a way to help them improve performance. Examples of ways to improve the performance of a high values, low productivity employee are to provide additional training and mentoring, or reassigning them to tasks for which they will prove to be productive.

Employees in Quadrant 3 (high productivity, low values) are usually the employees who create the most problems for leadership. Productivity is usually easier to measure than values. If love covers over many sins, high productivity masks them. But such employees will become a cancer in an organization at the first time a change, driven by values and mission, competes with either their existing productivity achievements or their hopes to achieve gains in the future. When the rules change, they resist. Therefore, it is vital for leaders to evaluate the integrity of their high producers against the organization's core values. Consider the following proverbs:

> *A good man obtains favor from the Lord,*
> *but a man of evil devices he condemns.*
> ~ Proverbs 12:2 ESV

> *No ill befalls the righteous,*
> *but the wicked are filled with trouble.*
> ~ Proverbs 12:21 ESV

One who is righteous is a guide to his neighbor,
but the way of the wicked leads them astray.
~ Proverbs 12:26 ESV

Even a child makes himself known by his acts,
by whether his conduct is pure and upright.
~ Proverbs 20:11 ESV

Bread gained by deceit is sweet to a man,
but afterward his mouth will be full of gravel.
~ Proverbs 20:17 ESV

Traditional business wisdom believes Quadrant 3 (high productivity, low values) employees are extremely difficult to change—they will seldom adopt values that are inconsistent with their overarching goal of winning. As a Christian leader, you must try and move such employees into the high productivity, high values box. As with Paul, sometimes values can be present but are misguided. Through leading by example, speaking the truth in love, and never compromising values for productivity gains, all employees have the opportunity to align their values with those of the organization. Opportunity for "repentance" is to be given in a work-setting too.

In life, the opportunity to accept Christ will end at some undetermined time in the future. In business, the opportunity for a Quadrant 3 employee to change and adopt the values of the enterprise is not open-ended either. If a change in values is not adopted, an employee will need to be released from service. This fact should not be a difficult problem for a Christian leader to accept. We act in love toward all and leave the consequences of discharging our duties as leaders to God and our clear conscience. We can be comforted when a decision to end employment must be made through the knowledge that God is at work in the lives of everyone, and He will use all circumstances to bring about good for the believer and opportunity for salvation to the lost.

And if you have high values, high productivity employees—thank God for them. Honor them with your time, your sincere expressions of thanks, opportunities for further advancement, and if the time comes for them to leave for opportunities you cannot provide, celebrate their time with you and wish them peace and success. Such people will become leaders in their own right and will remember you as their role model. In this way, goodness is advanced in the world.

REFLECTIONS FOR THE WEEK

1. Have you ever confronted a decision to replace an employee who has demonstrated the ability to be highly productive but who does not exhibit the characteristics and values espoused by your organization? What was the result of your deliberations?

2. Spend time this week meditating on employees who you would categorize as Quadrant 4 (high values, high productivity). As a leader, what can you do to further advance their careers? As a leader, what can you do to demonstrate your appreciation for their service?

3. Spend time this week meditating on employees who you would categorize as Quadrant 2 (high values, low productivity). What are you doing to move their productivity to an acceptable level?

PRAYER

Dear God, evaluation of performance is a difficult assignment for any leader. I know that You love all of us, that You are not preferential, and that You have a plan for each of us. With sober insight and a loving spirit, help me to guide those who work for me so that their lives are enriched and their usefulness to You is increased. I pray that everyone who works for me sees Your Son within me.

Amen

OCTOBER—WEEK THREE

RECOGNIZING WHEN CHANGE IS NECESSARY

Then the word of the Lord came to Jonah the second time, saying, "Arise, go to Nineveh, that great city, and call out against it the message that I tell you." So Jonah arose and went to Nineveh, according to the word of the Lord. Now Nineveh was an exceedingly great city, three days' journey in breadth. Jonah began to go into the city, going a day's journey. And he called out, "Yet forty days, and Nineveh shall be overthrown!" And the people of Nineveh believed God. They called for a fast and put on sackcloth, from the greatest of them to the least of them. The word reached the king of Nineveh, and he arose from his throne, removed his robe, covered himself with sackcloth, and sat in ashes. And he issued a proclamation and published through Nineveh, "By the decree of the king and his nobles: Let neither man nor beast, herd nor flock, taste anything. Let them not feed or drink water, but let man and beast be covered with sackcloth, and let them call out mightily to God. Let everyone turn from his evil way and from the violence that is in his hands. Who knows? God may turn and relent and turn from his fierce anger, so that we may not perish."
When God saw what they did, how they turned from their evil way, God relented of the disaster that he had said he would do to them, and he did not do it.

~ Jonah 3:1–10 ESV

The ear that listens to life-giving reproof
 will dwell among the wise.
Whoever ignores instruction despises himself,
 but he who listens to reproof gains intelligence.
The fear of the Lord is instruction in wisdom,
 and humility comes before honor.

~ Proverbs 15:31–33 ESV

When was the last time you were the agent of change in others? Were the circumstances personal or business related? What type of prior relationship did you have with the person or people you were leading toward change? Did the opportunity excite you, or would you rather have been swallowed by a fish than be the agent of change in others?

When was the last time someone asked you to change? How would you describe your first impression of the "advice" being offered or the command being given? Would King Solomon have described you as wise or as a despiser of your soul?

There is nothing about change that is easy. Change is hard whether you are the object or the agent of it. When we are asked to change something about ourselves, we resist, and our resistance comes naturally. I believe our resistance is deeply rooted in our human nature and springs from one of two human characteristics. The first is fear. The second is pride.

Fear comes into play because change involves risk, and risk carries uncertainty with respect to outcomes. Whenever a change is undertaken, there is always a risk of failure. The risk of failure often blocks adopting or embracing the steps necessary to change.

Human pride impedes acceptance that there is something about ourselves or our work that needs to change. There is a huge difference in knowing that something about you needs to change and being told by someone else that they have reached the same conclusion. In the Old Testament, God continually referred to the ancient Jewish people as a "stiff necked and rebellious people." They did not want to change their ways, and neither do we.

Our own experience in resisting change warns us how difficult a challenge lies before us when we are the agents of change in others. Acting as a seed of doubt, this knowledge can sap courage and perseverance at crucial times in the change process. Leaders must gird themselves against emotional pitfalls if they are to sustain the effort necessary to bring about a successful change in the lives of others.

Personal experience can provide a leader with strength and courage. Trying times can produce perseverance and perspective. A leader who has previously navigated a change process approaches future changes with more confidence; leaders build on successes or study times of failure

OCTOBER—WEEK THREE

to discern better strategies the next time around. And while personal experience is important, knowledge and wisdom can also be gained by studying what others have done in similar circumstances. For a Christian leader, the Bible is an important resource for studying and understanding the process of change.

The Bible tells one long story of God calling His people—His creation—to change (repent) from an attitude and desire to disobey (sin) to an attitude of trust in Him, love of Him, and obedience to Him (salvation and righteousness). The call to change weaves a continuous thread from Genesis to Revelation. The thread is deeply woven into the stories and multi-faceted impressions that the Bible makes upon us. The Bible reveals that change is a natural part of human life, and accepting change is difficult to do. The Bible also reveals that God is in control of the outcome of all things.

CONSIDER—

The Bible is an interpretive history of the origins of the world and all that is in it. From the beginning, God has patiently worked to reveal His plans for us. Although we are surrounded by change, by people and events that we cannot control and struggle to understand, God alone stands unchanging, calling us to anchor our souls in Him.

> In the beginning, God created the heavens and the earth. The earth was without form and void, and darkness was over the face of the deep. And the Spirit of God was hovering over the face of the waters.
> ~ Genesis 1:1–2 ESV

When I look at your heavens, the work of your fingers,
the moon and the stars, which you have set in place,
what is man that you are mindful of him,
and the son of man that you care for him?
Yet you have made him a little lower than the heavenly beings
and crowned him with glory and honor.
You have given him dominion over the works of your hands;
you have put all things under his feet.
> ~ Psalm 8:3–6 ESV

I lift up my eyes to the hills.
From where does my help come?
My help comes from the Lord,
who made heaven and earth.

~ Psalm 121:1–2 ESV

The Bible is also an interpretive history of a particular people and their relationship with God. Through their relationship we see that God is steadfast, faithful, and just. In their stories we see that God will act in the world to fulfill His purposes in spite of acts of disobedience from the people. From God's chosen people came Jesus Christ, for us the "image of the invisible God, the firstborn of all creation" (Colossians 1:15 ESV). Jesus Christ impels all people to change, to "seek first the kingdom of God," and to live within His love and mercy. Jesus Christ says, "Come to me, all who labor and are heavy laden, and I will give you rest" (Matthew 11:28 ESV). If we believe the story of Jesus, we gain access to God's power and peace in this ever changing world.

> Now the Lord said to Abram, "Go from your country and your kindred and your father's house to the land that I will show you. And I will make of you a great nation, and I will bless you and make your name great, so that you will be a blessing. I will bless those who bless you, and him who dishonors you I will curse, and in you all the families of the earth shall be blessed."
>
> ~ Genesis 12:1–3 ESV

Seek the Lord while he may be found;
call upon him while he is near;
let the wicked forsake his way,
and the unrighteous man his thoughts;
let him return to the Lord, that he may have compassion on him,
and to our God, for he will abundantly pardon.
For my thoughts are not your thoughts,
neither are your ways my ways, declares the Lord.

~ Isaiah 55:6–8 ESV

He has told you, O man, what is good;
and what does the Lord require of you

> *but to do justice, and to love kindness,*
> *and to walk humbly with your God?*
> ~ Micah 6:8 ESV

Or is God the God of Jews only? Is he not the God of Gentiles also? Yes, of Gentiles also, since God is one—who will justify the circumcised by faith and the uncircumcised through faith
~ Romans 3:29–30 ESV

The Bible reveals that order has been called out of chaos, and our God is a God of order. This is good to know in times when changes are occurring too fast for us to understand or are too difficult for us to bear.

"For God is not a God of confusion but of peace"
~ 1 Corinthians 14:33 ESV

> *For behold, I create new heavens*
> *and a new earth,*
> *and the former things shall not be remembered*
> *or come into mind.*
> *But be glad and rejoice forever*
> *in that which I create;*
> *for behold, I create Jerusalem to be a joy,*
> *and her people to be a gladness.*
> ~ Isaiah 65:17–18 ESV

The Bible proclaims God's love for us. The love of God stands in perfect balance to the righteousness of God. Righteousness demands justice and judgment. Love showers the penitent heart with forgiveness, mercy, and grace. Truth, spoken in love, heals wounds and imparts trust that moving toward God will be for our great good. To change toward God is to move toward a safe-haven in an uncertain world.

These things I command you, that you love one another.
~ John 15:17 NKJV

Then Jesus, looking at him, loved him, and said to him, "One thing you lack: Go your way, sell whatever you have and give to the poor, and you will have treasure in heaven; and come, take up the cross, and follow Me."
~ Mark 10:21 NKJV

> Repent therefore and be converted, that your sins may be blotted out, so that times of refreshing may come from the presence of the Lord, and that He may send Jesus Christ, who was preached to you before.
>
> ~ Acts 3:19–20 NKJV

The Bible acts as a compass, guiding us into contemplation of self that has as its purpose a call to change—to move away from self-righteousness, self-realization, and self-sufficiency toward selflessness and obedient, loving, hopeful, faithful, enduring, and reverent worship of God. The Bible provides us with clear examples of leaders guiding others through change.

In the first century, evangelists and apostles began to preach the message of Jesus Christ to the Jews and Gentiles. The books of Acts to Revelation all contain stories of the growth of the church and how the leaders of the early church achieved success in gaining converts to Christ. The success of the early ministers of the Christian church was clearly attributable to the worth of both the message and the messenger. But their success was also guided, in part, by how they delivered their message and how they behaved relationally with their target audiences. Studying what they did provides useful information to anyone assigned the task of leading others to change.

What did they do? They exhibited seven behaviors to guide their target audiences through the process of change.

1. **They made excellent first impressions.**

    > For neither at any time did we use flattering words, as you know, nor a cloak for covetousness—God is witness. Nor did we seek glory from men, either from you or from others, when we might have made demands as apostles of Christ. But we were gentle among you, just as a nursing mother cherishes her own children. So, affectionately longing for you, we were well pleased to impart to you not only the gospel of God, but also our own lives, because you had become dear to us. For you remember, brethren, our labor and toil; for laboring night and day, that we might not be a burden to any of you, we preached to you the gospel of God. You are witnesses, and God also, how devoutly and justly and blamelessly we behaved ourselves among you who believe; as you know how we exhorted, and comforted, and charged every one

of you, as a father does his own children, that you would walk worthy of God who calls you into His own kingdom and glory.

~ 1 Thessalonians 2:5–12 NKJV

2. **They were trustworthy; they were not hypocrites.**

For our boasting is this: the testimony of our conscience that we conducted ourselves in the world in simplicity and godly sincerity, not with fleshly wisdom but by the grace of God, and more abundantly toward you.

~ 2 Corinthians 1:12 NKJV

For we do not preach ourselves, but Christ Jesus the Lord, and ourselves your bondservants for Jesus' sake.

~ 2 Corinthians 4:5 NKJV

We give no offense in anything, that our ministry may not be blamed. But in all things we commend ourselves as ministers of God: in much patience, in tribulations, in needs, in distresses, in stripes, in imprisonments, in tumults, in labors, in sleeplessness, in fastings; by purity, by knowledge, by longsuffering, by kindness, by the Holy Spirit, by sincere love, by the word of truth, by the power of God, by the armor of righteousness on the right hand and on the left, by honor and dishonor, by evil report and good report; as deceivers, and yet true.

~ 2 Corinthians 6:3–8 NKJV

3. **They cared more about others than themselves.**

For out of much affliction and anguish of heart I wrote to you, with many tears, not that you should be grieved, but that you might know the love which I have so abundantly for you.

~ 2 Corinthians 2:4 NKJV

For this reason I bow my knees to the Father of our Lord Jesus Christ, from whom the whole family in heaven and earth is named, that He would grant you, according to the riches of His glory, to be strengthened with might through His Spirit in the inner man, that Christ may dwell in your hearts through faith; that you, being rooted and grounded in love, may be able to comprehend with all the saints what is the width and length and depth and height— to know the love of Christ which passes knowledge; that you may be filled with all the fullness of God.

~Ephesians 3:14-19 NKJV

4. They never let the people forget what had been learned and gained as a result of change.

You are our epistle written in our hearts, known and read by all men; clearly you are an epistle of Christ, ministered by us, written not with ink but by the Spirit of the living God, not on tablets of stone but on tablets of flesh, that is, of the heart.

~ 2 Corinthians 3:2-3 NKJV

I marvel that you are turning away so soon from Him who called you in the grace of Christ, to a different gospel, which is not another; but there are some who trouble you and want to pervert the gospel of Christ. But even if we, or an angel from heaven, preach any other gospel to you than what we have preached to you, let him be accursed.

~ Galatians 1:6-8 NKJV

As you therefore have received Christ Jesus the Lord, so walk in Him, rooted and built up in Him and established in the faith, as you have been taught, abounding in it with thanksgiving.

~ Colossians 2:6-7 NKJV

5. They taught what they had seen and witnessed—the truth.

But I make known to you, brethren, that the gospel which was preached by me is not according to man. For I neither received it from man, nor was I taught it, but it came through the revelation of Jesus Christ.

~ Galatians 1:11-12 NKJV

That which was from the beginning, which we have heard, which we have seen with our eyes, which we have looked upon, and our hands have handled, concerning the Word of life— the life was manifested, and we have seen, and bear witness, and declare to you that eternal life which was with the Father and was manifested to us— that which we have seen and heard we declare to you, that you also may have fellowship with us; and truly our fellowship is with the Father and with His Son Jesus Christ.

~ 1 John 1:1–3 NKJV

6. They answered two important questions, "What's in it for me?" and "What would you have me do?"

Now the Lord is the Spirit; and where the Spirit of the Lord is, there is liberty.

~2 Corinthians 3:17 NKJV

Therefore, if anyone is in Christ, he is a new creation; old things have passed away; behold, all things have become new. Now all things are of God, who has reconciled us to Himself through Jesus Christ, and has given us the ministry of reconciliation, that is, that God was in Christ reconciling the world to Himself, not imputing their trespasses to them, and has committed to us the word of reconciliation.

~ 2 Corinthians 5:17–19 NKJV

7. They encouraged the people in times of difficulty to pick up and continue to persevere.

Now I rejoice, not that you were made sorry, but that your sorrow led to repentance. For you were made sorry in a godly manner, that you might suffer loss from us in nothing. For godly sorrow produces repentance leading to salvation, not to be regretted; but the sorrow of the world produces death.

~ 2 Corinthians 7:9–10 NKJV

My little children, these things I write to you, so that you may not sin. And if anyone sins, we have an Advocate with the Father, Jesus Christ the righteous. And He Himself is the propitiation for our sins, and not for ours only but also for the whole world.

~ 1 John 2:1–2 NKJV

Therefore, as the elect of God, holy and beloved, put on tender mercies, kindness, humility, meekness, longsuffering; bearing with one another, and forgiving one another, if anyone has a complaint against another; even as Christ forgave you, so you also must do.

~ Colossians 3:12–13 NKJV

Our God never changes; but we are constantly changing. God, our rock, provides a constant point of orientation in the midst of change. When we keep our focus on living our lives in obedience to Christ, we can act as godly agents of change in the lives of others. Moreover, we are able to "remove the plank from our eyes so that we are able to see the speck in our brother's eyes." We can, with God's help, be godly agents of change, helping to bring into our work, our homes, and our communities the kingdom of God today.

REFLECTIONS FOR THE WEEK

1. The New Testament stories show the early evangelists interacting with the people in five relational roles: stranger, close friend, coach/mentor, parent, and boss. Do you believe the seven steps above would be effective when the relationship is that of a boss and subordinate? Why?

2. We may make a mistake in our leadership of others. How will you respond in such a situation?

PRAYER

O God, You have called me to be a leader and to be mindful of those in my care. You have placed me with a family, among friends, within a business and a community, and You have commanded that I be faithful to You and diligent in serving others in my care. I pray that You will guide me in my role as a leader. Hear my prayer, forgive my errors, bless my endeavors, and encourage me in times of weakness.

> *But let all those rejoice who put their trust in You;*
> *Let them ever shout for joy, because You defend them;*
> *Let those also who love Your name*
> *Be joyful in You.*
> *For You, O Lord, will bless the righteous;*
> *With favor You will surround him as with a shield.*
> ~Psalm 5:11–12 NKJV

Amen

OCTOBER—WEEK FOUR

DEFINING THE MISSION OF THE ORGANIZATION

> Then one of them, a lawyer, asked Him a question, testing Him, and saying, "Teacher, which is the great commandment in the law?" Jesus said to him, "'You shall love the Lord your God with all your heart, with all your soul, and with all your mind.' This is the first and great commandment. And the second is like it: 'You shall love your neighbor as yourself.' On these two commandments hang all the Law and the Prophets."
>
> ~ Matthew 22:35–40 NKJV

> Now Peter and John went up together to the temple at the hour of prayer, the ninth hour. And a certain man lame from his mother's womb was carried, whom they laid daily at the gate of the temple which is called Beautiful, to ask alms from those who entered the temple; who, seeing Peter and John about to go into the temple, asked for alms. And fixing his eyes on him, with John, Peter said, "Look at us." So he gave them his attention, expecting to receive something from them. Then Peter said, "Silver and gold I do not have, but what I do have I give you: In the name of Jesus Christ of Nazareth, rise up and walk." And he took him by the right hand and lifted him up, and immediately his feet and ankle bones received strength. So he, leaping up, stood and walked and entered the temple with them—walking, leaping, and praising God.
>
> ~ Acts 3:1–8 NKJV

February 7, 2010 dawned as a crisp, beautiful day in South Florida. My son and I were on a mission. Our destination: Sun Life Stadium for Super Bowl XLIV. Tired from a red-eye flight out of Louisiana the day before and a night of restless sleep, we were nonetheless energetic and eagerly looking forward to participating with the thousands of other fans in cheering on our team.

Sun Life Stadium is off the beaten path, and a large grassy field separates the transportation and shuttle areas and the stadium gates. Stepping off the shuttle bus, we merged into the mob of enthusiastic and festive people forming a restless sea of color—blue and white or black and gold, depending on their allegiance. It was an electric moment. Suddenly, in the middle of that great green field, we were accosted by a half-dozen or so Christian evangelists handing out tracts on Christ and passionately pleading with everyone within earshot to "repent and hear the good news." Their presence and message were unexpected, and the crowd met them with amusement and, in some instances, hostility. The evangelists had to have expected that, but they persevered, regardless. They too, it seems, were on a mission.

Approaching them, I wondered in my heart how a soapbox messenger would appeal to anyone, let alone this particular crowd. But I reminded myself that God can use all circumstances to break into our world and our self-awareness. I remembered another time when my feet were hurrying me along, not on a wonderful outing with my son, but on a darker mission of deceit and betrayal, and I wondered what might have been my reaction then had I ventured upon a soapbox evangelist. Would I have turned aside? I took a tract and thanked the person who handed it to me. In my mind, anyone who proclaims Christ deserves to have other Christians thank them for their labor.

Negative reaction from a crowd hearing the call of Christ has been the evangelist's circumstance since Jesus departed. The Apostle Paul said, "Where is the wise? Where is the scribe? Where is the disputer of this age? Has not God made foolish the wisdom of this world? For since, in the wisdom of God, the world through wisdom did not know God, it pleased God through the foolishness of the message preached to save those who believe. For Jews request a sign, and Greeks seek after wisdom; but we preach Christ crucified, to the Jews a stumbling block and to the Greeks foolishness, but to those who are called, both Jews and Greeks, Christ the power of God and the wisdom of God" (1 Corinthians 1:20–24 NKJV).

Although my personality is not drawn to a street-corner (grassy field) soapbox orator, I realize their message is the same as Billy Graham's. And since I know what Christ has done for me, I will not impede the message being preached to anyone else.

Looking back, I think a lot of the negative reaction of the Super Bowl crowd was a self-defense mechanism, as if the context and message of the evangelists somehow implied the football game and the fun such an event provides was sinful and, worse, that we were a sinful people for participating. Perhaps the evangelists thought that, but it seems more likely to me they chose the venue because it would host a great crowd—like Jesse James' reason for robbing banks (when asked why he robbed banks he is reported to have said, "because that is where the money is"). If you are an evangelist, you go where the people are.

I find it difficult to think of these evangelists as cheerless individuals. Surely, if we truly knew them by name, they too would reveal a "life" where events are celebrated and the joy of life is realized. They must step down from the soapbox sometime and go home. I believe they were just "working" on Super Bowl Sunday.

So, in retrospect, I cannot fault them for intruding on our gaiety. Sin can be found everywhere because it is everywhere—even at a Super Bowl. On that day, like any day, the odds favor that some there had real problems—drinking, gambling, abusive behaviors, or dishonesty. Others, I am sure, were back-sliding in their faith, and a message to heed the call of Christ again was as a lighthouse in foggy weather. Certainly, some of the people at Sun Life Stadium that day were unsaved. Had that group listened to the evangelists, it would have been Son Life Stadium—a double win—a Super Bowl and Salvation!

Mission statements express the "why" companies and organizations exist. As such, they provide a context and framework by which decisions are reached and plans are executed. It seems to me that even a poorly written mission statement can bring clarity and unity of purpose within an organization. It is easy to see the benefit of employees and coworkers sharing common beliefs about businesses and using the same measuring sticks to judge performance, identify trouble, and respond to opportunity.

My experience is that business life often mirrors personal life. For example, walking past a problem at work gives tacit approval for others to walk past problems. And, walking past a problem at home also leads to regret later on. Procrastination is another example—to procrastinate is never good—at home or at work. Choosing to refrain from starting a project without the necessary resources to complete it is wise at work and home. A kind word timely spoken is well received at work and at home.

So if life mirrors work, what about mission statements? Is there any benefit in developing a personal mission statement for ourselves? Where would we begin? How would we approach such an assignment?

Dr. Rick Warren[5], pastor of Saddleback Church in California, wrote a blockbuster bestseller, *The Purpose Driven Life: What on Earth Am I Here For?* dealing with this topic. Dr. Warren asserts the "quest for personal fulfillment, satisfaction and meaning can only be found understanding and doing what God placed you on earth to do." According to Dr. Warren, the starting place for an individual to answer the fundamental questions of "Why am I here?" and "What is my purpose?" must be with God and His eternal purposes for each life. In his words, Dr. Warren says, "it is not about you." The Purpose Driven Life outlines five purposes for each individual, based upon God's plan when we were created:

- We are planned for God's pleasure, so the first purpose is to offer real worship.
- We were formed for God's family, so the second purpose is to enjoy real fellowship.
- We were created to become like Christ, so the third purpose is to learn real discipleship.
- We were shaped for serving God, so the fourth purpose is to practice real ministry.
- We were made for a mission, so the fifth purpose is to live out real evangelism.

I agree with Dr. Warren that our purpose in life is found in God. Apart from a relationship with God, whatever we do in life will, in the final judgment, be less than what could have been. The wonderful news is that God wants to have a relationship with us. The biggest obstacle we face in obtaining a relationship with God is ourselves.

---

5   Quotes from Dr. Warren were obtained from *The Purpose Driven Life* home page.

> Behold, I stand at the door and knock. If anyone hears My voice and opens the door, I will come in to him and dine with him, and he with Me.
>
> ~ Revelation 3:20 NKJV

> Jesus answered and said to him, "If anyone loves Me, he will keep My word; and My Father will love him, and We will come to him and make Our home with him.
>
> ~ John 14:23 NKJV

> Come to Me, all you who labor and are heavy laden, and I will give you rest.
>
> ~ Matthew 11:28 NKJV

> O Jerusalem, Jerusalem, the one who kills the prophets and stones those who are sent to her! How often I wanted to gather your children together, as a hen gathers her chicks under her wings, but you were not willing!
>
> ~ Matthew 23:3 NKJV

While I can agree with Dr. Warren that realization of the human self starts with having a relationship with God, I disagree with his assertion that it is not about us. Finding our purpose in life is rooted in understanding and appreciating just how much God cherishes us.

I think it is important to remember just how much God loves us for "us." After all: God created us, God loves us, and God sent Christ to us. Those things are pretty personal to me.

> For God so loved the world that He gave His only begotten Son, that whoever believes in Him should not perish but have everlasting life.
>
> ~ John 3:16 NKJV

> We love Him because He first loved us.
>
> ~ 1 John 4:19 NKJV

> But God demonstrates His own love toward us, in that while we were still sinners, Christ died for us.
>
> ~ Romans 5:8 NKJV

> For you were bought at a price; therefore glorify God in your body and in your spirit, which are God's.
>
> ~ 1 Corinthians 6:20 NKJV

Christian music artist tobyMac summed up our importance to God in his song "Made to Love."[6] Because God knew us before He formed us and because He has promised never to leave or forsake us, we know that we were "made to love, and be loved by [God]."

Because God created us, we have a hidden hunger for relationship with Him. Because God loves us, His love is available to everyone, all the time. It is like an electrical outlet in a wall—the power is there, but to be useful it must be accessed and a switch turned on. Experiencing God's love is a potential reality that becomes true reality immediately upon our being plugged into Him. The first and greatest commandment calls us to plug ourselves into a relationship with God—to "love the Lord our God with all our heart, all our mind and all our strength." Our true power, purpose, wisdom, and gifts are found in God.

And what are we to make of God's greatest gift—the gift of Christ to us? We are to take that gift and share Christ with our neighbor. Yes, the Golden Rule teaches us to treat people the way we would like to be treated—i.e. with respect, with integrity, with good intentions, with kindness, with empathy—all personal and human emotions and characteristics of behavior. But lately I have come to think there is much more involved in loving our neighbor as ourselves.

John Wesley, the founder of the Methodist church, was famous for admonishing his fellow ministers to "offer them [the people] Christ." What other act of love could we ever show to anyone that would compare with offering people Christ? On February 4, 2010, some soapbox evangelists in South Florida considered the derision of the crowd to be of no consequence as they offered Christ to everyone who passed by. Peter and John, upon entering the temple, offered Christ to a lame man, and then to all who came to see the miracle. Billy Graham, perhaps more eloquently than the South Florida

---

6   tobyMac. "Made to Love." Portable Sounds. Forefront Records, 2006.

evangelists, has offered Christ to millions of people around the world in a ministry spanning 70 years.

In your town, this Sunday, in churches everywhere, a minister will offer Christ to those who attend and hear. And in Samaria, over two thousand years ago, "many of the Samaritans of that city believed in Him because of the word of the woman who testified, 'He told me all that I ever did'" (John 4:39 NKJV).

Offering Christ to the world is an inescapable and integral component of every Christian's personal mission statement. We are not all called to stand on soapboxes, but we are called to be prepared to share the hope that is in us, that transforms our lives and gives us peace.

But sanctify the Lord God in your hearts, and always be ready to give a defense to everyone who asks you a reason for the hope that is in you, with meekness and fear; having a good conscience, that when they defame you as evildoers, those who revile your good conduct in Christ may be ashamed (1 Peter 3:15–16 NKJV).

REFLECTIONS FOR THE WEEK

1. A number of years ago, I attended a conference on setting life goals and developing plans to achieve them. Each member of the conference was asked to prepare a personal mission statement. Here is mine:

> I am a child of the living God. I worship Him with gladness, and the knowledge of His presence illuminates my life. I find my purpose in Him, to be a loving husband and father and to work out his will for my life and my salvation with awe and trembling. I desire to walk in the light, to be a witness to the light and to do, faithfully, whatever He asks of me. He is my all, in all, and my sure hope and shelter in times of need.

2. Spend time this week developing your own personal mission statement. Remember, a mission statement should guide your actions, spell out your overall life goal, provide a path, and guide your daily decision making. Your personal mission statement will provide the framework or context within which you will set goals, evaluate objectives, and formulate strategies to achieve them.

3. Imagine a close friend has been diagnosed with a terrible illness. He or she comes to you and asks why you believe in God. How will you offer Christ to your friend?

PRAYER

Father God, I cannot comprehend why You chose to love me. And having become aware of Your love, I cannot comprehend living without it. Let me plunge headfirst into the love of Christ, the hope of Christ, and daily rejoice over the life of Christ that saved me and keeps on saving me. Through Your Holy Spirit, enable me to express the fruit of Your Spirit in my life: love, joy, peace, patience, kindness, goodness, gentleness, faithfulness, and self-control. With a grateful and humble heart, let me have opportunities to share Christ with a fallen world. Let me make a friend, be a friend, and lead a friend to Christ.

Amen

NOVEMBER

Make a joyful noise to the Lord, all the earth!
Serve the Lord with gladness!
Come into his presence with singing!
Know that the Lord, he is God!
It is he who made us, and we are his;
we are his people, and the sheep of his pasture.
Enter his gates with thanksgiving,
and his courts with praise!
Give thanks to him; bless his name!
For the Lord is good;
his steadfast love endures forever,
and his faithfulness to all generations.

~ Psalm 100 ESV

You keep him in perfect peace
whose mind is stayed on you,
because he trusts in you.
Trust in the Lord forever,
for the Lord God is an everlasting rock.

~ Isaiah 26:3-4 ESV

And a highway shall be there,
and it shall be called the Way of Holiness;
the unclean shall not pass over it.
It shall belong to those who walk on the way;
even if they are fools, they shall not go astray.
No lion shall be there,
nor shall any ravenous beast come up on it;
they shall not be found there,
but the redeemed shall walk there.
And the ransomed of the Lord shall return
and come to Zion with singing;
everlasting joy shall be upon their heads;
they shall obtain gladness and joy,
and sorrow and sighing shall flee away.

~ Isaiah 35:8-10 ESV

Whether events and circumstances have proven to be in your favor or against, the coming of November marks the beginning of the home stretch for this year. The holiday calendar and vacations compress the number of work days available. As a result, November and December will literally hurtle past. In a few short weeks, businesses will begin to receive Christmas and holiday cards from suppliers, friends, and affiliates. Offices will begin to receive holiday foods and treats for sharing with coworkers. Holiday decorations on streets and houses will brighten up the ever pressing dreariness of the winter season. Soon, the visible signs of celebration, thanksgiving, and joy will surround us. Some of us, perhaps most of us, will gleefully move into this time of feasting and holiday with great anticipation and gladness. Some, however, will feel more like Ebenezer Scrooge than Bob Cratchit. For them, the decorations, crowds, traffic, and songs of the season will impart little joy.

Just because the calendar has moved into the holiday season does not mean everyone is required to feel joyful and thankful. Sorrow and disappointment, disease and death, unfortunate circumstance and bad luck happen throughout the year. Expressing joy and thanksgiving in the midst of difficulties, trials, and uncertainties is not easy. Yet the record is clear, the example is undeniable—people of faith are called to express joy and thanksgiving in all circumstances (cf. Philippians 4:6-7 and Colossians 3:15). Should we feel worse if we do not feel joy and thanksgiving when our hearts are sad?

I confess that joy and thanksgiving hide from me in my dark hours. The human psyche is not geared toward joy and thanksgiving in the midst of trials, pain, and grief. Psychologists have tracked the progress of the human psyche moving through grief in five distinct phases: denial and isolation, anger, bargaining, depression, and acceptance. Joy and thanksgiving are not in the list. But I can also assert that my life is filled with joy and thanksgiving now. The reason? God has given me grace in each and every dark circumstance. I have persevered, endured, withstood, and passed through all troubles heretofore. I have a clear record of God's presence leading me toward His peace and His joy. He has never left me alone, He has never let me down, and I can think of no circumstance that He has not turned for my good. My life and times are my own testimony, and my goal is to continually shorten the time it takes to move through periods of darkness, anxiety, and stress, and into the peace and joy that flows from God.

And this, I believe, is the important distinction between Christians' and non-believers' experience of trials, sadness, difficulty, and uncertainty. When Little Orphan Annie sings, "The sun'll come out, tomorrow"[7] the source of her optimism is self-generated—the result of pep talks and human nature—perhaps an innate wisdom that says "what goes up, must come down" and no circumstance will remain the same forever. But optimism for believers is not worldly and self-generated. It is rather generated by the Holy Spirit through the operation of faith and hope.

Faith and hope for a believer are not at all subject to whim or chance, and that is what makes them so powerful. The world may view faith and hope as mere possibilities—sometimes things will work out for a person's good, sometimes they will not—but that is not to be the view of a Christian.

FAITH

> Now faith is the assurance of things hoped for, the conviction of things not seen.
>
> ~ Hebrews 11:1 ESV

The *Harper-Collins Dictionary of Religion* notes that faith is "the act or virtue or spiritual disposition by which people accept the reality, promises, and love of God. The term faith can refer to what one believes, or the power by which one believes, or the state of soul that belief creates." In dark times, faith becomes the power needed to uplift our hearts, reminding us that God is in control and that God is ever directing His love and will for the good of those who believe in Him and are called by His name. Faith is like a muscle, however, in that it must be exercised if it is

---

[7] "Tomorrow" by Charles Strouse and Martin Charnin, from the musical *Annie*, 1977.

to grow stronger. We do not know if what we confess to believe by faith is powerful until we are in need of it and are forced to find it in ourselves. We must walk through the valley of the shadow of death to know that God is walking with us.

Faith allows a Christian to be able to eagerly look forward to life everlasting in the presence of God. The Christian's eternal destiny is a settled matter, although not yet seen. With such an important matter firmly settled, there is immense freedom to focus on eternity while living in a temporal setting, to not succumb to anxieties whose source is a world that is passing away.

HOPE

Hope is another virtue that empowers Christians to express joy and thanksgiving in all circumstances. In an article entitled "Hope" (Bible.org), J. Hampton Keathley III eloquently discussed the role of hope in activating a believer's optimism in pressing circumstances. Mr. Keathley (a graduate of Dallas Theological Seminary and a pastor for 28 years, who died in 2002) observed that hope is a "strong and confident expectation" as opposed to a modern viewpoint that hope is wishful thinking and without certainty. Mr. Keathley's article illustrates that biblical hope accomplishes wonders in the lives of believers in the following ways:

- It changes how we see ourselves.
- It changes what we value.
- It affects what we do with our lives—our talents, time, treasures.
- It gives us joy and peace.
- It gives us protection.
- It gives us strength, courage, and boldness.
- It gives endurance, comfort, and confidence in the face of death.
- It gives us confidence in ministry.

No one makes it through life untouched by difficulty. Our ability to express joy and thanksgiving in all circumstances will be tested. Perspective is gained at the conclusion of a matter. We gain increasing measures of faith and hope by God's grace—and in faith and hope, we can rejoice.

> Therefore, since we have been justified by faith, we have peace with God through our Lord Jesus Christ. Through him we have also obtained access by faith into this grace in which we stand, and we rejoice in hope of the glory of God. Not only that, but we rejoice in our sufferings, knowing that suffering produces endurance, and endurance produces character, and character produces hope, and hope does not put us to shame, because God's love has been poured into our hearts through the Holy Spirit who has been given to us.
>
> ~ Romans 5:1–5 ESV

My Christian friends, if this is a season of darkness rather than joy and light for you, recall how God has acted in your life in the past and be renewed. Recall how He loves you. Recall how He did not withhold His Son from us. Be full of faith and hope. Today, offer a prayer of thanks for what God will do and is doing in your life at this difficult time, and pray for patient endurance until the trial has passed.

REFLECTIONS FOR NOVEMBER

1. Spend time drafting a prayer of thanksgiving for Thanksgiving Day. Include in your prayer a petition for God's blessing and peace upon those whom you know are going through difficult times.

2. Find the time to discuss the concepts of joy and peace with other Christians. What has been their experience in finding joy and peace in difficult circumstances? Use these stories to build up one another's spiritual reserves against the day when trials and uncertainties arise again.

PRAYER

Father God, thank You for being with me in difficult times. Through Your Holy Spirit, remind me of Your faithfulness and Your promises. Forgive me when in dark times I struggle to cling in hope and faith to You. Use those times to guide me into a deeper relationship with You, and let me help others who are struggling with their own dark times.

Surely he has borne our griefs
 and carried our sorrows;
yet we esteemed him stricken,
 smitten by God, and afflicted.
 But he was pierced for our transgressions;
 he was crushed for our iniquities;
 upon him was the chastisement that brought us peace,
 and with his wounds we are healed.

~ Isaiah 53:4–5 ESV

Amen

NOVEMBER—WEEK ONE

PRACTICING GOOD STEWARDSHIP THROUGH THE DILIGENT MANAGEMENT AND ALLOCATION OF RESOURCES

Do not toil to acquire wealth;
be discerning enough to desist.
When your eyes light on it, it is gone,
for suddenly it sprouts wings,
flying like an eagle toward heaven.

~ Proverbs 23:4–5 ESV

Do not eat the bread of a man who is stingy;
do not desire his delicacies,
for he is like one who is inwardly calculating.
"Eat and drink!" he says to you,
but his heart is not with you.
You will vomit up the morsels that you have eaten,
and waste your pleasant words.

~ Proverbs 23:6–8 ESV

I charge you in the presence of God and of Christ Jesus, who is to judge the living and the dead, and by his appearing and his kingdom: preach the word; be ready in season and out of season; reprove, rebuke, and exhort, with complete patience and teaching. For the time is coming when people will not endure sound teaching, but having itching ears they will accumulate for themselves teachers to suit their own passions, and will turn away from listening to the truth and wander off into myths. As for you, always be sober-minded, endure suffering, do the work of an evangelist, fulfill your ministry. For I am already being poured out as a drink offering, and the time of my departure has come. I have fought the good fight, I have finished the race, I have kept the faith. Henceforth there is laid up for me the crown of righteousness, which the Lord, the righteous judge, will award to me on that Day, and not only to me but also to all who have loved his appearing.

~ 2 Timothy 4:1–8 ESV

Each Christian, at a precise and specific point in time, was changed into a new person, and the old self, the former person of consciousness that had ruled and defined life, values and relationships, was obliterated. The old self lived life in rebellion against God; the new self lives life in harmony with God and His purposes. Each of us was irrevocably changed the moment we confessed Jesus Christ as Lord, the Savior of our souls, and the Redeemer of all our sins; on the basis of His righteousness alone, we stand blameless in the presence of Almighty God. Theologians say we have been ***justified*** before God. Thereafter, the process of internalizing and comprehending in a personal way the gravity of God's gift of grace begins. For the rest of our lives, with the help and guidance of the Holy Spirit, we are shaped and molded into the person that God wants us to be. More and more, we become like Jesus. "He must increase, but I must decrease" (John 3:30 ESV).

The process by which Christians change into new, self-aware creatures becoming more and more like Christ is called "sanctification." *The Harper-Collins Dictionary of Religion* defines sanctification as "the procedure for making a person sacred." Wayne Grudem, in his book *Systematic Theology: an Introduction to Biblical Doctrine*, defines sanctification as "a progressive work of God and man that makes us more and more free from sin and like Christ in our actual lives." God is truth; becoming more like God reveals our true selves. The status quo must change once Jesus has touched our lives and the Holy Spirit has indwelt us. Happiness—being blessed in all circumstances—is an outcome of sanctification.

Our journey of sanctification is lifelong. It proceeds at an uneven pace. Sometimes the pace is fast, and spiritual growth and renewal abound; other times spiritual growth seems slow and delayed, and our faith can even be challenged. No Christian is perfect. Even the Apostle Paul said, "Not that I have already obtained this or am already perfect, but I press on to make it my own, because Christ Jesus has made me his own" (Philippians 3:12 ESV).

Because we are not laboring solely on our own—God is at work in us—and God will not fail (Philippians 1:6), we are encouraged in all circumstances, confident that God will succeed in changing us into what He wants us to be.

Sanctification deals with two fundamental issues of self: are we our own master, or do we belong to another; and, how are we to use and deploy ourselves in life? A significant doctrine of Christianity, and a stumbling block for some, is that we must lose ourselves when we find Christ. In fact, to gain Christ, we must lose ourselves and forfeit allegiance to anyone or anything else other than Christ.

> Whoever loves father or mother more than me is not worthy of me, and whoever loves son or daughter more than me is not worthy of me. And whoever does not take his cross and follow me is not worthy of me. Whoever finds his life will lose it, and whoever loses his life for my sake will find it.
> ~ Matthew 10: 37–39 ESV

> And they came to Capernaum. And when he was in the house he asked them, "What were you discussing on the way?" But they kept silent, for on the way they had argued with one another about who was the greatest. And he sat down and called the twelve. And he said to them, "If anyone would be first, he must be last of all and servant of all."
> ~ Mark 9:33–35 ESV

> At that time the disciples came to Jesus, saying, "Who is the greatest in the kingdom of heaven?" And calling to him a child, he put him in the midst of them and said, "Truly, I say to you, unless you turn and become like children, you will never enter the kingdom of heaven. Whoever humbles himself like this child is the greatest in the kingdom of heaven."
> ~ Matthew 18:1–4 ESV

Spiritual maturity gained through the process of sanctification yields awareness that God has claims on our lives—our thoughts, our actions, our relationships, our work. God's claim upon our lives is often characterized as that of a Master toward a servant—even that of a Master toward a slave. In the first issue of self we realize who owns us. God owns us; we are His. "Know that the Lord, he is God! It is he who made us, and we are his; we are his people, and the sheep of his pasture" (Psalm 100:3 ESV).

The relationship of God as Master and ourselves as servants can be thought of as that between an owner (God) and a steward of the owner's property (us). A steward is someone entrusted with someone else's property for the purpose of managing it in accordance with the owner's wishes. It is an interesting paradox that we belong to God, but God has entrusted us with the safekeeping of His property. The result can be the same as asking the fox to guard the henhouse. But unlike foxes, we possess intellects and the power of the Holy Spirit to guide our choices about managing God's property.

A steward is required to make choices with respect to the property in their care. Those choices usually entail two broad alternatives—spend (use up) some of the property, or conserve the property.

Choices to spend (use up) some of the property, in turn, can be characterized in one of three ways: invest, sustain, and waste. Choosing to invest a portion of the property has as its goal an increase in the overall property at some time in the future. An investment is to return both the amount invested (the principal) and a gain.

Choosing to sustain the property may entail using some of the property for upkeep and protection. Using a portion of the property in this way will not result in a return, but is designed to avoid a loss greater than the amount used. Using up some of the property in ways that are neither investing nor sustaining is to waste the property—there is no benefit inuring to the owner for such use of the property.

Sometimes a decision to invest will not be successful. There is always an element of risk in any investment. Where circumstances result in a loss of gain or principal, understanding the attitude of the steward is necessary to evaluate whether the use of property was wasteful.

In the parable of the talents (Matthew 25:14–30), Jesus commends the actions of two good stewards and condemns the actions of one unfaithful steward. While it is true the parable records both good stewards earning a return for their Master, the actions of the stewards to use their

Master's property in accordance with their abilities and their Master's wishes are the true source of their Master's commendation. Similarly, the heart (attitude) of the unfaithful manager was not directed toward the Master's best interests, nor did the unfaithful manager use his best ability to bring gain to the Master. The unfaithful manager's decision to conserve the property by hiding it in the ground was foolish and wrong.

As a leader of your business, you are charged with behaving as an honest and faithful steward of the assets entrusted to your care. Although a leader who is also an owner of a business has more flexibility in choosing to invest, sustain, or waste resources than a leader working for an owner, there are still third parties with vested interests associated with any enterprise that should restrain and constrain waste. For example, employees want to be paid, creditors want to be paid, and partners want to realize a return on their investment commensurate with the risk taken in making an investment in the enterprise; governments and communities want taxes paid, property maintained, and community services enriched. Wasting resources can put the interests of third parties at risk.

As God's steward of your own life—*the life he owns*—you are also charged to be an honest and faithful manager. You are charged to choose between using up your life in accordance with God's will, or conserving your life and standing on the sidelines. The wishes of God are clear on how He wants you to behave.

> Son of man, I have made you a watchman for the house of Israel. Whenever you hear a word from my mouth, you shall give them warning from me. If I say to the wicked, 'You shall surely die,' and you give him no warning, nor speak to warn the wicked from his wicked way, in order to save his life, that wicked person shall die for his iniquity, but his blood I will require at your hand. But if you warn the wicked, and he does not turn from his wickedness, or from his wicked way, he shall die for his iniquity, but you will have delivered your soul.
> ~ Ezekiel 3:17–19 ESV

You are the light of the world. A city set on a hill cannot be hidden. Nor do people light a lamp and put it under a basket, but on a stand, and it gives light to all in the house. In the same way, let your light shine before others, so that they may see your good works and give glory to your Father who is in heaven.

~ Matthew 5:14–16 ESV

So we are both servants of Christ (charged to follow Him) and stewards of Christ's possessions—namely, ourselves. All that we own and possess—our intellects, our financial resources, our energy and capacity to do work, our time, our relationships, our physical health, and our attitudes—are gifts of God and, at the same time, owned by God. Moving through life on a journey of sanctification, Christians expend those resources and invest in the kingdom of God. Christians use the blessings God has given them to grow and sustain His kingdom.

Christ is more than an intellectual exercise for us. We are called to live lives that draw others to Christ, to serve others, to build up the church, and to glorify God. We are called to invest ourselves in God's kingdom. We are heirs of the kingdom of God and are not merely spectators of it.

> For as in one body we have many members, and the members do not all have the same function, so we, though many, are one body in Christ, and individually members one of another. Having gifts that differ according to the grace given to us, let us use them: if prophecy, in proportion to our faith; if service, in our serving; the one who teaches, in his teaching; the one who exhorts, in his exhortation; the one who contributes, in generosity; the one who leads, with zeal; the one who does acts of mercy, with cheerfulness.
>
> ~ Romans 12:4–8 ESV

Above all, keep loving one another earnestly, since love covers a multitude of sins. Show hospitality to one another without grumbling. As each has received a gift, use it to serve one another, as good stewards of God's varied grace: whoever speaks, as one who speaks oracles of God; whoever serves, as one who serves by the strength that God supplies—in order that in everything God may be glorified through Jesus Christ. To him belong glory and dominion forever and ever.

~ 1 Peter 4:8–11 ESV

Just as no Christian is perfect, no Christian lives in a perfect world. It is difficult to determine if what we are doing in the world is consistent with God's plan. The world changes, and our lives and circumstances change too. But I believe we can discover God's plan for using us in His kingdom in five distinct areas of our lives, regardless of our present circumstances.

1. **Take stock of your natural abilities.** What are your interests, your training, your experiences, your talents, and your strengths? In their book, *Now, Discover Your Strengths,* Marcus Buckingham and Donald O. Clifton, Ph.D. assert that a person's best use of time and energy is against their strength and not in shoring up an area that is not strength. They note, "To excel in your chosen field and to find lasting satisfaction in doing so, you will need to understand your unique patterns. You will need to become an expert at finding and describing and applying and practicing and refining your strengths." Similarly, applying your natural abilities in Christian work will bring confidence, productivity, and satisfaction.

2. **Be alert to any circumstance God places in your path that requires a decision of involvement or restraint.** The circumstances I mean are spontaneous and not part of your daily routine. Responding to a beggar, offering assistance to a stranded motorist, rebuking foolish and bad behavior in others, and offering a kind word to one in sorrow are all examples of learning to stretch your role in God's kingdom beyond what you already perceive it to be.

3. **Be intentional in your understanding of the primary relational roles you hold in life.** Are you a parent of young children or old, are you caring for elderly parents or others in poor health or special circumstances, are you a spouse, are you an employer or employee, are you retired, are you a friend, are you a coach, teacher, or mentor to others? We are not here to "go along to get along." We are here to make a difference. Someday we will be held accountable before God for how we responded to the persons that God placed in our lives.

4. **Adopt a Christian perspective on financial and other resources that have been entrusted to you.**

> For if the readiness is there, it is acceptable according to what a person has, not according to what he does not have.
> ~ 2 Corinthians 8:12 ESV

> The point is this: whoever sows sparingly will also reap sparingly, and whoever sows bountifully will also reap bountifully. Each one must give as he has decided in his heart, not reluctantly or under compulsion, for God loves a cheerful giver. And God is able to make all grace abound to you, so that having all sufficiency in all things at all times, you may abound in every good work.
> ~ 2 Corinthians 9:6-8 ESV

5. **Take stock of the circumstances in which you find yourself.** God has placed you in a particular geographic location. God has placed you in a specific job with specific circumstances associated with it. God walks with you every day and is intimate with everything affecting you. In all circumstances, you can be of service to God.

> Do you not know that in a race all the runners run, but only one receives the prize? So run that you may obtain it. Every athlete exercises self-control in all things. They do it to receive a perishable wreath, but we an imperishable. So I do not run aimlessly; I do not box as one beating the air. But I discipline my body and keep it under control, lest after preaching to others I myself should be disqualified.
> ~ 1 Corinthians 9:24-27 ESV

Finally, what should be the goal of our service to God? If we are truly good stewards of what God has given us, what should be the evidence of our effort?

Many years ago I heard a joke that poked fun at the stewardship of a certain John Doe. According to the joke, it came to pass that John Doe died, and at the reading of his last will and testament, these words were written: "I, John Doe, being of sound mind and body, spent it all." When I heard the joke, I confess I thought it reflected, at least in some measure, a very astute point of view. John Doe left nothing behind. John Doe had exhibited perfect timing in his death. On the other hand, it is clear that if John Doe was survived by family or had obligations that outlived him, then condemnation of John Doe is the better point of view. We cannot judge John Doe in a vacuum.

But the joke has stuck with me over a number of years. And I have come to reflect on the joke in a new light. John Doe ends his life with nothing left. Whatever had interested John Doe in life was no longer important. We do not know how John Doe invested his life, but we know his ending left nothing. We do not know how hard he tried to accomplish his goals. And all of this leads to a very important question that echoes the question of Ecclesiastes, "What does man gain by all the toil at which he toils under the sun?" (Ecclesiastes 1:3 ESV). Is anything worth exhausting yourself completely in its pursuit? Jesus told two parables that say the answer is "yes."

> The kingdom of heaven is like treasure hidden in a field, which a man found and covered up. Then in his joy he goes and sells all that he has and buys that field.
>
> Again, the kingdom of heaven is like a merchant in search of fine pearls, who, on finding one pearl of great value, went and sold all that he had and bought it."
>
> ~ Matthew 13:44–46 ESV

The pursuit of the kingdom of God is worth exhaustion. And this implies an interesting paradox in discharging the role of being a steward of God's property. As a Christian steward of my life and my gifts and my resources, my goal is to exhaust them. My goal is to restate the joke this way: "I, Don Moore, being of sound mind and body, spent it all for Jesus." I want to finish the race depleted, used up, tired, but exhilarated from the journey of sanctification. Let me say as Paul, "For I am already being poured out as a drink offering, and the time of my departure has come. I have fought the good fight, I have finished the race, I have kept the faith. Henceforth there is laid up for me the crown of righteousness, which the Lord, the righteous judge, will award to me on that Day, and not only to me but also to all who have loved his appearing" (2 Timothy 4:6–8 ESV).

REFLECTIONS FOR THE WEEK

1. Meditate and pray this week on the five areas of your life listed above. What areas do you believe are being used effectively in your role as steward of your life for Christ? What areas might be worth exploring?

2. Sometimes people hesitate to commit to becoming involved because of uncertainty as to the legitimacy of the perceived call on their life or confusion about how God has gifted them for service. Wayne Grudem, in his book *Systematic Theology: an Introduction to Biblical Doctrine*, offered the following advice for people struggling to understand their spiritual gifts and ways in which to be of service to God. "The person wondering what his or her spiritual gifts are should simply begin to try ministering in various areas and see where God brings blessing." Where do you feel drawn to help at church or in your community?

PRAYER

Dear Jesus, embolden me to more service. Let me say with the psalmist,
"Search me, O God, and know my heart!
Try me and know my thoughts!
And see if there be any grievous way in me,
and lead me in the way everlasting!" (Psalm 139:23–24 ESV).
                                                                Amen

NOVEMBER—WEEK TWO

PROTECTING THE REPUTATION OF THE ORGANIZATION

"And now, behold, the cry of the people of Israel has come to me, and I have also seen the oppression with which the Egyptians oppress them. Come, I will send you to Pharaoh that you may bring my people, the children of Israel, out of Egypt." But Moses said to God, "Who am I that I should go to Pharaoh and bring the children of Israel out of Egypt?" He said, "But I will be with you."

~ Exodus 3:9–12a ESV

Then Moses answered, "But behold, they will not believe me or listen to my voice, for they will say, 'The Lord did not appear to you.'" "If they will not believe you," God said, "or listen to the first sign, they may believe the latter sign. If they will not believe even these two signs or listen to your voice, you shall take some water from the Nile and pour it on the dry ground, and the water that you shall take from the Nile will become blood on the dry ground."

But Moses said to the Lord, "Oh, my Lord, I am not eloquent, either in the past or since you have spoken to your servant, but I am slow of speech and of tongue." Then the Lord said to him, "Who has made man's mouth? Who makes him mute, or deaf, or seeing, or blind? Is it not I, the Lord? Now therefore go, and I will be with your mouth and teach you what you shall speak." But he said, "Oh, my Lord, please send someone else." Then the anger of the Lord was kindled against Moses.

~ Exodus 4:1, 8–14a ESV

What then? Are we Jews any better off? No, not at all. For we have already charged that all, both Jews and Greeks, are under sin, as it is written:

"None is righteous, no, not one;
no one understands;
no one seeks for God.

~ Romans 3:9–11 ESV

> So Pilate entered his headquarters again and called Jesus and said to him, "Are you the King of the Jews?" Jesus answered, "Do you say this of your own accord, or did others say it to you about me?" Pilate answered, "Am I a Jew? Your own nation and the chief priests have delivered you over to me. What have you done?" Jesus answered, "My kingdom is not of this world. If my kingdom were of this world, my servants would have been fighting, that I might not be delivered over to the Jews. But my kingdom is not from the world." Then Pilate said to him, "So you are a king?" Jesus answered, "You say that I am a king. For this purpose I was born and for this purpose I have come into the world—to bear witness to the truth. Everyone who is of the truth listens to my voice." Pilate said to him, "What is truth?"
>
> ~ John 18:33–38a ESV

One of the most successful television shows, based upon longevity and viewer interest statistics, was "America's Most Wanted" that aired on the Fox Television Network from February 1988 through March 2013. According to a TV Guide article, the program played a major role in the capture of more than 1,200 fugitives worldwide. Americans, it seems, not only watched the show, they also paid attention.

On the FBI website it is reported the genesis of the "FBI Ten Most Wanted Fugitives" list began when a reporter made an inquiry about the names and descriptions of the "toughest guys" the FBI wanted to capture. After the story ran, publicity was so great that J. Edgar Hoover, then Director of the FBI, made the list permanent.

Is it safe to say we are fascinated with villains? It certainly seems so.

For some, the fascination with criminal and aberrant behavior is akin to the "rubber necking" of bystanders passing a traffic accident. We are curious creatures and have a natural interest in accidents, crimes, and tragedies. Human curiosity in turn drives the focus of purveyors of news; very little news reported on a daily basis deals with good news.

For others, interest in criminal behavior undoubtedly relates to the human intellect trying to come to grips with the darker side of human nature. Continual news reports of the evil that exists and is rampant in the world still leaves us unprepared when faced with crimes and violence occurring in our neighborhoods. Thoughts of "how could" and "why" and "what type of person" cross our minds when confronted with stories of murder, theft, battery, assault, fraud, abuse, betrayal, and terrorism.

The Bible includes many stories of villains—it is, after all, a mirror into humanity. As such, the Bible clearly reflects mankind's penchant for evil. The stories of villainy and evil impact us the same way as stories on the evening news, in our newspapers, or on the radio.

Just like our times and headlines, the villains in the Bible come from all people, socioeconomic classes, and all places. The villains presented in the Bible commit different offenses, but each of the stories is unambiguous about the villainy of the individual. In this regard the Bible record differs from our human experience with today's headlines because the villainy is truly exposed. The Bible peers into the minds and hearts of the persons in its stories, and we know their crimes and their guilt. Their character demonstrates sin and evil. In keeping with the FBI Ten Most Wanted List, here are some of the villains in the Bible and the evil they caused.

1. Cain—the first son of Adam and Eve. Cain was envious and jealous of his brother Abel and allowed a terrible thought to enter into his mind. Cain did not master his evil impulse but rather acted upon it and murdered his brother Abel—the first murder (Genesis 4).

2. Lamech—a son of Cain. Lamech was filled with pride and avarice. He was also the first bigamist reported in the Bible. Lamech's pride and wrath led him to commit murder, just as his father had done. And just like Cain, Lamech expressed no remorse; in fact, he justified his actions. "I have killed a man for wounding me, a young man for striking me. If Cain's revenge is sevenfold, then Lamech's is seventy-sevenfold" (Genesis 4:23b-24 ESV).

3. Pharaoh—king of Egypt who subjected the Israelites to cruel slavery and captivity. Pharaoh cared nothing for human life. Being afraid of the increasing numbers of the Israelites, Pharaoh ordered the death of all male infants born to Jewish families. Pharaoh did not know God and did not respect or honor God's call to release the Israelites into Moses's care. Pharaoh's obstinacy and pride cost Egypt the lives of all firstborn

sons—other than the protected Israelites—and ultimately cost him his life and the lives of many of his soldiers (Exodus 4:18–14:31).

4. Jeroboam—the first king of Israel following the separation of the united kingdom under Saul, David, and Solomon. Jeroboam was envious of the Temple and worship in Jerusalem and fearful that over time his subjects would want to rejoin Judah in order to participate in festivals, worship, and Temple sacrifice. Accordingly, "He also made temples on high places and appointed priests from among all the people, who were not of the Levites" (1 Kings 12:31 ESV). Jeroboam thus dishonored God and led his people into disobedience, false worship, and apostasy. Through the prophet Ahijah, God pronounced the following condemnation of Jeroboam:

> "Go, tell Jeroboam, 'Thus says the Lord, the God of Israel: "Because I exalted you from among the people and made you leader over my people Israel and tore the kingdom away from the house of David and gave it to you, and yet you have not been like my servant David, who kept my commandments and followed me with all his heart, doing only that which was right in my eyes, but you have done evil above all who were before you and have gone and made for yourself other gods and metal images, provoking me to anger, and have cast me behind your back.'"
> ~ 1 Kings 14:7–9 ESV

5. Ahab—a king of Israel and the husband of Jezebel. The Bible describes Ahab in this way:

> And Ahab the son of Omri did evil in the sight of the Lord, more than all who were before him. And as if it had been a light thing for him to walk in the sins of Jeroboam the son of Nebat, he took for his wife Jezebel the daughter of Ethbaal king of the Sidonians, and went and served Baal and worshiped him.
> ~1 Kings 16:30–31 ESV

Ahab's lust for Jezebel led him to allow worship of Baal in Israel and to allow Jezebel to murder many priests of God. God confronted Ahab through the prophet Elijah, but even the miracles of God performed through Elijah did not turn Ahab from his evil ways. During his reign, Ahab delivered false testimony against a man in order to have him killed so that Ahab could seize his property. Ultimately, Ahab is killed in battle, and the prophecy of God's judgment against him and Jezebel is fulfilled (1 Kings 16:29-22:39).

6. Haman—an advisor and high ranking official of Xerxes, king of Babylon. Haman was a descendant of the Amalekites, a people that God had sworn to Moses he would forever war against (Exodus 17:16). Haman was a bigot and hated the Jews. He devised a plot to have the Jewish people utterly destroyed by decree of King Xerxes. Haman was filled with pride, wrath, and envy against everyone. His hatred of the Jews put him in direct conflict with God. Ultimately, Esther, a Jew and the wife of King Xerxes, was able to reveal Haman's true nature, and King Xerxes had Haman executed (Esther).

7. Herod the Great—a king in Israel at the time of the birth of Jesus. The historical record of Herod is one of a ruthless and possibly mad man who ruled with an iron fist. Although he was a significant supporter and contributor in the building of the Temple, he was also a murderer. When the wise men visited Herod to inquire about the birth of the king of the Jews, Herod conspired to have the baby found and killed. When the wise men departed without informing Herod the whereabouts of the baby, Herod ordered all male infants two years of age or younger in Bethlehem to be killed (Matthew 2:16-18). Herod was not a Jew, and although he seemed to respect Jewish prophesies, he did not worship God or honor Him.

8. Caiaphas—the High Priest in Jerusalem who captured Jesus and demanded his crucifixion before Pilate, even refusing to allow Pilate to release Jesus when Pilate seemed reluctant to have Jesus killed. Although he was a Pharisee and publicly practiced acts of piety and worship, the Bible reveals his hypocrisy and self-interest rather than godliness. Caiaphas, like most of the Pharisees, believed that acts of worship were what counted before God and not contrition and humility of heart. Caiaphas refused to believe that Jesus was the Son of God (Matthew 26:3-5, 57-67; 27:20-26).

9. Pilate—the Roman governor of Israel who ordered the crucifixion of Jesus. Pilate was a bigot who hated the Jews. On one occasion, Pilate ordered the murder of Jewish citizens, including a group of worshipers at the Temple. When he questioned Jesus about the charges brought against Him by the chief priests and the elders, Pilate found no fault

with Jesus. Nonetheless, his fear of a bad report being sent against him by the Jews to Caesar compelled him to acquiesce to the demands to have Jesus crucified. Prior to having Him crucified, Pilate ordered Jesus flogged—again without any evidence against Jesus—in the hope that the flogging would satisfy the anger of the Jews. Pilate symbolically tried to excuse his behavior by washing his hands of the blood of Jesus—but it was his order that confirmed Jesus' death.

10. Judas—one of the twelve disciples of Jesus and the one who betrayed Him to the chief priests and elders. Judas was a thief and filled with avarice and greed. Although he was a disciple, he did not believe Jesus' testimony. For the price of thirty pieces of silver, he agreed to betray Jesus to the Temple soldiers. He identified Jesus to the Temple guards with a kiss. Judas committed suicide when the gravity of his betrayal became too much for him to bear (Matthew 26:14-16, 47-50; 27:3-10).

Most all of the Ten Commandments were broken by the individuals listed above, but they also committed other acts and exhibited character traits that most of us would find shameful. All of them acted without respect (fear) toward God. Murders were committed. The villains often exhibited sinful pride, envy, lust, wrath, greed, and betrayal. For many, confronted with God's awesome power and majesty, they persisted in defiance and would neither repent nor change from their actions that were against God and His will. These villains caused many people to suffer.

When I was growing up, I used to hear the phrase "There, but for the grace of God, go I" used to describe others in a difficult position—health, wealth, or wisdom. My friends and I would often discuss the meaning of that phrase, but, as seven year olds, none of us could truly understand its meaning. We reluctantly concluded that God had some purpose in making some people suffer and in allowing others to not suffer. Therefore, the saying was as if a "God-lottery" had been won by some and lost by others. That seemed unfair to us, but a lot of life is unfair to a seven-year-old child.

The phrase takes on new meaning for me now, particularly in light of Romans 9:3-11 quoted above: "none is righteous, no, not one." I haven't murdered anyone, but I have committed many (too many) of the sins on the list in the previous paragraphs. Christians, as they grow in their faith, love, and devotion to God, become acutely aware of all sin in their life—past and present. Christians, as they grow in their faith, love, and devotion to God, remain sadly aware that they will sin again somewhere in the future.

When a Christian stumbles, it makes the news largely because the secular world believes Christians hold themselves out as holy and righteous in comparison over and against all others. This is not true, of course, because the Bible says that "sin is crouching at the door. Its desire is for you" (Genesis 4:7b ESV). Sin is part of our human condition. Jesus knew we would struggle with sin in this life, and He gave His followers instructions for calling sinning believers to repentance (see Matthew 18:15–35). The process of sanctification lessens our proclivity to sin, but until we die and go to heaven, we will continue to stumble and sin. The one thing sin is not is surprising. Sin is one of the basic characteristics of humanity.

Consider some of the heroes of the Bible. Moses committed murder and had to flee from Egypt. Moses angered God in his initial refusal to trust God and go on the mission God had called him to. David committed adultery and murder. Solomon allowed pagan religions to flourish in Israel. Neither David nor Solomon was a good parent. Joseph's arrogance about his gift of interpreting dreams was at least a part of the reason his brothers sold him into slavery in Egypt. Paul persecuted the church and played some role in the death of Stephen. Peter denied Christ three times. The list goes on. No one is righteous; all have fallen short of the glory of God.

But the good news is that those of us who believe in Jesus, His righteousness, and His act of sacrifice for the atonement of sins can find forgiveness. The psalmist said,

> *For as high as the heavens are above the earth,*
> *so great is his steadfast love toward those who fear him;*
> *as far as the east is from the west,*
> *so far does he remove our transgressions from us.*
> ~ Psalm 103:11–12 ESV

We are clean because of what Jesus did on the cross. And we will continue to move toward perfection with each passing day until our last day passes.

Therefore, the saying I first heard as a seven year old is a remarkably concise and accurate assertion of God's acts of salvation. I am a sinner, yet I am also clean because of Jesus and my profession of faith in Him. God sees Jesus whenever He sees me. God's grace through Jesus Christ is what differentiates us from every other person.

It is not our acts of righteousness. We could all be Pharaoh, we could all be Pilate, we could all be Cain, and we could all be Judas. But, praise God, **there but for the grace of God go I.** In a fallen world, with ample opportunity to sin and fall short of the glory of God, we can still rest assured in our salvation. We walk in grace, grace greater than all our sin.[8]

REFLECTIONS FOR THE WEEK

1. Read Matthew 6:21–48. If Jesus truly meant what He said in this discourse on righteous behavior, what would be your response? How does this passage of Scripture relate to Romans 3:9–11?

2. Which of your sins are you most pleased and grateful that God removed as far as east is from west? Are there any sins that you are unwilling to believe have been removed from you?

PRAYER

Almighty God, I so want to please You. You have done such acts of kindness in my life, such acts of beauty and blessing, that when I think of betraying Your love, I am undone. I struggle to come again to the foot of the cross and ask again for Your forgiveness—that You take me back—that You once again extend Your grace into my life. I weep. I chastise myself. I try. O God, do not give up on me. Extend Your blessings again in my life. Let me know the love of Christ that covers all my shame, all my sin. O God, thank You for sending Jesus to a sinner like me.

Amen

---

[8] From the hymn, "Grace Greater Than All Our Sin," lyrics by Julia H. Johnston, in the public domain.

NOVEMBER—WEEK THREE

ACCUMULATING SUFFICIENT RESOURCES TO ACHIEVE THE GOALS AND OBJECTIVES OF THE ORGANIZATION

I cry aloud to God,
aloud to God, and he will hear me.
In the day of my trouble I seek the Lord;
in the night my hand is stretched out without wearying;
my soul refuses to be comforted.
When I remember God, I moan;
when I meditate, my spirit faints. Selah
You hold my eyelids open;
I am so troubled that I cannot speak.
I consider the days of old,
the years long ago.
I said, "Let me remember my song in the night;
let me meditate in my heart."
Then my spirit made a diligent search:
"Will the Lord spurn forever,
and never again be favorable?
Has his steadfast love forever ceased?
Are his promises at an end for all time?
Has God forgotten to be gracious?
Has he in anger shut up his compassion?" Selah
Then I said, "I will appeal to this,
to the years of the right hand of the Most High."
I will remember the deeds of the Lord;
yes, I will remember your wonders of old.
I will ponder all your work,
and meditate on your mighty deeds.
Your way, O God, is holy.
What god is great like our God?
You are the God who works wonders;
you have made known your might among the peoples.
You with your arm redeemed your people,

> the children of Jacob and Joseph. Selah
> When the waters saw you, O God,
> when the waters saw you, they were afraid;
> indeed, the deep trembled.
> The clouds poured out water;
> the skies gave forth thunder;
> your arrows flashed on every side.
> The crash of your thunder was in the whirlwind;
> your lightnings lighted up the world;
> the earth trembled and shook.
> Your way was through the sea,
> your path through the great waters;
> yet your footprints were unseen.
> You led your people like a flock
> by the hand of Moses and Aaron.
>
> ~ Psalm 77 ESV

But God said to Jonah, "Do you do well to be angry for the plant?" And he said, "Yes, I do well to be angry, angry enough to die." And the Lord said, "You pity the plant, for which you did not labor, nor did you make it grow, which came into being in a night and perished in a night. And should not I pity Nineveh, that great city, in which there are more than 120,000 persons who do not know their right hand from their left, and also much cattle?"

~ Jonah 4:9–11 ESV

My family, like many, has followed a tradition of celebrating Thanksgiving with a feast and family gathering. The "historical" Moore family feast, the one held while my parents were alive, was something to behold—turkey, dressing, mashed potatoes, giblet gravy, sweet potatoes, green bean casserole, corn pudding, cranberries, fruit salad, homemade yeast rolls, broccoli and cheddar casserole, oyster casserole, pecan pie, pumpkin pie, and homemade whipped cream topping. In those days my motto was "eat early and eat often."

With the passing of my parents, the gatherings now are smaller, but the menu is roughly the same. We fondly remember feasts of the past, and new memories are created each year. Preparations for the Moore Thanksgiving celebration are meticulous, time constrained, and menu specific. Ensuring adequate resources exist to deliver the feast is an important task for the leaders of our family. Memories of past family dinners provide context and comfort when preparations miss a beat and sometimes go awry.

Gathering sufficient resources at the right time and of the right quality is an ongoing job of every leader of every enterprise. But what are the ramifications for the leader and the enterprise when valuable and necessary resources are not available and not obtainable when they are most desperately needed?

An unfortunate truth of life and leadership is that resources are sometimes not available and cannot be made available, no matter what is tried to secure them. One measure of this truth is the number of bankruptcy filings in the U.S. Federal Court system. For the year ending December 31, 2013, 1,038,720 non-business and 33,212 business bankruptcy filings were made (according to the Administrative Office of the U.S. Courts). Each of these filings undoubtedly had unfortunate effects on the people and businesses making the filing. And each bankruptcy filing undoubtedly had some negative effect on others, particularly those who were owed money or earned a portion of their income from the now bankrupt party. An inability to obtain financial resources can result in economic calamity, and calamity can occur regardless the efforts taken by individuals or leaders to prevent it from happening.

Life itself often hangs in the balance of a need for specific resources. People succumb to illness and disease each year and too often, in spite of advances in medicine and knowledge, people die. Illness, disease, and tragic accidents are not respecters of persons. Rich and poor alike contract serious illnesses; rich and poor alike suffer from the effects of serious accidents. On October 5, 2011, Steve Jobs, a co-founder of Apple, Inc. and one of the wealthiest men in the world (Forbes Magazine estimated his net worth at $8.3 billion in 2010), died from pancreatic cancer. Christopher Reeve was a successful and well-known actor. One of his most memorable roles was Superman. In 1995, Reeve was thrown from a horse and became a quadriplegic. He died in 2004.

Both Steve Jobs and Christopher Reeve were famous and possessed great financial resources, but they were not cured. Their passing made headlines. All over America and all over the world, each day, people die from illness and accident, and this in spite of Herculean efforts by medical professionals and the expenditure of great sums of money to prevent its occurrence.

Sometimes, what is needed is not available.

A leader grappling with a shortage of important resources must manage two separate responses—that of the business or enterprise they lead, and their own personal response to the situation. Of the two, the personal response is often the most difficult to navigate since leaders invest a lot of their personality into their businesses. The typical business response, once it is certain that the resources needed are not forthcoming, is to search for and work at a modification of the business goal or objective that is now in jeopardy of failure.

A leader attempting to solve a problem of resources follows a series of steps, and a decision-tree type of logic takes over: the leader (1) assesses the implications, (2) reassigns priorities, (3) resets expectations to those needing to know, (4) establishes new goals and objectives in light of the resource deficit, (5) communicates the new direction to others, and (6) pursues the new objectives including obtaining the resources needed to accomplish them. This hierarchy of activities will continue to be followed in a loop for each successive situation where resources either remain inadequate or unavailable to accomplish the new goal.

At some point, the leader will declare victory or surrender. Sometimes surrender is forced upon the leader through loss of job or legal proceedings. Other times, surrender becomes a personal decision when fighting the good fight no longer is palatable.

Leaders also respond emotionally to situations and circumstances where resources needed for important goals and objectives are not available. People whose significant hopes and dreams are thwarted by uncontrollable events and circumstances experience a wide range of emotions. For example, each of the phases of grief can be experienced (denial, anger, bartering, acceptance, and sorrow/depression). But people can also experience renewed energy and sense of purpose in the face of loss, and courage and resilience can also be fostered. Sometimes, people grow spiritually through times of difficulty and trial.

The human response to tragedy and hopelessness is profoundly illustrated in the Book of Job. It is widely accepted as one of the oldest books in the Bible. Job is a book of wisdom—wisdom about God and about a man, Job, confronting life circumstances that are horrendous and undeserved.

The reader of the book knows what Job does not know: all of the terrible circumstances that have befallen him are the result of a test and argument between God and Satan. In heaven, in front of the heavenly host, God commended Job for being a righteous man. Satan disputed God's commendation of Job and accuses Job of loving God only because of the blessings God has bestowed upon him. Satan accuses Job of false piety and lack of true conviction of his faith and knowledge of God.

> And the Lord said to Satan, "Have you considered my servant Job, that there is none like him on the earth, a blameless and upright man, who fears God and turns away from evil?" Then Satan answered the Lord and said, "Does Job fear God for no reason? Have you not put a hedge around him and his house and all that he has, on every side? You have blessed the work of his hands, and his possessions have increased in the land. But stretch out your hand and touch all that he has, and he will curse you to your face." And the Lord said to Satan, "Behold, all that he has is in your hand. Only against him do not stretch out your hand." So Satan went out from the presence of the Lord.
> ~ Job 1:8–12 ESV

Satan immediately goes and strikes Job's children and his possessions. In spite of the loss of all that he held dear, Job remained upright and righteous. When it was reported to Job the enormity of the calamity that had overtaken him, he said, "Naked I came from my mother's womb, and naked shall I return. The Lord gave, and the Lord has taken away; blessed be the name of the Lord" (Job 1:21 ESV). Job's righteousness remained intact.

After the passage of some time, God spoke to Satan once more of Job's integrity and righteousness, and again Satan challenged Job's integrity.

> Then Satan answered the Lord and said, "Skin for skin! All that a man has he will give for his life. But stretch out your hand and touch his bone and his flesh, and he will curse you to your face." And the Lord said to Satan, "Behold, he is in your hand; only spare his life."
>
> So Satan went out from the presence of the Lord and struck Job with loathsome sores from the sole of his foot to the crown of his head. And he took a piece of broken pottery with which to scrape himself while he sat in the ashes.
>
> Then his wife said to him, "Do you still hold fast your integrity? Curse God and die." But he said to her, "You speak as one of the foolish women would speak. Shall we receive good from God, and shall we not receive evil?" In all this Job did not sin with his lips.
>
> ~ Job 2:4–10 ESV

The details of Job's infirmities at the hands of Satan are horrific. Job's suffering was real and profound.

Soon after his affliction, Job is visited by three friends who are dumbfounded at the sight of Job and the depth of his suffering. They sit with Job for seven days in silence "for they saw that his suffering was very great" (Job 2:13b ESV).

After seven days and nights, Job speaks, and he curses the day he was born. Job gives a poignant voice to his suffering, saying,

> "For the thing that I fear comes upon me,
> and what I dread befalls me.
> I am not at ease, nor am I quiet;
> I have no rest, but trouble comes"
>
> ~ Job 2:25–26 ESV

With the silence broken, Job's friends also begin to speak. They attempt to offer comfort to Job by asking him to confess whatever sin he had (must have) committed against God that caused him to be treated as he was being treated. Imagine how Job felt—he knew he had done nothing; their assessment was not true. His friends in part give voice to his own questions because they speak of the awesome majesty and power of God, and they cannot bring themselves to believe Job is innocent and undeserving of his fate. No, their paradigm of God leads them to believe Job sinned against God, even if he sinned unwittingly, because God (as they understand Him) would not punish a righteous man.

One of the friends, Bildad, even accuses Job's children (who were killed by a sudden storm at the hands of Satan) of deserving their fate. Through the give and take of the dialogues between Job and his friends, Job must wrestle with a new enlightenment for himself: bad things do happen to good people. This leads Job to consider why—why has such tragedy befallen him, and why is God doing this to him? Searching within himself and finding no wrong deserving such treatment, Job longs to speak with God and defend himself. Job, it seems, has also attributed his calamities to God. Job longs to be justified.

Job recalls with sadness times past when his life was pleasant and he felt the loving presence of God. Job says,

> "Oh, that I were as in the months of old,
> as in the days when God watched over me,
> when his lamp shone upon my head,
> and by his light I walked through darkness,
> as I was in my prime,
> when the friendship of God was upon my tent,
> when the Almighty was yet with me,
> when my children were all around me,
> when my steps were washed with butter,
> and the rock poured out for me streams of oil!"
> ~ Job 29:2–6 ESV

But in this lament, unlike the psalmist above who remembered God as a comfort in his time of need, no comfort or solace is found in his sweet memories.

In the end, after Job has withstood all of the "wisdom" and advice of his friends, God visits Job and, in response to Job's desire for a hearing before God, questions Job. Through those questions, God reveals to Job important information about his character. He reveals that His wisdom is beyond understanding. Through the conversation with God, Job becomes fully convinced of this fact: God's wisdom, power, majesty, glory, and purposes cannot be fathomed by man.

Prior to God's speaking with him, Job, like his friends, had shared an opinion about the "fear" of the Lord that was more about being "fearful" than trusting. But as a result of his trials and God's response, Job learned the fear of the Lord must also be encapsulated in worship and trust. Job's faith in God was confirmed. Job learned that even though he had not deserved what happened to him, God had a purpose in it. Job learned there is not always, if even often, a correlation between material blessings and poverty, or good times and bad times, and sin. Job learned God is just and righteous and will ultimately judge rightly the actions and fate of man.

Here is another interesting observation. Even though God had, in a way, taken Job to the woodshed with his questions, the experience helped Job to heal. Contrast that with how Job felt at the hands of his friends "comfort." Job's trials created loneliness. Tragedy that includes loss, any loss—friends, family, self-esteem, health, employment, or possessions—creates loneliness. His friends brought further alienation rather than wholeness.

Job's nightmare of existence also robbed him of God's presence. Job thought he was alone—that God had forsaken him. This was untrue. God had a purpose in allowing the unspeakably tragic events to unfold in Job's life, but Job was never apart from God. Consider the verse from Psalm 77 above. "Your way was through the sea, your path through the great waters; yet your footprints were unseen." The psalmist knew that even if God's physical presence could not be felt (His footprints were not seen), He nonetheless was leading His flock through all difficulties. God had never forsaken Job and was always with him. Job's friends wounded him in spite of their good intentions. But Job learned to stay near to God, to call upon His name for help and relief, even when God does not seem to be listening.

We learn all of these things too in the story of Job. We also learn that God has an adversary who is also against us. Notwithstanding the adversary, we learn God's plans will not be thwarted; God is sovereign, even over his enemy. And we learn our only source of comfort in an uncertain world that is beyond our control is to rest in the presence of God. We learn to follow God's unseen footprints.

Someday, for you and me, calamity may strike. Someday, God may seem distant and uncaring about our suffering. Someday, we may even be too overwhelmed with grief and sorrow to find the desire or strength to pray for relief. Against the prospect of an evil day overtaking us, here are some things to do and practice now to provide resources against an evil day.

- Build a personal record of faith. Keep a journal record of all you have been through and how God worked in your life to overcome each obstacle or to comfort you. Such a written record of your life will aid you in dark hours where memories fade.
- Cultivate Christian friends. Be a Christian friend to others. Do not judge others too harshly, but love them as Jesus has commanded us to do. We help ourselves when we help others. We gain perspective on tragedy and comfort and hope when we walk through difficulties and when we assist others in their walk.
- Ask God to build your faith, even at the risk of trials.
- Learn everything you can about God. Study the Bible. Meditate on passages that confuse you. Find passages that comfort you. Memorize passages that remind you of His grace, His love, His power, His justice, His mercy, and His glory.
- Make it a practice to pray, every day, at all hours of the day. Include God in a running and continuous dialogue in your mind.

Build your relationship with God. Have conversations with Him and not just pleas.

- Become introspective of your motives and your feelings. Become self-aware of things in your life that might be displeasing to God. Repent of those things immediately.
- Practice acts of piety, particularly fasting. Charles Stanley, a well-known minister and evangelist, describes fasting as essential in hopeless situations or in overcoming strongholds in a life. He also says fasting is useful to prepare for what is to come, to prepare for what God has called you to do, and to cleanse you by the inward renewing of mind and spirit—to equip yourself for the battle in which you find yourself. Personally, fasting has been one of the most amazing acts of spiritual discipline I have discovered in my walk with God.
- Cling to Jesus. Jesus suffered unfairly for our sins. Jesus knew what it was like to be human. Study Jesus, love Jesus, imitate Jesus, desire Jesus, and beseech Jesus to strengthen you in all things.

Jesus said, "My sheep hear my voice, and I know them, and they follow me. I give them eternal life, and they will never perish, and no one will snatch them out of my hand. My Father, who has given them to me, is greater than all, and no one is able to snatch them out of the Father's hand. I and the Father are one" (John 10:27–30 ESV).

Trust God to preserve His children, even in the midst of Job-like struggles.

REFLECTIONS FOR THE WEEK

1. Read again the list of spiritual armament above. Begin to practice at least one of them this week.

2. Using a concordance, track usage of "fasting" in the Bible. Ponder how fasts were done, when they were done, why they were done,

and the results attributed to fasting. Ask yourself under what circumstances you would be willing to fast before the Lord.

PRAYER

Almighty God, I, like all of Your creation, have so many concerns and so many troubling thoughts. How loud the cry that must come to Your ears each moment of the day! My difficulties separate me from You as I become absorbed in my conflicts and my pain, as I become involved in dealing with the issue before me that demands my time and attention. In Your great compassion and mercy, hear my pleas. And in Your great compassion and mercy, teach me to rest safely and securely in the knowledge of Your faithfulness, mercy, and love. Protect me from times of testing, but if they must come, strengthen me for the ordeal. Help me to build a treasure trove of spiritual weapons to use when my courage fails, my wisdom fails, and my heart is heavy.

Amen

NOVEMBER—WEEK FOUR

INCREASING SALES AND REVENUES

Jude, a servant of Jesus Christ and brother of James,
To those who are called, beloved in God the Father and kept for Jesus Christ:
May mercy, peace, and love be multiplied to you.
Beloved, although I was very eager to write to you about our common salvation, I found it necessary to write appealing to you to contend for the faith that was once for all delivered to the saints. For certain people have crept in unnoticed who long ago were designated for this condemnation, ungodly people, who pervert the grace of our God into sensuality and deny our only Master and Lord, Jesus Christ.

~ Jude 1:1–4 ESV

But you, beloved, building yourselves up in your most holy faith and praying in the Holy Spirit, keep yourselves in the love of God, waiting for the mercy of our Lord Jesus Christ that leads to eternal life. And have mercy on those who doubt; save others by snatching them out of the fire; to others show mercy with fear, hating even the garment stained by the flesh.

~ Jude 1:20–23 ESV

What good is it, my brothers, if someone says he has faith but does not have works? Can that faith save him? If a brother or sister is poorly clothed and lacking in daily food, and one of you says to them, "Go in peace, be warmed and filled," without giving them the things needed for the body, what good is that? So also faith by itself, if it does not have works, is dead.

~ James 2:14–17 ESV

Come, everyone who thirsts,
 come to the waters;
and he who has no money,
 come, buy and eat!
Come, buy wine and milk

NOVEMBER—WEEK FOUR

without money and without price.
Why do you spend your money for that which is not bread,
and your labor for that which does not satisfy?
Listen diligently to me, and eat what is good,
and delight yourselves in rich food.
Incline your ear, and come to me;
hear, that your soul may live;
and I will make with you an everlasting covenant,
my steadfast, sure love for David.

~ Isaiah 55:1–3 ESV

I bought my first new car when I was eighteen years old. It was a bright orange hatchback Chevrolet Vega with a white racing stripe. I am uncertain now, but I do not think it had air conditioning. It did have an A.M. radio though, and a few years after I bought the car, I put in an F.M. radio adapter that never really worked very well.

It was not a very powerful car, notwithstanding the racing stripe. The motor had four cylinders, and it was made out of aluminum, a shortcoming that became apparent to me about three years later.

My Vega had an automatic transmission, but its shift stick was on the floor between the two vinyl bucket seats—I really thought it was ultra cool, for a while. I have a photograph of me standing next to it, smiling.

In cold weather the celluloid in the ignition would fail and the engine would not turn over. This feature was fairly vexing. My friends thought it sounded like a Cessna single prop airplane. Ha.

A particularly useful feature was the hatchback. I was a musician back then, and I used to haul my music gear (including a very heavy electric piano) all over the country in the hatchback. On some of those journeys, I would watch in helpless amazement as various pieces of my car fell off as I traveled the byways of America. Once, a side window in the rear rattled around for a while and then peeled off—the car behind me managed a nifty maneuver to avoid it. Fortunately, I quickly learned junkyards everywhere kept a full stock of Vega parts.

Did I mention I paid the window sticker price for the car? I remember shopping for it. The radio in my old car had announced a big Chevrolet tent sale, and I had gone to see what was on sale. As it turned out, the orange Vega I had set my eye on was on sale—the window sticker said so. When I asked, "How much?" the salesman merely pointed at the sticker. My father was pretty disappointed in my judgment about this matter when I told him about it later that day. I became pretty disappointed in my judgment as the next three years rolled by. In those days, three years was the most a bank would allow to repay a car loan. The aluminum engine burned up within days of my last payment.

Most salesmen have to work harder at gaining sales than the salesman of my Chevy Vega did. I laugh sometimes at thinking how badly I treated that salesman. After all, if he struggled with the belief that all sales were as easy as mine, he probably died penniless.

The truth is most sales are hard to get. That is why so many books are written by salesmen for salesmen, why so many seminars are given by salesmen for salesmen, why so many sales consultants are employed by leaders and sales managers alike to look for ways to increase sales, and why leaders of enterprises search high and low to find "good" salesmen. Leaders spend significant amounts of time and money designing incentive programs to reward salesmen in order to balance a human desire to achieve with an equally human desire to coast. I have known salesmen (perhaps you have also) who, having a sales goal and commission goal in mind, will work only hard enough to achieve the goal. Thereafter, they are on their own time. Good for them, not great for their employer.

Brian Tracy, in his book, *Be a Sales Superstar: 21 Great Ways to Sell More, Faster, Easier in Tough Markets*, notes that he often opens his seminars by asking who in the audience is in sales. His goal in asking the question is to have everyone in the room realize they are all involved in sales. In Tracy's opinion, "everyone is in sales, no matter what you do." Tracy points out that "your ability to 'sell' others on your ideas will determine your success in your life and career as much as any other factor." There is truth in that statement. We may differ, however, on the definition of success.

I enjoyed reading Tracy's book. His confidence and the stories of his achievements undoubtedly help people hoping to improve their sales performance. In particular, I liked his summary of the four common steps in any sale: attention, interest, desire, and action.

Before any sale can occur, the customer's attention must be caught. Once attention has been gained, a level of interest must be aroused, and this interest must ultimately be expressed as desire for the product or services. Desire is brought about usually through identification of particular benefits that will attract and draw in the buyer. Last, some action must be taken to close the sale or the effort was a waste of time (from, at least, the vantage point of the salesman).

In my Vega case, the radio announcement caught my attention. My interest was aroused when I saw the cool orange Vega with bucket seats and center stick shift. My desires included the ideas that I was an eighteen year old "man" with the ability to enter into a legal contract, and the car I was driving was not "what I wanted." It turned out closing the sale was pretty easy.

Something else struck me about Tracy's book. He said, "Selling has often been called a transfer of enthusiasm. The more enthusiastic and convinced you are about what you are selling, the more contagious this enthusiasm will be and the more your customers will sense it and act on it." I do not remember if my Vega salesman was enthusiastic—I had enough enthusiasm for both of us. Later, I had sole possession of buyer's remorse. But the wisdom gained, now ***that*** was worth the price I paid.

I cannot say I ever recommended a Vega to anyone else. Nor did I ever buy another Chevrolet—and I have had fifteen automobiles since then. I have, however, recommended other cars and other manufacturers. For that matter, I have also recommended movies, televisions, appliances, restaurants, books, classes, people, neighborhoods, schools, careers, and countless other things during the course of my life. My enthusiasm for things often finds expression in recommendations to others. The converse is also true: when things are not what I had hoped for, I withhold a recommendation or express my dissatisfaction.

Christians, at the most basic and individual level, have been granted the most significant and priceless gift of all time—eternal life and fellowship with God. Though we would give all we have for God's gift, our currency is worthless.

For me, the magnitude of this gift never grows dull, but in fact it continues to astound, amaze, inform, bless, comfort, inspire, protect, and overwhelm me with each passing day. Therefore, I am extremely enthusiastic about my relationship with God through Jesus Christ. I am already realizing the benefits of that relationship, and I am convinced that in this life I will never see the end of them, nor will they cease to grow. I am not alone in holding this view. No Christian is a provisional Christian who has to go through a period of waiting to be fully granted membership with all its privileges. Every Christian is as I am, or should be.

There are thousands of books on how to become a good salesman. Most people accept as true that everyone sells something everyday—ourselves, ideas, products, services, or just points of view. But most people, even many salespeople, according to Tracy, are not aware of the extent that our lives are filled with selling activities, nor are many people actually comfortable with the idea of being thought of as "salesmen." I remember being shocked to hear at Arthur Andersen & Co. (once one of the largest public accounting firms in the world) that I was expected to "sell" services to clients and potential clients. But retaining existing and obtaining new clients was how the firm grew and made openings for future partners.

At Arthur Andersen, I learned one of the easiest ways to grow sales was to sell our services to people who already knew about us and liked us. It helped that I was also enthusiastic about my career and my employer, and my enthusiasm was apparent to others—and as Tracy said, enthusiasm is a trait every salesman should possess. Enthusiasm about what Christ has done is an important trait for a Christian to have and to share.

At Arthur Andersen I also learned that both my own and my staff's behavior around clients had a direct effect on their perception of our talent and services and their willingness to use us again and to refer our work to others. The behavior of Christians in the world is also important. Christians are expected to have a positive effect on the world. Humility may step in on this point and you may say, "Who am I to make any effect on the world?" That is a good question. Frankly, if it were up to each Christian alone to make a positive contribution on the world, the effort would result in failure. But it is not us who are making the contribution—it is Christ. And Christ will not fail.

Christians, living daily in Christ, become more and more like Christ. Even though Christians, just as non-Christians, possess many, many different talents and capabilities, every Christian has this singular difference from non-Christians: every Christian has the same Spirit living in them. Every Christian has the very Spirit of God living inside. As a result, we are all alike even though we are all different. Have you ever noticed that couples who have been married for a long time tend to begin to look like each other? The same thing applies to Christians. We begin to "look" like each other from the inside. What is the image that we take on, the image that we all are being conformed to? Light in a world filled with darkness.

> In the beginning was the Word, and the Word was with God, and the Word was God. He was in the beginning with God. All things were made through him, and without him was not any thing made that was made. In him was life, and the life was the light of men. The light shines in the darkness, and the darkness has not overcome it.
>
> ~ John 1:1–5 ESV

We are becoming a special type of "light" in the world, and we cannot help it. I hold this opinion on very great authority. Jesus said, "You are the light of the world. A city set on a hill cannot be hidden. Nor do people light a lamp and put it under a basket, but on a stand, and it gives light to all in the house. In the same way, let your light shine before others, so that they may see your good works and give glory to your Father who is in heaven" (Matthew 5:14–16 ESV).

God, through the Holy Spirit, is making each of us into a lighthouse.

God's work is going on whether or not we are conscious of it. And God will not stop His work in our lives because we are slow learners. God is patient, and He loves us—oh how He loves us!

God's love, manifested in our life circumstances, will sometimes lead us to desire to deepen the relationship with God, to quicken it. Sometimes this desire will occur in a season of difficulty, and God's grace is desperately needed. Sometimes this desire will occur in times of celebration when our hearts are bursting with joy and we know our blessings were sent from God. Sometimes someone else may need to hear about our faith and the hope we have, and being aware of their needs will draw us into a deeper dialogue with God so that we can feel more equipped to speak about Him to others. And sometimes, someone or something will cross our path that will spark a question in our lives that only God can answer. Because God loves us, and because God desires a relationship with us, we can be assured that time spent seeking Him will be fruitful.

In the passage from Jude above, it is clear that the name of Christ can be sullied by impersonators who use the guise of Christianity to seek their own gain. Such impersonators hinder God's work of salvation. The apostles Paul and Peter also warned of this threat and the besmirching of the reputation of Christians. The impostors referred to above were individuals without belief who had chosen the mantle of Christ in which to "sell" their views in pursuit of their personal, albeit short-term, gain. But it is not only "wolves in sheep's clothing" that undermine the truth of Christ. Joining the impersonating crowd are vocal non-believers who develop arguments, laws, and persecutions to attack the beliefs of Christians. And, since no one is perfect, Christians in their own sin can negatively affect others and obscure the wonder and the glory that is truly ours in Christ. The warnings of the New Testament writers are necessary to us—we must remain vigilant and introspective about our motives and actions.

I believe there are four things we can do to strengthen our relationship with God. They are:

1. **Practice Obedience**. Jesus said the first great commandment was to "love the Lord your God with all your heart and with all your soul and with all your mind" (Matthew 22:37 ESV). Jesus also said, "If you love me, you will keep my commandments" (John 14:15 ESV). Love toward God

is best expressed in obedience. Obedience is an act of will that is made possible with knowledge, trust, faith, and hope. Knowledge is gained by experience and study. Trust, faith, and hope are gained through personal introspection of one's life's circumstances.

2. **Serve Others**. Be of service to others using the gifts that God has given you. In so doing, you express Christ's love to others. After Jesus had expressed the first great commandment, He went on to say, "And a second is like it: You shall love your neighbor as yourself" (Matthew 22:39 ESV). Jesus also said, "A new commandment I give to you, that you love one another: just as I have loved you, you also are to love one another" (John 13:34 ESV). On the night before His Crucifixion, Jesus washed the feet of His disciples in demonstration of service toward one another and humility (John 13:2–5). Another time, Jesus told the disciples, "Whoever would be great among you must be your servant, and whoever would be first among you must be your slave, even as the Son of Man came not to be served but to serve, and to give his life as a ransom for many" (Matthew 20:26b–28 ESV). Being of service to others is pleasing to God and good for our souls.

3. **Abide in Christ.** Jesus said, "Abide in me, and I in you. As the branch cannot bear fruit by itself, unless it abides in the vine, neither can you, unless you abide in me. I am the vine; you are the branches. Whoever abides in me and I in him, he it is that bears much fruit, for apart from me you can do nothing" (John 15:4–5 ESV). We abide in Christ in a number of ways. When we attend church and worship God, we abide in Christ. When we take the sacraments, we abide in Christ. When we read the Bible and participate in Bible study, we abide in Christ. When we pray, we abide in Christ. When our lives are measured in relation to Christ and His yardstick and not our own, we abide in Christ. When we form friendships with other believers, we abide in Christ.

4. **Evangelize**. Share with others the gifts that have been granted to you. God has given you two immeasurable gifts—eternal life and the forgiveness of sins. God loves a cheerful giver. Give to others what has been given to you. Let God's bounty in your life flow out to others. It

is right and proper to have humility about everything except Christ. Be as Paul who said, "Therefore I will boast all the more gladly of my weaknesses, so that the power of Christ may rest upon me. For the sake of Christ, then, I am content with weaknesses, insults, hardships, persecutions, and calamities. For when I am weak, then I am strong (2 Corinthians 12:9b–10 ESV).

Apostle Paul also said, "If possible, so far as it depends on you, live peaceably with all" (Romans 12:18 ESV). And Apostle Peter said, "Beloved, I urge you as sojourners and exiles to abstain from the passions of the flesh, which wage war against your soul. Keep your conduct among the Gentiles honorable, so that when they speak against you as evildoers, they may see your good deeds and glorify God on the day of visitation" (1 Peter 2:11–12 ESV).

You are the light on a hill. People are going to notice you because you are a Christian. You will gain their **attention** even if you do not wish to or seek to. People will also be **interested** in what you have that they do not have. As you live your life a light before others, you will arouse in them a **desire** to know more about your beliefs that bring you such comfort, such hope, such joy, and such peace. Your life may lead others to take **action** and open their hearts to the Lord. I am confident such a sale will not lead to buyer's remorse or a withheld recommendation. Wouldn't it be wonderful, someday, to hear that your life led another to Christ?

REFLECTIONS FOR THE WEEK

1. Spend time thinking about "peddlers" of Christianity that offend you. Prepare a list of those things about them or their message that offends you. Record your concerns over message or doctrine and contemplate your concerns as you study the Bible and listen to other messages. Lift up your concerns in prayer to God.

2. Now think about how you can gain confidence in recommending Christ to others in a way that is not offensive to you. What are you willing to say to others about Jesus?

PRAYER

Father, I again give You thanks for the gift of Jesus and the salvation that is mine. I do not understand it, but I claim it by faith. Encourage me to be able to express my faith to others. Whatever fears I have, answer them and quiet my mind so that all I say and do is pleasing to You. Jesus said, "I am the good shepherd. My sheep hear my voice." I humbly pray that others will hear the voice of Jesus through me.

Amen

DECEMBER

And in the same region there were shepherds out in the field, keeping watch over their flock by night. And an angel of the Lord appeared to them, and the glory of the Lord shone around them, and they were filled with great fear. And the angel said to them, "Fear not, for behold, I bring you good news of great joy that will be for all the people. For unto you is born this day in the city of David a Savior, who is Christ the Lord. And this will be a sign for you: you will find a baby wrapped in swaddling cloths and lying in a manger." And suddenly there was with the angel a multitude of the heavenly host praising God and saying,
"Glory to God in the highest,
and on earth peace among those with whom he is pleased!"

~ Luke 2:8–14 ESV

Lord, you were favorable to your land;
you restored the fortunes of Jacob.
You forgave the iniquity of your people;
you covered all their sin. Selah
You withdrew all your wrath;
you turned from your hot anger.
Restore us again, O God of our salvation,
and put away your indignation toward us!

~ Psalm 85:1–4 ESV

Steadfast love and faithfulness meet;
righteousness and peace kiss each other.
Faithfulness springs up from the ground,
and righteousness looks down from the sky.
Yes, the Lord will give what is good,
and our land will yield its increase.
Righteousness will go before him
and make his footsteps a way.

~ Psalm 85:10–13 ESV

In 1965, Charlie Brown asked a question that has been asked for over two thousand years: "What is the meaning of Christmas?" Charlie Brown had been overwhelmed with the commercialization of Christmas, and he was feeling alienated from the celebrations around him. Charlie Brown wanted an answer; he wanted to know if there was any purpose, any reason for the season.

Charles Shultz, the creator of the syndicated cartoon Peanuts, in a brilliant piece of writing, had Linus, the younger brother of Lucy and a friend of Charlie Brown, give the reply. Linus recited the passage from Luke 2:8–14 (King James Version), and a national television audience equal to 50% of all television sets in America heard again, clearly, what all the fuss and celebration is really about.

"A Charlie Brown Christmas" has been aired every year since then through the date that I am writing this. I still get tears in my eyes when I hear Linus's child's voice reciting the passage from Luke that announces the birth of a Savior who will impart true life to the world—a passage that illuminates the overwhelming love of God toward us. Psalm 8:2 reads, "From the lips of children and infants you have ordained praise." Charles Shultz understood the true meaning of Christmas, and through his cartoon character Linus, gave Jesus to everyone who would listen.

My parents had an aluminum Christmas tree, a kind of tree that the children in "A Charlie Brown Christmas" preferred over real trees. Somewhere along the way we stopped using it, but I confess I absolutely loved that tree. Even now I warmly and fondly remember lying underneath the silvery frond-like branches, surrounded by wrapped presents, and watching the tree change colors as the three-color light underneath the tree quietly whirred around and around. Lying there, I had a sense of child-like wonder. Certainly I was thinking about the presents under the tree and those still to arrive on Christmas Eve, but there was much more going on in my mind. There was mystery in Christmas, and there always has been. Even Mary did not fully comprehend everything going on around her. Luke records, "But Mary treasured up all these things, pondering them in her heart" (Luke 2:19 ESV).

In 1897, an editorial appeared in The (New York) Sun, a New York City newspaper at the time, concerning whether or not Santa Claus existed. The now famous editorial by Francis Pharcellus Church resoundingly answered, "Yes, there is a Santa Claus!"

The language of Mr. Church's editorial is remarkable to read in light of the debate here in the second decade of the 21st century over the political correctness of keeping Christ in Christmas at all! Santa Claus is no longer the question. In my mind, it is a sad situation when a number of large corporations do not want their employees to wish people a "Merry Christmas!" greeting. Rather, some employers would prefer employees use the more non-controversial "Happy Holidays!" If Christ is not in Christmas, what is there to celebrate and be happy about?

Listen to what Mr. Church had to say about Santa:
> Virginia, your little friends are wrong. They have been affected by the skepticism of a skeptical age. They do not believe except that they see. They think that nothing can be which is not comprehensible by their little minds. All minds, Virginia, whether they be men's or children's are little.
>
> Yes, Virginia, there is a Santa Claus. He exists as certainly as love and generosity and devotion exist, and you know that they abound and give to your life its highest beauty and joy. Alas! how dreary would be the world if there were no Santa Claus.

My sense is that in 1897, there were few people who took umbrage that Christmas is celebrated to honor the birth of Jesus Christ of Nazareth. Over 100 years later, we could substitute the name of Jesus for Santa Claus, and in the words of Mr. Church read: **"Yes, Virginia, there is a Jesus!"** to remind us, just as Linus did, that Christmas without Christ is nothing at all. It is bluster and a waste of time if Jesus is not at the center of our hearts at Christmas.

But the joy of the gift of God—entering into the world as a human baby in order to bring salvation to the world—can neither be celebrated in stony silence, nor can its joy be diminished by Christmas-police who over-emphasize decorating and gift giving as being out of touch with the solemnity of the occasion. Do we not deserve the benefit of the doubt, here? Paul says, "Rejoice in the Lord always; again I will say, rejoice. Let your reasonableness be known to everyone. The Lord is at hand" (Philippians 4:4–5 ESV).

I enjoyed my parent's aluminum tree. I enjoyed cookies and treats. I enjoyed lights in our home town and on people's houses. For me, the accoutrements of Christmas make it impossible to ignore that something is going on that is worth the celebration—and it is not crass commercialism. Jesus Christ came into the world to save sinners, and I am chief among them. Jesus Christ was fully human and fully divine. I do not understand it, but it makes Jesus more approachable to me.

Christmas tells us that Jesus once was a baby, just as we were. He grew under the care of His earthly parents into a boy, then an adolescent and, finally, a man. He ate and drank, and He celebrated the joyful events of life, from holy festivals of the Jewish people to weddings.

Even though He was in the very nature God, He did not escape the hurts and trials of life. Rather, He was tempted just as we are, and He was betrayed by His friends. In spite of this, He endured and persevered, trusting the Father with His whole heart.

He worked very hard, and from time to time He was tired. He wept at death in the world and met His own death with resolute courage. In the end, He was physically beaten and abused. He bled and He died.

Through all the times of His life, Jesus Christ loved the Father, and He loved me. And on the third day, praise God, Jesus rose from the dead! Because He lives, I have hope in this world for a better world tomorrow. Because He lives, I will live too. Hallelujah! Merry Christmas!

REFLECTIONS FOR DECEMBER

1. The month of December marks Advent—for Christians, the celebration of the coming of Christ into the world. Spend time this month reflecting and remembering times and circumstances where God met your particular needs. Dig deeper than the true but too broad understanding that he meets all your needs. Find the few where he met your particular need when only he could

do it. Treasure that moment in your heart this month. Wrap that moment in a gift box for yourself.

2. The wise men followed a star to find the place where Jesus was. Surround yourself this month with evidence of the star leading to Jesus today: lights, songs, parties, presents, sermons, stories, memories, and Charlie Brown. Be joyful and be sentimental. Christmas is a human holiday of God's gift to us.

PRAYER

Jesus, some people, too many people, do not yet know You. Allow this time of Advent to quicken the hearts of an unbelieving world. Some believers, too many believers, are going through difficult times in the midst of Christmas. Comfort them and cover them with compassion. Speak to our hearts; sing to our souls that the love of the Father is greater than the world we live in. You are the only reason for this season. Meet me, I pray, where I most need You.

Amen

DECEMBER—WEEK ONE

HOLDING YOURSELF AND OTHERS ACCOUNTABLE TO KEEP PROMISES AND COMMITMENTS

He came to his own, and his own people did not receive him. But to all who did receive him, who believed in his name, he gave the right to become children of God, who were born, not of blood nor of the will of the flesh nor of the will of man, but of God.

And the Word became flesh and dwelt among us, and we have seen his glory, glory as of the only Son from the Father, full of grace and truth. (John bore witness about him, and cried out, "This was he of whom I said, 'He who comes after me ranks before me, because he was before me.'") For from his fullness we have all received, grace upon grace. For the law was given through Moses; grace and truth came through Jesus Christ.

~ John 1:11–17 ESV

Fear not, for you will not be ashamed;
  be not confounded, for you will not be disgraced;
for you will forget the shame of your youth,
  and the reproach of your widowhood you will remember no more.
For your Maker is your husband,
  the Lord of hosts is his name;
and the Holy One of Israel is your Redeemer,
  the God of the whole earth he is called.
For the Lord has called you
  like a wife deserted and grieved in spirit,
like a wife of youth when she is cast off,
  says your God.
For a brief moment I deserted you,
  but with great compassion I will gather you.
In overflowing anger for a moment
  I hid my face from you,
but with everlasting love I will have compassion on you,
  says the Lord, your Redeemer.

> *This is like the days of Noah[a] to me:*
> *as I swore that the waters of Noah*
> *should no more go over the earth,*
> *so I have sworn that I will not be angry with you,*
> *and will not rebuke you.*
> *For the mountains may depart*
> *and the hills be removed,*
> *but my steadfast love shall not depart from you,*
> *and my covenant of peace shall not be removed,*
> *says the Lord, who has compassion on you.*
> ~ Isaiah 54:4–10 ESV

According to Craig Gotsill (author of an article entitled "How Effective is a Money-back Guarantee?" posted June 15, 2010 on Zendesk.com), the money-back guarantee was an innovation developed by J.R. Watkins in 1868 as a means of enticing would-be customers to try his liniments. The money-back guarantee was a feature designed to take some of the risk out of the purchasing decision by consumers. The tactic apparently worked, because Mr. Watkins' company continues to exist today. Mr. Gotsill goes on to report that use of the money-back guarantee was also a prominent feature of Sears and Roebuck as they grew their catalogue business in 1888. Money-back guarantees are now commonplace in the retail industry.

The money-back guarantee is a form of promise that makes two assertions. The first is that the buyer will be pleased with their purchase, and the second is that the seller will live up to the promise to make a full refund if asked to do so.

As with any promise, reliance on a money-back guarantee is only as good as the integrity of the person making the promise. I am certain you have experienced the pain of broken promises—whether ones broken against you or by you. Humanly speaking, broken promises are part of the human condition. Satan lied to Eve in the Garden of Eden. Jesus said of Satan, "He was a murderer from the beginning, and does not stand in the truth, because there is no truth in him. When he lies, he speaks out of his own character, for he is a liar and the father of lies" (John 8:44 ESV).

How does one judge the integrity of the person making a promise?

Reputation is one way. It is often possible to gain perspective about the reputation, or integrity, of someone through references and the recommendations of others. A person who historically keeps promises will develop a reputation of integrity. A promise breaker will gain a poor reputation.

Jesus said, "Beware of false prophets, who come to you in sheep's clothing but inwardly are ravenous wolves. You will recognize them by their fruits. Are grapes gathered from thornbushes, or figs from thistles? So, every healthy tree bears good fruit, but the diseased tree bears bad fruit. A healthy tree cannot bear bad fruit, nor can a diseased tree bear good fruit. Every tree that does not bear good fruit is cut down and thrown into the fire. Thus you will recognize them by their fruit" (Matthew 7:15–20 ESV).

I read these words and know that honesty and integrity are what God expects of us. Yet, I still commit sins against God and others, and so do you. How are we to understand Jesus' message as it pertains to us, to followers and believers of Jesus who are still capable of personally succumbing to temptation and sin?

I believe the answer is found not in us but only in the veracity of God.

The Apostle Paul said, "Let God be true though every one were a liar" (Romans 3:4 ESV). No one but God is capable of keeping all promises all the time and always, always, always bearing good fruit. The passage from Matthew above is taken from Jesus' Sermon on the Mount. Jesus gives many other absolutes in the Sermon on the Mount discourse that listeners then and now find remarkable because they are impossible for humans to keep. But, just because the directives are hard to keep (even impossible to keep) does not make them void from God's perspective. It is their very impossibility that drives home the point that we are all in need of a Savior if requirements such as those in the Sermon on the Mount are necessary for righteousness.

The Bible, from Genesis to Revelation, is a story of God's faithfulness set against the unfaithfulness of man. The unfaithfulness of man offers keen instruction. By the time we humans are grown, we are informed judges of the character of each other—we know we are each capable of doing good and evil in different circumstances. In the Sermon on the Mount, Jesus touches on lust, fidelity, anger, bearing grudges, use of oaths and promises to promote personal gain, revenge, hate, pride, worry, greed, self-seeking, prejudice, and judgmental thinking as sins of the human condition. Jesus' words convict us of our sins in these areas.

Because we are fallen people living in a fallen world, methods have been developed over the years to provide added safeguards for promise making and promise keeping. Verbal promises accompanied by a handshake are the simplest method and likely the oldest method of demonstrating an agreement has been reached or a promise made between two people.

Adding an "oath" to God is another way individuals try and persuade each other of respective veracity.

There are consequences associated with breaking promises, and threats of retaliation were added to promises to impress upon the promise maker the seriousness of infidelity. In ancient times, threats were often graphically depicted by the two parties to an agreement butchering an animal and cutting the carcass in two halves, implying to each other that the fate of the animal would befall the one breaking the promise. Such an example is present in a covenant between God and Abraham (cf. Genesis 15:8–10, 17, and Jeremiah 34:17–18).

Corroboration by witnesses provides an added incentive for keeping promises as well as evidence that an assertion is true or a promise was made in the case of a subsequent dispute. The integrity of the witness is now added to the integrity of the promise maker to further ensure promises made are kept or enforced. The Ninth Commandment is, "You shall not bear false witness against your neighbor" (Exodus 20:16 ESV).

The importance of witnesses is depicted in an exchange between Jesus and the Pharisees over Jesus' true identity:

> Again Jesus spoke to them, saying, "I am the light of the world. Whoever follows me will not walk in darkness, but will have the light of life." So the Pharisees said to him, "You are bearing witness about yourself; your testimony is not true."

> "I am the one who bears witness about myself, and the Father who sent me bears witness about me."
> ~ John 8:12–13, 18 ESV

God, being fully aware of our mistrust of each other and our interest in gaining assurance as to the veracity of a promise, also adopted some of these same methods in His interactions, promises, and covenants with man. We have, in part, come to trust God and honor His reputation through His acts of keeping His promises.

Of all the signs of covenant that God has given man, two stand out as remarkably different from the rest. Those are the rainbow set in the sky that reminds us (and God) of His promise to never again completely destroy men from the earth by flood, and the atoning sacrifice of Jesus Christ on the cross that reminds us (and God) of His acts of love and mercy to redeem man from sin and death. Both vividly display God's righteousness and mercy.

The rainbow frames the time in which God will fulfill His plans of redemption and ultimate judgment; God will not destroy the earth by flood until His acts of redemption and salvation have been completed. The atoning death of Christ on the cross and His resurrection from the dead frames God's mighty acts to complete His plans of redemption. Jesus' sacrificial death and resurrection from the dead stand as a beacon to guide sinners into relationship with God until the time of the end comes. Jesus' death on the cross and His resurrection from the dead demonstrates God's everlasting promises of hope and restoration to those who believe in His Son.

These two signs—the rainbow in heaven and Jesus, the Light of Heaven—have never faded away; they are visible to both God and men. Both signs were created by light passing through a medium. Light passing through the medium of water molecules creates the beauty of the rainbow. Jesus Christ, the true light that brings life to the world, passed through the medium of death in order to win for us freedom from the law of sin and death. He is the Light that lets us see the beauty of God and His mercy and grace toward us. Jesus is even now seated at the right hand of the Father, displaying His wounds that brought us healing, and interceding on our behalf with the Father. Heaven and earth sing His praises!

> Crown Him the Lord of love;
> Behold his hands and side,
> Those wounds, yet visible above,
> In beauty glorified.
> All hail, Redeemer, hail!
> For thou hast died for me;
> Thy praise and glory shall not fail, throughout eternity.[9]

God is trustworthy. The Old and New Testaments testify God is trustworthy. When you next see a rainbow, remember God's promise to withhold for a time His righteous judgment against a sinful world. Then give thanks to Jesus the Christ, the Savior of the sinful world, whose light we bask in and whose light we are to reflect to others groping in the darkness.

REFLECTIONS FOR THE WEEK

1. Many Christians do not study the Old Testament. Some struggle to find solidarity with an ancient culture, one that was often brutal in nature. Some struggle to understand God's judgments on ancient peoples—Jews and Gentiles alike. But Jesus said the Law of Moses, the prophets, and the Psalms all point to Him. With Jesus' words in mind, read Isaiah chapters 40 to 56 and make notations in your Bible whenever you read a passage that you believe points to Jesus. As you read, consider what Isaiah's original hearers might have thought He was saying to them.

2. What insights do you gain about Jesus and His death on the cross from these passages from Isaiah?

---

[9] From the hymn, "Crown Him with Many Crowns," composed by Matthew Bridges and Godfrey Thring. Public domain.

PRAYER

Hear this, all peoples!
Give ear, all inhabitants of the world,
both low and high,
rich and poor together!
My mouth shall speak wisdom;
the meditation of my heart shall be understanding.
I will incline my ear to a proverb;
I will solve my riddle to the music of the lyre.
Why should I fear in times of trouble,
when the iniquity of those who cheat me surrounds me,
those who trust in their wealth
and boast of the abundance of their riches?
Truly no man can ransom another,
or give to God the price of his life,
for the ransom of their life is costly
and can never suffice,
that he should live on forever
and never see the pit. But God will redeem my life from the grave;
he will surely take me to himself.
But God will ransom my soul from the power of Sheol,
for he will receive me.

~ Psalm 49:1–9, 15 ESV

Amen

DECEMBER—WEEK TWO

RETAINING AND RECRUITING TALENTED EMPLOYEES

Now Naomi had a relative of her husband's, a worthy man of the clan of Elimelech, whose name was Boaz. And Ruth the Moabite said to Naomi, "Let me go to the field and glean among the ears of grain after him in whose sight I shall find favor." And she said to her, "Go, my daughter." So she set out and went and gleaned in the field after the reapers, and she happened to come to the part of the field belonging to Boaz, who was of the clan of Elimelech. And behold, Boaz came from Bethlehem. And he said to the reapers, "The Lord be with you!" And they answered, "The Lord bless you."

~ Ruth 2:1–4 ESV

And the hand of the Lord was with them, and a great number who believed turned to the Lord. The report of this came to the ears of the church in Jerusalem, and they sent Barnabas to Antioch. When he came and saw the grace of God, he was glad, and he exhorted them all to remain faithful to the Lord with steadfast purpose, for he was a good man, full of the Holy Spirit and of faith. And a great many people were added to the Lord. So Barnabas went to Tarsus to look for Saul, and when he had found him, he brought him to Antioch. For a whole year they met with the church and taught a great many people. And in Antioch the disciples were first called Christians.

Now in these days prophets came down from Jerusalem to Antioch. And one of them named Agabus stood up and foretold by the Spirit that there would be a great famine over all the world (this took place in the days of Claudius). So the disciples determined, every one according to his ability, to send relief to the brothers living in Judea. And they did so, sending it to the elders by the hand of Barnabas and Saul.

~ Acts 11:21–30 ESV

John Maxwell has made a remarkable career of studying, analyzing, and teaching leadership principles to millions of people all over the world. I can personally testify his books have inspired and instructed me in my role as a leader in my organization. In his book *The Twenty-one Indispensable Qualities of a Leader: Becoming the Person Others Will Want to Follow,* Maxwell identifies and discusses the qualities of leaders that enable them to effectively lead others and achieve their personal and business goals and objectives. Maxwell begins his book with the human quality of character. According to Maxwell, "The development of character is at the heart of our development not just as leaders, but as human beings." With his gift of insight, Maxwell goes on to say, "We don't get to pick our talents or IQ. But we do choose our character. In fact, we create it every time we make choices—to cop out or dig out of a hard situation, to bend the truth or stand under the weight of it, to take the easy money or pay the price. As you live your life and make choices today, you are continuing to create your character."

In a business setting, I have been designated a leader of people since 1981. Initially, and for a good number of years, I led small groups of people to accomplish tasks and discrete projects. Later, I led larger groups of people in both strategic activities and in the pursuit of goals and objectives. Eventually, I became the chief executive of an organization and became fully responsible strategically and operationally for leading it to achieve its mission.

Sometime in the years after I became a chief executive, I noticed in the Book of Ruth a leader and businessman named Boaz. In the few short verses quoted above and in his story, the Bible makes clear Boaz is a man of character. Since reading about Boaz, I have had a personal goal of becoming "Boaz-like" in my relationships with employees. Boaz illustrates the profound and positive effect that a leader can have upon those being led. Leadership is not about honor or glory; it is about responsibility and accountability. Boaz sets a tough standard to achieve.

The Book of Ruth is a wonderful piece of literature. Out of the everyday trials and uncertainties of life, the actors in the Book of Ruth reveal and demonstrate character-building at its finest. Historically, the book takes place in the time of the Judges—a time when the Jewish people had taken possession of the Promised Land but had not petitioned God to give them a king. In times of civil uncertainty and war, God would raise up judges to lead the people. In times of peace, the people governed themselves according to their tribes and allotments of land. Some of the more famous judges were Samson, Gideon, and Samuel.

The three central characters in Ruth are Naomi, Ruth, and Boaz. Naomi is a widow who lost her husband and two sons while living in the foreign land of Moab. Although her two sons married Moabite women while living in Moab, they died childless. In that time and culture, such life circumstances placed Naomi in dire straits. Her life in shambles, Naomi determines to return to Israel. She instructs her daughters-in-law to return to their own families, where they might be able to find other husbands and rebuild their lives. Ruth is one of her daughters-in-law, and Orpah is the other. Orpah decides to leave Naomi, but Ruth persists in staying with Naomi. Ruth says, "Do not urge me to leave you or to return from following you. For where you go I will go, and where you lodge I will lodge. Your people shall be my people, and your God my God. Where you die I will die, and there will I be buried. May the Lord do so to me and more also if anything but death parts me from you" (Ruth 1:16–17 ESV). Together, Ruth and Naomi return to Bethlehem.

Safely back in Bethlehem, Ruth goes to gather grain from the fields of others in a practice known as gleaning. Gleaning was a method established by God to allow the poor to obtain food. As it turns out, Ruth gleans in a field owned by Boaz, and he notices her working and befriends her. Eventually, Ruth boldly asks Boaz to "redeem" her under the Mosaic law of kinsman-redeemer, a practice that allowed a childless widow to take as her husband a relative for the purpose of having a son to whom the name and estate of the deceased father would pass. Boaz qualified as a kinsman-redeemer for Ruth. Although the practice of kinsman-redeemer existed, it was a difficult assignment for the redeemer because of conflicts of interest over their own progeny and property.

Boaz is much older than Ruth and is flattered by her offer. Boaz, a man of noble character, sees in Ruth a similar noble quality of character, and he accepts her offer. But Boaz also realizes there is a redeemer closer to Naomi and Ruth than himself. Accordingly, in an act that further demonstrates his noble character, Boaz allows the other relative the opportunity to redeem the property of Naomi and to take Ruth as wife. When that relative refuses, Boaz and Ruth are married. Three generations later, out of their union comes David, the beloved king of Israel.

The story of Ruth presents Boaz in sufficient detail to gain an understanding and appreciation of his strong and noble character traits. Here are the character traits that I have seen in Boaz.

- Although Boaz was a man of standing in his community and regarded as successful (he owned property and had employees), the personal regard of the community and the employees for Boaz was for his character much more than for his wealth. When he entered his field, Boaz greeted his employees in a heartfelt way with the blessing of the Lord. They returned the blessing. Boaz instructed his men not to harm Ruth and to allow her to glean even in areas where gleaning would not have been allowed. Boaz fed Ruth and gave her water, and he asked Ruth to stay only in his fields where he could assure her of protection. When Ruth came to Boaz at night, he treated her with respect and cared about her reputation.
- Boaz was a man of God. Not only did he bless his workers, but he understood the law of kinsman-redeemer as God had intended it. He did not covet Naomi's property and did not lust after Ruth. Boaz accepted the role of kinsman-redeemer.
- Boaz was very observant of all that went on around him in his business and in his community. He had taken note of Naomi's return to Bethlehem, and he had noticed Ruth's kindness toward her. Aware of the treacherous times of the Judges, Boaz advised Ruth to be careful for her safety, and he was careful about his own property, standing guard over his own harvest.
- He was a man of compassion toward others. Boaz lived out his values for his employees and others to see. In his instructions to his workers concerning Ruth, he demonstrated integrity and a willingness to be generous to others.

- Boaz was a man of action. He was present in his fields at the time of harvest even though he had enough wealth to employ overseers. He was present and working at the threshing of the grain, and he took an active and personal role in protecting his property. At the end of the work process, he celebrated with food and drink.
- Boaz followed the law. He did not skirt it or interpret it to his advantage. Although he wanted to be the kinsman-redeemer for Naomi and Ruth, he realized there was another with a closer claim. In the presence of witnesses, he offered the other relative the opportunity to exercise the lawful rights of kinsman-redeemer. In all that he did, Boaz followed the letter of the law and the heart of the law.

The Book of Ruth demonstrates, without God speaking, that God is aware of His creation and is actively accomplishing His plans to be our "kinsman-redeemer." There is a thread that runs through the Bible of God causing His plan of salvation to unfold. In Ruth, we see God's hand at work in the ancestors of David. From David's line comes Jesus, the Christ. And Jesus is our hope and salvation.

The Bible reveals that God is at work in the lives of all people. Whomever God chooses to use will have success because He will provide the power and resources to accomplish His purpose. If He did not do so, no one would succeed.

The Apostle Paul, in the book of Romans, discusses God's choice—His election—of individuals and peoples as part of His sovereign right. The idea that God is truly active in the affairs of men was an affront to certain people in Paul's day and is an affront to some today. In answer to the question over God's right to choose whom He will bless and use, Paul said, "But who are you, O man, to answer back to God? Will what is molded say to its molder, 'Why have you made me like this?' Has the potter no right over the clay, to make out of the same lump one vessel for honorable use and another for dishonorable use?" (Romans 9:20–21 ESV).

Paul was truly a Christian leader; in addition to writing much of the New Testament, he sponsored churches in numerous communities and established a church structure that allowed those communities to continue to grow and prosper after he had moved on.

Early in his career, however, Paul had been a persecutor of the church. Trust was not easy for Paul to come by among the Christian believers. But as Acts 11:21–30 reveals, Paul had a "Boaz-type" benefactor in Barnabas. Because Barnabas took an active interest in befriending Paul, Paul was more quickly accepted in the young Christian community. Paul was also able to gain experience and skill in evangelizing the message of Christ with Barnabas at his side. God had plans for Paul, and Barnabas was useful in assisting God in Paul's ministerial preparations.

With this in mind, how is God using you in His plans? He has gifted you with opportunity and the privilege of leading others. Can you see the possibility that you are situated somewhere in the middle of the story that God is writing? Boaz did not realize that his great-grandson would be king of Israel. Boaz did not know that God would promise to David that his progeny would rule over Israel for all time. Boaz did not know how his little link in the chain of time would impact our lives through the birth of Jesus Christ. But God knew. And God is aware of you; He has lovingly created you and placed you in your particular circumstances. When you accepted Jesus as your Savior, God put His Spirit in your life to shape it, mold it, and make it beautiful. Your character is being shaped by God's Holy Spirit. Everything you do and say is meaningful to God and His plans for you and the world around you.

David was overwhelmed by the thought that God was intimately aware of him and cared about him. He said, "O Lord, what is man that you regard him, or the son of man that you think of him? Man is like a breath; his days are like a passing shadow" (Psalm 144:3–4 ESV).

And again, David said, "Who am I, O Lord God, and what is my house, that you have brought me thus far? And this was a small thing in your eyes, O God. You have also spoken of your servant's house for a great while to come, and have shown me future generations, O Lord God!" (1 Chronicles 17:16b–17 ESV). David was like us in this respect: When his eyes were focused on God, he made wise choices; when his eyes turned from God, he chose poorly. Through all of his choices, David was still an instrument in God's plan, and God's plan cannot help but be confirmed.

Boaz was used by God for a noble purpose, but he did not know God as a person or a friend. David, Barnabas, and Paul were used by God for noble purposes, and they did know God as a person and a friend. Because you know Christ, God knows you as His child. Through Jesus, God knows you as a friend. Greet today with confidence, knowing that whatever you do today matters to God. Be aware, be conscious, be wise, and be blessed.

REFLECTIONS FOR THE WEEK

1. Proverbs 15:3 says, "The eyes of the Lord are in every place, keeping watch on the evil and the good." Proverbs 15:30–33 says, "The light of the eyes rejoices the heart, and good news refreshes the bones. The ear that listens to life-giving reproof will dwell among the wise. Whoever ignores instruction despises himself, but he who listens to reproof gains intelligence. The fear of the Lord is instruction in wisdom, and humility comes before honor." Consider your role as a leader to those who report to you at work. Apply the wisdom of the proverbs quoted above to your interaction this week with those people.

2. Many successful companies use a form of employee evaluation (known as a 360 degree evaluation) that asks a broad range of coworkers to evaluate key attributes and skills of a leader. If your company does not utilize this method of evaluation, research it and consider how you might benefit personally as a leader from such an evaluation by those you lead.

PRAYER

Father, thank You for caring about me. Grant me the wisdom to see Your guiding hand in my life, in the mundane and the important. Awaken within me the understanding that coincidence is not in Your vocabulary. Otherwise, I would have to conclude You are not careful for Your creation and my hope would flounder, my peace would dissipate, and my heart would fail within me. Rather, let me rejoice in the thought that Your eyes are everywhere, keeping watch on the wicked and the good.

Amen

DECEMBER—WEEK THREE

RECOGNIZING WHEN CHANGE IS NECESSARY

See what kind of love the Father has given to us, that we should be called children of God; and so we are. The reason why the world does not know us is that it did not know him. Beloved, we are God's children now, and what we will be has not yet appeared; but we know that when he appears we shall be like him, because we shall see him as he is. And everyone who thus hopes in him purifies himself as he is pure.

Everyone who makes a practice of sinning also practices lawlessness; sin is lawlessness. You know that he appeared in order to take away sins, and in him there is no sin. No one who abides in him keeps on sinning; no one who keeps on sinning has either seen him or known him.

~ 1 John 3:1–6 ESV

"Let all the house of Israel therefore know for certain that God has made him both Lord and Christ, this Jesus whom you crucified." Now when they heard this they were cut to the heart, and said to Peter and the rest of the apostles, "Brothers, what shall we do?" And Peter said to them, "Repent and be baptized every one of you in the name of Jesus Christ for the forgiveness of your sins, and you will receive the gift of the Holy Spirit. For the promise is for you and for your children and for all who are far off, everyone whom the Lord our God calls to himself."

~ Acts 2:36–39 ESV

For while we were still weak, at the right time Christ died for the ungodly. For one will scarcely die for a righteous person—though perhaps for a good person one would dare even to die—but God shows his love for us in that while we were still sinners, Christ died for us. Since, therefore, we have now been justified by his blood, much more shall we be saved by him from the wrath of God. For if while we were enemies we were reconciled to God by the death of his Son, much more, now that we are reconciled, shall we be saved by his life. More than that, we also rejoice in God through our Lord Jesus Christ, through whom we have now received reconciliation.

~ Romans 5:6–11 ESV

Would you say you are a forgiving person? Are you the type of person who holds short accounts with others? Or do you find it difficult to forgive someone who has injured you?

Before we were married, my wife and I decided our future relationship would benefit from attending joint counseling sessions with a marriage counselor. Just like all couples, married or dating, we had experienced issues from time to time that seemed difficult to sort through on our own. For us, the counseling sessions were helpful and instructive. Through them we learned two important lessons for resolving conflict in our relationship. The first was to postpone for a time conflict resolution if either of us was feeling Hungry, Angry, Lonely, or Tired. The best choice when one of us is feeling any of these characteristics (and we added an S for sick) is to table serious discussion until HALTS has passed.

The second great lesson we learned was to always fight fair. Unfair fighting was defined as either of us dredging past mistakes that had no bearing on a current event or circumstance into a current fray. A good relationship is built upon trust and forgiveness. In the face of trust and forgiveness, past mistakes cannot be used as a weapon or an argument. This little rule keeps us centered on the present circumstances only. What happened in the past was dealt with in the past. The troubles for today are always sufficient for today, to paraphrase Jesus.

Of the two, the second lesson is more difficult to keep because wounds are memorable—it is hard to truly forget and forgive past mistakes. Humans harbor grudges. My mother was notably adept at remembering past mistakes in arguments with my father. But unfair fighting was not limited to just my home; because all parents argue from time to time, I witnessed similar behavior and unfair fighting techniques in the homes of my childhood friends too.

In the 1950s and 1960s, the commonplace nature of couples arguing was comically displayed in the wildly popular television show "The

Honeymooners," starring Jackie Gleason. Most of the comedy of "The Honeymooners" was obtained through the arguments of husband Ralph Kramden with his wife, Alice. Alice was skilled at recalling all of Ralph's faults in any current argument. Ralph could not escape his past. As a child observer of arguments both real and televised, I learned the grudge tactic was not a good one to bring peace—regardless of accuracy and relevance.

It is difficult to forgive and forget. This is true for slights and offenses others make against us and also true for our own self-inflicted wounds that we obstinately cling to. Hebrews 12:1 encourages us to "throw off the sin that so easily entangles." In that passage I hear the admonition of Jesus to let go past sins and disappointments.

The passage from Romans 5:6–11 above tells us that all our sins have been forgiven by Christ. There is no parsing of sins by Christ—all are alike and all are damnable. But all are forgiven by His act of salvation. An inability or unwillingness to forgive yourself what Christ has already forgiven you will rob you of God's peace. If you have confessed a sin to God and believe that Jesus Christ died for your sins, you are forgiven. There is no greater truth or gift of God to humans than this: Christ came into the world to save sinners.

Satan enjoys our inability to forgive ourselves of past sins, because our refusal to let go of them denies the majesty of Christ's death on the cross. Such behavior belittles Christ. But there is more for Satan to enjoy as well. Holding onto past sins already forgiven you by God will entangle your life and keep you from knowing the peace of God. Holding onto past sins will block the joy and freedom that flows out of forgiveness and hinder your service to God and to others.

Obstinately clinging to past sins is prideful; it is prideful to think your sins are so gross and grievous they are above Christ's redemption. It is prideful and foolish to think that you must do something about sin—that you will find a way to rise above it. Satan will remind you of the sins you keep locked in your mind and rob you of peace, joy, and service to God.

I fly a lot in my business. Hundreds of times I have heard flight attendants recite before take-off that if cabin pressure is compromised while in flight, oxygen masks will fall from overhead compartments. Their instructions remind passengers that when traveling with an infant, it is of vital importance to first secure your own mask before assisting others. These same instructions apply to anyone who still harbors grudges or wounds against themselves for past sins. Before we can be counted on to assist others in God's kingdom, we first have to take care of our own immediate needs. Jesus is our oxygen mask whose forgiveness gives us power and a favorable testimony to assist others.

    I know firsthand the difficulty of letting go of past sins that feel so gross and grievous that Christ's death on the cross seems too little to fit the offense. The circumstances of my awakening to the foolishness of self-loathing over past sins were remarkable and came at a most opportune time. I had spent months grappling with my past. I had spent months in remorseful reflection and longed to have peace with myself and with God. I had confessed my sin and my heart to God, but I refused to accept forgiveness. For a time I would forget my anguish, but it would rise unbidden to my mind again and again. My mistakes were blocking grace and healing.

    While driving home alone late one evening, I chanced to find on the radio a Christian broadcast of a sermon that had been delivered by a preacher (I do not remember his name) who had at that time been deceased for ten years. I had made this same drive on the same road at the same time for many weeks and had never found a Christian broadcast before. And I never found that radio station again. But that night, the radio was clear as a bell and the preacher spoke of the all-surpassing value of Christ's death on the cross. He read from Romans a number of passages dealing with Christ's sacrifice for the full and complete forgiveness of sins. His message went straight to my heart. I had been harboring guilt and conviction of past sin that was crippling my future. I listened with rapt attention. I cried. Upon arriving home, I rushed to my bedroom and read the book of Romans. I saw that my sin, awful as it was, was no match for God's mercy and grace. My Christian life changed that night. One of Satan's most potent weapons against me was removed by Christ and Christ alone.

If you are struggling with a sin from your past that you cannot be rid of, it may help to think about it in this way: when we sin, we sin against Jesus. As I reflect back to that emotional ride home and that time in my life, I now see I was being held hostage by the weight of sin (pain) I had caused another. It felt like my sin was more against another than God. Intellectually, I knew I had broken God's rules, but I did not understand that my sin was truly more against God than against another person.

While it is true another person may also be injured by our acts, the heart of the matter is that Jesus bore the brunt of our sins in His body when He went to the cross. Otherwise, why did He die? Why did He go? Was Christ's life that cheap? I had hurt another person and that was bad, but they never hung on a cross with the sins of the world on their shoulders because of me. On the other hand, Jesus did.

My friend in Christ, there is only one mediator of our sins before God—Jesus, the Christ. He willingly gave His life for ours. He has the right to grant us forgiveness. Truth be told, He has the preeminent right of forgiveness. John says in the verse from 1 John above, "no one who abides in him keeps on sinning." If we refuse to give Him all of our sins—if we allow some sins to keep us in bondage, are we not still sinning? Who is master, our sins or Jesus?

Jesus describes His love for us this way: "Greater love has no one than this, that someone lay down his life for his friends" (John 15:13 ESV). Jesus proved His love for us by going to the cross and dying for the sins of the world. As you reflect on sins that even now cling to you and entangle your joy and peace in this world, consider what would happen if you laid down that part of your life for Jesus' sake. Jesus gave His life for you. Give that last part of your life—the part that is holding you in bondage and robbing you of your life in Christ, robbing you of joy, peace, and hope, and robbing you of Christian service and sacrifice—give that part of your life to Jesus and be free.

REFLECTIONS FOR THE WEEK

1. There is a variation of the Lord's Supper where the minister hands out the bread of life with the instruction to take it but refrain from eating it. Rather, the recipient is instructed to hold on

to the piece of bread and contemplate what sin is holding them in bondage. After prayer and reflection, the recipient silently names their sin, places it mentally on the bread, and returns the bread to the minister. Once all the bread has been re-collected, the Lord's Supper proceeds and each person eats the bread that Christ has sanctified. It is a powerful service of healing and wholeness. If you were given a piece of bread today, what would you name as the sin that holds you in bondage? Can you give that sin to Christ today?

2. Is there someone you know who is in bondage to their past? Can you speak a word of comfort to them?

PRAYER

Jesus, there is peace and freedom in You and You alone. You said that apart from You, I can do nothing. The same message applies to repairing broken lives. You know everything about me. You were aware of me as You bled and died on the cross. Your love was sufficient then and is still sufficient to heal me today. Grant me the strength to let go. Grant me the strength to let You restore my life to fullness of purpose and peace. Let me bring into the light of Your presence those hurtful and hidden things that keep me in darkness.

Amen

DECEMBER—WEEK FOUR

DEFINING THE MISSION OF THE ORGANIZATION

You, however, have followed my teaching, my conduct, my aim in life, my faith, my patience, my love, my steadfastness, my persecutions and sufferings that happened to me at Antioch, at Iconium, and at Lystra—which persecutions I endured; yet from them all the Lord rescued me. Indeed, all who desire to live a godly life in Christ Jesus will be persecuted, while evil people and impostors will go on from bad to worse, deceiving and being deceived. But as for you, continue in what you have learned and have firmly believed, knowing from whom you learned it and how from childhood you have been acquainted with the sacred writings, which are able to make you wise for salvation through faith in Christ Jesus. All Scripture is breathed out by God and profitable for teaching, for reproof, for correction, and for training in righteousness, that the man of God may be complete, equipped for every good work.

I charge you in the presence of God and of Christ Jesus, who is to judge the living and the dead, and by his appearing and his kingdom: preach the word; be ready in season and out of season; reprove, rebuke, and exhort, with complete patience and teaching. For the time is coming when people will not endure sound teaching, but having itching ears they will accumulate for themselves teachers to suit their own passions, and will turn away from listening to the truth and wander off into myths. As for you, always be sober-minded, endure suffering, do the work of an evangelist, fulfill your ministry.

For I am already being poured out as a drink offering, and the time of my departure has come. I have fought the good fight, I have finished the race, I have kept the faith. Henceforth there is laid up for me the crown of righteousness, which the Lord, the righteous judge, will award to me on that Day, and not only to me but also to all who have loved his appearing.

~ 2 Timothy 3:10–4:8 ESV

DECEMBER—WEEK FOUR

The Christmas season and the rapidly approaching New Year are the perfect time to reflect on the circumstances of the past year. Almost twelve months ago, you began the year with hopes and expectations, plans and objectives. Good planning and forecasting is important, but one thing is certain; plans and expectations do not turn out exactly as forecast. There is always a variance between actual and forecasted results. Evaluating how things worked out for you requires an interpretation using both fact, what actually happened, and opinion, why the actual result occurred instead of the hoped for result.

Measuring what truly happened is almost always fact based—it is like a light switch—either the light is on (goals were met) or the light is off (goals were missed). The facts, however, shed little light on how the enterprise and its leaders and employees actually reacted to changing circumstances. Opinions are formed to add qualitative judgment: Did the enterprise do what needed to be done in the face of current events, changing circumstances, and uncertainty?

Both types of evaluations are important. To some (those in the "winning isn't everything—it is the only thing" crowd), missing a goal but displaying quality character traits in trying but yet failing is cold comfort—it is really no comfort at all. Depending on the stakes involved, the difference in making goals or missing them can mean the very life of the enterprise. When the stakes are that high, there is little solace found in watching a business cease to exist "with style." To others (who belong to the Teddy Roosevelt crowd), honor is always found in the struggle and the cause being pursued, even if victory is not achieved. Roosevelt himself said, "If he fails, at least (he) fails while daring greatly, so that his place shall never be with those cold and timid souls who neither know victory nor defeat."

Winning and losing are facts, but perspective is gained through honest self-reflection. The ability of a leader to discern wisdom and gain perspective is invaluable because, unless the "men in the arena" cease to exist, each will live to fight another day and will carry into the next venture personal characteristics (perseverance, applied wisdom, endurance, insight, intuition, courage) as part of the experiences gained from the last. Experiences—both good and bad—count, in my opinion.

Over a lifetime, experience builds and provides a leader with valuable insight, foresight, and wisdom. However, the role of being a leader is not permanent. The time will come when leadership will be relinquished to someone else. Human brevity dictates an important and significant responsibility of leadership—to prepare those who follow for leadership so that continuity of the mission is preserved.

What future leaders do with the position they inherit will be their responsibility; you have the responsibility to equip them to succeed to the best of your ability. Your responsibility remains while you are in the position of leadership. Training future leaders is an active and ongoing responsibility. Each circumstance and event can provide great material to shape future leaders and to impart meaning in the context of mission.

In the book of 2 Timothy, the author, Paul, has neared the end of his leadership roles of missionary and apostle. In his time of active leadership and work, Paul established churches throughout the known world and labored greatly to impart to them sound doctrine and structure. In his work and travels, Paul met and associated with many others. Some of them, like Timothy, had been trained and equipped to carry on Paul's work of bringing the message of Christ and salvation to the world and caring for the body of Christ—the church. Timothy was one of Paul's most beloved students. At the end of his career, Paul's love for Christ and the church pressed upon him an urgent desire to pass on the mantle of leadership to others. The letter to Timothy gives us excellent insight into certain godly leadership skills to accomplish that purpose.

Paul demonstrates seven godly leadership skills that are important in times of transition from one leader to another:

1. Paul hand-picked future leaders and spent significant time with them. Because Paul had assumed personal and hands-on involvement in the training of Timothy, he had great confidence in Timothy's ability to assume a position of leadership. Paul knew his faith in Timothy was sound—he knew Timothy could carry on in his absence. "For this reason

I remind you to fan into flame the gift of God, which is in you through the laying on of my hands" (2 Timothy 1:6 ESV).

In this leadership characteristic, Paul imitated Christ. Paul had received hands-on training from Jesus, and Paul had received additional strengthening and encouragement from the other eleven original apostles. Paul gave to his students and disciples the same level of training, encouragement, and time that he had benefited from and received from others. There is no substitute for spending time and energy training future leaders.

2. Paul retraced the past and gave it "fresh eyes" and context for Timothy. Paul's life and experiences had been hard, and his hardships, when judged by the world, implied failure and not success. Paul had faced persecution and imprisonment, he had been run out of many towns, and he had sometimes been deserted by his companions. But Paul's perspective on all that he had been through was one of great success—he had been triumphant in each instance. "You, however, have followed my teaching, my conduct, my aim in life, my faith, my patience, my love, my steadfastness, my persecutions and sufferings that happened to me at Antioch, at Iconium, and at Lystra—which persecutions I endured; yet from them all the Lord rescued me" (2 Timothy 3:10–11 ESV).

Without hearing from Paul the context in which these trials occurred, their purpose from Paul's perspective, and their ultimate good for the mission itself, Timothy might have misunderstood them. Equally important, the knowledge that Paul imparted would safeguard Timothy and the mission now being entrusted to him when Timothy experienced his own trials.

3. Paul was open and honest about the difficulty that would face Timothy in the days ahead. "But understand this, that in the last days there will come times of difficulty. For people will be lovers of self, lovers of money, proud, arrogant, abusive, disobedient to their parents, ungrateful, unholy, heartless, unappeasable, slanderous, without self-control, brutal, not loving good, treacherous, reckless, swollen with conceit, lovers of pleasure rather than lovers of God, having the appearance of godliness, but denying its power. Avoid such people" (2 Timothy 3:1–5 ESV).

Jesus did the same thing with His disciples (cf. Luke 17:22–37; Luke 21:7–36). Leaders know and anticipate risks. Future leaders must quickly learn to do the same.

4. Notwithstanding the anticipated risks and trials to come, Paul encouraged Timothy to persevere. The encouragement was not merely wishful thinking and empty words. Paul called Timothy to remember the power of God and Timothy's own gifts. "The saying is trustworthy and deserving of full acceptance. For to this end we toil and strive, because we have our hope set on the living God, who is the Savior of all people, especially of those who believe. Command and teach these things. Let no one despise you for your youth, but set the believers an example in speech, in conduct, in love, in faith, in purity. Until I come, devote yourself to the public reading of Scripture, to exhortation, to teaching. Do not neglect the gift you have, which was given you by prophecy when the council of elders laid their hands on you" (1 Timothy 4:9–14 ESV).

5. Paul assured Timothy of his positive feelings and his hope for Timothy's success. A leader who cares about others only because it helps the leader achieve success is a hypocrite. A godly leader cares about employees on a personal level, hoping for their success and well-being, knowing that God is watching. "I thank God whom I serve, as did my ancestors, with a clear conscience, as I remember you constantly in my prayers night and day. As I remember your tears, I long to see you, that I may be filled with joy" (2 Timothy 1:3–4 ESV).

6. Paul reiterated his confidence in Timothy, and reminded Timothy of his training and the resources readily available to him in his mission. Paul had confidence in Timothy, but Timothy needed to have confidence in himself. "But as for you, continue in what you have learned and have firmly believed, knowing from whom you learned it and how from childhood you have been acquainted with the sacred writings, which are able to make you wise for salvation through faith in Christ Jesus. All Scripture is breathed out by God and profitable for teaching, for reproof, for correction, and for training in righteousness, that the man of God may be complete, equipped for every good work"(2 Timothy 3:14–17 ESV).

7. Paul clearly restated the mission. There was no ambiguity about the mission Paul was assigning Timothy. "I charge you in the presence of God and of Christ Jesus, who is to judge the living and the dead, and by his appearing and his kingdom: preach the word; be ready in season and out of season; reprove, rebuke, and exhort, with complete patience and teaching" (2 Timothy 4:1–2 ESV). A leader must always communicate the mission statement to others. It can never be over-communicated.

Was Paul effective in transferring his ministry to others? Did Timothy succeed in carrying on the mission of Paul, or more accurately, carrying on the mission of Christ?

I believe the answer is yes based on two observations. First, Christianity did spread across the entire world and continues to grow today. Second, we know of no subsequent letter from Timothy to any other successor. There was no need for a different letter other than the one written by Paul to be written. What Paul wrote to Timothy was completely satisfactory for Timothy and for all who followed Timothy. This fact testifies to the power of Paul as a leader. Timothy got the message. Timothy was successful. Others have also gotten the message from Paul. The gospel continues to advance.

As you spend quiet time at the end of the year reflecting on your mission statement and formulating plans for the New Year, find time to impart wisdom to others. It is an obligation of a leader. Be confident and enthusiastic about your life experiences and your hope in Christ. Christ has been good to you this year. Thank Him privately and publicly. Finally, as long as God allows you to be a leader, lead. In season and out of season, in good times and bad times, lead others to the best of your ability to do so. Be strong and very courageous, and God's hand will not depart from you.

REFLECTIONS FOR THE WEEK

1. In sports it is not unusual to see a particularly successful coach leave a legacy of other successful coaches at different teams. This week, recall leaders in your past that have helped you become

successful today. Then consider who you have helped to be successful. Who in your organization could you devote time with in the coming year to shepherd into a future leadership position?

2. Over the past year, what events and circumstances called for you to lead "in season and out of season"? Make it a point to discuss those times with your teams in order to share wisdom and set a foundation for positive experiences in the future.

PRAYER

Almighty God, my time is limited. What I hold dear now, what I passionately seek, will someday disappear or will fall to the hands of others to pursue. This is the way of the world that You designed. Only You are constant, Lord. Only You are everlasting. You have given me desires and talents. You have created me for a purpose. Bless me and enable me to fulfill Your plans for me. Let me not hold too tightly to what is transient. Rather, let me hold tightly to what is everlasting—a faithful and obedient relationship with You. Help me to help others become leaders in your kingdom.

Amen

DECEMBER—WEEK FIVE

HARVESTING AND PRUNING THE ORGANIZATION

And when a great crowd was gathering and people from town after town came to him, he said in a parable, "A sower went out to sow his seed. And as he sowed, some fell along the path and was trampled underfoot, and the birds of the air devoured it. And some fell on the rock, and as it grew up, it withered away, because it had no moisture. And some fell among thorns, and the thorns grew up with it and choked it. And some fell into good soil and grew and yielded a hundredfold." As he said these things, he called out, "He who has ears to hear, let him hear."
And when his disciples asked him what this parable meant, he said, "To you it has been given to know the secrets of the kingdom of God, but for others they are in parables, so that 'seeing they may not see, and hearing they may not understand.' Now the parable is this: The seed is the word of God. The ones along the path are those who have heard; then the devil comes and takes away the word from their hearts, so that they may not believe and be saved. And the ones on the rock are those who, when they hear the word, receive it with joy. But these have no root; they believe for a while, and in time of testing fall away. And as for what fell among the thorns, they are those who hear, but as they go on their way they are choked by the cares and riches and pleasures of life, and their fruit does not mature. As for that in the good soil, they are those who, hearing the word, hold it fast in an honest and good heart, and bear fruit with patience.

"No one after lighting a lamp covers it with a jar or puts it under a bed, but puts it on a stand, so that those who enter may see the light. For nothing is hidden that will not be made manifest, nor is anything secret that will not be known and come to light. Take care then how you hear, for to the one who has, more will be given, and from the one who has not, even what he thinks that he has will be taken away."

~ Luke 8:4–18 ESV

There is something remarkable about planting something and watching it grow. Even though we stand in the midst of a green world, the ubiquity of it dulls our senses to it. We pass by living plant material everyday and do not give it a second thought. We mow grass every weekend in season and are not amazed at the vibrant vitality of nature. We are displeased by the resiliency of weeds in our lawns and flower beds that grow despite our chemicals and the sweat of exertion to eradicate them from our yards. In autumn, leaves beyond count fall and fall and fall, and we rake and rake and rake, but we do not stand in amazement of the magnitude of the breath of life that foliage represents for us.

But if you buy seeds and plant the seed yourself, your interest in what happens next is keen. If you have ever put a seed in the ground, patted the soil over the top, and watered the seed, you know the thrill that is experienced when the tender green shoot emerges and straightens itself to drink in sunlight and life. That same tender green shoot will capture our attention for days, and we will nurture the plant with water, ample exposure to sunlight, and protection from predators. Yes, there is something remarkable about planting a seed and watching it grow. We are drawn into creation by becoming part of it.

Humanly speaking, we are like plants in this regard: in the mass of humanity that surrounds us, our uniqueness and beauty can be lost. We are told we are cogs in the wheel. We come to doubt that there is something special about us. We can believe the lie that our circumstances were chance and fate; either a fortunate puff of wind carried our lives to rich soil, or a harsh wind carried us to rocky soil. We can say with some human equanimity, "C'est la vie," (such is life) over our circumstances, whatever those circumstances may be. But, dear friend in Christ, we are also like plants in this regard: the Creator of the earth lovingly gave you life and has watched in delight your tender shoot springing up and stretching for the light, and life. You matter and possess a significance to the only One to whom an opinion about you counts.

Because our world is fallen in sin, we do not begin our lives in good soil. Rather, we begin along the path, on rocky soil, or amid thorns and weeds.

But God is persistent and caring and refuses to abandon us. He is, after all, the Creator. At His mighty word the world and all that is in it sprang into existence from nothing. Life exists in God and God alone. God moved you from the path or the rocky soil or the weed-filled field into good soil—where His Son could offer you life and liberty and fill you with good things, a future, and a purpose. The Word of Life gave you new life, and since that glorious day when Christ filled your heart, your life has not been the same. These are powerful and hope-filled words, and they are true, but they do not always seem true. Because our world is fallen in sin, we suffer the effects of sin, and we do not always do or say or act as if we are God's true seed planted in rich, verdant soil. We remain human and act like humans, but we are not without hope.

Over the last fifty-two weeks, you have read a lot of Scripture and have pondered its meaning. Notwithstanding your desire to know God and please Him, I am certain there have been weeks in the last fifty-two that you are not proud of. I am certain you have been tested and in certain instances found wanting. I am also certain you have experienced some prosperity, that you have overcome some hardships and obstacles, and that you have demonstrated leadership in struggles and good fortune alike. You are a child of God, and that is remarkable. But you are not yet what you shall be one day. Life provides the background and environment in which God shapes and molds your life for His purpose. A new circumstance will occur each day of your life. God uses life's circumstances to both test and nurture you, for both are necessary for your growth. And God's effort is making a positive difference in your life. Reading God's Word has changed you. It cannot do otherwise.

> *For as the rain and the snow come down from heaven*
> *and do not return there but water the earth,*
> *making it bring forth and sprout,*
> *giving seed to the sower and bread to the eater,*
> *so shall my word be that goes out from my mouth;*
> *it shall not return to me empty,*
> *but it shall accomplish that which I purpose,*
> *and shall succeed in the thing for which I sent it.*

> *For you shall go out in joy*
> *and be led forth in peace;*
> *the mountains and the hills before you*
> *shall break forth into singing,*
> *and all the trees of the field shall clap their hands.*
> *Instead of the thorn shall come up the cypress;*
> *instead of the brier shall come up the myrtle;*
> *and it shall make a name for the Lord,*
> *an everlasting sign that shall not be cut off.*
> ~ Isaiah 55:11–13 ESV

God has filled you with His Word. Rejoice in that news! Resolve in this season of resolutions to remain close to Him. Abide in Him. He will bring the sun, the rain, the nourishment, the hope, the faith, the protection, and the increase.

Let your heart well up with the springs of eternal water that will sustain and cleanse you in the midst of a fallen world. Peace belongs to God; it does not belong to the world. Because God holds you in His hands, because you stand in the shelter of His wings, approach the New Year in hope. Build on what you have done this past year. Resolve to study His Word, to listen for His voice, to seek Him with all your heart, to worship Him with gladness of heart, and to offer your life and service to Him out of love. God will equip you to bear much fruit, even in a fallen world.

> *The Lord bless you and keep you;*
> *the Lord make his face to shine upon you and be gracious to you;*
> *the Lord lift up his countenance upon you and give you peace.*
> ~ Numbers 6:24–26 ESV

REFLECTIONS FOR THE WEEK

1. Matthew 7:7–8 says, "Ask, and it will be given to you; seek, and you will find; knock, and it will be opened to you. For everyone who asks receives, and the one who seeks finds, and to the one who knocks it will be opened." Prayerfully consider your requests of God for the coming year. Record your requests in your Bible and refer to them throughout the next year. Use them to deepen your faith, your hope, and your love of God.

2. John 13:6–7 says, "He came to Simon Peter, who said to him, 'Lord, do you wash my feet?' Jesus answered him, 'What I am doing you do not understand now, but afterward you will understand.'" Jesus meets us in our humanity. Our feet get dirty. Our faces get marred. We know our situation and do not want Jesus to see that for Himself. Here, at the end of the year, pause and remember how Jesus met your needs in the past year. Jesus said that we do not realize now what He is doing, but later we will understand. What is your understanding of Jesus' work in your life this past year?

PRAYER

Father, You are active and present in all of the seasons of our lives. Even when it seems like You are standing far off, You are near. Nothing about me escapes Your notice. Let me remember You when the day is mundane or difficult. Let me remember You when joy abounds. In all circumstances, let me remember this: Apart from You I can do nothing; apart from You I am nothing. In this surpassing knowledge I stand and have hope. In joyful confidence I know my life has meaning and purpose because of You. In You I shall be fruitful, and my harvest will be bountiful.

Amen

NOTES

FEBRUARY WEEK TWO

1. Kalas, J. Ellsworth. Easter From the Backside (Nashville: Abingdon Press, 2008), 14-15.

2. Maxwell, John. Make Today Count, The Secret of Your Success is Determined by Your Daily Agenda (New York: Center Street, 2008), 2.

MARCH WEEK THREE

1. *Ernst and Young website,* http://www.ey.com/US/en/About-us/Our-values.

2. Brown-Forman Corporation website, http://www.brown-forman.com/company/values/

3. Berkshire Hathaway Inc., http://www.berkshirehathaway.com/govern/ethics.pdf.

4. Arby's, Inc. website, http://arbys.com/about, found under the caption, "Some things we believe in."

5. Hall, Roger PhD. *Expedition (United State of America: Arete Press, 2015),* 126.

APRIL WEEK THREE

1. Chambers, Oswald. My Utmost for His Highest, (Uhrichsville, Ohio: Barbour Publishing, with permission from Discovery House Publishers), cf. May 14, May 15, and May 22.

MAY WEEK TWO
1. Department of the Air Force, AFP 35-49, 1 September 1985; see http://www.au.af.mil/au/awc/awcgate/readings/afp35-49-nocover.pdf, page 2 of 11.

2. Bernstein, Elizabeth. "The Many Powers of Maybe, Refusing to Commit Has Never Been Easier, and It Says a Lot About Us," published in the Wall Street Journal, November 1, 2010, found at http://online.wsj.com/articles/SB10001424052748704141104575588460082408950.

JUNE WEEK TWO
1. Ylvisaker, Joh. *The Gospels: a Synoptic Presentation of the Text in Matthew, Mark, Luke, and John With Explanatory Notes* (Minneapolis, MN: Augsburg Publishing House, 1932), 503.

2. Greenwood, Marcia, in an article entitled, "Mustard Seed Faith" found at *https://www.tgm.org/MustardSeed.html*.

3. From a blog (author unknown) found at http://dailyexegesis.blogspot.com/2009/11/if-you-have-faith-size-of-mustard-seed.html.

JUNE WEEK FOUR
1. White, Charles Edward, in an article entitled, "What Wesley Practiced and Preached About Money," found at http://www.christianitytoday.com/le/1987/winter/87l1027.html?start=1.

2. Unknown author, *Riches: A Biblical Perspective (Ministry in the Marketplace)*, (edited by Vision Foundation, Inc., published 1994).

JULY WEEK FOUR
1. Lewis, C. S. *Mere Christianity* (HarperSanFrancisco, a division of Harper Collins Publishers, 2001), 6.

2. Strobel, Lee. *The Case for Faith: a Journalist Investigates the Toughest Objections to Christianity* (Grand Rapids, MI: Zondervan, 2000).

3. Ewan, Pamela Binnings. *Faith on Trial: an Attorney Analyzes the Evidence for the Death and Resurrection of Jesus* (Nashville: Broadman & Holman Publishers, 1999).

4. Lutzer, Erwin. *The Doctrines That Divide: a Fresh Look at the Historic Doctrines That Separate Christian* (Grand Rapids, MI: Kregal Publications, second edition, 1998).

5. Wilke, Richard Byrd and Julia Kitchens. *Disciple: Becoming Disciples Through Bible Study, Study Manual, second edition* (Abingdon Press, 1993).

AUGUST WEEK TWO
1. Young, William P. *The Shack* (Los Angeles: Windblown Media, 2007).

AUGUST WEEK THREE
1. From notes taken at a seminar conducted by H. Martin Blacker, retired medical doctor and neurosurgeon for Vistage International Group 113, New Orleans, Louisiana.

2. *The Covenant Prayer of John Wesley* was found at http://godspace-msa.com/2014/03/14/john-wesleys-covenant-prayer-a-good-reminder-for-lent/.

SEPTEMBER
1. The quote from Franklin D. Roosevelt can be found at http://www.brainyquote.com/quotes/authors/f/franklin_d_roosevelt.html.

SEPTEMBER WEEK ONE
1. For a discussion of the evil represented by the legion of demons, see MacArthur, John. *The MacArthur Study Bible* (Crossway, 2010); footnote 5.13 in the book of Mark; and Ylvisaker, Joh. *The Gospels: a Synoptic Presentation of the Text in Matthew, Mark, Luke, and John With Explanatory Notes* (Minneapolis, MN: Augsburg Publishing House, 1932), 191.

SEPTEMBER WEEK THREE
1. Kotter, John P. from an article entitled, "Leading Change: Why Transformation Efforts Fail," published in the Harvard Business Review, January 2007, found at http://hbr.org/2007/01/leading-change-why-transformation-efforts-fail/ar/1.

2. Dawson, Mark J. and Mark L. Jones. "Human Change Management: Herding Cats," originally published on the PwC website (2006) at www.pwc.com/gx/en/people-change-consulting-services/herding-cats-human-change-management.jhtml.

3. Additional information and a description of the change management method known as the ADKAR model developed by Jeff Hiatt can be found at http://www.prosci.com/adkar-model/overview-3/.

4. The quote from Mark Twain can be found at http://www.goodreads.com/quotes/150120-if-a-cat-sits-on-a-hot-stove-that-cat.

SEPTEMBER WEEK FOUR

1. A description of Abraham Maslow's Hierarchy of Needs can be found at http://www.simplypsychology.org/maslow.html in an article written by Saul McCloud, published 2007, updated 2014.

SEPTEMBER WEEK FIVE

1. Kalas, J. Ellsworth. *I Bought a House on Gratitude Street: and Other Insights on the Good Life*, (Nashville: Abingdon Press, 2011), 8-9.

OCTOBER

1. Randy Pausch, *Last Lecture: Achieving Your Childhood Dreams*, delivered September 18, 2007 at Carnegie Mellon can be viewed at http://www.youtube.com/watch?v=ji5_MqicxSo.

OCTOBER WEEK ONE

1. Reiss, Moshe. "Jephthah's Daughter" can be found at http://jbq.jewishbible.org/assets/Uploads/371/371_jephthahs.pdf.

OCTOBER WEEK FOUR

1. Warren, Rick. *The Purpose Driven Life: What On Earth Am I Here For?* (Grand Rapids: Zondervan, 2002). See also http://purposedriven.com/books/pdlbook/#purpose for a description of the five purposes God intended for each individual.

2. The quote of John Wesley to "offer them Christ" is discussed in an article by Joshua Toepper entitled *John Wesley's Clarity of Vision and Strategy: a Necessary Step for the 21st Century Church*, posted November 19, 2012 at http://seedbed.com/feed/john-wesleys-clarity-in-vision-and-stategy-a-necessary-step-for-the-21st-century-church-pt-1/.

NOVEMBER WEEK ONE
1. Grudem, Wayne. *Systematic Theology: An Introduction to Biblical Doctrine*, (Leicester, England: Inter-Varsity Press, 1994), 746.

2. Buckingham, Marcus, and Donald O. Clifton, Ph.D. *Now, Discover Your Strengths,* (New York: The Free Press, 2001), 3.

3. Grudem, Wayne. *Systematic Theology: An Introduction to Biblical Doctrine*, (Leicester, England: Inter-Varsity Press, 1994), 1029.

NOVEMBER WEEK TWO
1. Information about America's Most Wanted television show can be found at http://www.tvguide.com/news/americas-most-wanted-canceled-1063277.aspx

2. *A history of the FBI's Ten Most Wanted program can be found at* http://www.fbi.gov/stats-services/publications/ten-most-wanted-fugitives-60th-anniversary-1950-2010/fbi_ten_most_wanted_fugitives_program.

3. Stanley, Charles. *The Glorious Journey,* (Nashville: Thomas Nelson Publishers, 1996), 473.

NOVEMBER WEEK FOUR
1. Tracy, Brian. *Be A Sales Superstar: 21 Great Ways to Sell More, Faster, Easier in Tough Markets* (San Francisco, CA: Berrett-Koehler Publishers, Inc. 2002), page x.

2. Ibid, page 52.

DECEMBER
1. Information about the long-running television cartoon A Charlie Brown Christmas, written by Charles Schulz and produced by Lee Mendelson, can be found at http://usatoday30.usatoday.com/life/television/news/2005-12-05-charlie-brown-christmas_x.htm in an article by Bill Nichols in an article entitled, "The Christmas Classic That Almost Wasn't," published in USA Today, December 6, 2005.

DECEMBER WEEK TWO
1. Maxwell, John. *The Twenty-one Indispensable Qualities of a Leader: Becoming the Person Others Will Want to Follow* (Nashville: Thomas Nelson, 1999), 4.

DECEMBER WEEK FOUR
1. The quote from Theodore Roosevelt can be found at http://www.theodore-roosevelt.com/trsorbonnespeech.html.

INDEX

OF LEADERSHIP ACTIVITIES AND DEVOTIONAL MESSAGES

DEFINING THE MISSION OF THE ORGANIZATION— ITS REASON FOR BEING IN EXISTENCE

March—Week Five
June—Week One
October—Week Four
December—Week Four

ESTABLISHING THE VALUES AND THE CULTURE OF THE ORGANIZATION—THE WAY IN WHICH IT WILL ACHIEVE ITS MISSION

March—Week Two
March—Week Three
July—Week One
July—Week Two

DETERMINING PRIORITIES, SETTING GOALS, AND COMMUNICATING THEM TO OTHERS

January—Week Three
January—Week Four
May—Week One
September—Week Two

HOLDING YOURSELF AND OTHERS ACCOUNTABLE TO KEEP PROMISES AND COMMITMENTS

January—Week Two
March—Week Four
May—Week Two
October—Week One
December—Week One

ACCUMULATING SUFFICIENT RESOURCES TO ACHIEVE THE GOALS AND OBJECTIVES OF THE ORGANIZATION

February—Week Three
May—Week Three
June—Week Two
September—Week Four
September—Week Five
November—Week Three

PRACTICING GOOD STEWARDSHIP THROUGH THE DILIGENT MANAGEMENT AND ALLOCATION OF RESOURCES

January—Week One
June—Week Three
June—Week Four
November—Week One

RETAINING AND RECRUITING TALENTED EMPLOYEES

April—Week One
April—Week Two
August—Week One
October—Week Two
December—Week Two

INCREASING SALES AND REVENUES

February—Week One
April—Week Three
September—Week One
November—Week Four

MANAGING THE BALANCE SHEET AND ANTICIPATING TROUBLE

April—Week Four
May—Week Four
August—Week Two
August—Week Three

PROTECTING THE REPUTATION OF THE ORGANIZATION

February—Week Two
July—Week Three
July—Week Four
November—Week Two

RECOGNIZING WHEN CHANGE IS NECESSARY

February—Week Four
March—Week One
September—Week Three
October—Week Three
December—Week Three

HARVESTING AND PRUNING THE ORGANIZATION

June—Week Five
August—Week Four
December—Week Five

For more information about
Donald C. Moore
&
What If Jesus Carried A Briefcase?
please visit:

www.donaldcmoore.com

For more information about
AMBASSADOR INTERNATIONAL
please visit:

www.ambassador-international.com
@AmbassadorIntl
www.facebook.com/AmbassadorIntl